Fodor's

BUDAPEST

Welcome to Budapest

Situated on both banks of the Danube, Budapest unites the colorful hills of Buda and the wide, businesslike boulevards of Pest. Wander the inner city districts to admire the architecture and soak in the history, relax in a thermal bath, explore nearby castles and caves, or shop your way down Váci utca. There is no wrong way to experience Budapest. This book was updating during the COVID-19 pandemic. As you plan your upcoming travels, please confirm that places are still open and let us know when we need to make updates by writing to us at this address: editors@fodors.com.

TOP REASONS TO GO

★ **It's gorgeous:** Grand boulevards, cobblestone streets, and an embarrassing wealth of geographic and architectural splendor.

★ **Architectural splendor:** From Roman ruins to the Gothic Revival Hungarian Parliament Building, the Neoclassical St Stephen's Basilica, and the modernist apartment complexes in Újlipótváros.

★ **Thermal spas:** Nothing quite compares to a long, hot soak in mineral-rich waters in opulent settings.

★ **Vibrant nightlife:** Ruin bars in the Jewish District and Sparties (spa parties) are top attractions.

Contents

2 New York Café

Built in Italian Renaissance-style, with chandeliers dangling from ceilings adorned by frescoes, New York Palace Café is one of the oldest in Budapest. *Ch. 7*

3 Museum Hopping

From history museums like the House of Terror to art museums like the Ludwig Museum of Contemporary Art, there's a museum for every interest. *Ch. 6, 9*

4 Tram Ride

Pest's Tram 2 follows the Danube River, providing views of Buda, Buda Castle, and Parliament along with several UNESCO World Heritage Sites. *Ch. 6*

5 Zwack Unicum Museum

Taste Hungary's signature liqueur straight from a cask at a quirky museum dedicated to the drink that first caught the attention of the Habsburg Emperor and is still widely popular. *Ch. 6*

6 Visit a Wine Region

Hungary is divided into 22 wine regions. The most popular are Tokaj, famous for its sweet or dry white wines, and Villány, famous for its full-bodied and spicy reds. *Ch. 12*

7 Red Budapest Tour

Take a walking tour past sites like Memento Park, House of Terror, Soviet Army Memorial, Hospital in the Rock, and Poster Gallery to get some context on the communist period in Hungary. *Ch. 3, 4, 9*

8 Lake Balaton

Lake Balaton is a stunning body of water in western Hungary that's popular with water-sports fans, foodies, and music lovers. All just over an hour's drive from Budapest. *Ch. 12*

9 The Views from Castle Hill

Take in the panoramic views of Budapest atop Castle Hill while looking through the fairy-tale arches of Fisherman's Bastion. *Ch. 3*

10 Shopping Streets

Váci utca and Deák Ferenc "Fashion Street" are some of the most popular shopping streets in the city. Pozsonyi út in Újlipótváros is home to more local stores and cafés. *Ch. 5, 6*

11 Walk the Chain Bridge

The Széchenyi Chain Bridge spans the River Danube between Buda and Pest. Before it was built, locals relied on a pontoon bridge that often left them stranded on either side. *Ch. 3*

12 City Park

At the end of Andrassy út and just beyond Heroes' Square, this lush park is home to Vajdahunyad Castle, one of the oldest zoos in Europe, and the exquisite Szechenyi Bath House. *Ch. 8*

13 Shoes on the Danube

Just steps from the Hungarian Parliament building, the Shoes On The Danube memorial honors the Jews who were killed by Arrow Cross militiamen in Budapest during World War II. *Ch. 9*

14 The Opera

The Hungarian State Opera House has been undergoing extensive updates to restore this building to its former glory. Until then, catch a performance at the Erkel Theater. *Ch. 6*

15 Hike the Buda Hills

The Buda side has a collection of hiking trails to choose from that offer fascinating views of the cityscape, including Gellert Hill, Normafa, and Janos Hill. *Ch. 11*

16 Danube Cruise

Whether you take a candlelit dinner cruise past the Hungarian Parliament or a pleasant day trip to Szentendre, the Danube River is a relaxing way to take in the city. *Ch. 12*

17 Ruin Bars

Occupying dilapidated pre-war buildings in Budapest's old Jewish Quarter, ruin bars in Budapest reimagine abandoned warehouses and historic buildings as characterful places to party. *Ch. 1, 7*

18 Szabo Ervin Library

This hidden treasure set in the beautifully preserved Wenckheim Palace is a working library with gilded and grand reading rooms and galleries. *Ch. 6*

19 The Danube Bend

Enchanting and picturesque old towns like Esztergom, Visegrád, and Szentendre are an easy—and required—day trip from Budapest. *Ch. 12*

20 Great Market Hall

Part souvenir bazaar, part street-food mecca, this neo-Gothic masterwork is the city's largest indoor market, with food on the ground floor and crafts on the top floor. *Ch. 6*

WHAT'S WHERE

1 Várkerület (Castle District). This UNESCO-designated neighborhood boasts narrow cobbled streets and some of the city's crowning glories, including the Royal Palace and ornate Matthias Church.

2 Gellérthegy and Tabán. Hike to the top of Gellért Hill to find the imposing Liberation monument then soothe your muscles in the healing Rudas Baths or Gellért fürdő.

3 Belváros. Budapest's District 5 is the city's true inner city. It's walkable, well-connected by public transport, and home to lots of attractions, restaurants, and shopping along Váci utca and Deák Ferenc "Fashion Street."

4 Southern Pest. Józsefváros is a welcome break from the tourist-heavy Jewish Quarter nearby. The once-sleepy Ferencváros is a hip and trendy suburb with a vibrant café and nightlife scene.

5 Erzsébetváros and the Jewish Quarter. The old Jewish Quarter is home to the city's famed ruin bars making it the center of nightlife. You'll also

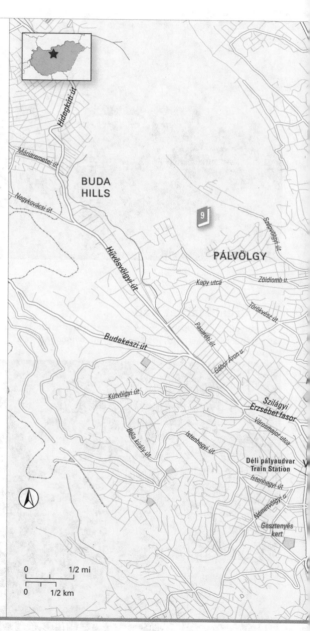

find Europe's biggest synagogue on Dohány utca.

6 Városliget (City Park). Budapest's largest park sits at the end of Andrássy út. You'll find sweeping lawns and a lake, the famous Széchenyi Baths, Budapest Zoo and botanical gardens, the Museum of Fine Arts, and Vajdahunyad Castle.

7 Parliament and Around. Hungary's Parliament, a neo-Gothic structure top-heavy with ornamental stonework, visually dominates this part of town.

8 Margitsziget (Margaret Island) and Northern Pest. Budapest's car-free island park is a tranquil getaway within reach of the city. You'll find the ruins of a 13th-century Dominican convent, a musical fountain, and a small zoo. Northern Pest's Újlipótváros is a lively and well-off residential area.

9 Óbuda and Buda Hills. Óbuda (Old Buda) is the oldest and second largest Budapest district. You'll find the remains of the Roman settlement of Aquincum and some great eateries. Hike Buda's verdant rolling hills, then tour the labyrinthine caves beneath them.

What to Eat and Drink

PÁLINKA
This fermented fruit brandy contains a minimum of at least 37.5% alcohol in every shot, which means you'll be able to pronounce the Hungarian word for cheers—*Egészségére*—in no time! Served in a traditional tulip-shaped pálinka glass and available in pear, apricot, or cherry flavor.

GOULASH
Gulyás, meaning "herdsman" in Hungarian, is one of Hungary's national dishes and was named for cowherds in eastern Hungary. This classic recipe is created with the best local ingredients, including beef, potatoes, vegetables, pinched egg noodles, paprika, and Hungarian spices.

SAVANYÚSÁG
Instead of a salad course, a plate of *savanyúság* (pickled vegetables), often shredded cabbage, cucumbers, beets, or tomatoes, will accompany your main course. Shop for juicy-sour Hungarian pickles and jars of pickled veg at Great Market Hall.

LANGOS
Langos is a traditional Hungarian fried bread, sold everywhere by street carts and vendors across the city. The traditional toppings for this deep-fried delight are a dollop of sour cream and shredded cheese, but other options include bacon, sausage, red onion, garlic, and paprika.

PAPRIKA CHICKEN
This dish can be served with pork or beef, but it's commonly ordered with chicken. Served with a side of egg noodles and a dollop of sour cream, the real star of this hearty recipe is the creamy paprika sauce.

PASTRIES GALORE
Dedicated pastry shops known as cukrászdas serve as a thriving cultural hub where locals come to socialize over coffee and baked goods. For a savory treat similar to a bread roll, try a *kifli*. If you like cheesy, buttery biscuits, you'll love a *pogácsa*. If you have a sweet tooth you have to sample the variety of filled *rétes* (strudels). *Bejgli* is a sweet bread rolled with your choice of poppy seed, walnut, or minced chestnuts. Leave room for *fánk* (doughnuts) and *palacsinta* (crepes).

ERŐS PISTA
Spice up your meals in Hungary and at home with Hungary's version of hot sauce. *Erős Pista* is a paste made from ground fresh chili peppers that you will find at your table in most restaurants and served alongside every soup and main course in Hungary.

Kürtőskalács (Chimney Cake)

Hungarians frequently use a teaspoon of the paste in the preparation of various dishes.

KÜRTŐSKALÁCS (CHIMNEY CAKE)

Watch in awe as street vendors all over Budapest wrap dough around a cylinder baking spit and cook it over charcoal. Once caramelized to golden-brown perfection, choose a coating of cinnamon, vanilla, cacao, or walnut. In the summer months, some vendors give you the choice to add ice cream in the center of the cone.

HUNGARIAN WINE

Hungary produces a variety of wines from across 22 regions in the country. The terrain is rich in volcanic and limestone soil, and unique microclimates help to produce different signature Hungarian grapes like *furmint, hárslevelű, juhfark* (white), and *kadarka* (red). Visit local wine bars, or venture out to one of the wine regions to sample delicious wines like Tokaji, Egri bulls blood, Portugeiser, and Kreinbacher, to name a few.

FRÖCCS

During the Soviet era the wine was so bitter and undrinkable that Hungarians would dilute it with soda water. Even with the improvement of wine, the trend stuck, and locals still love to cool down with a refreshing *fröccs* (spritzer) in summer.

STUFFED VEG

Töltött káposzta (stuffed cabbage) and *töltött paprika* (stuffed peppers) are a Hungarian favorite. Cabbage and peppers are stuffed with meat, rice, or vegetables, boiled, decorated with a tomato sauce, and topped with Hungarian sour cream.

Under The Radar

STREET ART TOURS

Get a unique three-hour walking tour of the Jewish Quarter and 8th District with context on Budapest's thriving street art scene. See the coolest graffiti and murals and learn about the artists, themes, and sociopolitical background as you get an accidental lesson in local history and culture.

ROOFTOP BARS

While tourists are busy trying to figure out how to explore Budapest's caves, locals are on the city's rooftops sipping cocktails and enjoying panoramic views of Budapest. Some of the most popular include 360 Bar, Leo, High Note Skybar, Toprum, and St. Andrea Wine and Skybar.

ROMAI PART

Look like a local in summer and fall by escaping the city center and settling into a deck chair with a *fröccs* (spritzer), some lángos, and fried fish on this 10-kilometer-long (6-mile-long) stretch along the Danube riverbank, peppered with cute riverside restaurants, cafés, food trucks, and bars.

FŐVÁROSI SZABÓ ERVIN KÖNYVTÁR (METROPOLITAN ERVIN SZABÓ LIBRARY)

Budapest's central library is located in the lavish Wenckheim Palace, a building that was originally built in 1889 and repurposed in 1931 by Ervin Szabó, who helped establish the public library system in Budapest. Head to the fourth floor to find students and professors studying in the same grand, jaw-droppingly gorgeous rooms where a Hungarian aristocrat once entertained. You'll want to dance in the converted ballroom but try to control yourself, it's still a working library. Part of what makes this a true hidden gem is that the lavish rooms are not immediately obvious. Buy a pass from the front desk (this gives you permission to enter but not to borrow books), then go through the entry gates and take the elevator to the 4th floor. Enter a room across from the elevator and follow the sign for "Palace."

DISTRICT 8

What was once considered a somewhat dodgy area of Budapest has become the favorite neighborhood of most locals, especially since tourists claimed the Jewish Quarter nearby. District 8, Józsefváros, has underground ruin pubs, liberal cafés, and is home to the Palace District. Just steps from the city center you will find cheap beers, local prices on food, and the real Budapest. Check out Lumen Café, Csendes ruin bar, Auróra, and the Szabó Ervin Library.

Akvárium Klub

AKVÁRIUM KLUB

Akvárium Klub is one of the city's most popular meeting spots and hangouts with a big terrace, steps, and a hip underground bar with a glass roof that shows the pool above—hence the name, aquarium. Young locals gather in the square above to picnic around the pool, listen to the music, and watch people below.

HOSPITAL IN THE ROCK NUCLEAR BUNKER MUSEUM

Under Castle Hill sits an elaborate cave system that was used as an emergency first-response hospital during WWII and the 1956 revolution. During the Cold War, the hospital was repurposed as a nuclear bunker. This former top-secret location was turned into a museum in 2007 and houses more than 40 waxwork figures as well as original machinery and furniture.

GO MOBILITY ON MARGARET ISLAND

Surrounded by the Danube river and famous for its manicured gardens and outdoor activities, Margaret Island is one of the most popular and pleasant sightseeing destinations in the city. The best way to explore the island is to rent bikes, go-karts, or electric vehicles from Go Mobility.

BUDAPEST JAZZHOUSE

What started as a jam between musician friends, eventually grew to intimate living-room concerts of some of Budapest's best jazz talent. Each event is a one-time experience, set in a home or secret garden (in summer) in Budapest. The location is revealed once you book tickets at ⊕ budapestjazzhouse.com

A38
A38 is a concert venue, restaurant, and exhibition space on a converted Ukrainian cargo ship that's docked on the Buda side of the Danube River just south of the Pertrofdi Bridge. Head to the deck with a drink in hand and enjoy the views.

Budapest with Kids

THE GYERMEKVASÚT (CHILDREN'S RAILWAY)
This narrow-gauge retro railway line staffed and operated by children (with some adult supervision) is a throwback to the days of communism when it was created to give children a chance to learn responsibility.

BUDAVÁRI MÁTYÁS KIRÁLY JÁTSZÓTÉR
If your little one needs to expend some royal energy, or play at the changing of the guards after seeing them in action at Buda Castle, take them to Budavári Mátyás király játszótér, a castle-themed playground with equipment for all ages, popular with local parents in the know. To get here, make your way to the beautiful St. Matthias Church where it meets Fisherman's Bastion, and take the almost hidden path to the right.

PALATINUS FÜRDŐ
In operation since 1919, the Palatinus Baths on Margaret Island were Budapest's first outdoor baths and today are one of Budapest's top attractions for local families year-round. You'll find a spa, open-air bath, a wave pool, a fun indoor pool, thermal pools, fountains, a water-slide park, a playground, outdoor fitness equipment, tennis courts, and a colorful range of spa and wellness treatments.

GELLÉRT HILL
Hiking Gellért-hegy or Gellért Hill is a must when visiting Budapest. Walk up the hill from the Liberty Bridge and stop at an older park that is great for younger kids, complete with slides, swings, and traditional favorites.

Continue up the hill a bit more and you'll hear the laughter of kids playing in a fun new park with large slides down the hillside, cool obstacles to climb, and in-ground trampolines for kids to jump on. But don't stop there: you have to head to the top to see Lady Liberty towering over Budapest. In addition to the amazing view, you'll be rewarded with stalls that sell delicious snacks and treats.

CHAIRLIFT UP TO NORMAFA (BUDA SIDE)
Take Bus 291 from the city center and get off at the last stop to make your way up to János Hill and the Elizabeth Lookout Tower by chairlift. The chairlift was built in 1970 and is a favorite with locals who enjoy taking the two-seater chairs on a track length of 1,040 meters covering a 262 meter difference in elevation, in about 12 minutes each way. The beloved lift is scheduled for an overhaul (to increase capacity and add four-seater cars), so be prepared to walk in case it is not in service.

VÁROSLIGET (CITY PARK)
Pack a picnic and head to City Park for a day of family-friendly activities. There's a castle, museums, a zoo, a circus, a playground, and so much more. At the man-made lake, families can rent canoes and paddle boats in the summer or ice skates in the winter. If you come on the right weekend, there are often outdoor festivals happening with stalls for vendors and food.

Chairlift up to Normafa

DINÓ PARK

With thirty life-sized dinosaur sculptures throughout this park, young paleontologists get to explore the many carnivorous and herbivorous species that once roamed the earth all the while living out *Jurassic Park* dreams. Journey through the park, check out exhibits, pose with dinosaurs, and learn more about paleontology.

ICE-SKATING

From mid-November until February, outdoor ice-skating rinks across the city are open to the public. During the holiday season, skating is free for kids at the Christmas markets, so head over to the biggest outdoor ice-skating rink in Europe at Városliget (City Park) and enjoy gliding on the ice against the backdrop of the Vajdahunyad castle.

THE CASTLE HILL FUNICULAR

Buda Castle sits atop the hill at a 40-degree incline and rises over 300 feet. Skip the strenuous walk up the hill and take the kids on the Funicular for views and fun. This 70-year-old transport is a UNESCO World Heritage Site that was bombed in WWII but later restored.

RIVER RIDE TOUR

The River Ride tour bus travels on land and water and offers an unforgettable tour of the city and the Danube for kids. Watching the bus drive directly into the water and float down the Danube River is always a winner with kids.

HUNGARIAN RAILWAY MUSEUM

This interactive outdoor museum is one of the largest in Europe with over fifty vintage steam engines

to explore and admire. Fun for kids of all ages.

PINBALL MUSEUM

More arcade than museum, this rainy-day hangout suits kids of all ages with its pinball machines dating back to the 1920s that you can actually play on. Pay an admission fee to enter and then play on all the machines for free for as long as you like.

MUSICAL FOUNTAIN

On the hour from 10am to 10pm (from May to October), Margaret Island's musical fountain dances and sprays water in sync with varied musical accompaniment. Music is tailored to younger kids earlier in the day but the mesmerizing evening light shows are a lovely way to wind down with a picnic supper after a day of sightseeing.

What to Buy

HAND-PAINTED EGGS
Beautifully hand-painted and incredibly detailed, wooden eggs are an Easter and Christmas ornament tradition, but can be found year-round in markets and stores across Budapest.

HEREND PORCELAIN
Beautiful hand-painted porcelain is available across Hungary, but the Herend company is the brand synonymous with quality and tradition. The company was founded in 1826 and has been making luxurious hand-decorated porcelain products ever since. Figurines, vases, and plates make great souvenirs.

AJKA CRYSTAL
The Ajka Crystal factory has been making handmade crystal tableware and decor for over 200 years. The small town of Ajka is located about two hours from Budapest if you want to visit the factory. Each piece is handmade and unique and available in over 20 different colors. Bowls, stemware, vases, and candleholders make great gifts.

PAPRIKA
A Hungarian scientist was awarded the Nobel Prize in 1937 for discovering that fresh red pepper is rich in vitamin C and other important minerals. It also just makes everything taste good. Locals get their favorite sweet, mild, or hot paprika from the grocery store, but tourists can buy it in packages that include a wooden spoon at Great Market Hall.

EMBROIDERY
While the colorful and detailed embroidery of Hungarian traditional dress is not the everyday style of locals today, hand-embroidered aprons, oven mittens, lace tablecloths, and runners are still very popular and widely available in Budapest's markets. Patterns and colors vary from region to region.

TOKAJI WINE
Tokaji is Hungary's most famous wine region and a UNESCO World Heritage Site. Its sweet Tokaji Aszú is known as the "King of Wines" and has been the preferred wine of popes, royalty, and artists for centuries.

HUNGARIAN DOLLS
Handcrafted Hungarian dolls dressed in traditional Hungarian peasant costumes with colorful embroidery or elegant ball gowns are a beautiful souvenir of Hungary.

RUBIK'S CUBE
The Rubik's Cube was invented by Hungarian Erno Rubik in 1974, and it still holds up as a fun puzzle for kids of all ages.

HUNGARIAN SECRET BOX
At first glance, this beautiful hand-painted and hand-carved intricate wooden box is an ordinary jewelry box. But its secret compartment can only be opened by solving a puzzle to release the hidden panels and locks that are guarding, ideally, a very important object.

PÁLINKA AND UNICOM
Palinka and Unicom are Hungary's most popular alcoholic beverages, both manufactured and bottled within the country. If you're looking for a one-of-a-kind souvenir with a rich and tasty history, shop for these libations at duty-free.

HUNGARIAN LEATHER
Whether you shop for tiny leather change purses or leather-bound books at holiday markets or custom, splurgeworthy leather shoes at Vass Shoes, Hungary is one of the best places to find quality leather craftsmanship in Europe and the world.

Ruin Pubs

MAZEL TOV

This wildly popular Jewish Quarter restaurant elevated the ruin bar concept. Drink fancy cocktails and Hungarian wines and nibble on Middle Eastern cuisine in a stylish setting under twinkling lights and tumbling greenery.

FÜGE UDVAR

This enormous ruin bar features a covered courtyard with a large *füge* fig tree in the middle. The seemingly countless side rooms have everything from street art, table tennis, billiards, and foosball. Don't stop wandering until you find the freshly baked, delicious pizza. If you're seeking even more challenging entertainment, get in on the hugely popular escape-room trend at the MindQuest escape room upstairs. The venue has five escape rooms including one with a Cold War bomb to diffuse. Be sure to reserve ahead if you plan to play on weekends.

SZIMPLA KERT

Pay your respects at Budapest's original ruin bar, the bar that started the ruin bar trend in the early 2000s and somehow never lost its appeal. In fact, it's one of the city's top attractions and so much more than just a bar. A massive abandoned residential building, furnished with eclectic found furniture and local art, you'll find lively crowds, big name DJs, local musicians, great food, drinks, and events. There's a weekly farmers' market here on Sundays, with local farmers selling cheeses, honey, jams, meats, and local specialties. The on-site design shop features ceramics, jewelry, and other crafts from local designers as well as vintage and repurposed toys and knickknacks.

AN'KERT RUIN PUB

A series of connecting courtyards creates space to lounge, dance, or dine at this whitewashed brick building and abandoned factory. During the day, the space lends itself to vegan markets, fashion shows, art shows, and other events.

INSTANT–FOGAS HÁZ

If you're looking to drink cheap drinks and dance the night away, then head to the biggest ruin bar in the city housed in a former apartment building with a crumbling facade. Wander through the huge nightclub and find over a dozen bars and rooms with different genres of music. Given its popularity and the fact that it's more "clubby," drinks here are a little more expensive than in other ruin bars.

CSENDES LÉTTEREM

Tucked away on a quiet back street in the 5th District, the laid-back Csendes Létterem Vintage Café & Bar features high ceilings, an eclectic mix of art, secondhand treasures, knickknacks, and century-old chandeliers. It's a café by day and lively bohemian bar by night and affordable at any time.

ÉLESZTŐHÁZ

This charming ruin bar has an open-air terrace and a huge selection of craft beers. The gigantic complex offers beer tastings, a restaurant, a "hopstel" (a hostel for beer lovers), and a wine and tapas bar.

Szimpla Kert

PÚDER BÁRSZÍNHÁZ

Part ruin pub, part culture hub, Púder is known for its floor-to-ceiling mural by artist Bertalan Babos Zsili as well as its creative menu of literary readings, live music, and theatrical performances. You'll also find an international menu, Hungarian craft beer, and creative cocktails.

SZATYOR

Decorated in typical ruin-bar style with an assortment of eclectic furnishings and high ceilings strung with a variety of pendants and chandeliers, Szatyor is outside the city's party district and set on the other side of the Danube on the fashionable Bartók Béla Boulevard in District 11. Instead of party-groups sipping low-priced beers, Szatyor draws a local and less rowdy crowd who come for good food and pricey craft beers.

CINTÁNYÉROS

Just steps away from the city center, the under-ground ruin bar scene in the 8th District is where locals go to avoid the tourists who have taken over the Jewish District's ruin bars. Cintányéros, a wine tavern, offers Hungar-ian wines from all over the country, a great selection of pálinka, and authentic Hungarian food.

AURÓRA

Another 8th District ruin bar, Auróra is a well-known site of the city's under-ground music and art scene. If you're interested in what's new and now on the local art scene, you'll want to stop here for drinks and a show. It's also a multi-purpose community center providing subsidized office spaces to a dozen NGOs, so stay a while and channel your tourist dollars to a good cause.

A GRUND

A Grund is a kid-friendly ruin bar in the shadow of a tall residential building in the 8th District, popular with locals for its great courtyard and big screens for watching sports. Most ruin bars are playgrounds for adults, but this one has an actual playground for kids, with toys, swings, a jungle gym, and a sandbox—*Grund* means sandlot.

What to Watch and Read

THE PAUL STREET BOYS BY FERENC MOLNAR

This young-adult novel revolves around two gangs of schoolboys in 1889 who are in a war to win the territory of a Józsefváros playground. This book is considered a classic in Hungary, and it is one of the most famous Hungarian novels outside the country.

ENEMIES OF THE PEOPLE: MY FAMILY'S JOURNEY TO AMERICA BY KATI MARTON

Based on real-life events, award-winning journalist Kati Marton tells the powerful and absorbing story of how her family in Budapest was targeted by the secret police during the communist regime and the tale of their inspiring escape to America.

THE INVISIBLE BRIDGE BY JULIE ORRINGER

In this novel, a young, Jewish Hungarian boy goes to Paris with a scholarship to study architecture. The story entangles readers in a passionate romance set during the Nazi occupation of WWII that ultimately causes him to return home to Budapest.

STRANGERS IN BUDAPEST: A NOVEL BY JESSICA KEENER

This novel follows an American on her journey in discovering life in Budapest. While settling in to her new city, a friend from back home asks her to check in on an elderly man named Edward Weiss. She quickly becomes entangled in the recent death of Edward's daughter in this murder mystery/thriller.

ECLIPSE OF THE CRESCENT MOON BY GÉZA GÁRDONYI

This journey to medieval Hungary focuses on the Siege of Eger in 1552, an epic battle where 2,000 Hungarian men, women, and children defended and defeated a Turkish force of more than 200,000 men under the leadership of István Dobó.

FATELESSNESS BY IMRE KERTÉSZ

In 2002, Hungarian novelist Imre Kertész won the Nobel Prize for Literature for his explorations of individuality in the face of the "barbaric arbitrariness of history." His debut novel Fatelessness was written between 1960 and 1973 and first published in 1975. The novel is a semi-autobiographical story about a 14-year-old Hungarian Jew's experiences in the Auschwitz and Buchenwald concentration camps.

ATTILA DIRECTED BY DICK LOWRY

Attila was king of the Huns, a nomadic people based on the Great Hungarian Plain in the 5th century AD. At its height, the Hunnic Empire stretched across Central Europe. This 2001 made-for-TV movie revolves around the legend of Attila (Gerard Butler), the leader and warrior who strategically brought several Hun clans under his rule. Throughout several epic battles, he attempts to assume power over the Roman Empire, but with the distraction of romance, and the betrayal of enemies, Attila's plan backfires.

DIARY FOR MY CHILDREN DIRECTED BY MÁRTA MÉSZÁROS

Márta Mészáros's is a key figure of Hungarian cinema whose films masterfully explore women's lives in contemporary society. Her feature film debut was in 1968 with *The Girl*, a poignant study of a young woman's search for affection. Here, and in later features such as *Riddance* (1973) and *Adoption* (1975), Mészáros brings stylish camerawork and her powers of observation to bear on contemporary sexual, psychological, social, and intergenerational relationships. She is perhaps best known for her autobiographical account of the Stalinist period, *Diary for My Children* (1982).

THE LAST DAYS PRODUCED BY STEVEN SPIELBERG

In 1944, over 425,000 Hungarian Jews were deported or killed in what the Nazis called the "cleansing" of Hungary. This powerful documentary follows five Hungarians who survived the horrific Auschwitz concentration camp.

SUNSHINE DIRECTED BY ISTVÁN SZABÓ

Set during the Nazi occupation, a Jewish-Hungarian family changes their name in an attempt to survive. From the Austro-Hungarian empire to the postwar communist era, we follow this family in their journey to fight for their life, religion, and status.

TIME STANDS STILL BY MEGÁLL AZ IDÖ

Set after the uprising of the 1956 revolution, this movie follows two brothers over the course of a decade as they grow up in Hungary and ultimately fall in love with the same woman.

THE WITNESS DIRECTED BY PÉTER BACSÓ

This satirical film about the communist era is a cult classic that was financed in Hungary at a tense political time but ultimately banned for over a decade because its portrayal was too close to home. Set in the 1950s, it portrays in a satiric tone a corrupt and deceitful system of government.

Budapest Today

Vibrant and vivacious, Budapest is endowed with all the romantic, picture-perfect charm of the grand old European capital that it is, albeit with a few scars that add a character all its own. In its center, baroque, neo-Gothic, and neoclassical architecture is decked in neo-Gothic, art deco, and art nouveau facades. The inner city's periphery is trimmed with communist-era gray cement-block buildings and new apartment complexes. Fairy-tale-like architecture, stirring public works of art, grand theaters, trendy nightlife hubs in formerly abandoned buildings, and innovative pop-up shops share space with bullet-pocked walls, cobblestone Holocaust memorials, and other sad reminders of wars and revolutions past.

While life in some Hungarian villages has stood still, complete with horse-drawn wagons, village water pumps, and dirt roads, change constantly reshapes the Budapest landscape. Currently, about one-third of the Hungarian population lives in Budapest, where both job opportunities and social services are concentrated. Dusty neon shop signs from the '80s remind you a high-end shoemaker or a tailor once worked here, now replaced by an international chain. Farther down the street, their rival successor continues business 40 years on, having never updated their sign either. It's a city full of real stories, real people, and a history that transcends historical borders, cardinal directions, and international trends. There is no wrong way to experience Budapest, just many options for the right way. That said, Budapest also happens to be a popular location for international film productions, making it even harder sometimes to tell the difference between life and art and to determine which is imitating which around here.

HUNGARY'S INVENTIVE SPIRIT

The Hungarian saying *kicsi a bors, de erős* (the peppercorn is small, but strong) can be applied to Hungarians and Hungarian intellectual achievement, too. From musicians like Ferenc Liszt, Zoltán Kodály, and Béla Bartók to Ignác Semmelweis, the doctor who popularized handwashing in hospitals, to the inventors of the Rubik's Cube, the Biro pen, and Prezi, all the way up to biochemist Katalin Karikó's groundbreaking research on mRNA that helped pave the way for the Pfizer Covid-19 vaccine that was released in December 2020, this small pastoral country is also the birthplace of thinkers who have made a worldwide impact, claiming a total of 13 Nobel Prizes since 1905.

POLITICS

Hungary has had just eight election cycles since the fall of communism (also known as the change in regime) and continues to undergo transformation. Viktor Orbán, head of the right-wing, national-conservative party Fidesz, is currently the longest-serving Prime Minister in Hungarian history. Despite contending with harsh criticism from the EU and at home for what is seen as his disregard of the rule of law, disenfranchisement of minorities and consolidation of power, he maintains high ratings in local polls.

Demonstrations are a new phenomenon in the culture but are now so frequent that they have even become social events of their own. People march out in the hundreds (and sometimes thousands) to protest everything from European migrant crisis policy, government controls over educational institutions, anti-LGBT legislation, the law banning the Central European University from operating in Hungary, the government smear campaign against George Soros, EU-Hungarian relations, and once even a proposed Internet usage tax. The public also has a plethora of corruption scandals (notably prevalent in every regime so far) to keep up with and, due to the statistically significant number of Hungarian guest workers abroad, Brexit is also a timely issue affecting many families. Just to lighten things up, the spoof party, *Magyar Kétfarkú Kutya Párt* (the Hungarian Two-Tailed Dog Party), occasionally throws its own demonstrations on themes like "Tomorrow should be yesterday!" and "Eternal life, free beer, tax-deduction!" Sadly, these are not as well-attended as they should be!

FOOD

Hungarians love to eat, to cook, and to talk about food. Not just at home and on TV, but in transit, too, and no train journey is complete without a course or two consumed on the way. The country's tastes have changed in the last 10 years as a range of new flavors have been introduced to the Budapest palate. Hungarians have a growing appetite for international cuisine and sushi, tapas, and pho are increasingly popular. You can even find vegetarian and vegan options in town. Classics like the Tabáni Gösser Étterem, Kádár Étkezde, and the Pozsonyi Kisvendéglő remain popular because Hungarians still prefer the rich, hearty flavor of traditional home cooking, full of meat and potatoes. For a taste of the bounty of local ingredients, head to the local market, where you can sample what local chefs have to work with.

LANGUAGE

Hungary's melodic tongue has created some of the most beautiful poetry and prose in the world, and also long baffled linguists with its complexity. Hungarian is considered one of the hardest languages in the world for a reason, so don't expect to catch on with your knowledge of neighboring Germanic, Slavic, or Latin-based languages. That said, if you want to win over your new Hungarian friends, and possibly score a pálinka in the process, make the effort to learn a few basic phrases. It's also useful to remember that last names come first here and szia can mean hello or goodbye.

NIGHTLIFE

On breezy, blossom-scented spring evenings and in the swelter of dark summer nights, downtown Budapest becomes like a Mediterranean city. Almost the entire District 7 is buzzing and you can easily find places open until the break of dawn. Take your pick of watering holes, ruin bars, or dance clubs to revel the night away. Whatever you do, be sure to include Szimpla Kert in your circuit: open night and day, this iconic spot ranges from an alternative, hopping artistic backdrop for your night out to a trendy, green afternoon chill-out corner (check out the farmers' market on Sunday morning). In the same vicinity, you have the Instant-Fogas dance club complex, and plenty of places to pop into on the way. If you are looking for something more polished, Districts 5 and 6 have plenty to offer, too.

RUIN BARS HAVEN'T RUINED EVERYTHING

Ruin bars changed social life in Budapest for good, drawing droves of tourists and aggressively loud and gawdy European stag (bachelor) and hen (bridal) parties. The cheap drinks and cool venues draw Airbnb backpackers to the city throughout the summer months, a trend that has driven many locals out of the Jewish Quarter. On the positive side, the interest in local art and design has spurred a renaissance of creative entrepreneurships in fashion and food, and what are just buzzwords elsewhere—environmentally friendly, upcycled, boutique, bio, and vegan—are threaded into everyday life here. Visit top designer showrooms along Andrássy út and in Districts 5, 6, and 7, or check out retro shops like Sputnyik Boutique, to see for yourself.

A WORK IN PROGRESS

Budapest ranked 57th out of a hundred cities on the Sustainable Cities Index of Arcadis, which measures cities based on their measures and investments in impact mitigation and sustainable growth. Meanwhile, Vienna—only 240 kilometers (149 miles) away—ranked fifth on the list.

Instead of renting a car or taking taxis, rely on Budapest's public transport when you visit. Despite roadwork, construction, and renovation of public spaces supported by endless EU funds and projects, Budapest has an excellent public transportation system. Buses and trams may be a bit run down, but public transportation is both affordable, accessible, and extremely reliable. Alternatively, rent a scooter or hop on one of the city's BuBi bikes. While Budapest traffic is only slowly adapting to sharing the road with cyclists, the reward is a totally different perspective on some breathtaking cityscapes and the respect of Budapest's hipsters, who will be sharing the bike lane with you.

WHAT'S NEW?

Whether it's an Ottoman-era thermal bath, Roman ruins, revival architecture, or a contemporary subway station, Budapest offers plenty of eye candy for architecture lovers, and it never stops evolving. The House of Hungarian Music designed by Sou Fujimoto opened in 2021 as part of the Liget Budapest Project—a major overhaul of Budapest's City Park. The museum is topped with a white roof punctuated with almost 100 holes for trees to grow through and wrapped in a wall of glass panels. It's dedicated to music and contains a range of interactive exhibitions on musical history as well as venues for hosting concerts. Next up for the Liget Budapest Project are the National Gallery of Hungary and the skateboard-ramp-shaped Museum of Ethnography.

The grand Hungarian Opera House on Andrássy út, designed by Miklós Ybl, is one of Budapest's most stunning buildings. Closed at the end of the 2016–17 season, the Opera House was originally scheduled to reopen in early 2019, but the scale of the restoration and modernization project kept growing, as did the costs, and the delays pushed into 2021. When complete, visitors will benefit from refreshed frescoes, updated facilities, and a substantial overhaul of the auditorium, as well as high technology additions that improve the experience for the visitor and the performer.

TRAVEL SMART

Updated by
Patti McCracken

★ **CAPITAL:**
Budapest

👤 **POPULATION:**
1.75 million

💬 **LANGUAGE:**
Hungarian

$ **CURRENCY:**
Forint (HUF)

☎ **COUNTRY CODE:**
36

⚠ **EMERGENCIES:**
112

🚗 **DRIVING:**
On the right

⚡ **ELECTRICITY:**
220v/50 cycles; electrical
plugs have two round prongs

🕗 **TIME:**
Six hours ahead of New York

⊘ **TRAVEL DOCUMENTS:**
Up to 90 days with valid
passport; Schengen rules
apply

✈ **AIRPORTS:**
BUD; DEB

🌐 **WEBSITES:**
www.visit-hungary.com
www.budapest.com
www.gotohungary.com

Know Before You Go

Chances are you won't master the Hungarian language. Luckily, penetrating the mysteries of day-to-day life in the Hungarian capital is much easier. You just need a heads-up on a few things. Is it Budapest or Boo-dah-pesht? Which side is better, Buda or Pest? What's the sad curse? Should you tip? How do you say "cheers" in Hungarian?

POTATO, POTAHTO?

You've probably heard the name Budapest pronounced a couple of different ways, so what's the right way to pronounce it? The "s" in Hungarian is pronounced "sh," and therefore Hungarians say "Budapesht." No one will correct or judge you for omitting the "sh" sound and using the basic English-language version, but if you want to sound like a local, or like a traveler who knows better, say "Budapesht."

BUDA OR PEST

Buda and Pest are separated by the Danube River and so you will hear people refer to the Buda side of the river and the Pest side of the river. Which side is best really depends on what kind of experience you are looking for. Buda is hillier and sits higher than Pest, so it offers great viewpoints. It's also home to the Várkerület (Castle District), one of the city's top attractions, as well as Matthias Church and Fisherman's Bastion. That said, many top attractions, including the Széchenyi Baths, elegant cafés, ruin bars, Opera House, Central Market Hall, Parliament Building, and shopping streets like Váci utca are in Pest. First-time visitors may want to stay in Pest because its sights are more numerous and more spread out and Buda's highlights are still easy to access as they are mostly concentrated along the river. Return visitors who have already gotten the lay of the land may opt for quieter Buda.

TAKE THE THERMAL WATERS

Ancient Romans were the first to exploit the city's thermal springs by building baths around them 2,000 years ago. These baths are still an integral part of the fabric of life here and must be tried, if only to soothe muscles after a long day of walking. For a veritable Turkish experience, try the Rudas baths (there's a rooftop hot tub) or the historical and atmospheric Kiraly baths. For a host of services plus an outdoor-wave pool experience in a stunning setting, visit the art nouveau Gellért baths. The Szechenyi baths are the city's biggest and most popular and you'll find a variety of pools, treatments, and even "sparties" (spa parties). Pack a bathing suit and flip-flops, and plan to spend most of a day. Thermal baths are open year-round.

BUDAPEST IS ENGLISH-FRIENDLY

Ahhh, Hungarian. It's a trickster's tongue. It makes sense that both Houdini and the inventor of the Rubik's Cube were Hungarian. They started out life trying to figure out a puzzling language, and as a result became experts at untangling things. Case in point, Hungarian greetings. *Csókolom* means both hello and goodbye which, at least, is one less thing to remember. But then locals often use slang for greetings so they might say *Sziya*, which means "see you," and leave you with a wave and a "hello." To keep things interesting, Hungarians put last names first. It's worth making an effort to learn a few key phrases but most locals speak English fluently and many restaurants will have menus available in English.

MONEY MATTERS

Hungary never adopted the Euro, despite its membership in the EU. Its currency is the Forint, represented either as HUF or Ft. Don't think you can come to Hungary from, say, Austria, and spend the rest of your euros here. A few five-star hotels may accept euros, but no one else will. If you do need to change a wallet-full of euros, your best rate of exchange will be at a Hungarian bank. Stay away from the HUF/euro currency exchange ATMs as they are a rip-off.

DON'T CLINK

Hungarians like to drink, but they don't like to clink, so when you make a toast, raise your glass, make eye contact, and channel your clinking energy into trying to say cheers in Hungarian. *Egészségedre!*, pronounced egg-a-shag-a-dre, will take a little practice, so you might want to ask a local to coach you.

VALIDATE OR PAY A FINE

You bought your metro ticket, you pushed your way through the turnstyle, but you forgot to validate your ticket. To Hungarian controllers—who like to stand near the turnstyle in plainclothes—this is akin to stealing a free ride. No amount of pleading with them, or waving the unvalidated ticket in their face, will get you off. You'll have to pay that fine. So, be sure to take a minute and run your ticket through one of the machines at metro station entrances to validate.

DOWNLOAD A TAXI APP

Uber was banned in Hungary after a taxi driver lobby in 2016 and you won't find Lyft here either. Instead, download taxi-hailing apps like Bolt or Taxify to arrange a licensed cab. Avoid freelance cabs and you'll also avoid inflated charges.

THE JEWISH DISTRICT IS NOT FOR LIGHT SLEEPERS

Twenty years ago, the ruin bar trend was born in the then-deserted Jewish District when some industrious entrepreneurs set up a bar in an abandoned building with a tumbledown courtyard and found furnishings. Ruin bars attracted the young and cool and soon more bars followed and the entire neighborhood started to feel the love. These days, the Jewish District's ruin bars are one of the city's top attractions, and while you can easily find "characterful" shabby-chic apartments for rent, you might want to think twice on that good deal. In recent years, the area has become known for 24-hour bars and loud partying groups from all over Europe, and the party vibes are less fun when A. you are not invited and B. you're trying to sleep. Also, it's worth noting that ruin bars are more or less "controlled decay;" the apartment or room you rent may just be decay.

TIP AWAY!

Tips are accepted and even encouraged in Hungary. The gratuity is often included with the bill. If not, 10% is standard for good service, 15% for outstanding service. Be sure to hand the tip to your server directly; it's considered rude to leave it on the table.

DON'T TELL PEOPLE TO CHEER UP

If you think locals look a little down, don't judge: they're cursed, or at least they believe they are, and who are you to say otherwise when these people have suffered misfortune, repression, and catastrophes for centuries? The most popular root of the Curse of Turan dates to King Stephen, who in AD 1000 brought Christianity to the kingdom by force, quelling ancient traditions and rites. Those who resisted cast a malicious spell on Hungary, a curse felt in an overwhelming sense of pessimism and melancholy. For ages, the curse has been blamed for losses from the invasion of the Mongols, to the invasion of the Turks, the losses of the Hungarian Revolution to the Treaty of Trianon where Hungary lost over 70 percent of its territory. There is a popular adage that "Magyars take their pleasures mournfully," so maybe don't be too chirpy.

PÁLINKA

Pálinka, or fruit brandy, is something of a national treasure. It is still homemade in the villages, using whatever fruits are abundant, usually plums, pears, cherries, or apricots. The alcohol content is high, ranging anywhere from 35%–85%, but the point for most isn't to get drunk. If you're invited to have a drink, it's impolite to turn the offer down, although if you need to, just turn your glass upside down to indicate "no." It's worth noting that if you do engage, you don't sip this drink, you knock it back.

Getting Here and Around

Air

Hungary has not had a flagship carrier since 2012, but there are still nonstop flights to be found on some U.S. airlines, and even a few European airlines. Travel time from New York to Budapest is eight and a half hours. From Chicago, it is nine and a half hours. American Airlines offers direct flights from New York to Budapest, and Polish airline LOT offers direct flights to Budapest from both New York and Chicago. However, be careful when booking to make sure you've got the direct flight, and not one that makes a stop in Warsaw.

AIRPORTS
Franz Liszt International Airport (BUD), still commonly referred to by its former name Ferihegy (pronounced "Ferihug") is, by far, Hungary's largest commercial airport, and is located 24 km (16 miles) southeast of central Budapest. A temporary closure of Terminal 1 nearly a decade ago has turned into a permanent one, and all airlines operate out of Terminal 2A and Terminal 2B. Pier B, a new passenger terminal, opened in 2018. Hubs located here are LOT Polish Airlines Smartwings Hungary, WizzAir, and RyanAir. There are also commercial airports with regular, albeit relatively limited, service in Debrecen and at Sármellék, near the western end of Lake Balaton, which services mostly charter flights.

Bicycle

Budapest is no Amsterdam, but there is a decided push to get people out of their cars and onto bikes. The city now has 300 km (186 miles) of bike routes and a growing number of dedicated bike paths. MOL Bubi is a popular bike sharing program that has 128 bike stations and 1,500 bikes available throughout the city. Most riders use the bikes for short distances, when it's quicker to travel by bike than tram or bus.

Bus

Buses, trams, and trolleybuses all are abundant and convenient for travel within Budapest. When looking at a transit map, busses are blue, trams are yellow, and trolleybuses are red. A single-fare ticket is valid for only one ride in one direction, unless you purchase a transfer. Tickets are widely available in metro stations and newsstands and must be validated on board. Alternatively, you can purchase a one-, three-, or seven-day tourist ticket, which allows unlimited travel on all services within the city limits. You can also purchase a group card for 24 hours, which allows up to five passengers to travel together on the same card. Hold on to whatever ticket you have; spot checks by aggressive officials (look for the red armbands) are numerous and often targeted at tourists. Note, if you are traveling on the seven-day card and get stopped by a ticket controller, he or she has the right to request your passport as proof of identity. Trolleybus stops are marked with red rectangular signs that list the route stops; regular bus stops are marked with similar light blue signs. Tram stops are marked by light blue or yellow signs. Most lines run from around 4:30 am and stop operating between 11 pm and midnight. However, there is all-night service on certain key routes—night buses are identifiable because they are numbered between 900 and 999. Consult the separate night-bus map posted in most metro stations for all-night service. Note that while it's possible to buy tickets directly from bus drivers, it costs more, they have no change, and you'll be holding up a grumbling line of passengers impatient to board.

Car

If you're considering renting a car just to drive around Budapest, reconsider. Parking is a horror and the fines for illegal parking are high, as is the probability of getting towed or booted. It's also important to note that if you're visiting a lot of the smaller cities that fan out from Budapest, they are easy trips to make by train or bus. However, driving is the most convenient way to get from Eger to Tokaj, for example, or to travel between Debrecen and Szeged without having to return to Budapest (though there are a couple of buses each day that will also save you the trouble). Of course, assuming you can afford the time and the high fuel cost, and are not rattled by the prospect of encountering Hungarian drivers who pass whenever the opportunity does or does not present itself, a car will allow you to explore the countryside at your leisure. It's a small country, so even driving from one end to the other is manageable.

The main routes into Budapest are the M1 from Vienna (via Gyor), the M2 from the north, the M3 from Romania and Debrecen, the M5 from the southeast (Szeged, Serbia, and Romania), the M6 from Pecs, and the M7 from Balaton. The M4 is under construction and will eventually connect the city of Oradea (Romania) to Budapest. Like any Western city, Budapest is plagued by traffic jams during the day, but motorists should have no problem later in the evening. Motorists unaccustomed to sharing city streets with trams should pay extra attention. You should be prepared to be flagged down numerous times by police conducting routine checks. Be sure all your papers are in order and readily accessible; unfortunately, the police have been known to give foreigners a hard time.

■TIP➔ It's important to note that driving on motorways, except those that ring Budapest, requires a vignette, or toll sticker. This is now in the form of an e-vignette (or e-matrica), and can be purchased for around €12 for a 10-day vignette, and €16.50 for a one-month vignette. They can be purchased at gas stations or shops located at border crossings, as well as online at various sites, including hungary-vignette.eu and ematrica. nemzetiutdij.hu, both of which can be navigated in English. You will need to input your license tag number and registration, and at the time of purchase, you'll be asked to give the start date regarding when you want the vignette to be activated.

CAR RENTALS

An important thing to keep in mind when renting a car in Hungary is that the vast majority of cars are manual. There are few cars on the road that are automatic, so if you must have an automatic, it's imperative that you secure the rental in advance. If you're okay with a manual transmission, be sure the dealer familiarizes you with any safety features, i.e., getting the car into reverse. Many European car rentals are diesel, so you will also need to reserve ahead if you want a gas-fueled car.

The easiest way to rent a car is at the airport. Drivers must be at least 21 years old and have been driving for at least a year. This is the minimum age and experience, and rental companies are free to set more restrictive policies. Some companies will also impose a surcharge for drivers who are under the age of 25. Further, the age requirement can vary based on the type/class of car you want to rent. This is all at the rental company's discretion.

Getting Here and Around

If you plan to enter Hungary with a car you rented in another European country, check the policy. Not all rental agreements allow for this. Some agreements will allow budget cars to enter, but not higher-end vehicles. Be sure to sort this out at the time you make the reservation. Furthermore, if you plan to rent in Hungary, and tour other countries before returning, check the policy to ensure that is permitted. Be specific about which countries you plan to visit, because some may be permitted, and others not.

If you're planning to rent a car in Hungary and drop it off in another country, you're out of luck. There are no one-way rental options available.

Don't assume that the rental clerk will speak flawless English, and definitely don't assume that the rental agreement will be in English, as it most likely will be in Hungarian. Best to make use of a translator app and to make sure ahead of time what kind of rental agreement you're signing. In any case, the further ahead you plan, the better.

DRIVING

Hungarians drive on the right and observe the usual European rules of the road. Unless otherwise noted, the speed limit in towns, villages, and other such developed areas is 50 kph (30 mph), on main roads 90 to 110 kph (55 to 65 mph), and on highways 130 kph (78 mph). Stay alert: speed-limit signs are few and far between. Towns and villages are marked by a white rectangular sign with the town name written in black; slow down to 50 kph (or less if so marked) as soon as you pass one. You can speed up again once you pass a similar sign with the town name crossed out in red. Signs that show a yellow triangle with a white border indicate a main route. The driving age is 17. Like all Schengen countries, you must have an international driver license that

has been translated into the language of the country in which you're driving. Headlights must always be on, day and night, no matter the weather. Infants and toddlers must sit in a car seat in the back seat of the car. Phones must be hands free. Drinking alcohol is prohibited—there is a zero-tolerance policy, and penalties are severe.

GASOLINE

Unless you are out in rural areas or old villages, gas stations are plentiful in Hungary, and many on the main highways stay open all night, even on holidays. Major chains, such as MOL, Shell, and OMV, have Western-style, full-facility stations with restrooms, brightly lit convenience stores, and 24-hour service. Unleaded gasoline (bleifrei in German or ólommentes in Hungarian) is available at all stations (leaded fuel is no longer sold in Hungary) and is usually the 95-octane-level choice. Credit cards are widely accepted, and you should automatically get a receipt. If you don't, ask for a blokk (pronounced "blowk"). Bear in mind that diesel is widely used in Hungary. Always check to make sure you are putting the proper fuel into your car, or you may end up needing to get your fuel tank flushed. Or worse.

PARKING

Street parking in Budapest is hard to come by, and you'll likely have an easier time in the Buda part of the city, than in Pest. But both will be tricky and signs are often impossible to decipher. Most streets in Budapest's main districts have restricted, fee-based parking. Parking meters accept both credit cards and coins and give you a ticket to display on your dashboard (usually for a maximum of three hours). The cost is hourly and divided by zone. For example, Zone 1 is 525 HUF per hour ($1.75), Zone 2 is 440 HUF ($1.45), and Zone 3 is 350 HUF

($1.15). Parking is enforced from 8 am–6 pm weekdays, and Saturday 8 am–noon. It's free evenings, and Saturday afternoon to Sunday. The minimum parking time is 15 minutes; the maximum in one place is three hours.

⚠ **It cannot be stressed enough that parking is strictly controlled and cars will be towed or booted for seemingly minor infractions.**

ROAD CONDITIONS

There are four classes of roads: expressways (designated by the letter "M" and a single digit), main highways (a single digit), secondary roads (a two-digit number), and minor roads (a three-digit number). Main highways will also have a European-wide equivalent, marked with the letter "E" followed by the highway number. Expressways, highways, and main roads in towns are fairly well maintained. The condition of minor roads varies considerably, with some being so deeply rutted you'd presume they're still used for horse-drawn carts. In rural parts of central Hungary, for example, it can take well over an hour to drive 15 miles because of poor conditions on the back roads. In planning your driving route with a map, opt for the larger roadways whenever possible; you'll generally end up saving time even if there is a shorter but smaller road. Be especially carefully on the motorways that cut through the plains in Central Hungary: Some of these routes are known as among the most deadly in Europe because of the intense speeding.

Ⓜ Public Transport

Service on Budapest's subways is cheap, fast, and frequent; stations are easily located on maps and streets by the big letter "M" (for metro). Tickets—valid on all forms of mass transportation—can be bought at hotels, metro stations, newsstands, and kiosks. They are valid for one ride only, including transfers to different trains within one line (i.e., M1 to M2) for one hour; you can't change direction or interrupt your trip at a station. All tourist tickets and passes are equally valid for the subway, too. Tickets must be validated in the time-clock machines in station entrances and should be kept until the end of the journey, as there are frequent checks by undercover inspectors; a fine for traveling without a ticket is 16,000 HUF ($53) or 8,000 ($26.50) when paid on the spot. Cash and debit cards are accepted for on-the-spot payments, but be sure to ask for a receipt. If you purchased a ticket but forgot to validate it, you'll still get fined. If you cannot pay on the spot, you will have to pay the fine via cash or check through a transaction that must be conducted at the post office.

Ride-Sharing

Uber pulled out of Budapest after protests by local taxi drivers and being cited by Hungarian officials for unfair practices in 2016, which essentially shut down ride-sharing in the city. Download Bolt or Taxify before you visit for the same e-hailing convenience and to avoid "freelance" cab drivers and inflated fares. These apps allow you to hail and pay with your phone and fares and drivers are regulated.

🚖 Taxi

In 2013, the government imposed new regulations on taxis in Budapest. All taxi rates have been standardized so that there should be no difference in the cost of hailing a taxi on the street or ordering one by phone. Additionally all licensed taxis are yellow and the rates are printed

Getting Here and Around

on the back window. All taxi companies have English-speaking operators. The base fare is 700 HUF ($2.35) and 350 HUF ($1.20) per km (½ mile). There are freelance taxis available, also yellow, and they will have a "*független szolgáltató*" (freelance) sign displayed on their doors. Try to avoid these.

🚆 Train

International trains—and there is a steady stream of them, from all directions—are routed to two stations in Budapest. Keleti Pályaudvar (East Station) receives most international rail traffic coming in from the west, including Vienna. Nyugati Pályaudvar (West Station) handles a combination of international and domestic trains. Déli handles trains to the Lake Balaton region and to Pécs. Within Hungary, there is frequent and convenient rail service to many smaller cities and towns on the many routes that radiate in all directions from Budapest.

Many domestic trains have only second-class (*másod osztály*, pronounced "mahshould oh-sty") cars. First class (*elso osztály*, pronounced "ell-she oh-sty"), which costs around 50% more, will give you somewhat larger seats, fewer fellow passengers crowding in and slicing their odorous salami beside you, and velvety upholstery that you won't stick to on a hot summer day, unlike the vinyl-like seat fabric found in most second-class cars. On generally newer Intercity (IC) trains even second class is considerably more comfortable than the same class on older trains that ply slower routes.

For travel only within Hungary, Eurail offers a Eurail National Pass, with a range of options for second-class travel. They are all one-month passes, limited to a specified number of travel days within that month. A pass offering three days of travel is $109; four days is $135; five days is $158; six days is $182, and a pass for eight days is $224. The same package is available for first class, although it costs more, of course. MÁV Hungarian Railways offers a one-month travel pass that might make sense if, during a short stay, you take separate trips from Budapest to Eger, Pécs, and Lake Balaton, for example. Czech train company RegioJet began offering train services within Hungary in summer of 2020, MAV's first real competitor.

Travel by train from Budapest to other large cities or to Lake Balaton is cheap and efficient. Avoid *személyvonat* (local trains), which are extremely slow; instead, take Intercity (IC) trains or *gyorsvonat* (express trains). On timetables, *vágány* (tracks) are abbreviated with a "v"; indul means departing, and *érkezik* means arriving. Trains get crowded during weekend travel in summer, especially to Lake Balaton; you're more likely to have elbow room if you pay a little extra for first-class tickets—assuming first class is an option on your train.

Intercity (IC) trains—which ensure relatively comfy, clean, and fast service on domestic routes to the largest towns outside of Budapest—require a *helyjegy* (seat reservation, roughly pronounced "heyyedy" as three distinct syllables). But you should automatically receive one at the time of purchase, for around 500 HUF extra beyond the normal cost of the ticket for the distance you're going. Before leaving the ticket window, though, check to see that you get two ticket-like slips of paper: one is your ticket, the other is your seat reservation.

Essentials

⚽ Activities

SOCCER

The men's national team is hardly a showstopper: Hungary had a thirty-year drought before squeaking into the Euro 2016 Championship annals by reaching the 16th round. Hardly something to cheer about, but Hungarians are diehard supporters of their national team, the Magyars. Historically, the team has done well. It has made nine FIFA appearances, three European Championship appearances, three Olympic bronze medals, and was runner up in two World Cup championships. A new arena opened in Budapest in 2019, and was named for one of its most beloved players, Ferenc Puskás.

The women's team is controlled by the same body that governs the men's team, the Hungarian Football Federation. It is struggling to get the same recognition that the men's team gets. A highlight came in 2019, when Hungary hosted the UEFA Women's Championship League Final.

HANDBALL

Handball Planet, an aggregator of handball enthusiasm worldwide, gives the top spot to Hungary, claiming the sport is more popular here than anywhere else on the globe. The women's team won the European Championship in 2020. The team has won two bronze medals in the Olympics and consistently places well in the World Championship and the European Championship. The men's team has won several bronze medals in the Olympics—the latest in 2012—and made it to the quarterfinals of the 2017 World Championship.

SPAS

There are more than one thousand thermal springs streaming through Hungarian earth, more than any other place in the world. Hungarians tapped into this bounty long ago, and to this day nurture a treasured spa culture. The Gellért spa, located in a 1918 masterpiece art nouveau building on Gellért Hill, is perhaps the most famous. It has ten geothermal baths, which draw from hot spring waters first discovered in the 12th century. There are also salt rooms, which are great detoxifiers, and several common swimming areas. The most unusual site to tourists, however, will probably be the expansive pools, or baths, that are not meant for swimming, but relaxing. You might spot a group of men playing a game of chess while standing waist deep in water, while others read a book or a newspaper.

Like at any spa, it's best to keep chatter and laughter to a minimum. People are here for quiet time. Swimming is encouraged, but splashing or anything that would be disruptive to other patrons is not. Also note that thermal baths are not recommended for children, but check the spa first to see if they have facilities for kids.

All nine of Budapest's spas are unisex, though Rudas Bath reserves Tuesday for women only.

🍴 Dining

Budapest's culinary scene is lively and varied and these days often described as emerging international. The city has six Michelin star restaurants and hosts European-wide chef competitions. Along with the traditional eateries, you'll find a host of fine-dining restaurants offering modern takes on classic Hungarian dishes, as well as a growing variety of vegan restaurants and street food options.

Essentials

Navigating Budapest

As in Paris, neighborhoods in Budapest are known and referred to locally not by name but by their district number, the equivalent of the Paris arrondissement. The standard format for written street addresses is: first the district number—on maps Roman numerals designate each of Budapest's 22 districts, while on envelopes the middle two numerals of the four-digit zip code indicate the district (e.g., a specific neighborhood in District 7 might have a 1072 zip code)— followed by the word "Budapest" (sometimes followed by the Roman numeral, just to be certain); and then the street name and street number.

Although the lower-numbered districts are generally downtown and the farther you go into the outskirts in all directions the higher the district number, it's not quite as simple as that: the first several numbers—Districts 1 (including Castle Hill), 2, and 3—are in Buda and border the Danube, while District 4 somehow ended up in northern Pest (along the Danube) well away from downtown, and Districts 5 through 9 are all wholly or at least partly in downtown Pest (parts of 5 and 9 border the river). Whereas District 10 is in eastern Pest, far from the Danube, some areas of downtown Buda by the river fall within District 11. Districts 5, 6, 7, and some of 9 are in downtown Pest; District 1 includes Castle Hill, Buda's main tourist district.

You will find few reminders among street names of the era of communist rule, when streets and squares were named after Soviet heroes and concepts. If you look carefully at street signs, you may still find some with the old names crossed out with a triumphant red line. Today many of Budapest's streets and squares are named after famous Hungarian composers, poets, and painters, reflecting the nation's strong regard for music and the arts. ■ TIP→ **Keep in mind that Hungary numbers building levels starting from zero (i.e., the ground floor is 0, next floor up is 1, etc.).**

A few clues to navigating:

út (sometimes útja) means road or avenue

utca (u.) means street

tér (sometimes tere) means square

körút (krt.) means ring road

körtér and köröndmean circle

kerület (ker.) means district

emelet (em.) means floor

földszint (fsz.) means ground floor

Lunch-only eateries, or *étkezdes*, can still be found, and serve good food for low prices, Monday through Friday.

Dining in Budapest will make the budget-minded happy, because the dollar will go a long way. Expect to pay around $2 for a cappucino, and less than $1.50 for a half-pint of beer. A sandwich from a street vendor will empty no more than $3 from your wallet, and even dinner at an upscale restaurant likely won't cost more than $50 per person.

If you need a break from goulash and chicken paprikash, you're in luck, because Budapest has one of the largest Chinese communities in Europe, and the best Chinese restaurants are in Chinatown, just outside the city.

DISCOUNTS AND DEALS
Restaurants in the city center (District 5) cater to tourists and ex-pats, and are more expensive. Better deals can be found a bit farther out of the tourist zone. But regardless of what part of town you're in, many places offer low-cost, prix-fixe lunches, so it's worth checking. Ask for tap water to avoid paying high rates for bottled water.

PAYING
Most restaurants take credit cards, but some smaller places do not. It's worth asking. A gratuity of 10% will often be added to the bill. If the service was exceptional, it's customary to tip beyond the gratuity.

MEALS AND MEALTIMES
Many restaurants are closed Sunday, and upscale restaurants are often closed Sunday and Monday. It is rare to get a hot meal past 10 pm at any place any night of the week, so night owls, beware.

SMOKING
Smoking has been banned in restaurants and bars since 2012. It is permitted outside, however, which includes restaurant terraces and outdoor cafés.

What It Costs in HUF			
$	$$	$$$	$$$$
AT DINNER			
under 1,500 HUF	1,500– 3,000 HUF	$3,001– 5,000 HUF	over 5,000 HUF

⊕ Health and Safety

COVID-19
COVID-19 brought all travel to a virtual standstill in 2020, and interruptions to travel have continued into 2021. Although the illness is mild in most people, some experience severe and even life-threatening complications. Once travel started up again, albeit slowly and cautiously, travelers were asked to be particularly careful about hygiene and to avoid any unnecessary travel, especially if they were sick.

Older adults, especially those over 65, have a greater chance of having severe complications from COVID-19. The same is true for people with weaker immune systems or those living with some types of medical conditions, including diabetes, asthma, heart disease, cancer, HIV/AIDS, kidney disease, and liver disease. Starting two weeks before a trip, anyone planning to travel should be on the lookout for some of the following symptoms: cough, fever, chills, trouble breathing, muscle pain, sore throat, and new loss of smell or taste. If you experience any of these symptoms, you should not travel at all.

And to protect yourself during travel, do your best to avoid contact with people showing symptoms. Wash your hands often with soap and water. Limit your time in public places, and, when you are out and about, wear a face mask that covers your nose and mouth. Indeed, a mask may be required in some places, such as on an airplane or in a confined space like a theater, where you share the space with a lot of people. You may wish to bring extra supplies, such as disenfecting wipes, hand sanitizer (12-ounce bottles were allowed in carry-on luggage at this writing), and a first-aid kit with a thermometer.

Essentials

Given how abruptly travel was curtailed at the onset of COVID-19, it is wise to consider protecting yourself by purchasing a travel insurance policy that will reimburse you for any cancellation costs related to COVID-19. Not all travel insurance policies protect against pandemic-related cancellations, so always read the fine print.

HOSPITALS

Hungarian hospitals don't have dedicated general emergency rooms that one can just walk into. If you call an ambulance, the paramedics assess you and, based on your condition and location, take you to the relevant department of the hospital, where you are immediately treated. Hungarian doctors are well trained, and most speak English or German. Over the last decade, an attempt has been made to modernize hospitals throughout Hungary, but Budapest appears to be last on the list. Its facilities are still sadly outdated, and doctors and nurses are severely underpaid and overworked. The private Telki Hospital just outside of Budapest or one arranged by the American Clinic are the best options.

PHARMACIES

Most pharmacies (*gyógyszertár*) close between 6 pm or 8 pm, but several stay open at night and on weekends, offering 24-hour service, with a small surcharge for items that aren't officially stamped as urgent by a physician. You must ring the buzzer next to the night window and someone will respond over the intercom. Staff are unlikely to speak English, so try to get at least a rough translation of what you need before you go. A small extra fee (100 HUF–200 HUF) is added to the bill. Pharmacies are usually well stocked. Late-night pharmacies are usually found across from the train stations.

 Immunizations

There are no immunization requirements for visitors traveling to Hungary for tourism.

Lodging

Many of the city's grand dame edifices—built during the Austro-Hungarian empire and still standing after two world wars and the Soviet love of concrete—are now the sites of luxe accommodations and they drip in opulence. Five-star hotels including the Corinthia, the New York Palace, Four Seasons, Kempinski, Sofitel, and so many more are abundant in Budapest, and none spare expense in living up to the modern idea of luxury. That being the case, there are still a lot of less conspicious places to stay, whether it be a family-run, three-star hotel on a tranquil street in Buda hills, or a pension on a side street in Pest. There is also a robust boutique hotel scene, and plenty of reputable budget chains.

FACILITIES

Basic facilities should include TV, Wi-Fi, and a private bathroom, although you cannot always expect a tub. Air conditioning is often hard to come by, as many of the older buildings cannot adequately be adapted to offer it. Further, Hungarians believe AC is bad for your health. The weather in Budapest is generally so pleasant that it is rarely a huge problem.

PRICES

All room rates indicated here are based on double-occupancy rack rates in high season. It's important to note, however, that these rates often double during the week Formula I racing comes to Budapest every year, usually in mid-August. On the other hand, most large hotels offer significant discounts, frequently including breakfast, for weekend bookings and during special sale periods throughout the year. If a property seems too expensive at first glance, it's worth looking into special rates by calling them as well as checking their website. Most hotels include all taxes as well as breakfast in their regular quoted rates. Luxury hotels usually do not include VAT of 18% and a tourist tax of 4% in the room rate, nor do they usually include breakfast.

Most hotels allow children under 16 to stay in their parents' room for free, though age limits vary from property to property. For single rooms with a bath, count on paying about 80% of the double-room rate. With the possible exception of family-run pensions, credit cards are widely accepted.

As in many post-communist bloc countries, hotels in Budapest had a special corner on the tourism market for a long time. With few big chains in town and few local investors who could afford the capital risk, there was minimal competition and hotel rates in no way reflected the local economic situation. Their guests were people from far-off places for whom it was irrelevant that one night's stay was worth 25% of an average monthly salary on the local economy. This changed about 10 years ago when the Airbnb boom arrived in Budapest and average Hungarians anted up and joined the game. As the Sziget Festival increased in popularity and the new tourist wave in Budapest included a lot more backpackers, these guests liked both the unique, rough and tumble style of the Jewish District's ruin bars and the prices of these informal residential rentals. It wasn't long before foreign investors took advantage of this niche and began buying property purely for Airbnb speculation and running full-time businesses on this model. In the meantime, boutique hotels also started to find their place on the market, too. As a result, basically no one in the hotel industry has raised their prices in the last ten years. In fact, prices have actually dropped. So, if you think a swank hotel you fancy might be out of your price range, think again. There are a wide range of sophisticated, charming, off-beat, and homey places to choose between and there are a great deal of bargains to be had across the board.

RENTALS

Apartment hotels are a good option for business travelers or families. Luxury apartments can be rented for approximately 20% less than a room in a five-star hotel. Regardless of what you pay, there can be a minimum rental imposed, anywhere from a few nights to a few weeks. Some companies insist on a month-to-month rental. You can rent from ⊕ apartmentsinbudapest.com, ⊕ vrbo.com, or ⊕ airbnb.com, among others.

RESERVATIONS

Advance reservations are strongly advised in summer, especially at the smaller, lower-priced hotels and during the week in August that Formula I racing descends upon Budapest. In winter it's not anywhere near as difficult to find a hotel room, even at the last minute, and prices are usually reduced by 20% to 30%. The best budget option is to book a private room or an entire apartment. Expect to pay around $50–$60 for a double at a three-star hotel, and keep in mind, three-star in Europe is quite adequate. If you have a feather allergy, notify the staff when making your reservation. Otherwise, assume that all pillows and duvets are down. Visitors who prefer a room unsullied by cigarette smoke will be happy to know that most of Budapest's large hotels offer some smoke-free rooms, and in some cases entire wings or floors. The situation changes

Essentials

dramatically, however, once you travel far from the capital.

Money

While Hungary is part of the European Union, it does not use the euro as its currency (although hotels and sightseeing tours often quote prices in euros). The Hungarian currency is the forint, which you will see abbreviated to "HUF" and "Ft" interchangeably. ■TIP→ **Nobody calls it "HUF" in speech; just refer to forints when talking about money.**

🍸 Nightlife

Budapest seems to have every kind of drinking establishment you might imagine, from discos and bars to quiet indoor courtyards, live-music joints, and artsy bohemian spaces. Local pubs, where you can get mostly beer and wine, called sörözo (beer joints) or a borozó (wine bars), are scattered across the city. In the last decade, the city's nightlife has become concentrated in the Jewish District, (the smallest region of the Pest city center) where the city's ruin bars are concentrated, with some spillover into the Lipótváros neighborhood. Buda also boasts some excellent spots, although nighttime there is typically much quieter and concentrated in neighborhood pubs.

Thursday night is a big party night in Budapest, especially in Pest, and is often busier than a weekend evening. Underground bars are popular among locals, particularly the college crowd and twentysomethings. Some are laid-back art spots, others are beer-specialty bars. The most popular bars in recent years are the ruin bars, and tourists are particularly attracted to them. A lot of ex-pats like to go there, and you'll usually find them packed and very loud. Wine bars are in abundance, and if you go, ask for a spitzer, a half-wine/half-carbonated water drink that really hits the spot in summer.

Bars are more popular than clubs, which wasn't the case even a few years ago, but if it's midnight and you still want to party, there are plentiful club options that carry on until 4 or 5 am. Most nighttime spots in Budapest are open quite late, with the exception of several outdoor terrace squares, where bars close around midnight or 1 am. There are also numerous 24-hour bar options.

🎭 Performing Arts

Budapest is a city deeply rooted in its love and appreciation for the performing arts. During the main season, which runs from September through June, you can find ballet, opera, classical music, and theater performances any night of the week. And compared to those for performances in many European cities, tickets to events in Budapest are affordable indeed to Western pocketbooks.

Hungary is, perhaps, best known for modern classical music, having produced two of the most famous composers of the 20th century, Béla Bartók and Zoltán Kodály, both of whose works are widely played throughout the city by numerous orchestras. Budapest is also home to the world-renowned Liszt Ferenc Music Academy (named after Hungarian composer Franz Liszt), which has by far the city's finest classical concert hall.

The Hungarian State Opera House, a grandiose hall on the beautiful, tree-lined Andrássy út in the city center, is one of Budapest's most famous buildings, built in 1884 and celebrated at that time as the most modern opera house in all of Europe. It is home to the Hungarian State Opera and the National Ballet, which, in addition to their regular performance schedules, put on a special Summer Opera & Ballet Festival for two to three weeks in July or August.

The Palace of the Arts, or Müpa, is a state-of-the-art facility that opened in 2005, and was an immediate sensation. It is located near Rákóczi Bridge along the Danube, and is next to the National Theatre, which opened in 2002. Both venues are part of the city's new Millenium City Center, which is still being developed. Müpa houses within it the Bartók National Concert Hall, the Ludwig Museum, and Festival Theatre, the technological master of them all.

The most noteworthy orchestras are the Budapest Festival Orchestra and Hungarian Radio Symphony. Most play at the Liszt Ferenc Music Academy, but for up-to-date information, pick up Fidelio, a free monthly booklet listing every classical music event available at ticket and Tourinform offices.

There are very few theater performances held in English, but Red Ball Theater, which opened in 2015, offers English-language programming, as does MU Theater, a noted venue for contemporary dance.

Several of Budapest's most famous churches host concerts by pianists, orchestras, and sometimes singers, mostly during the summer months from May to September. We highly

recommend taking in an orchestra concert in the Gothic Mátyás Templom in the Castle District, as it overlooks the entire city and the Danube River.

TICKETS
Tickets for arts events can be bought at the venues themselves, but many ticket offices across the city sell them without an extra charge. Prices are low compared to much of Europe. It's usually possible to get tickets a few days before most shows, but performances by major international artists sell out early. Tickets to Budapest Spring Festival events also go particularly quickly. Tickets can be purchased at ⊕ budapestconcert.com, which also has a complete listing of events. You can also check out ⊕ expat-press. com/category/hungarian-culture for more listings and options. ⊕ Budapest.com is another good resource for ticket outlets.

⬛ Shopping
Meandering around District V can delight with unusual treasures, too, and perhaps the best shopping can be done in Pest's side streets and udvars (passages). The Great Market Hall (aka Central Market) is vibrant and full of locals and foreigners alike any day of the week. You can buy everything there from hog tails to hats. The areas around Király utca and Ferenciek tere are dotted with stylish design shops. The streets off Váci utca, toward Petofi Sándor, are good places to poke around in for both old-style shops and ateliers. Andrássy út—perhaps Budapest's most beautiful shopping boulevard—is a must for strolling in any case, and serious shoppers will certainly enjoy the many upscale furniture and housewares shops lining the street between Oktogon and Deák Ferenc tér. If you just want to window shop, Falk Miksa utca is a lovely tree-lined street in the heart of

Essentials

the arts trade to amble down, filled with galleries and antique stores.

Hungary is famous for its age-old Herend porcelain, which is hand-painted in the village of Herend near Lake Balaton. High-quality, hand-cut crystal is considerably less expensive here than in the United States. Crystal and porcelain dealers also sell their wares at the Ecseri Piac flea market, often at discount prices, but those looking for authentic Herend and Zsolnay should beware of imitations. There are many folk-art vendors along Váci utca, selling hand-painted wooden eggs and embroidered fabrics. For tablecloths and traditional Hungarian costumes, head to the second floor of the Vasárcsárnok.

Shops are generally open until 5 or 6 pm on weekdays and 1 pm on Saturday (only shops in the malls are open on Sunday, for the most part).

Taxes

As a tourist in Hungary you will generally encounter two kinds of tax. Value-Added Tax (VAT) of up to 27% is included in the price of most consumer goods and services. An additional tourist tax is added to hotel bills in some parts of the country—it's 4% in Budapest.

Tipping

Tipping is appreciated in Hungary, but not expected. At restaurants that don't already include a gratuity, it is acceptable to tip 10%, or 15% if the service is exceptional. Tipping beyond that can be seen as patronizing, or worse. In spas, tips top out at 400 HUF (masseurs) and 100 HUF (attendants). There are attendants in some restrooms, and a tip

of 100 HUF is expected. Taxi drivers are tipped 10%. Most often tipping is done by making it clear when paying that you don't need the change (just nod and say *köszönöm* (thank you), pronounced kuh-suh-num).

Visitor Information

There are two Visitor Information locations in the city center. The main office is near Deák Square on Sütő utca, and the second is near Heroes' Square inside the City Park Ice Rink. In addition, there are two smaller tourist points at the airport.

When to Go

High Season: Budapest is very busy from June through August, when many of the major music and culinary festivals take place.

Low Season: Winters are dark and long in Hungary, and Hungarians are notoriously grumpy in these months, but hotels are cheaper.

Value Season: You can catch the tail end of the wine festival and the Jewish festival in September when the weather is gorgeous.

Top Tours

BUDAPEST ARCHITECTURAL TOURS

Budapest Architectural Tours offers private tours of Hungary, with a special focus on Budapest. The groups are small, limited to five, making the experience more personal with time for questions and photo ops. ⊕ www.tourguideofhungary.com

BIKE TOURS

Budapest Bike Breeze offers a variety of tours that allow you to hit the highlights, find the photo ops, and sample local cuisine. Tours cater to all levels and are family-friendly, too. The Szentendre Bike and Boat Tour includes a scenic bike ride out of Budapest along the Danube (swimming stops possible in good weather) to the medieval town of Szentendre. After lingering a while in this cute arts-filled town, make your way back to Budapest by boat. ⊕ budapestbikebreeze.com

BOAT TOURS

Legenda Tours offers a range of sightseeing cruises, both day and night, as well as a popular romantic candlelit dinner cruise. ⊕ www.legenda.hu

BUS TOURS

Big Bus Budapest is not only economical, it's also the most widely used bus tour in the city. Get the lay of the land on your first day in Budapest with this hop-on, hop-off tour or use it to hit the highlights so that you don't need to stress validating your ticket on the metro. ⊕ www.bigbustours.com/en/budapest/budapest-bus-tours

FAMILY-FRIENDLY BUS-BOAT TOURS

Bus tour or boat tour? Why choose when you can do both! RiverRide's amphibious sightseeing tour takes you to all of Budapest's top sights on four wheels and then takes you into the Dunube for views from the river. ⊕ riverride.com

ART NOUVEAU TOUR

WithLocals offers a three-hour private art and culture tour of all things art nouveau in the city. As its name indicates, all guides are local with proven expertise in the field. ⊕ www.withlocals.com

COMMUNIST HISTORY TOUR

Don't miss the true stories of the most dramatic period in Hungary's history on Generation Tours' 2.5-hour free walking tour of Red Budapest. Stops include Freedom Bridge, Liberty Square, Parliament, Imre Nagy, Liberty Statue, and more. ⊕ www.generationtours.com/budapest/free-red-budapest-tour

See Budapest's top sights through the lens of a local who shares what life was like behind the Iron Curtain. How did Hungary end up being a Red country? Who were the actual heroes and traitors in the 1956 Revolution? ⊕ www.gonative-guide.com/en/tours/budapest/125-red-budapest-communism-tour-eng

WALKING TOURS

EUrama offers private walking tours that take you to the main sites, but also to the lesser known, off-the-beaten path sites, revealing much of Budapest that cannot be gotten on your own. ⊕ www.eurama.hu

WINE TOURS

Wine Tours has a menu of options available for wine tours all over the region. You can spend one or two days touring the wine region of Lake Balaton, or a half day in Etyek, a famed wine region just outside of Budapest. ⊕ wine-tours.hu

50

Helpful Hungarian Phrases

BASICS

Hello	Szia/ szervusz	see-ya/ ser-voose
Yes/No	Igen/ nem	ee-gen/nem
Please	Kérem (szépen) legyen szíves	kay-rem (say-pen)/ le-dyen see-vesh
Thank you	Köszönöm (szépen)	kuh-suh-nuhm (saypen)
You're welcome	Színesen	see-vesh-en
I'm Sorry (apology)	Sajnálom/ bocsánat	shai-nal-ohm / boh-chah-nut
Sorry (Excuse me)	Elnézést	el-nay-zaysht
Good morning	Jó reggelt	yo rag-gehlt
Good day	Jó napot	yo nah-pot
Good evening	Jó estét	yo esh-tate
Goodbye	Viszlát/ viszontlátásra	vees-lot/ vees-ohnt-lot-osh-ra
Mr. (Sir)	Uram	oo-ram
Mrs.	Asszonyom	ah-sun-yum
Miss	Hölgyem	huh-l-dyem
Pleased to meet you	Örülök, hogy találkoztunk	ehr-rul-ook, hodyah tall-all-cause-tunk
How are you?	Hogy vagy?	Hoj vaj?

NUMBERS

one-half	fél	fail
one	egy	edge
two	kettő	ket-tuh
three	három	hah-rome
four	négy	neigh-dge
five	öt	uht
six	hat	hut
seven	hét	hate
eight	nyolc	nyolts
nine	kilenc	kee-lents
ten	tíz	teez
eleven	tizenegy	teez-en-edge
twelve	tizenkettő	teez-en-ket-tuh
thirteen	tizenhárom	teez-en-hah-rome
fourteen	tizennégy	teez-en-neigh-dge
fifteen	tizenöt	teez-en-eurht
sixteen	tizenhat	teez-en-hut
seventeen	tizenhét	teez-en-hate
eighteen	tizennyolc	teez-en-nyolts
nineteen	tizenkilenc	teez-en-kee-lents
twenty	húsz	whose
twenty-one	huszonegy	whose-on-edge
thirty	harminc	harm-mince
forty	negyven	n-edge-van
fifty	ötven	uht-van
sixty	hatvan	hut-vahn
seventy	hetven	hat-van
eighty	nyolcvan	nyolts-vahn
ninety	kilencven	kee-lents-ven

one hundred	száz	sahz
one thousand	ezer	ehzer
one million	egymillió	edge-milly-oh

COLOR

black	fekete	feck-eta
blue	kék	cake
brown	barna	barn-a
green	zöld	zh-hewld
orange	narancssárga	nah-ranch-shahr-gah
red	piros	peer-oosh
white	fehér	faye-hair
yellow	sárga	shahr-gah

DAYS OF THE WEEK

Sunday	Vasárnap	va-shahr-nahp
Monday	Hétfő	hate-fuh
Tuesday	Kedd	ked
Wednesday	Szerda	ser-duh
Thursday	Csütörtök	chew-tur-took
Friday	Péntek	pain-tek
Saturday	Szombat	soam-but

MONTHS

January	Január	yawn-ew-are
February	Február	feb-rew-are
March	Március	mar-ce-ush
April	Április	ap-rill-ish
May	Május	my-ush
June	Június	you-knee-ush
July	Július	you-lee-ush
August	Augusztus	agh-us-tush
September	Szeptember	sap-tam-bear
October	Október	ok-toe-bear
November	November	no-vam-bear
December	December	debt-sam-bear

USEFUL PHRASES

Do you speak English?	Beszél angolul?	Beh-sail angle-ul?
I don't speak [Language]	Nem beszélek [magyarul].	Nem beh-sail-ek [madya-rule].
I don't understand.	Nem értem.	Nem ert-em.
I don't know.	Nem tudom.	Nem two-dome.
I understand.	Értem.	Ert-em.
i'm American.	Amerikai vagyok.	Am-erikay-e vadge-ok.
I'm British.	Brit vagyok.	Brit vadge-ok.
What's your name.	Mi a neve?	Me ah neh-veh?
My name is ...	A nevem ...	Ah neh-vehm ...
What time is it?	Mennyi az idő?	Men-ye oz e-dur?
How?	Hogyan?	Hodge-on?
When?	Mikor?	Me-core?
Yesterday	Tegnap	tag-nah-p

Today	Ma	ma
Tomorrow	Holnap	hole-nah-p
This morning	Ma reggel	ma rag-gehl
This afternoon	Ma délután	ma dale-ew-tawn
Tonight	Ma este	ma esh-teh
What?	Mi?	Me?
What is it?	Mi az?	Me oz?
Why?	Miért?	Me-air-t?
Who?	Ki?	Key?
Where is ...	Hol van ...	Hole vahn ...
... the train station?	... a vasútállomás?	... ah vah-shoot-all-oh-mash?
... the subway station?	... a metróállomás?	... ah metro-all-oh-mash?
... the bus stop?	... a buszmegálló?	... ah boose-meg-all-oh?
... the airport?	... a repülőtér?	... ah rap-ew-l-ew-t-air?
... the post office?	... a posta?	... ah posh-tah?
... the bank?	... a bank?	... ah bahnk?
... the hotel?	... a hotel?	... ah hotel?
... the museum?	... a múzeum?	... ah moo-zeh-um?
... the hospital?	... a kórház?	... ah core-haas?
... the elevator?	... a lift?	... ah lift?
Where are the restrooms? (toilet)	Hol van a mosdó? (W.C.)	Hole vahn ah mosh-dough? (Vay-tsay)
Here/there	Itt/ ott	eat/ oat
Left/right	Bal/ jobb	ball/ yo-b
Is it near/far?	Közel van/ messze van?	Kew-zal vahn?/ Mess-se vahn?
I'd like ...	Szeretnék	S-air-et-n-ache
... a room	... egy szobát	... edge sob-aht
... the key	... a kulcsot	... ah cool-chot
... a newspaper	... egy újságot	... edge uhy-sha-got
... a stamp	.... egy bélyeget	... edge bay-egg-et
I'd like to buy ...	Szeretnék venni...	S-air-et-n-ache ven-knee
... a city map	... egy várostérképet	... edge vahr-osh -t-air-cape-et
... a road map	... egy autóstérképet	... edge ow-toe-sh-t-air-cape-et
... a magazine .	... egy magazint	... edge ma-ga-scene-t
... envelopes	... borítékokat	... bore-eat-ach e-ok-at
... writing paper	... levélpapírt	... leh-veil-pup-ear-t
... a postcard	... egy képeslapot	... edge cape-ash-lap-oat
... a ticket	... egy jegyet	... edge ye-edge-et
How much is it?	Mennyibe kerül?	Many-beh care-ul?
It's expensive/ cheap	Drága/ olcsó	draw-guh/ ol-cho

A little/a lot	Kevés/ sok	kev-esh/ sh-oal
More/less	Több/ kevesebb	t-oh-b/ kev-esh-eb
Enough/too (much)	Elég/ túl sok	el-ehg / t-ew-l sh-oak
I am ill/sick	Beteg vagyok	Beh-tag vadge-
Call a doctor	Hívjon orvost	Heeve-yon or-vosh-t
Help!	Segítség!	Shag-eat-shag!
Stop!	Állj (meg)!/ Elég!	Aye!/ El-egg!

DINING OUT

A bottle of ...	Egy üveg ...	Edge ew-v-egg
A cup of ...	Egy csésze ...	Edge chase-eh
A glass of ...	Egy pohár ...	Edge poh-haar
Beer	Sör	sure
Bill/check	Számla	saam-la
Bread	Kenyér	ken-yer
Breakfast	Reggeli	rag-ghehly
Butter	Vaj	v-aye
Cocktail/aperatif	Koktél	cock-tail
Coffee	Kávé	ka-vee
Dinner	Vacsora	vah-cho-rah
Fixed-price menu	Napi menü	nah-pee men-e'
Fork	Villa	vill-ah
I am a vegetarian/I don't eat meat	Vegetáriánus vagyok/ Nem eszem húst	Veh-geht-ar-ee anush vadge-ol Nem es-em who-sht
I cannot eat ...	Nem ehetek ...	Nem eh-et-ek ..
I'd like to order ...	Rendelni szeret-nék ...	Rendel-knee s-air-et-n-ache
Is service included?	Benne van a borravaló?	Ben-neh vahn a bore-ra-val-oh?
I'm hungry/thirsty	Éhes vagyok/ szomjas vagyok	A-hesh vadge-ok/ Som-yash vadge-ok
It's good/bad	Jó/ rossz	yo/ roass
It's hot/cold	Forró/ hideg	for-row/ he-dag
Knife	Kés	kay-sh
Lunch	Ebéd	eb-aid
Menu	Menü	men-ew
Napkin	Szalvéta	sal-vate-ah
Pepper	Bors	bore-sh
Plate	Tányér	taa-n-yair
Please give me ...	Legyen szíves odaadni ...	L-edge-en see-vesh auda-ad-knee ... show
Salt	Só	show
Spoon	Kanál	khan-al
Tea	Tea	teh-ah
Water	Víz	v-ease
Wine	Bor	boar

Great Itineraries

Six Days in Budapest

Let's be honest: you can blow through Budapest's big-ticket attractions in three days and still have time to quaff down the requisite bowl of goulash. But this city has as many "must-dos" as "must-sees." So if you want to really experience Hungary's capital, plan on spending five days, setting a sixth day to visit Szentendre.

DAY 1: TAKE IT FROM THE TOP

There's a good reason why Castle Hill is the undisputed first stop on everyone's itinerary. This UNESCO World Heritage Site has a genuine "wow factor," yet it is compact enough for jet-lagged—or late-arriving—visitors to cover on their first day. Begin by poking around the Royal Palace (time permitting, tour the Hungarian National Gallery in its center block). Next, stroll along the cobblestone streets between colorful baroque, Gothic, and Renaissance facades, stopping in for a look at Matthias Church; then head for Fishermen's Bastion. The view from its Disneyesque turrets isn't just achingly beautiful: it will help you get your bearings! If you need a caffeine fix to keep you going—or just want to get a fix on Budapest's coffee culture—drop into Ruszwurm, the city's oldest café.

DAY 2: ANDRÁSSY ÚT

Today, turn your back on hilly Buda and get acquainted with blessedly flat Pest. Start with a look inside massive Szent István Bazilika. Views from the cupola are worth the climb; though you may want to save your energy for the walk along Andrássy út, another UNESCO World Heritage Site. En route, pick and choose between the attractions (the Operaház and Terror Háza are favorites), leaving time to ogle other architectural treasures. The boulevard comes to a climatic finish at Hősök tere, where the Millennial Monument is flanked by two more museums. After perusing Old Masters in the Szépmuvészeti, take the Millennial Underground back to the opera house for an evening performance. Then wrap things up by toasting the good life with an alfresco nightcap on nearby Liszt Ferenc tér.

DAY 3: PEST

Kick off your day the Budapest way by breakfasting at Café Gerbeaud on Vörösmarty tér; then spend the morning browsing around Váci utca. Even if shopping's not your bag, you'll find the street to be a fascinating study in contrasts as it runs south past Euro-style boutiques, through the university area, to the venerable Vásárcsarnok Market. In the afternoon, treat yourself to a tour. Commercial ones cater to almost every taste—and cover almost every mode of transportation, from boats and bikes to balloons. Major sites, like Parliament, also offer tours or you can take a guided walk of the Jewish District to learn about the Jewish Ghetto, see the synagogues, and visit the ruin bars.

DAY 4: PARK YOURSELF

Budapesters love their parks—and you will, too, because the best of the bunch offer both gorgeous greenery and plentiful bathing opportunities. If you happen to be staying at either the Danubius Grand Hotel Margitsziget or the Ensana Thermal Margitsziget, Margaret Island is a serendipitous place to take the plunge. Otherwise, head for City Park, at the northeast end of Andrássy út. Developed as the centerpiece of Hungary's 1896 millennial celebrations, this urban oasis is the setting for the Széchenyi Baths. You could while away hours in its indoor and outdoor thermal pools. But before your toes get too wrinkled, consider City Park's other attractions. Beyond the baths, kids can kick back at the zoo, while adults can enjoy a smattering of museums and concert venues, plus one of Budapest's best-loved restaurants (Gundel).

DAY 5: HEAD FOR THE HILLS

Want to escape the urban scene without leaving the city limits? No problem. Gellért Hill is laced with trails leading up—waaay up—to the towering Liberation Monument and the Citadella behind it. (Don't worry about aching muscles: you can lounge later in one of three vintage baths located on the hill). More outdoorsy adventures are available in the Buda Hills: and you don't have to be a die-hard hiker to take advantage of them. János Hill, for example, can be accessed via a panoramic chairlift or a narrow-gauge train that's operated primarily by children. You'll find equally intriguing sites beneath these hills: namely some 200 caves, several of which are open to sightseers and spelunkers. Whatever you choose, reward yourself afterward with a down-home Hungarian dinner, complete with noodle pudding and live music.

DAY 6: AROUND THE BEND

By now you've probably crisscrossed the Danube on countless occasions, so it's high time you actually got out on the water. The ideal way to do it is by taking a leisurely two-hour boat trip upriver to Szentendre. Although it's known primarily as an artists colony, there's more to this picturesque little town than galleries and cutesy crafts shops but do leave room in your suitcase for souvenirs. Those who wish to linger can gain precious sightseeing time by opting for the shorter land route when returning to Budapest. Once back, you can compensate for your abbreviated boat trip by booking a moonlight dinner cruise through the city itself.

Seven Days: Budapest + Day Trips

For a first-time visitor with a week to enjoy, focus on the central and western part of the country and you'll have more than your share of places to go and sites to see. Base yourself in Budapest and hit the road every day with your rental car, or spare the morning and evening trips and base yourself in Szentendre or Visegrád to explore the surrounding towns.

DAY 1: BUDAPEST HIGHLIGHTS

The **Hungarian Parliament Building** on the Pest side at Kossuth Square can be viewed from many spots in the city, but to take in the magnificence of this Gothic Revival building, which took some 100,000 workers to complete, you need to see it up close. If you decide to take a tour, allow for about an hour. Nearby is "Shoes on the Danube," a moving memorial dedicated to the 20,000 Hungarian Jews executed by Nazis at the river. Next, stop at the **Great Market Hall,** a good spot early in the day before the crowds descend. You can have a coffee and pastry, and head up to the second floor for a good view of the whole market. Stroll around the **Jewish Quarter** for shopping, cute cafés, and history. Take a walking tour if you are interested in more historical context as you wander. Note, this is where the now famous ruin bars are located if you want an atmospheric afternoon drink. Walk across the **Chain Bridge** and take the funicular up to the Buda Hills. Check out **Matthias Church** and the **Fishermen's Bastion,** then end the day with panoramic views from **Buda Castle,** looking across the Danube to the stunningly lit Parliament building and the Chain Bridge.

Great Itineraries

Logistics: Walking or public transportation will be your best bet. Even in a taxi, traffic can be bad and will just eat into valuable time.

DAY 2: SZENTENDRE

A colorful, charming town about 10 miles north of Budapest, Szentendre is located along the river. There you can view artists at work, or buy some local art, as this is where one of Hungary's famed artist colonies is located. You can also visit Hungary's Open-Air Ethnographic Museum (a site that re-creates village life from centuries past) on the outskirts, or take in the National Wine Museum if you're scouting wines to take home. You'll feel a bit like you're in the Mediterranean as you amble along the winding cobbled paths and narrow alleyways. The houses are painted vibrant colors, a refreshing contrast to the muted colors of Budapest. There are a lot of folk art stores and handicraft workshops, perfect for buying keepsakes and souvenirs. Enjoy a traditional meal and the magic of this riverside town by evening and overnight here.

Logistics: This is an easy train ride from Budapest. Once here, it's entirely walkable.

DAY 3: VÁC.

The riverside city of Vác sits across the river from Szentendre and Visegrád. With 18th-century bridges, plazas, and baroque churches, the little riverside town is both fascinating and romantic and a perfect day trip. Jump on a river cruise to marvel at the town's beautiful skyline.

Logistics: EuroVelo, a network of the best cycle routes in Europe, has a route that runs along the banks of the Danube, and the Vác section is considered one of the most picturesque spots. Rent a bike for the afternoon to take it in.

DAY 4: VISEGRÁD

Visit fortress ruins and tour the **Palace of King Matthias,** who ruled the Hungarian Kingdom in the 13th Century, in Visegrád, a small town about a half hour from Szentendre. The mountaintop **Citadel** offers awe-inspiring views of the landscape and the Danube Bend. Brave travelers can opt to slide down the canopy zipline to take in the Danube and Visegrád views with an infusion of adrenaline. **The International Palace Games of Visegrád,** one of the largest medieval festivals in Europe, takes place here every summer.

Logistics: Drive or take a bus from Szentendre. It makes sense to base yourself here for a few nights while you take in the surrounding areas of Vác and Esztergom.

DAY 5: ESZTERGOM

Continue west to Esztergom, which is located about 48 km (30 miles) north of Budapest. Esztergom is one of the oldest towns in Hungary, and the current town sits atop the ruins of a medieval town. As it is where Christianity began in Hungary, it is not surprising that it is home to one of the largest cathedrals in Europe. Don't miss the Castle Hill area, famed for the Hungarian Royal Palace ruins. If you've got time, venture up into the adjacent Pilis Mountains where you can explore oak and beech forests dotted with caves and beautiful chalk cliffs.

Logistics: If you walk across the Mária Valéria bridge, it will bring you right into Štúrovo, Slovakia. Plan ahead by bringing some euros along, or alert your credit card company before your walk so that you may use your card in Slovakia as well as Hungary.

DAY 6: GYŐR

Győr is situated halfway between Vienna and Budapest, about an hour and a half drive from Budapest if you travel here

directly. It's known as the City of Waters because it is at the confluence of three rivers, the Mosoni-Duna River, a branch of the Danube, the Rába River, and the Rábca River, which flow through the historic old town of the city. Győr is one of the three wealthiest towns in the country (second to Budapest and Sopron), and it shows. The baroque architecture in the old town square is well maintained and boasts brightly painted facades, and the riverside boardwalks are vibrant and romantic. If you need a break from the beauty and old-world charm (impossible), there are thermal spas throughout the city if you didn't get a chance to take the waters in Budapest.

Logistics: Public transportation will be your best bet in getting around town.

DAY 7: LAKE BALATON

Round out your tour with a trip to **Lake Balaton.** This was where the wealthy used to vacation under the communist regime, and where Austrians and West Germans came for an affordable escape. It's not as cheap as it used to be, but it's still a good deal for what you get. If you have extra time in your itinerary, you'll want to allow a few days to explore the varied offerings of this area. The mountainous area around Lake Balaton is known for its wine making, while the shore to the south is full of

resort towns. And if it's beaches you're after, you can choose the resort town that best fits the kind of experience you want. **Siófok** is famous for its beaches and nightlife. **Zamárdi** is attractive to families because it offers a large adventure park and the longest stretch of free beach in the region. The bobsled track doesn't hurt either.

In **Keszthely** tour the baroque **Festetics Palace,** a stunning national landmark, to get a sense of what life was like for the aristocrats of the 18th and 19th centuries.

Lake Hévíz at the western tip of Lake Balaton is really just an enormous thermal bath. The eleven-acre lake is covered in water lilies and the temperature is welcoming year-round—the lowest it will ever get is 75°F—even in the often brutal cold of February. The medicinal muds extracted from the yards-thick lake bed are routinely used to treat muscle pain and even rheumatism—treatments are prescribed by doctors—but the mud is also used in beauty treatments. You'll want to allow time for mud masks and mud body wraps and general rolling in the therapeutic mud.

Logistics: The Lake Balaton region can get packed in summer, so plan ahead and accordingly.

On the Calendar

February

Mangalica Pork Festival. Also known as the Hairy Pig food festival, this two-day food and culture fest on Szabadsag Square in the heart of the city is named for the Mangalica pig breed (also known as curly-hair hog), a unique pig breed indigenous to Hungary. Entry is free and you'll find a variety of local foods and crafts. ⊕ *mangalicafesztival.hu.*

The annual **Busójárás Festival** in the southern Hungarian town of Mohács is such an ingrained local tradition that it has been named a UNESCO cultural heritage event. Usually held between the end of February and the first few days of March, this ritual carnival involves six days of strange characters in masks and furry costumes making as much noise as possible to chase away winter. Mohács is also known as being the site of two seminal battles, one in 1526 which ushered in the Ottoman occupation, another in 1687 that helped end it. Plan to take in the most raucous of the Mohács processions which takes place on Farsang Sunday. ⊕ *www.mohacsibusojaras.hu*

***Farsang* (Carnival) Season.** Costume parades and carnival masks mark Hungary's farewell to winter and ushering in of spring. Farsang celebrations take place across Hungary to scare off evil spirits and the capital is filled with themed events, colorful crowds, and masquerade balls. The festive period stretches from early March until Easter and involves a lot of rich sweets and meats. Most event spaces in Budapest host parties and celebrations. Be sure to sample the staple of the season, a carnival doughnut at the Carnival Doughnut Festival ⊕ *www.facebook.com/farsangifankfesztival.*

March

Revolution Day. On March 15th, Hungarians commemorate the Revolution and the following War of Independence against the Austrian-Habsburg rule. Events are held throughout the city, including Buda Castle and the National Museum where you will find folk dance demonstrations and folk concerts. Dress in red, white, and green to join the fun.

Budapest Spring Festival. One of the most popular of Hungarian festivals is held for two weeks beginning in mid-March. Spread across 50 to 60 venues around the city, the festival hosts renowned classical musicians, performers, and orchestras from across Europe and beyond, and also includes various theater productions, performances, and film screenings. Tickets to its more than 200 events go fast, so it's wise to plan ahead if you hope to attend. ⊕ *www.btf.hu*

April

The Titanic Film Festival. One of the leading film festivals in Central Europe, Titanic International Film Festival surprises Hungarian audiences with works of cinema of the Far East, visually stunning Korean and Japanese thrillers, period action dramas and animation, concert films, and Scandinavian crime dramas. ⊕ *titanicfilmfest.hu*

June

Budapest Summer Festival. Hailed as one of Europe's best summer festivals, music events are hosted throughout the summer at various venues. Catch open-air theater performances, concerts, and special events for the kids, too. Margaret Island's Open-air stage makes for a wonderful summer day out if you can catch an event. ⊕ *szabadter.hu/en*

Danube Carnival Inernational Culture Festival. Folk dancing, classical music, wind bands, world music, and contemporary dance performances are held at a variety of venues across the capital city for two weeks in mid-June. ⊕

July

Red Bull Air Race. This annual air show features performance flights over the Danube in some of the world's fastest and lightest planes. ⊕ *airrace.redbull. com/en*

August

Festival of Folk Arts. The most renowned local artists and craftsmen from different regions of the country introduce their skills handed down from many generations at this annual festival in Budapest's Castle District. ⊕ *www.mestersegekun-nepe.hu*

Sziget Festival. The first Sziget Festival was organized back in 1993 as a small gathering and has since evolved into one of Europe's largest music festivals with over 1,000 shows across 60 stages, for seven days straight. ⊕ *szigetfestival.com/en*

September

Budapest Wine Festival. In mid-September, a wine exhibition in the Buda castle features the country's best wine producers, including a wine auction. The arts component includes classical and jazz concerts each evening. ⊕ *www.winefestival.hu*

October

Budapest Design Week. For ten days in October, Budapest hosts the best of Hungarian and international designers with a variety of events, including workshops, markets, presentations, and awards. ⊕ *designweek.hu/2020*

December

Christmas Markets. There are a multitude of Christmas markets where you can get your mulled wine and chimney cake fix, but perhaps the most famous is the one at Vörösmarty tér, in front of the famous Gerbeaud coffeehouse, which is decorated beautifully for the holidays. Goods at this market are handmade and traditional so it makes a great spot for quality souvenir shopping. The Christmas Market at St. Stephen's Basilica features festive lights and music and hearty street food as well as a skating rink for children.

Contacts

Activities

Escape Room. ☎ *30/185–6996* ⊕ *escaperoom-budapest.com*. **Bubble Football.** ☎ *30/185–6996* ⊕ *www.bubble-football-budapest.com*.

BUDAPEST SPAS CONTACTS Gellért Baths. ☎ *1/466–6166* ⊕ *www.gellertfurdo.hu*. **Király fürdő.** ✉ *Fő utca 84, Budapest* ☎ *1/202–3688* ⊕ *en.kiralyfurdo.hu*. **Palatinus Baths.** ✉ *Margitsziget, Margit-sziget* ☎ *1/340-4500* ⊕ *en.palatinusstrand.hu*. **Rudas Baths.** ☎ *1/321–4568* ⊕ *www.rudasbaths.com*. **Széchenyi Baths.** ✉ *Városliget* ☎ *1/363–3210* ⊕ *szechenyispabaths.com*.

✈ Air

AIRPORT Ferenc Liszt International Airport (BUD). ☎ *1/296–9696* ⊕ *www.bud.hu*. **Debrecen International Airport.** ✉ *Mikepércsi út* ☎ *20/467–9899* ⊕ *www.debrecenairport.com/en*.

AIRLINES LOT Polish Airlines. ☎ *22/577–7755* ⊕ *www.lot.com*. **Ryan Air.** ⊕ *www.ryanair.com*. **Smartwings.** ☎ *284/000–612* ⊕ *www.smartwings.com*. **WizzAir.** ⊕ *www.wizzair.com*.

🚌 Bus

CONTACTS Volán. ☎ *1/382–0888* ⊕ *www.volanbusz.hu*.

Ⓜ Public Transport

CONTACTS Center for Budapest Transport (BKK). ☎ *1/325–5255* ⊕ *bkk.hu*.

Taxi

CONTACTS Bolt Taxi. ☎ *1/444–5154* ⊕ *www.bolt.eu*. **Budapest Taxi.** ☎ *1/777–7777*. **City Taxi.** ☎ *1/211–1111* ⊕ *www.citytaxi.hu*. **Főtaxi.** ☎ *1/222–2222* ⊕ *www.fotaxi.hu*. **6X6 Taxi.** ☎ *1/666–6666* ⊕ *new.6x6taxi.hu*. **Taxi 4.** ☎ *1/444–4444*. **Taxi Plus.** ☎ *1/888–8888*. **Tele 5 Taxi.** ☎ *1/555–5555*.

🚆 Train

CONTACTS Eurail. ⊕ *eurail.com*. **MÁV.** ☎ *1/349–4949* ⊕ *www.mavcsoport.hu/en*. **Regiojet.** ☎ *22/222–2221* ⊕ *www.regiojet.com*.

Chapter 3

VÁRKERÜLET (CASTLE DISTRICT)

DISTRICT 1

Updated by
Joseph Reaney

 Sights
★★★★★

 Restaurants
★★★★☆

 Hotels
★★★★☆

 Shopping
★★☆☆☆

 Nightlife
★★★☆☆

NEIGHBORHOOD SNAPSHOT

TOP EXPERIENCES

- **Taste wine in a cave:** Delve deep down into the medieval Faust Wine Cellar, situated in the caves below the Hilton Budapest, for a truly unique wine tasting experience.

- **Catch a dance show:** Watch one of the world's finest folk dance ensembles put on a show at the architecturally fascinating Hagyományok Háza (Hungarian Heritage House).

- **Up, up, and away:** Feeling too lazy to climb all the way from Víziváros to Buda Castle? Hop on the quaint, 19th century sikló (funicular) and you'll be up there in a jiffy.

- **Drink in the view:** Sip a delicious cocktail as you admire the city below from the Leo Rooftop bar; a clever sliding-window system means it's now open year-round.

GETTING HERE

Víziváros is easy to reach from anywhere in Budapest. The metro station Batthyány tér is at the heart of the district, trams run along the riverside street Bem rakpart, and it's just a short walk across the river to Belváros and Lipótváros. Getting up to Várhegy (Castle Hill) is trickier, as it's a climb from any of the metro stations or tram stops. If you don't want to walk, catch the frequent Bus 16, to hop on the historic sikló (funicular), or to take the free escalator up from the Várkert Bazár (Castle Garden Bazaar). Most of the neighborhood is pedestrianized or limited to traffic, so leave the car at home.

PLANNING YOUR TIME

As one of the city's main tourist neighborhoods, the Castle District's attractions are typically open all week long and year-round. Most close in the early evening (between 5 and 7 pm), at which point Castle Hill can suddenly feel very deserted. However, it's worth sticking around for spectacular views of the lit-up city from the suddenly-free-to-visit Fisherman's Bastion, before heading down to Víziváros for some after-dark fun.

QUICK BITES

- **Royal Guard Café.** Set inside the seemingly historic Főőrség (Guard House), which was actually only built in 2020, this is a pleasant and convenient stop for a coffee. ⊠ *Lovarda utca, Castle District* Ⓜ *M2: Déli pályaudvar*

- **KedvesKrém.** Pop into this delightful ice cream and frozen yogurt parlor to cool down during the long walk up from Víziváros to Várhegy. ⊠ *Batthyány utca 26, Castle District* ⊕ *www.kedveskrem.hu* Ⓜ *M2: Széll Kálmán tér*

- **Home of Franziska.** With its floral prints, muted colors, and geometric patterns, this calm little café is an away-from-it-all stop for a tasty breakfast, light lunch, or afternoon snack. ⊠ *Iskola utca 29, Castle District* ⊕ *www.franziska.hu* Ⓜ *M2: Batthyány tér*

- **Rétesvár.** For a sweet treat any time of day, this tiny, tucked-away bakery serves traditional homemade Hungarian strudel, as well as delicious gingerbread. ⊠ *Balta köz 4, Castle District* ⊕ *www.budavari-retesvar.hu* Ⓜ *M2: Déli pályaudvar*

Most of Buda's major sights and many of its best restaurants can be found in the Castle District, which encompasses two areas: the attraction-packed Várhegy (Castle Hill), a long, narrow plateau laced with cobblestone streets, beautifully preserved baroque, Gothic, and Renaissance houses, and crowned by the magnificent Royal Palace; and the riverside district of Víziváros (Water City), which lies below the castle and is a popular spot for dining, drinking, and making merry.

The hill itself is home to Budapest's biggest historical draws, including the 700-year-old Royal Palace, the enormous medieval Matthias Church, and the neo-Renaissance Fisherman's Bastion. It also has several fascinating museums and exhibits, as well as some of the most jaw-dropping views in the city. Mostly pedestrianized, the area is best explored on foot, and you can easily spend a whole day doing so.

As the sun sets, venture down to Víziváros, the Danube-hugging district below the Buda Castle complex. While it has a few worthwhile sights of its own, such as the Church of St. Anne and the Király Thermal Bath, it's best known for its hip cafés, excellent restaurants, and rooftop cocktail bars.

 Sights

The vast majority of this district's note-worthy attractions, including big hitters like Matthias Church and the Royal Palace, can be found high up on Castle Hill. The exceptions are the Várkert Bazár, which sits below the castle in Víziváros, and the Széchenyi Chain Bridge.

Bécsi kapu tér (*Vienna Gate Square*)
PLAZA | This lovely square (well, triangle) at the northwestern end of Castle Hill is home to some fine baroque and rococo houses. It's dominated by the enormous neo-Romanesque headquarters of the Országos Levéltár (Hungarian National Archives), a cathedral-like shrine to paperwork built in the 1910s, but there are other gems here, too: check out the house at number eight, with its pink-and-white striped facade and unusual curved windows. Nearby is the medieval stone

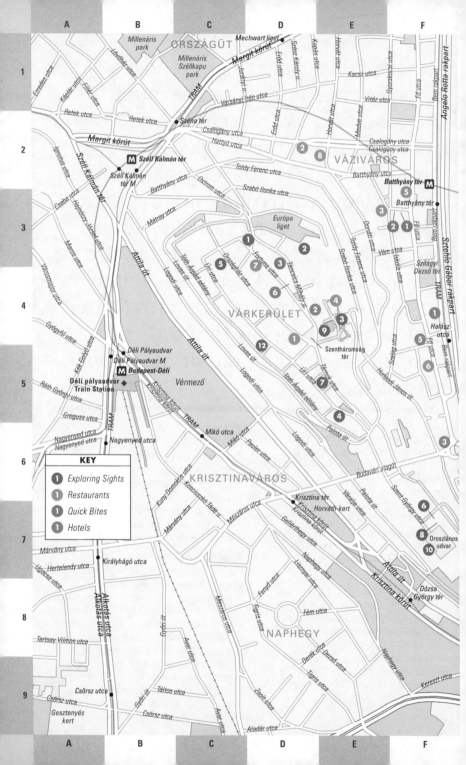

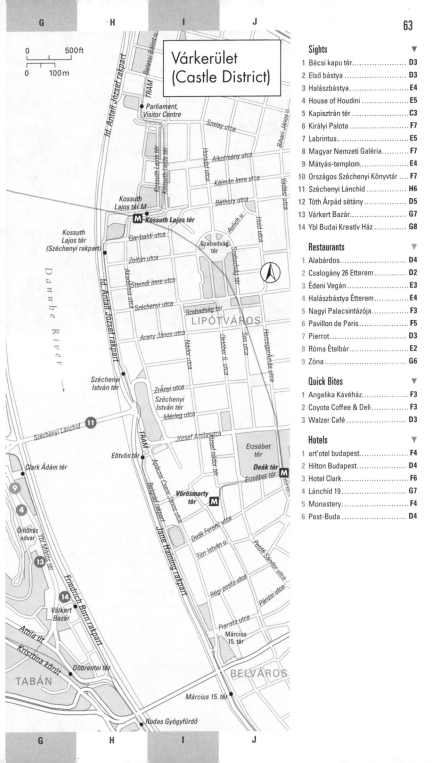

Várkerület
(Castle District)

Sights ▼

1 Bécsi kapu tér....................D3
2 Első bástya D3
3 Halászbástya......................E4
4 House of Houdini E5
5 Kapisztrán tér C3
6 Királyi Palota F7
7 Labrintus........................E5
8 Magyar Nemzeti Galéria..........F7
9 Mátyás-templom..................E4
10 Országos Széchenyi Könyvtár F7
11 Széchenyi Lánchíd H6
12 Tóth Árpád sétány D5
13 Várkert Bazár.....................G7
14 Ybl Budai Kreatív Ház G8

Restaurants ▼

1 Alabárdos.........................D4
2 Csalogány 26 Etterem D2
3 Édeni Vegán.......................E3
4 Halászbástya Étterem..............E4
5 Nagyi Palacsintázója..............F3
6 Pavillon de Paris...................F5
7 Pierrot............................D3
8 Róma Ételbár......................E2
9 Zóna...............................G6

Quick Bites ▼

1 Angelika Kávéház.................F3
2 Coyote Coffee & Deli..............F3
3 Walzer Café D3

Hotels ▼

1 art'otel budapest..................F4
2 Hilton Budapest...................D4
3 Hotel Clark.........................F6
4 Lánchíd 19 ....G7
5 Monastery.........................F4
6 Pest-Buda D4

The Halászbástya or Fisherman's Bastion with its panoramic viewing terrace and fairy-tale towers is one of the best known monuments in Budapest.

gateway (rebuilt in 1936) that marks the northern entrance to Castle Hill, and after which the square is named. As the name suggests, this Vienna Gate once marked the end of a highway that connected Buda Castle to the Austrian capital. ⊠ *Budapest* Ⓜ *M2: Széll Kálmán tér.*

Első bástya (*First Bastion*)
ARCHAEOLOGICAL SITE | Finally opened to the public in 2019, this area at the heart of Buda Castle was until recently a United States Marine Corps residence (the site was given to the US in 1948 as war reparations). Before that, it was used as a prison during the anti-Habsburg revolution of 1848–49, and way back in the 13th century, it was probably home to the royal residence of King Béla IV. Uncover the archaeological history of the site with a wooden-walkway audio guided tour of the excavated bastion and walls, all while enjoying spectacular views of the city below. ⊠ *9 Táncsics Mihály utca, Castle District* ☎ *30/153–0673* ⊕ *www.t9.hu/en* ⊠ *900 HUF* Ⓜ *M2: Batthyány tér.*

★ Halászbástya (*Fisherman's Bastion*)
VIEWPOINT | The wondrous porch overlooking the Danube and Pest is the neo-Romanesque Fisherman's Bastion, a merry cluster of white stone towers, arches, and columns above a modern bronze statue of St. Stephen, Hungary's first king. Medieval fishwives once peddled their wares here; today it's the turn of merchants selling souvenirs and crafts. During the day in high season, you must pay to get to the upper lookout level, but the very reasonable price is well worth the view. Nevertheless, if you don't want to pay it, you can still access the lower portion of the walkway, or come at night to freely explore the whole structure. ⊠ *Szentháromság tér, Castle District* ⊕ *www.budavar.hu/halaszbastya-belepodijai* ⊠ *1,000 HUF* Ⓜ *M2: Batthyány tér.*

House of Houdini
MUSEUM | FAMILY | Named for the renowned Budapest-born illusionist and escapologist, this entertaining, family-friendly museum is home to an

Tight on Time in the National Gallery?

Go right to the permanent exhibition halls focusing on the art of the great 19th-century Hungarian master, László Munkácsy. In the permanent exhibition *Variations on Realism – From Munkácsy to Mednyánszky*, you'll find Munkácsy's masterpieces *The Condemned Cell* and the *Woman Carrying Brushwood*, as well as works by László Paál, Lajos Deák Ébner, Adolf Fényes, József Koszta, Gyula Rudnay, and László Mednyánszky. Don't miss Pál Szinyei Merse, who quite on his own pursued a style akin to French impressionism but was not appreciated in his own era. If you're a fan of early ecclesiastical art, the medieval triptychs are something to behold. Have 15 minutes to spare yet? Go to the central rooms on the second floor to view *Modern Times – Hungarian Art between 1896 and World War II*.

enormous collection of Harry Houdini artifacts, from personal letters to stage magic props. Fun guided tours are topped by a live magic show performed by talented local conjurers. ✉ *Dísz tér 11, Castle District* ☎ *1/951–8066* ⊕ *www.houseofhoudinibudapest.com* 💰 *3,000 HUF* Ⓜ *M2: Déli pályaudvar.*

Kapisztrán tér (*Capistrano Square*)
PLAZA | This historic square at the northwestern end of Castle Hill is named after St. John of Capistrano, a 13th-century Italian friar who recruited a crusading army to fight the Turks who were threatening Hungary; you can find a statue of the honored Franciscan here. The square is also home to the remains of the 12th-century Gothic **Mária Magdolna templom** (Church of St. Mary Magdalene). With most of church destroyed by air raids during World War II, the main feature still standing is the tower; today you can climb its 172 steps for stunning city views. Also on the square is the **Hadtörténeti Múzeum** (Museum of Military History), set within a former barracks that still has cannonballs from the 1849 siege lodged in its walls. The exhibits, which include collections of uniforms and military regalia, trace Hungary's military history from the original Magyar conquest in the 9th century through the period of Ottoman rule to the mid-20th century. ✉ *Castle District* Ⓜ *M2: Széll Kálmán tér.*

Királyi Palota (*Royal Palace*)
CASTLE/PALACE | A palace originally built on this spot in the 13th century for the kings of Hungary was reconstructed in the Renaissance style under the supervision of King Matthias during the 15th century. That, in turn, was demolished as Buda was recaptured from the Turks in 1686.

The Habsburg empress Maria Theresa directed the building of a new palace in the 1700s. It was damaged during an unsuccessful attack by revolutionaries in 1849, but the Habsburgs set about building again, completing work in 1905.

Then, near the end of the Soviets' seven-week siege in February 1945, the entire Castle Hill district of palaces, mansions, and churches was reduced to rubble. Decades passed before reconstruction and whatever restoration was possible were completed. Archaeologists were able to recover both the original defensive walls and royal chambers, due in part to still surviving plans and texts from the reigns of Holy Roman Emperor Sigismund and King Matthias.

Freed from mounds of rubble, the foundation walls and medieval castle walls were completed, and the ramparts

Királyi Palota or the Royal Palace is a historic castle-and-palace complex atop Castle hill on the Buda side, hence it is also referred to as Buda Castle.

surrounding the medieval royal residence were re-created as close to their original shape and size as possible. If you want an idea of the Hungarian homelife of Franz Josef and Sissi, however, you'll have to visit the baroque Gödöllő Palace.

Today, the Royal Palace is used as a cultural center. The baroque southern wing contains the **Budapesti Történeti Múzeum** (Castle Museum), displaying a fascinating permanent exhibit of modern Budapest history from Buda's liberation from the Turks in 1686 through the 1970s. Viewing the vintage 19th- and 20th-century photos and videos of the castle, the Széchenyi Lánchíd, and other Budapest monuments—and seeing them as the backdrop to the horrors of World War II and the 1956 revolution—helps to put your later sightseeing in context. You will also find the **Országos Széchényi Könyvtár** (National Széchényi Library), which has a copy of everything ever published in the Hungarian language.

In front of the Royal Palace, facing the Danube by the entrance to Wing C, stands an equestrian statue of Prince Eugene of Savoy, a commander of the army that liberated Hungary from the Turks at the end of the 17th century. From here there is a superb view across the river to Pest. ⊠ *Szent György tér 2, Castle District* ⊕ *www.budavar.hu* 🖃 *Castle Museum 2,400 HUF* ⊙ *Castle Museum closed Mon.* Ⓜ *M2: Déli pályaudvar.*

Labirintus (*Labyrinth of Buda Castle*) **NATURE SITE | FAMILY |** Used as a wine cellar during the 16th and 17th centuries and then as an air-raid shelter during World War II, this 16-meter (52-foot) deep, 1,200-meter (3,900-foot) long labyrinth—entered at Úri utca 9 below an early-18th-century house—is perhaps best explored on the 6 pm evening tour, when the spooky, winding corridors are illuminated only by oil lamp. Special exhibits include a wax museum with elaborately costumed figures depicting the attendants of a "haunted" masked ball held by the Black Count—a legendary

18th-century inhabitant of the tunnels; medieval stone monuments, including a red marble parapet from the palace of King Mathias; the Maze of Darkness—a completely dark section of the tunnels; and "Count Dracula's" mist-filled tomb. ■ TIP→ **This attraction is a little overpriced for what it is and gets mixed reviews from visitors, but if you like caves and getting a little spooked, it might be worth a visit.** ⊠ *District I, Úri utca 9, Castle District* ☎ *1/212–0207* ⊕ *www.labirintus.eu* ✉ *3000 HUF* Ⓜ *M2: Széll Kálmán tér, take bus 16 or 16/A to Szentháromság tér, M3: Deák Ferenc tér, take bus 16 to Szentháromság tér.*

★ **Magyar Nemzeti Galéria** (*Hungarian National Gallery*)
MUSEUM | Spread across four wings (and four floors) of the Royal Palace, this national gallery exhibits Hungarian fine art, from medieval ecclesiastical paintings, statues, and triptychs, through to Gothic, Renaissance, and baroque art, to a rich collection of 19th- and 20th-century works. Especially notable are the works of the romantic master painter Mihály Munkácsy, the Impressionist Pál Szinyei Merse (who quite on his own pursued a style akin to French impressionism), and the Surrealist Mihály Tivadar Kosztka Csontváry, who was much admired by Picasso. There is also a large collection of modern Hungarian sculpture, as well as regular (paid) temporary exhibits. Labels and commentary for both permanent and temporary exhibits are in English, and there's an audio guide available. ■ TIP→ **There is a 1,000 HUF charge to make video recordings, which are limited to the permanent exhibitions.** ⊠ *Castle District* ☎ *1/201–9082* ⊕ *www.mng.hu* ✉ *From 3,200 HUF; audio guide 800 HUF* ☉ *Closed Mon.* Ⓜ *M2: Déli pályaudvar.*

★ **Mátyás-templom** (*Matthias Church*)
RELIGIOUS SITE | The ornate white steeple of the Matthias Church is the highest point on Castle Hill. It was added in the 15th century, above a 13th-century

View Finder

You can either pay a modest fee to enter the Halászbástya (Fishermen's Bastion)—right by Mátyás templom (Matthias Church)—or else walk 10 minutes (or hop on any Várbusz) to the Királyi Palota (Royal Palace), where the lovely vistas are free. To soak in the sublimity of the Buda hills, meanwhile, go to the other side of the castle district (a two-minute walk) and walk along Tóth Árpád sétány (Árpád Tóth Promenade).

Gothic chapel. Officially the Buda Church of Our Lady, it has been known as the Matthias Church since the 15th century, in remembrance of the so-called Just King who greatly added to and embellished it during his reign (though many of these changes were lost when the Turks converted it into a mosque). The intricate white stonework, mosaic roof decorations, and some of its geometric patterned columns seem to suggest Byzantium, yet it was substantially rebuilt again in the neobaroque style 87 years after the Turkish defeat in 1686. One fortunate survivor of all the changes was perhaps the finest example of Gothic stone carving in Hungary: the Assumption of the Blessed Virgin Mary, visible above the door on the side of the church that faces the Danube.

Inside, the Trinity Chapel holds an *encolpion,* an enameled casket containing a miniature copy of the gospel to be worn on the chest; it belonged to the 12th-century king Béla III and his wife, Anne of Chatillon. Their burial crowns and a cross, scepter, and rings found in their excavated graves are also displayed here. The church's treasury contains Renaissance and baroque chalices, monstrances, and vestments. Climb the steps in the church's northwest corner to visit

Did You Know?

The stunning Matyas-templom or Matthias Church located atop the Buda Castle hill has witnessed several Royal weddings and coronations, including that of Charles I in 1916 (the last ruler of the Austro-Hungarian Empire).

the Royal Oratory and the collection of ecclesiastical art, as well as (for an extra fee) the panoramic tower with spectacular views of the city. From here, you can also admire the baroque Trinity Column in the square opposite, erected in 1712–13 as a gesture of thanksgiving by survivors of a plague.

High Mass is celebrated every Sunday at 10 am, sometimes with full orchestra and choir and often with major soloists; get here early if you want a seat. During the summer there are organ recitals on some Fridays and Sundays at 7:30 pm. ⊠ Szentháromság tér 2, Castle District ☎ 1/355–5657 ⊕ www.matyas-templom. hu ☒ 1,800 HUF; Tower 1,800 HUF Ⓜ M2: Batthyány tér.

Országos Széchenyi Könyvtár (Széchenyi National Library)

LIBRARY | The western wing (Wing F) of the Royal Palace is the Országos Széchenyi Könyvtár, which houses more than 2 million volumes. Its archives include well-preserved medieval codices, manuscripts, and historic correspondence, as well as the newly added Sound Library, which includes more than 2,600 digitized sound recordings of jazz music operettas, military music, folk songs, and more. This is not a lending library, but the reading rooms are open to the public (though you must show a passport); the most valuable materials can be viewed only on microfilm, however. Temporary exhibits on rare books and documents, for example, are usually on display; the hours for these special exhibits vary, and admission for smaller exhibits is sometimes free, though major exhibits usually have a charge. Note that the entire library closes for one month every summer, usually in August. ⊠ District I, Királyi Palota (Wing F), I Szent György tér 4-6, Castle District ☎ 1/224–3745, 1/224–3700 to arrange English-language tours ⊕ www.oszk.hu ☒ 1200 HUF Ⓜ M2: Széll Kálmán tér.

Széchenyi Lánchíd (Széchenyi Chain Bridge)

BRIDGE/TUNNEL | The oldest and most elegant of the eight road bridges that span the Danube in Budapest—particularly when lit up at night—the Széchenyi Chain Bridge connects Víziváros on the west bank with Lipótváros on the east. Before it was built, the river could be crossed only by ferry or by pontoon bridge that had to be removed when ice blocks began floating downstream in winter. It was constructed at the initiative of the great Hungarian reformer and philanthropist Count István Széchenyi, using an 1839 design by the English civil engineer William Tierney Clark, and was finished by the Scotsman Adam Clark (no relation). After it was destroyed by the Nazis, the bridge was rebuilt in its original, classical and symmetrical form—though widened for traffic—and was reopened in 1949, on the centenary of its inauguration. At the Buda end of the Chain Bridge is **Clark Ádám tér** (Adam Clark Square), from which you can zip up to Castle Hill on the siklό (funicular); it's 1,400 HUF one way. The square is also home to the **0 kilométerkő** (Zero Kilometer Stone), a sculpture from which all highway distance signs are measured all over the country. ⊠ Széchenyi Lánchíd, Castle District Ⓜ Tram 19, 41.

Tóth Árpád sétány (Árpád Tóth Promenade)

PROMENADE | This romantic tree-lined promenade, often overlooked by sightseers, follows the castle's ramparts southeast from the Museum of Military History toward the Royal Palace. It offers a fascinating "behind-the-scenes" look at the matte-pastel baroque houses that face Úri utca, with their regal arched windows and wrought-iron gates. On a late spring afternoon the fragrance of the cherry trees and the sweeping view of the quiet Buda neighborhoods below may be enough to revive even the most weary. About halfway along the route is a staircase leading down to the **Sziklakórház** (Hospital in the Rock), a subterranean World War II medical facility turned Cold War nuclear bunker that's part of the extensive Castle Hill caves network; entry costs 4,000 HUF. ⊠ *Castle District* Ⓜ *M2: Déli pályaudvar.*

Várkert Bazár (*Castle Garden Bazaar*)

GARDEN | It may look centuries old, but this beautiful complex of palatial riverside buildings was actually only constructed in the late 1800s by architect Miklos Ybl; the use of neobaroque and neo-Renaissance architecture was very fashionable at the time. The buildings are today home to everything from theaters and art exhibitions to restaurants and shops, but the complex's highlights are the spaces in between, including the manicured ornamental gardens and the lovely, strollable footpaths. You can take an elevator and escalator from here up to the top of Castle Hill for free. ⊠ *Ybl Miklós tér 2–6, Castle District* ☎ *30/198–5274* ⊕ *www.varkertbazar.hu* 🎟 *Exhibitions 4,000 HUF* Ⓜ *Tram 19, 41.*

Ybl Budai Kreatív Ház (*Ybl Buda Creative House*)

ARTS VENUE | A self-described "open community cultural space" located in a beautiful former pump house on the banks of the Danube, this cool little gallery and art space also boasts a pleasant café and bar. ⊠ *Miklós tér 9, Castle District* ☎ *1/569–8597* ⊕ *budaikreativhaz.hu* Ⓜ *Trams 19, 41.*

🍴 Restaurants

Alabárdos

$$$$ | HUNGARIAN | Something of a Buda Castle institution, Alabárdos first opened it doors almost 60 years ago—and within a building several centuries older than that. It remains one of the area's best gourmet dining options, with a menu that takes Hungarian classics and adds international and experimental twists to create fusion dishes like fillet of duck thigh risotto and poached trout with

black olives. **Known for:** modern Hungarian cuisine; lovely enclosed garden and terrace; open kitchen showcases chefs at work. $ *Average main: 7,500 HUF* ⊠ *Országház utca 2, Castle District* ☎ *1/356–0851* ⊕ *www.alabardos.hu* ☉ *Closed Sun.* Ⓜ *M2: Déli pályaudvar.*

Csalogány 26 Etterem

$$$ | EUROPEAN | Perennially on the Michelin radar, Csalogány 26 is one of the few truly great restaurants on the Buda side, and it's an ideal place to dine before or after taking in the Castle District. It also offers one of the best prix-fixe lunches in the city for a fraction of the cost of dinner. **Known for:** roasted lamb; prix-fixe menus with wine pairings; advance reservations necessary. $ *Average main: 3,500 HUF* ⊠ *Csalogány utca 26, Castle District* ☎ *1/201–7892* ⊕ *www.csalogany26.hu* ☉ *Closed Sun. and Mon. No dinner Tues. and Wed.*

Édeni Vegán

$ | VEGETARIAN | In a city that isn't always friendly to strict dietary requirements, this canteen-style bistro caters to several of them. Not only is every dish on the menu entirely vegan, from the leafy salads and fresh pastas to the thick soups and hearty stews, but many are also sugar-free, fat-free, gluten-free, and preservative-free. **Known for:** entirely plant-based dishes; generous pick-and-mix portions; popular mushroom vegan burgers. $ *Average main: 1,000 HUF* ⊠ *Iskola utca 31, Castle District* ☎ *20/921–5276* ⊕ *www.edenivegan.com* Ⓜ *M2: Batthyány tér.*

★ Halászbástya Étterem

$$$$ | HUNGARIAN | With a blockbuster view like this, a restaurant could be forgiven for lacking a focus on food—but that's not the case at this romantic terrace restaurant, part of the Fisherman's Bastion. From the goat cheese and pomegranate salad, to the Mangalitza pork tenderloin with octopus, to the smoking chocolate and raspberry dessert, every dish on the minimum three-course menu is perfectly prepared

and appealingly presented. **Known for:** sweeping views of the Danube in both directions; innovative take on Hungarian cuisine; service can be slow when busy. $ *Average main: 14,000 HUF* ✉ *Halászbástya, Szentháromság tér, Castle District* ☎ *30/897–1517* ⊕ *www. halaszbastya.eu* ⊙ *Closed Mon. and Tues.* Ⓜ *M2: Batthyány tér.*

Pavillon de Paris

$$$ | **FRENCH** | The main draw of this popular French restaurant, set across the road from the French Institute, is the incredibly romantic summer garden, where wrought iron chairs and cloth-covered tables are bathed in the glow of a million fairy lights. But that's not all it has going for it: come for the ambience but stay for the delicious French fare, including foie gras with brioche, bourguignonne snails, and crème brûlée, all served with a smile. **Known for:** delightful garden setting; modern takes on classic French dishes; expensive mains. $ *Average main: 4,900 HUF* ✉ *Fő utca 20, Castle District* ☎ *20/509–3430* ⊕ *www.pavillon-deparis.hu* Ⓜ *Tram 19, 41.*

Pierrot

$$$$ | **HUNGARIAN** | When touring the sights of Castle Hill, this elegant, long-established restaurant (once a medieval bakery) is the perfect stop for lunch or dinner. Sit in the romantic vaulted dining room or out in the lovely garden to enjoy an array of delicious, beautifully presented dishes—it's mainly traditional Austro-Hungarian staples with inventive, 21st-century twists—along with a good selection of local wines. **Known for:** crispy panfried pike perch; building dates back to 13th century; nightly live piano music. $ *Average main: 6,000 HUF* ✉ *Fortuna utca 14, Castle District* ☎ *1/375–6971* ⊕ *www.pierrot.hu* Ⓜ *M2: Batthyány tér.*

★ Róma Ételbár

$$ | **HUNGARIAN** | A favorite local lunch stop for more than three decades, and recently revived by new owner Dániel Andrusch, this cozy streetside restaurant serves the neighborhood's most authentic Hungarian food. It's deliciously hearty, meaty stuff, from thick goulash stews to fist-sized *cordon bleu*, but make sure you save space for dessert—particularly the giant, lip-smacking *túrógombóc* (cottage cheese dumpling). **Known for:** long-time Róma resident hostess Cica; wooden chairs and gingham tablecloths; túrógombóc (cottage cheese dumpling). $ *Average main: 2,500 HUF* ✉ *Csalogány utca 20, Castle District* ☎ *30/190–7773* ⊕ *www.facebook.com/romaetelbar2020* ⊙ *No dinner* Ⓜ *M2: Batthyány tér.*

Zóna

$$$ | **INTERNATIONAL** | This cool and contemporary bistro consistently ranks as one of Budapest's best, with a choice of globally inspired menus offering elegant, seasonal, and beautifully presented dishes on the one hand (think pigeon breast and duck liver) and unfussy gastro-grub on the other (think gourmet burgers and fries). The interior is bright, snazzy, and fun, with pastel-colored walls, patterned wood floors, and precariously dangling lights, while the floor-to-ceiling windows make the most of the river views. **Known for:** extensive wine menu with bottles on display; cellist plays some evenings; service can be hit and miss. $ *Average main: 3,500 HUF* ✉ *Lánchíd utca 7, Castle District* ☎ *30/422–5981* ⊕ *www.zonabudapest.com* Ⓜ *Tram 19, 41.*

☕ Coffee and Quick Bites

Angelika Kávéház

$ | **CAFÉ** | This four-room café gets even bigger in the summer, when six small graduated terraces with awnings open up outside. You can get a full range of cakes here and an over-the-top iced coffee with ice cream and whipped cream. **Known for:** Parliament views; drinks and desserts; bustling terrace. $ *Average main: 1,000 HUF* ✉ *District I, Batthyány tér 7, Batthyány tér* ☎ *1/225–1653* ⊕ *www. angelikacafe.hu* Ⓜ *M2: Batthyány tér.*

Coyote Coffee & Deli

$ | **BAKERY** | This cute little local-feeling café offers good coffee and great baked treats. A friendly team, who all speak good English, is another plus, as are the street-side tables to watch the world go by in warm weather. **Known for:** bagels and breakfast; coffee made with care, sourced in Vienna; people-watching on the patio. ⑤ *Average main: 1500 HUF* ✉ *Markovits Iván ut 4, Batthyány tér* ☎ *20/283–6959* ⊕ *www.facebook.com/ CoyoteCoffeeDeli* Ⓜ *M2: Batthyány tér.*

★ Walzer Café

$ | **CAFÉ** | This cute little cafe is within walking distance of the Castle District's top sights, but far enough off the tourist path to not feel or operate like a tourist trap. You'll find warm and friendly service along with delicious cakes and sandwiches. **Known for:** convenient to Matthias Church, Fisherman's Bastion, and Buda Castle; delicious cakes; charming and local-feeling. ⑤ *Average main: 1000 HUF* ✉ *Tancsics Mihaly utca 12, Castle District* ☎ *30/250–5971* ⊕ *www.facebook.com/ walzercafe.*

Hotels

The fairy-tale surroundings of Castle Hill make it a delightful place to stay. Sure, walking home is a strenuous uphill affair, but buses, taxis, and the sikló (funicular) can help out. Hotels down by the Danube in Víziváros have great river views of Parliament and Pest, or of Castle Hill itself, and are a little easier to get to and from.

art'otel budapest

$$ | **HOTEL** | Encompassing a large, modern building and an 18th-century baroque wing on the Buda riverfront, the art'otel adroitly blends old and new, with the modern design elements—including a vast contemporary art collection—supplied by American artist Donald Sultan. **Pros:** colorful and distinctive design; luxury ELEMIS bathroom products; contemporary artworks by Donald Sultan.

Cons: breakfast isn't included in the rates; standard rooms have no tea and coffee facilities; design choices won't appeal to all. ⑤ *Rooms from: 38,000 HUF* ✉ *Bem rakpart 16–19, Batthyány tér* ☎ *1/487– 9487* ⊕ *www.radissonhotels.com/en-us/ hotels/artotel-budapest* ⤢ *165 rooms* ⑩ *No meals* Ⓜ *Tram 19, 41.*

Hilton Budapest

$$$$ | **HOTEL** | **FAMILY** | A quick walk around the exterior of this hotel quickly betrays its mixed architectural origins—it was built in 1977 around the remains of a 13th-century Gothic chapel—but the modern and tasteful rooms, proximity to Matthias Church (right next door), and great views from Castle Hill will soothe the most delicate of aesthetic sensibilities. **Pros:** dramatic river views; prime Castle Hill location; wine tastings in atmospheric medieval cellar. **Cons:** no pool and minimal fitness facilities; typical chain-hotel rooms; bizarre combo of Gothic stonework and 1970s tinted gold windows. ⑤ *Rooms from: 102,500 HUF* ✉ *Hess András tér 1–3, Castle District* ☎ *1/889–6600* ⊕ *www.budapest.hilton. com* ⤢ *322 rooms* ⑩ *No meals* Ⓜ *M2: Batthyány tér.*

★ Hotel Clark

$$$ | **HOTEL** | Commonly referred to as Hotel Leo—an easy mistake, as the bistro and rooftop bar are called Leo, and there are lion motifs everywhere—this is a trendy and contemporary boutique hotel at the Buda end of the Chain Bridge. **Pros:** elegant but down-to-earth decor; two-thirds of rooms face the river; excellent breakfasts (ask for the sweet bakery basket). **Cons:** corridors are perilously dark; wellness area comprises just a small gym and sauna; top-floor rooms book up fast. ⑤ *Rooms from: 55,000 HUF* ✉ *Clark Ádám tér 1, Castle District* ☎ *1/610–4890* ⊕ *www.hotelclark- budapest.hu* ⤢ *86 rooms* ⑩ *No meals* Ⓜ *Tram 19, 41.*

Lánchíd 19

$$$ | HOTEL | While the interior design is a big selling point of this modern boutique hotel—each of the 48 rooms and suites offers distinctive color palates, furnishings, and artworks (by talented local students)—its location between the Chain Bridge and the Várkert Bazár leading up to Castle Hill means you'll find yourself looking out more often than in. **Pros:** stunning city views from floor-to-ceiling windows; popular L19 Bistro is right downstairs; building exterior made up of color-changing panels. **Cons:** no fitness center or spa; trees can obscure river views in summer; two-day minimum stay in summer. *⑤ Rooms from: 47,500 HUF ✉ Lánchíd utca 19, Castle District ☎ 1/457–1200 ⊕ www.lanchid19hotel.hu ⇗ 48 rooms ⊗ No meals Ⓜ Tram 19, 41.*

Monastery

$$$$ | HOTEL | As the name suggests, this brand-new boutique hotel is located within a 300-year-old, baroque Franciscan abbey. **Pros:** fascinating history meets modern convenience; breakfast served in lovely covered courtyard; free parking available. **Cons:** not all rooms face the river; showers could be stronger; breakfast is nothing special. *⑤ Rooms from: 65,000 HUF ✉ Fő utca 30, Castle District ☎ 1/770–8210 ⊕ www.monasterybudapest.accenthotels.com ⇗ 47 rooms ⊗ Free breakfast Ⓜ Tram 19, 41.*

Pest-Buda

$ | HOTEL | Conveniently located in the heart of Castle Hill, this small, family-owned design hotel has a long and illustrious history stretching all the way back to 1696. **Pros:** spacious and stylish rooms; restaurant has hearty Hungarian cuisine; seasonal terrace with Matthias Church views. **Cons:** breakfast starts late and finishes early; room lights are unnecessarily complicated to use; no elevator. *⑤ Rooms from: 30,000 HUF ✉ Fortuna utca 3, Castle District ☎ 1/800–9213 ⊕ www.pest-buda.com ⇗ 10 rooms ⊗ Free breakfast Ⓜ M2: Batthyány tér.*

Nightlife

For the neighborhood's best bars and clubs, head down from Castle Hill and stroll the streets of Víziváros.

BARS

Belgian Brasserie Henri

BARS/PUBS | For beer aficionados, nowhere beats this dimly lit underground bar: there are more than a dozen Belgian brews available on draught, with many more bottles filling the fridges. The food, including Belgian staples like mussels and fries, is nothing special, but it does help keep you upright. *✉ Bem rakpart 12, Castle District ☎ 1/201–5082 ⊕ www.belgasorozo.com Ⓜ Tram 19, 41.*

Bereg

BARS/PUBS | Located around the back of the eye-catching Hattyú haz (Swan House), an example of the short-lived "organic" architectural style, this quirky little pub is a great place for a local craft beer and a bite to eat. If the weather is good, sit out in the leafy garden, complete with puddle-sized pond and wooden bridge. *✉ Batthyány utca 49, Castle District ☎ 1/615–1298 ⊕ www.beregbar. hu Ⓜ M2: Széll Kálmán tér.*

Lánchíd Söröző

BARS/PUBS | Next to Clark Ádám tér, a large square in Buda at the end of the Lánchíd (Chain Bridge), this tiny pub attracts tourists and locals alike. The walls are covered in black-and-white photos from Budapest and Paris. Ask for owner Róbert Nagy, who speaks excellent English and loves to meet visitors from abroad. *✉ District I, Fő utca 4, Batthyány tér ☎ 1/214–3144 ⊕ lanchidsorozo.hu.*

Leo Rooftop Bar

BARS/PUBS | An extension of the Hotel Clark, this chic and atmospheric rooftop bar offers a breathtaking view of the Chain Bridge below, as well as along the Danube to the Parliament. Soak up the views while sipping one of the bar's signature cocktails (the whisky sour is especially good). The seating area is covered and heated, meaning the bar is open year-round; though it's always hard to get a table so book ahead. ⊠ *Clark Ádám tér 1, Castle District* ☎ *70/944–6320* ⊕ *www.leo-budapest.hu* Ⓜ *Tram 19, 41.*

Oscar American Bar
BARS/PUBS | This hip Tinseltown-themed bar attracts a mixed Hungarian and international crowd, who come for its delicious cocktails and its classic Hollywood memorabilia. ⊠ *Ostrom utca 14, Castle District* ☎ *70/700–0222* ⊕ *www.oscarbar-budapest.hu* Ⓜ *M2: Széll Kálmán tér.*

🎭 Performing Arts

CHURCH CONCERTS
Budai Capuchin Templom (*Buda Capuchin Church*)
FILM FESTIVALS | The Capuchin Church holds monthly concerts on the last Thursday of every month starting at 7:30 PM. ⊠ *District I, Fo utca 30–32, Batthyány tér* Ⓜ *M2: Batthyány tér.*

Mátyás Templom (*Matthias Church*)
CONCERTS | The city's most famous church hosts concerts from Hungarian and international orchestras every Friday and Saturday night year-round. Most performances start at 7 pm. ⊠ *Szentháromság tér 2, Castle District* ☎ *1/355–5657* ⊕ *www.matyas-templom.hu* Ⓜ *M2: Batthyány tér.*

Szent Anna Templom (*St. Anne's Church*)
CONCERTS | The historic baroque church, which was built in 1761, hosts regular organ and classical music concerts throughout the year; performances typically start at 7:30 or 8 pm. ⊠ *Batthyány tér 7, Batthyány tér* ☎ *1/201–6364* ⊕ *felsovizivaros.plebania.hu* Ⓜ *M2: Batthyány tér.*

FOLK DANCE
Magyar Állami Népi Együttes (*Hungarian State Folk Ensemble*)
DANCE | The 30-member ensemble, formed in 1951, performs at the beautiful, eclecticist Hagyományok Háza (Hungarian Heritage House), known for its architectural motifs of flowers and birds. Choreography is based on authentic dances that date back hundreds of years. It's considered to be one of the top folk groups worldwide, having performed in 50 countries. The ensemble gives between 100 and 120 shows in Budapest annually at their venue. ⊠ *Hagyományok Háza, Corvin tér 8, Batthyány tér* ☎ *1/225–6000* ⊕ *www.hagyomanyok-haza.hu* Ⓜ *Tram 19, 41.*

🛍 Shopping

ART GALLERIES
★ **Koller Gallery**
ART GALLERIES | This charming little art gallery showcases contemporary works by Hungarian artists including Victor Vasarely, the leader of the Op Art movement. Everything you see here is for sale, including the sculptures in the beautiful garden out back. Climb the creaky stairs to the top floor for an exhibition on artist Amerigo Tot, who once lived here, as well as spectacular city views. ■ **TIP→ If the door is closed, it doesn't mean the gallery is; try ringing the doorbell.** ⊠ *Táncsics Mihály utca 5, Castle District* ☎ *1/356–9208* ⊕ *www.kollergaleria.hu* Ⓜ *M2: Batthyány tér.*

FASHION
Agnes Toth Studio
JEWELRY/ACCESSORIES | This small fashion and art store, owned by a contemporary Hungarian painter and embroiderer, has quickly gained a reputation for its unique, hand-crafted, floral-patterned designer handbags. ⊠ *Lánchíd utca 13, Castle District* ⊕ *www.agnestothstudio.eu* ⊘ *Closed Mon. and Tues.* Ⓜ *Tram 19, 41.*

Romani Design

CLOTHING | Gorgeous bright greens, reds, blues, and yellows make Romani Design dresses stand out in Hungary, but it's the quality of the cut that has made them stand out on international catwalks in recent years. Designer Helena Varga draws on her Roma roots to design clothes with an authentic Hungarian Romani flavor and modern chic appeal. Handmade accessories, including purses, bags, and jewelry complement flowing dresses, tight pants, and frilly shirts. One of the country's freshest clothing designers, every piece from this designer is an original. To find Romani Design, visit the Magma+ Hungarian Art&Design shop on Úri utca, Fian Koncept on Fortuna utca in Buda's Castle District, or take the long journey out to visit the Romani Design studio in District 15 on Batthyány utca 31/b (by appointment only). ⊠ *Magma+ Hungarian Art&Design, Úri utca 26-28, Castle District* ☎ *30/258-9774* ⊕ *www. romani.hu.*

FOOD AND WINE

Bortársaság

WINE/SPIRITS | There's an excellent selection of Hungarian vintners represented at this conveniently located little shop, with knowledgeable staff offering background and guidance on the country's wines, like this year's Tokaji or Kékoporto. There's a good selection of wine accessories as well, from oak wine racks to high-tech bottle openers. It's one of more than a dozen Bortársaság outlets in the city. ⊠ *Lánchíd utca 5, Castle District* ☎ *1/225-1702* ⊕ *www.bortarsasag.hu* ☉ *Closed Sun.* Ⓜ *Tram 19, 41.*

PORCELAIN

★ Herendi Majolikabolt (*Herend Village Pottery*)

CERAMICS/GLASSWARE | For the Herend name and quality without the steep price tag, visit this small shop where you can choose from Herend's practical line of informal ceramic cups, dishes, and table settings, all hand painted. The colorful pasta bowls are perfect for outdoor summer entertaining. ⊠ *Bem rakpart 37, Batthyány tér* ☎ *1/356-7899* ⊕ *www. herendimajolika.hu* ☉ *Closed Sun.* Ⓜ *M2: Batthyány tér.*

Chapter 4

GELLÉRTHEGY (GELLÉRT HILL) AND TABÁN

DISTRICTS 1, 11

Updated by
Jennifer Rigby

4

⦿ **Sights**
★★★★☆

🍴 **Restaurants**
★★★☆☆

🏨 **Hotels**
★☆☆☆☆

🛍 **Shopping**
★★★☆☆

🍸 **Nightlife**
★★☆☆☆

NEIGHBORHOOD SNAPSHOT

TOP EXPERIENCES

■ **Hike to the Citadella:** Bask in the views of the city below—particularly breathtaking by night.

■ **Gellért and Rudas baths:** Soak up—quite literally— some of Budapest's most famous and gorgeous thermal baths.

■ **Bartók Béla út:** Take a leisurely stroll along this boulevard, stopping for coffee and popping in and out of galleries along the way.

■ **Czakó Kert:** Brunch and browse the weekend farmers' market at one of the oldest surviving buildings in the area.

■ **Hadik Kávéház:** Go back in time to a restored version of one of the great coffeehouses of Budapest's past.

■ **Cheers:** Sample local beers, wines, and hospitality at KEG sörművház or Palack Wine Bar.

GETTING HERE

To get to Gellérthegy from Pest, it's a picturesque walk across Szabadság híd (Liberty Bridge), or a quick metro trip to Szent Gellért tér (Line 4). Neighboring Tabán, squeezed between the hill and the castle, is walkable from both the center of Pest (via Erzsébet híd, Elizabeth Bridge) and Gellérthegy itself. It doesn't have a metro, but it is well served by trams and buses, including the 19 and 41 trams, which run alongside the river, and the 5, 16, and 105 buses, which come over the river.

PLANNING YOUR TIME

Both of these neighborhoods are quieter than many of the tourist hot spots, so visiting them at any time of day is fine. They are very safe, too. It's worth bearing in mind that a few of the galleries and coffee shops don't open on Sunday. Gellérthegy is particularly lovely to approach as the sun sets and then to observe the twinkling city below at night.

QUICK BITES

■ **Pekmuhely2.** This little bakery serves some of the best bread in the city, plus smashing pastries ✉ *Bartók Béla út 15/b, Gellérthegy* ⊕ *pekmuhely.hu* Ⓜ *Szent Gellért tér*

■ **Gulyaskantin.** Fast-food goulash is a thing and it's good and affordable, too. ✉ *Bartók Béla út 41, Gellérthegy* e ⊕ *gulyaskantin. hu* Ⓜ *Móricz Zsigmond körtér*

■ **Picnic.** This café by the river in Taban—an area not overly blessed with caffeine stops—manages to be both cute and stylish at the same time, with a lovely open front in good weather and a cozy vibe in winter. ✉ *Döbrentei utca 22, Tabán* ⊕ *www.facebook.com/ Picnicbudapest*

Gellérthegy (Gellert Hill), 761 feet high, is the most beautiful natural formation on the Buda bank. It takes its name from St. Gellért (Gerard) of Csanád, a Venetian bishop who came to Hungary in the 11th century and, legend has it, was rolled off the top of the hill in a cart by pagans.

The Citadella and various statues on its slopes have a fairy-tale loveliness, and the views from the top over the city are knockout. The walk up can be tough, but take solace from the cluster of hot springs at its foot; these soothe and cure bathers at the magnificent Rudas and Gellért baths.

In recent years, Gellérthegy has also become a bit of a browsing and brunching destination, with Bartók Béla út boasting a selection of hip bars, shops, cafés, and galleries. Neighboring Tabán hasn't had the same 21st century makeover, but is still a pleasant spot to wander around, with lovely views over the river, some good local pubs and a museum or two. Its history is fascinating, too, although not, in the main, visible; there has been a settlement on the spot for centuries, including a Balkan community who thrived in its tiny, twisty streets. However, most of the area was demolished around 100 years ago after becoming a bit too tumble-down, as the authorities saw it, but there are still some echoes of its past to be found among the green spaces and more modern architecture.

Sights

From the hill itself to the thermal waters that make the baths so tempting, natural wonders—with some human improvements—take center stage in these neighborhoods.

Citadella

HISTORIC SITE | The sweeping views of Budapest from this fortress atop the hill were once valued by the Austrian army, which used it as a lookout after the 1848–49 Revolution. Some 60 cannons were housed in the citadel, and while never used on the city's resentful populace, they were briefly, ominously, pointed down towards the citizens below after the 1956 uprising. The building is closed, but you can walk around it (keep an eye out for bullet holes from the various battles it has witnessed) and the view from the hilltop still makes it a worthy visit, especially at night when the entire city and its bridges are illuminated. Avoid the tacky, overpriced tourists stalls.

Just below the southern edge of the Citadella and visible from many parts of the city, the 130-foot-high **Szabadság szobor** (Liberty Statue) was originally planned as a memorial to a son of Hungary's then-ruler, Miklós Horthy, whose warplane had crashed in 1942. However, by the time of its completion in 1947

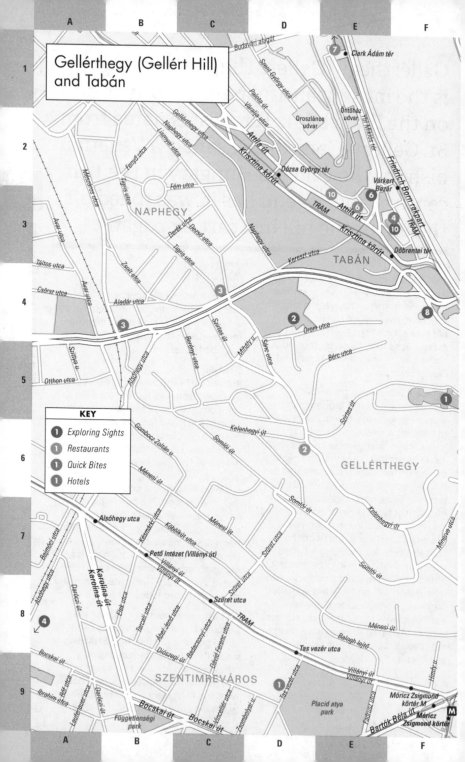

Gellérthegy (Gellért Hill) and Tabán

Sights ▼

1 Citadella F5
2 Filozófiai kertje D4
3 Gellért Termálfürdő H6
4 Memento Park A8
5 Rudas Gyógyfürdő G4
6 Semmelweis
Orvostörténeti Múzeum E3
7 Szabadság híd I6
8 Szent Gellért-szobor F4
9 Sziklatemplom H6
10 Tabán plébánia-templom F3

Restaurants ▼

1 Bölcső Bar H8
2 Búsuló Juhász D6
3 Czakó Kert C4
4 Grill Mánia H7
5 La Nube G9
6 Mr. & Mrs. Columbo E3
7 Nagyi Palacsintázója E1
8 Pagony kert H7
9 Rudas Bistro G4
10 Tabáni Gösser Étterem E3
11 Veganlove H7

Quick Bites ▼

1 Caphe by Hai Nam G8
2 Gdansk Bookstore Cafe G9
3 Hadik Kávéház Budapest H8
4 Libella Kávéház H7
5 MITZI H7
6 PupiCake H8

Hotels ▼

1 Danubius Hotel Flamenco D9
2 Danubius Hotel Gellért H7
3 Hotel Charles B4
4 Hotel Orion Várkert F3

(three years after Horthy was ousted), it had become a memorial to the Russian soldiers who fell in the 1944–45 siege of Budapest; and hence for decades it was associated chiefly with this.

A young girl, her hair and robe swirling in the wind, holds a palm branch high above her head. During much of the communist era, and for a couple of years after its close, she was further embellished with sculptures of giants slaying dragons, Red Army soldiers, and peasants rejoicing at the freedom that Soviet liberation promised (but failed) to bring to Hungary. Since 1992 her mood has lightened: in the Budapest city government's systematic purging of communist symbols, the Red Combat infantrymen who had flanked the Liberty Statue for decades were hacked off and carted away. A few are now on display among the other evicted statues in Szobor Park in the city's 22nd district, and what remains memorializes those who fought for Hungary's freedom. ⊠ District XI, Citadella sétány, Gellérthegy ⬛ Free Ⓜ Tram 47, 49 and a walk up the hill.

Filozófiai kertje (*The Garden of Philosophy*)

MEMORIAL | This quiet hilltop location (facing the river, turn left at the Liberty Statue) houses a peaceful and little-visited modern monument, designed to show the similarities in thought between what the sculptor saw as the world's leading religions. Around a little pool, there are statues of Abraham, Jesus, Buddha, Laozi, and Akhenaten, with others looking on. The most recognizable is probably Gandhi. Conceived by Hungarian sculptor Nándor Wagner, it has a double in Japan, and also offers panoramic views of the Danube and the city. ⊠ Gellérthegy ✛ Near the corner of Orum utca and Szirom utca.

★ **Gellért Termálfürdő** (*Gellért Thermal Baths*)

HOT SPRINGS | At the foot of Gellért Hill, the gorgeous Gellért Baths has beauty and history in spades, with hot springs that have supplied curative baths for nearly 2,000 years. The entrance to the spa is on a side street to the right of the palatial Danubius Hotel Gellért, although the pair are no longer run by the same company. These baths are unsurprisingly popular among tourists so you will want to book ahead online. Budapest's baths, once segregated, are now primarily co-ed (with special hours for segregated bathing for some baths), and it's the same story here. Men and women can now use all steam and sauna rooms as well as both the indoor pool and the outdoor wave pool—a Jazz Age classic that claims to be one of the first wave pools in the world—at the same time. Come for the lovely tiles, architecture, and painted glass, and stay for the range of treatments (some of which require a doctor's prescription). ⊠ District XI, Gellért tér 1, at foot of hill, Gellérthegy ☏ 1/466–6166 ⊕ www.gellertbath.hu ⬛ 3900 HUF weekdays for daily ticket, 4500 HUF weekends Ⓜ M4: Szent Gellért tér.

Memento Park

MEMORIAL | After the collapse of the Iron Curtain, Hungarians were understandably keen to rid Budapest of the symbols of Soviet domination. The communist memorials—including huge statues of Lenin, Marx, and Hungarian puppet prime minister János Kádár—that once dotted Budapest's streets and squares have been moved to this open-air "Disneyland of Communism." Somewhat tacky but amusing souvenirs are for sale, and songs from the Hungarian and Russian workers' movements play on a tiny speaker system. To get there, take the recently completed Metro 4 to Kelenföld vasútállomás (Kelenföld train depot) then, from the adjoining bus

Wander away from the major tourist attractions of the Citadel and the Liberty Statue and you'll find an intriguing cluster of statues at the Filozofiai kertje or Garden of Philosophy.

depot, catch the 101 or 150 bus in the direction of Budatétény vasútállomás (Campona). It's best to tell the driver when you get on that you want to get off at Memento Park. The park also operates its own bus from Deak tér daily at 11 am. There is a guided tour in English at 11:40 am daily during peak season; call ahead to confirm. You can also schedule a guide in advance for an additional fee (15,240 HUF). ⊠ District XXII, Balatoni út, corner of Szabadkai utca, South Buda ☎ 1/424–7500 ⊕ www.mementopark.hu ⊡ 1500 HUF; guided tours from 15240 HUF.

★ **Rudas Gyógyfürdő** (Rudas Baths)
HOT SPRINGS | This bath on the riverbank boasts perhaps the most dramatically beautiful interior of all of Budapest's baths, with the original Turkish pool the star of the show. A high, domed roof admits pinpricks of bluish-green light into the dark, circular stone hall with its austere columns and arches. The central octagonal pool catches the light from the glass-tiled cupola and casts it around the surrounding six pools, capturing the feeling of an ancient Turkish hammam. The Rudas's highly fluoridated waters have been known for 1,000 years—and the baths themselves date back to the 16th century. The baths vary in temperature from 16 to 42 degrees Celsius, and you can also drink the water from three springs in the 'drinking hall'. The thermal part is open by day Monday and Wednesday to Friday to men only, Tuesday to women only, and weekends to both sexes. A less interesting outer swimming pool is also co-ed. A 20-minute massage costs 7000 HUF. Soak after-hours here on Friday and Saturday nights from 10 pm to 4 am. ⊠ District I, Döbrentei tér 9, Gellérthegy ☎ 1/356–1322 ⊕ rudasbaths. com ⊡ 3700 HUF weekdays; 4300 HUF weekends; 5500 HUF night ticket Ⓜ M3: Ferenciek tere, then a 10-min walk to Buda, across Erzsébet híd.

Thermal Baths 101

Upon Arrival

The entrance procedure to *gyógyfürdők* (thermal baths) in Budapest can be baffling to visitors. Some baths post prices and treatments in English, but much of the information on the price list pertains to medical treatments offered at the spa for patients with prescriptions from their doctors, so it can be unclear what kind of ticket you need. Morning, afternoon, and evening tickets are usually available, as well as full-day tickets. It's worth purchasing a full-day ticket so you don't have to rush. Request treaments, choose a locker or cabin (cabins are slightly more expensive), and then pay all at once at admission. You can avoid some of the ticketing confusion by booking in advance: many baths now offer online tickets, and the separate costs for treatments, cabins, and sessions are spelled out a little more clearly. Upon payment or presentation of your online ticket, you get a watch-shaped electronic bracelet that serves as a key to a locker or cabin where you can leave your belongings.

What to Bring

As a rule, bring shower shoes to all thermal baths and a towel to all but the big wellness hotels. Swimsuits are required in most thermal baths, and a bathing cap is required in swimming pools. The Rudas Baths provides an apron-like garment to wear instead of swimwear on single-sex days. While almost everything you need is available to rent on site, lines can be long and dispensed towels can be scratchy. Bring a hat to wear on summer days.

TIP→ Keep some small change with you to tip locker attendants on your way out and in case you want a beverage in between soaks. Tip massage therapists before your treatment, not after.

FAQ

What now? Shower before entering the water (or risk being ejected). If you have long hair, tie it back.

Should I wear my birthday suit? No, nudity is not allowed, as most went coed within the past decade. The one exception: Rudas bath on single-sex days. Speak with your massage therapist before your massage to share if you are comfortable with or without a bathing suit for the treatment. It's up to you.

Is there a soaking strategy? It's recommended to stay in a thermal bath for 20 minutes, then rest on a recliner or dip quickly into a cool pool or take a cold shower to cool down before the next round. Work from medium-warm baths to hotter ones. If you feel dizzy, get out and cool down. Stay hydrated.

Inside voices only? Yes. Many locals come here to take the waters for medicinal and healing purposes, so you'll want to keep the noise down inside the pools. Speaking is not forbidden, but unless you're in an outdoor area, keep conversation to a minimum.

When to visit? Avoid the tourist rush and go to the larger baths as early as you can, even at 6 a.m., when most open; or linger on Friday or Saturday nights at Rudas, which stays open past midnight.

Thermal Terms

Don't worry if your Hungarian isn't up to scratch. We've translated a few common terms you will see on signs in thermal spas and wellness hotels throughout Hungary, so you can tell a dry brush massage from a medical exam.

Caldarium. A hot-water tub or tiled room of 40°C–50°C (104°F–122°F).

Értékmegőrző. Safe-deposit box. (*See Páncélszekrény.*)

Gőzfürdő. Steam room.

Gyógyfürdő. Any thermal bath that has naturally occurring water above 30°C (86°F). Most thermal baths contain minerals, which are listed at the entrance to the bath.

Hőlégfürdő. Sauna

Iszapfürdő. Mud bath.

Kezelés. Treatment.

Kleopátra Fürdő. Cleopatra Bath. A bath of milk and essential oils, known to be a moisturizing skin treatment.

Kneipp cure. This body of treatments is based on the theories of Sebastian Kneipp, a German priest who believed in the importance of water and herbs in treating stress and exhaustion. Treatments are designed for the individual based on a medical exam and are offered at most wellness hotels. An average treatment uses alternating hot and cold stimuli to increase blood circulation, followed by wrapping the body in herb infusions.

Laconium. A dry sauna of 55°C.

Masszázs. Massage. In general, massages are performed with light aromatic oil. Some, such as Thai massage, are performed with no oil.

Medence. Pool or basin—generally a thermal pool rather than a swimming pool (see Uszómedence). Nyirokcsomó kezelés. Lymph drainage. This treatment restores balance to the lymph system and rids the body of accumulated toxins.

Öltöző. Changing room.

Páncélszekrény. Literally "safe," but in this context refers simply to a safe deposit box. (*See also Értékmegőrző.*)

Szakorvosi vizsgálatok. Medical examination, which is required for some treatments.

Száraz kefe masszázs. Dry brush massage. This massage is performed with a soft bristle brush. It helps exfoliate the skin and increase blood circulation.

Szekrény. Locker.

Thalasso. This general term refers to any treatment using seaweed or sea algae, known to help combat cellulite.

Uszoda. Swimming (pool) facility (with one or more pools).

Uszómedence. Swimming pool.

Víz alatti masszázs. Underwater massage. This massage is performed under jets of cold and warm water treating specific body parts.

Semmelweis Orvostörténeti Múzeum (*Semmelweis Museum of Medical History*)
MUSEUM | This splendid baroque house was the birthplace of Ignác Semmelweis (1818–65), the Hungarian physician who proved the contagiousness of puerperal (childbed) fever, saving countless lives, and who became known—sadly, only after his death—as the "savior of mothers." It's now a museum that traces the history of healing and medicine, which sounds a bit niche but is actually fairly fascinating (if a little gross at times). Semmelweis's grave is in the garden. ⊠ *District I, Apród utca 1–3, Gellérthegy* ☎ *1/375–3533* ⊕ *semmelweismuseum. hu* ⌖ *1000 HUF* Ⓜ *M3: Ferenciek tere, then a 15-minute walk to Buda, across Erzsébet híd.*

Szabadság híd (*Liberty Bridge*)
BRIDGE/TUNNEL | It may play second fiddle to the Chain Bridge, but this pretty cantilevered river crossing is lit beautifully at night and makes for a pleasant stroll across the river in the day. Designed for the Millennium World Exhibition in 1896, and rebuilt after being blown up in the Second World War, keep an eye out for the interesting extras, like the mythological birds perched atop it. ⊠ *Szabadság híd, Gellérthegy* Ⓜ *M4: Szent Gellért tér.*

Szent Gellért-szobor (*Szent Gellért monument*)
MEMORIAL | This giant, multilevel monument halfway up the hill adds to the general fairy-tale feel on the Buda side of the river. The figure is St Gellért, Hungary's first missionary, whose preaching didn't sit very well with the locals. Legend has it he was thrown off the hill on this very spot in 1046. The monument is best viewed from the Pest side, at Erzsébet híd. ⊠ *Szent Gellért rkp. 16, Gellérthegy.*

Sziklatemplom (*Cave Church*)
CAVE | This atmospheric church built into a cave—one of several in the hill—lies just behind the landmark Danubius hotel. Mass is still held here (the church is run by the Pauline monks) and worth attending if so inclined, but it is also worth a look for its novelty value. Note: it was rebuilt in faux-cave style in the '90s so it is not quite as authentic as it could be. ⊠ *Sziklatemplom út, Gellérthegy* ☎ *1/775–2472* ⊕ *sziklatemplom.hu* ⊘ *Closed Sun. (except for mass)* Ⓜ *M4: Szent Gellért tér.*

Tabán plébánia-templom (*Tabán Parish Church*)
RELIGIOUS SITE | This church, whose steeple is a symbol of the old Tabán neighborhood, arose between 1728 and 1736 on the site of a Turkish mosque and was subsequently expanded several times, its present facade dating from 1880–81. Its form—mustard-colored stone with a rotund, green clock tower—could be described as restrained baroque, and it is dedicated to St Catherine of Alexandria. It is often closed on weekdays but worth noting as a truly ancient place of worship if you pass by: there has been a religious building on the site since the eleventh century. ⊠ *District I, Attila utca 11, Gellérthegy* Ⓜ *M3: Ferenciek tere, then a 15-minute walk to Buda, across the Erzsébet híd.*

 Restaurants

Dining options have improved greatly in these areas in recent years, with some swanky joints, good local and global options, and unique places too—including one where you dine among the abandoned pools of a thermal baths.

Bölcső Bar
$$ | **BURGER** | Sometimes you just need a good burger and a great beer, and Bölcső delivers. For that reason, and its proximity to the nearby university, it can be busy with students in the evening, but for lunch it is a relaxed stop. **Known for:** homemade burgers; vast selection of beers from local and farther afield breweries; popular student hangout. ⌖ *Average main: 2000 HUF* ⊠ *Zenta utca*

Szent Gellert-szobor is a grand monument to Hungary's first missionary who met a less-than-grand end when thrown off the hill here.

3, Gellérthegy ☎ 1/308–8210 ⊕ www.
facebook.com/bolcsobar Ⓜ M4: Szent
Gellért tér.

Búsuló Juhász

$$$ | HUNGARIAN | A special spot for high-end Hungarian cuisine, with huge windows to showcase the beautiful views of the trees and city unfolding below. From the outside, it looks a bit rustic, but inside it is decidedly polished (despite the fake tree). **Known for:** a beautiful outside terrace; lovely soups and refined dining; a proper sense of occasion. ⑤ Average main: 4000 HUF ✉ Kelenhegyi út 58, Gellérthegy ☎ 1/209–1649 ⊕ www.
busulojuhasz.hu Ⓜ M4: Móricz Zsigmond körtér; tram 17, 61.

★ Czakó Kert

$$ | HUNGARIAN | There is charm in spades at this historic barn and garden turned relaxed bistro. The setting is lovely, the food is good, and the service is friendly, plus there's a bakery, wine cellar, and shop to boot. **Known for:** located in the oldest surviving building in the area, with a pleasant garden; market-fresh ingredients; great breakfast. ⑤ Average main: 2500 HUF ✉ Czakó ut 15, Gellérthegy ☎ 1/501–4002 ⊕ www.czakokert.hu Ⓜ Tram 47, 49 and a walk; bus 8E, 108E, 112.

Grill Mánia

$$ | BARBECUE | This place may not look like much from the outside, particularly among the newer, trendier spots on Bartók Béla út, but it serves some of the most delicious authentic Balkan food out there. A Bulgarian known as Bárni is the proprietor, living out his dream of showcasing the chargrilled flavors of his childhood. **Known for:** chargrilled meats and fresh salads; unpretentious vibe; excellent house spreads and dips. ⑤ Average main: 2500 HUF ✉ Bartók Béla út 6, Gellérthegy ☎ 1/209–9220 ⊕ grillmania.hu Ⓜ M4: Szent Gellért tér.

La Nube

$$ | TAPAS | A lovely café and tapas bar run by a Hungarian-Spanish couple, La Nube offers traditional Spanish breakfasts,

great coffee, and brilliant tapas for lunch and dinner. **Known for:** cured meats and Spanish wines; churros; charming spot. $ *Average main: 3000 HUF* ⊠ *Bartók Béla út 41, Gellérthegy* ☎ *1/793–9123* ⊕ *www.lanubecafe.com* Ⓜ *M4: Móricz Zsigmond körtér.*

Mr. & Mrs. Columbo
$$ | **EASTERN EUROPEAN** | **FAMILY** | This warmhearted pub (look out for the picture of the American detective, Columbo, on the sign) serves a good range of tasty Czech beers as well as ten types—count 'em—of a traditional potato pancake dish with different stuffings and toppings. Family and dog friendly, it's cozy rather than rowdy. **Known for:** Czech lagers; variety of potato pancakes; cozy interior. $ *Average main: 1700 HUF* ⊠ *Szarvas tér 1, Tabán* ☎ *20/999–0388* ⊕ *www.facebook.com/Columboetterem* ☾ *Closed Sun.* Ⓜ *Tram 56.*

Nagyi Palacsintázója
$ | **CAFÉ** | This branch of the small chain, which means "Granny's pancake house" in English, is a decent stop for a very affordable Hungarian-style pancake. The location is quite picturesque, too, particularly compared to some of the other more modern branches, and there are tables outside in summer. **Known for:** nice spot for a quick stop; good value; sweet pancakes. $ *Average main: 350 HUF* ⊠ *Batthyány tér 5, Tabán* ⊕ *nagyipali.hu* Ⓜ *M2: Batthyány tér.*

★ Pagony kert
$$$ | **BISTRO** | This seasonal, outdoor bar and eatery set amoid the disused swimming pools of the neighboring Gellért Baths is a unique and appealing spot for a drink or a bite, from breakfast (open from a relaxed 10 am) through to cocktails. **Known for:** good vegan options alongside burgers; craft beers; drink or dine in a tiled pool (minus the water). $ *Average main: 3200 HUF* ⊠ *Kemenes utca 10, Gellérthegy* ☎ *70/885–8296* ⊕ *www.pagonykert.hu* ☾ *Summer only* Ⓜ *M4: Szent Gellért tér.*

Rudas Bistro
$$$ | **HUNGARIAN** | Splendid food and picture-perfect views across the river are on offer at this gorgeously situated restaurant attached to the baths of the same name. You can make a day of it with a soak and a feast, or come to the restaurant in its own right to enjoy the peerless panoramic vista from the fairy-lit terrace, often accompanied by music. **Known for:** brunch package with a spa ticket; one of the loveliest terraces in Buda; sauerkraut soup. $ *Average main: 4000 HUF* ⊠ *Döbrentei tér 9, Gellérthegy* ☎ *30/016–0125* ⊕ *rudasbistro.hu* Ⓜ *M4: Szent Gellért tér.*

Tabáni Gösser Étterem
$$$ | **HUNGARIAN** | Ask your concierge for decent traditional grub and chances are they will direct you to Tabáni Gösser Étterem, a traditional Hungarian restaurant, with hearty, tasty portions, a simple vibe, and good prices. **Known for:** hearty classics, from goulash to schnitzel; popular with locals; local beers on tap. $ *Average main: 3200 HUF* ⊠ *Attila út 19, Tabán* ☎ *1/375–9482* ⊕ *tabanigosser.eatbu.com* Ⓜ *Tram 19, 41; bus 5, 105, 16.*

Veganlove
$$ | **VEGETARIAN** | **FAMILY** | With its focus on goulash and rich meats, Budapest was not until recently considered a welcoming place for a vegan. But that's changed in recent years and this gem is one of the places leading the charge. **Known for:** a delicious broccoli burger (we aren't kidding); environmentally conscious; perfect for the vegan-curious. $ *Average main: 1700 HUF* ⊠ *Bartók Béla út 9, Gellérthegy* ⊕ *www.veganlove.hu* Ⓜ *M4: Szent Gellért tér.*

 Coffee and Quick Bites

Caphe by Hai Nam
$ | **VIETNAMESE** | Blending Vietnamese informality with professional service and simple, clean, and elegant Scandinavian style, this trendy café on Bartók Béla út

boasts one of only two ROCKET R9V coffee machines in the country and offers both light and dark roasted specialty coffees, the must-try Vietnamese coffee, and specialty teas and smoothies. Before you sample the tasty pastries and cakes, be sure to start with a Bánh mì sandwich (available in a variety of flavors and sizes, including a vegan version). **Known for:** excellent coffee; trendy spot; Bánh mì sandwiches. ⑤ *Average main: 1000 HUF* ✉ *Bartók Béla út, Gellérthegy* ⊕ *www. facebook.com/caphe.hainambudapest* Ⓜ *M4: Moricz Zsigmond Korter.*

Gdansk Bookstore Cafe

$ | **POLISH** | A hip coffeehouse, bar, and bookshop with a difference: namely, the pickled herring that hails all the way from the hometown of one of the proprietors, Gdansk, on the Baltic Sea. There are other Polish delicacies, too, as well as affordable drinks, dim lighting, shelves yawning with books, and strong eastern European intellectual vibes. **Known for:** Polish food, including herring and pierogis; good range of craft beers and vodka; varied closing times. ⑤ *Average main: 500 HUF* ✉ *Bartók Béla út 46, Gellérthegy* ☎ *20/988–1873* ⊕ *www.facebook. com/gdansk.konyvesbolt* Ⓜ *M4: Móricz Zsigmond körtér.*

Hadik Kávéház Budapest

$$ | **HUNGARIAN** | At the swankier end of the coffeehouse spectrum, Hadik is a looker, and knows it: bare brick walls, chandeliers, huge windows, and a mezzanine layer of seating. There's a full modern European-Hungarian-style lunch menu, too, as befits Hadik's status as one of the city's spruced up grand cafés. **Known for:** goulash and apple soups; historical chops but modern look; outdoor tables for people-watching. ⑤ *Average main: 2500 HUF* ✉ *Bartók Béla út 36, Gellérthegy* ☎ *1/279–0291* ⊕ *www.hadik. eu* ⊙ *Closed Mon. and Tues.* Ⓜ *M4: Szent Gellért tér.*

Libella Kávéház

$ | **CAFÉ** | The pretty little sidewalk tables offering a lovely view of the Liberty bridge are a big draw in the warmer months, but Libella is a good spot for a coffee or drink pretty much any time of the day—or year—thanks to its charm and relaxed vibes. **Known for:** popular with students from the nearby university; long opening hours 8 am–1 am; good range of beers. ⑤ *Average main: 500 HUF* ✉ *Budafoki út 7, Gellérthegy* ☎ *1/950–4994* ⊕ *www.facebook.com/ libellakavezo* ⊙ *Closed Sun.* Ⓜ *M4: Szent Gellért tér.*

MITZI

$$ | **INTERNATIONAL** | A short walk from the Gellért Baths, this cool little spot offers a broad and delicious breakfast and brunch menu as well as a lunch menu that changes weekly but always features Hungarian specialties, and great coffee and alcoholic drinks. The self-proclaimed 'dinky' coffeehouse, all stripped ceilings, huge plants, and globe lights, is a popular hangout with artsy locals and students. **Known for:** creative Hungarian specialities; laptop hangout; indulgent breakfasts and brunches. ⑤ *Average main: 2500 HUF* ✉ *Bartók Béla út 1, Gellérthegy* ☎ *70/659–1161* ⊕ *www.facebook.com/ mitzibudapest* Ⓜ *M4: Szent Gellért tér.*

PupiCake

$ | **BAKERY** | **FAMILY** | An extremely cute little café where the focus is on cakes, desserts, pies, puddings, and cookies. They are baked daily by the owner and make for a perfect energy-boosting treat for weary travelers. **Known for:** new cake, biscuit, and pie offerings daily; impressive baking skills; vegan treats. ⑤ *Average main: 500 HUF* ✉ *Bartók Béla út 25, Gellérthegy* ☎ *20/248–0230* ⊕ *pupicake. hu* Ⓜ *M4: Szent Gellért tér.*

Hotels

Beyond the palatial Danubius Hotel Gellért, the hotels in this area are a little uninspiring, although there are bargains to be had considering that the location is still very central.

Danubius Hotel Flamenco

$ | HOTEL | This glass-and-concrete socialist-era leviathan is right across the street from the supposedly (but not) bottomless Feneketlen Lake, and close to the pleasant lakeside restaurant, Hemingway, too. **Pros:** good value; great health and fitness facilities; lovely setting. **Cons:** out of the way; lacks personality; can get overtaken by conference guests. ⑤ *Rooms from: 14,500 HUF ⊠ District XI, Tas Vezér utca 7, Gellérthegy ☎ 1/889–5600 ⊕ www. danubiushotels.com/en/our-hotels-budapest/danubius-hotel-flamenco ↪ 355 rooms* †⊚⟊ *Free breakfast* Ⓜ *Tram 19, 49 to Kosztolányi Dezső tér.*

Danubius Hotel Gellért

$ | HOTEL | Budapest's most renowned art nouveau hotel is a truly astonishing building from the outside: the Hungarian capital can give you palace fatigue, but the Gellért's perch by the Danube, right by the Szabadság bridge, allows it to show off to maximum effect as you approach. **Pros:** beautiful architecture; discounted entrance to the amazing thermal baths included; elegant setting. **Cons:** room decor doesn't measure up to the architecture; bathrooms can feel dated; beds on the small side. ⑤ *Rooms from: 24,000 HUF ⊠ District XI, Szent Gellért tér 1, Gellérthegy ☎ 1/889–5500 ⊕ www.danubiushotels.com/hotelgellert ↪ 234 rooms* †⊚⟊ *Free breakfast* Ⓜ *M4: Szent Gellért tér.*

Hotel Charles

$ | HOTEL | It won't win points for its looks (externally at least), but the staff are extremely friendly and helpful, the food in the restaurant is delicious, and the location is actually more convenient than it seems—just behind the hill, and close to the castle, too. **Pros:** suprisingly tasty food at the restaurant; comfortable, spacious rooms, all with a kitchenette; low prices. **Cons:** needs some updating, mainly cosmetic; some noise for rooms on the street side; can feel out of the way, although there are buses. ⑤ *Rooms from: 12,000 HUF ⊠ Hegyalja út 23, Tabán ☎ 1/212–9169 ⊕ www.charleshotel.hu ↪ 60 rooms* †⊚⟊ *Free breakfast* Ⓜ *Bus 8E, 110, 112.*

Hotel Orion Várkert

$ | HOTEL | Despite the name (Várkert means "Castle Garden"), this friendly, modern little property is actually in Tabán, but in fairness, it is mere steps from the beautiful Várkert Bazár (Castle Garden Bazaar) and many of the attractions of Buda. **Pros:** reasonably priced; good location; comfortable and clean. **Cons:** fairly basic; no parking; could use sprucing up. ⑤ *Rooms from: 20,000 HUF ⊠ Döbrentei utca 13, Tabán ☎ 1/356–8583 ⊕ www.hotelorion.hu ↪ 30 rooms* †⊚⟊ *No meals* Ⓜ *Tram 19, 41; bus 5, 16, 105.*

Nightlife

On this side of the river, the nightlife is more about relaxed sipping and chatting with locals than wild partying.

BARS AND PUBS

Barba Negra

DANCE CLUBS | A stripped-back, summer-only venue with covered bars and a huge stage for big acts, both local and international, to perform. It's a little out of the way but worth it for the festival-feel of seeing live music here. ⊠ *Prielle Kornélia utca 4, Gellérthegy ☎ 20/563–2254 ⊕ www.barbanegra.hu* Ⓜ *Bus 153.*

Bartók-reggel. délben. este

BARS/PUBS | The name translates roughly to morning, dusk, evening, and this comfortable, slightly upscale gastropub is a welcoming spot at any of those times of day. The breakfasts and brunch, with live music, are lovely and worth booking in advance. And for evening imbibing, there's a convivial atmosphere and a wide range of beers and other drinks. ⊠ *Bartók Béla út 9, Gellérthegy* ☎ *1/211–2019* ⊕ *www.facebook.com/bartokgastropub* Ⓜ *M4: Szent Gellért tér.*

Béla. bár, étterem, lakás, arborétum

BARS/PUBS | Bar, eatery, loft, arboretum—Béla is pretty much what it says it is. A pleasingly eclectic bar that has the feel of someone's roomy loft apartment, though the cool bird mural on one wall and lots of plants don't an 'arboretum' make. The cocktails are good and the food isn't bad either. Check out the secret swing concerts in the cellar. ⊠ *Bartók Béla út 23, Gellérthegy* ☎ *70/590–7974* ⊕ *www.belabudapest.com* Ⓜ *M4: Szent Gellért tér.*

KEG sörművház

BREWPUBS/BEER GARDENS | **FAMILY** | Just a classic craft brewpub, run by friends, done right: a vast range of fresh beers, a cozy cellar location, and a relaxed atmosphere that entices people of all ages. There's traditional food on offer too, and sports and cultural events. ⊠ *Orlay utca 1, Gellérthegy* ☎ *1/616–8694* ⊕ *www.kegsormuvhaz.hu* Ⓜ *M4: Szent Gellért tér.*

Szatyor Bar and Gallery

CAFES—NIGHTLIFE | Located next to lovely coffeehouse Hadik, Szatyor has a similarly airy, contemporary central European feel, but with a bit more edge than its stately neighbor. There's art everywhere—even painted on the ceiling—and a cultural ethos pervades, even extending to literary quotes about soup on the menu. An arty and delightful place for a drink or two. ⊠ *Bartók Béla út 36, Gellérthegy* ☎ *1/279–0291* ⊕ *www.szatyorbar.com* Ⓜ *M4: Szent Gellért tér.*

NIGHTCLUBS

★ A38

DANCE CLUBS | Originally a Ukrainian stone-freighter, A38 is now a fantastic addition to the nightlife of Buda, permanently moored on this side of the Danube. It has a restaurant upstairs, an exhibition space, a bar, and a large dance floor downstairs. There's a different band on hand every night, from jazz to Latin, retro to electronic. ⊠ *District XI, near Petőfi Híd, on Buda side of river, Fovam tér* ☎ *1/464–3940 ticket office, 1/464–3946 restaurant* ⊕ *www.a38.hu* ✉ *Varies* Ⓜ *M4: Boráros tér; tram 4, 6 across river to Petőfi híd, budai hífő.*

Café del Rio

DANCE CLUBS | Calling itself a "fancy club for fancy people," one of Budapest's largest and hottest dance clubs—home to two dance floors, a "VIP lounge," and a restaurant—is near the Buda side of the Petőfi Bridge, close to the popular outdoor drinking garden Zöld Pardon. The club is open nightly 8 pm to 5 am. ⊠ *District XI, Goldmann György tér 1, South Buda* ☎ *30/397–3416.*

WINE BARS

Palack wine bar

WINE BARS—NIGHTLIFE | If you want to try Hungarian wines in relaxed but knowledgeable company, this is your spot. There are also tastings, snacks, a snatched view of the Liberty Bridge, and a sign that rather encapsulates the ethos: Wine not? ⊠ *Szent Gellért tér 3, Gellérthegy* ☎ *30/997–1902* ⊕ *www.facebook.com/palackborbar* Ⓜ *M4: Szent Gellért tér.*

🎭 Performing Arts

B32 Galéria és Kultúrtér

ART GALLERIES—ARTS | This nontraditional art gallery, stuffed with Budapest's leading creative types, showcases everything from theater performances to film, a design market, and exhibitions. It's a light, white space where there is always something interesting going on. Spot it via the large turquoise dot of its logo. ⊠ *Bartók Béla út 32, Gellérthegy* ☎ *1/787–0045* ⊕ *www.facebook.com/B32kulturter* Ⓜ *M4: Szent Gellért tér.*

Folklór Centrum

ARTS CENTERS | The center has been a major venue for folklore performances for more than 30 years. It hosts regular traditional folk concerts and dance performances from spring through fall. ✉ *District XI, Fehérvári út 47, South Buda* ☎ *1/203–3868.*

Fonó Budai Zeneház (Fonó Buda Music House)

MUSIC | Although it's a bit of a trek from the city center to Fonó, on the outskirts of Buda, it is a great place to see live folk acts. The music house has its own bar, several performance stages, and even its own folk-music CD shop. Concerts and dance houses are held on a near-nightly basis, and tickets are bought when you enter the music house. ✉ *District XI, Sztregova utca 3, South Buda* ☎ *1/206–5300* ⊕ *www.fono.hu.*

Tranzit Art Café

ART GALLERIES—ARTS | Once a bus station, this space is now a funky, airy café, art gallery, and cultural center, with a leafy courtyard and even hammocks. They also host various events and exhibitions, although be warned, it's about a 20-minute walk up from the river (or a 10-minute tram ride). ✉ *Bukarest utca 3-9, Gellérthegy* ☎ *1/209–3070* ⊕ *www.facebook. com/tranzitcafe* Ⓜ *M4: Újbuda-központ.*

Shopping

BOOKS
Pagony

BOOKS/STATIONERY | The Buda branch of this jolly mini-chain of bookstores, set up by three couples who wanted somewhere that sold both quality children's books and well-made toys in the same place. Pagony delivers on its promise, plus comfy armchairs and play areas, too. Kids will like the airships on the ceiling; adults, the café. ✉ *Bartók Béla út 5, Gellérthegy* ☎ *1/794–3719* ⊕ *www. pagony.hu* Ⓜ *M4: Szent Gellért tér.*

CURIOSITIES
Bélyeg Shop

ANTIQUES/COLLECTIBLES | For those who like their souvenirs a little unusual, as well as true enthusiasts, this traditional old stamp shop is a gem, clinging on to its patch on this increasingly cool street. Old Hungarian stamps, coins, and medals are all on offer, including some very rare items. ✉ *Bartók Béla út 33, Gellérthegy* ⊹ *The shop is in the yard, the gate code is 55* ☎ *1/365–8671* ⊕ *www.belyegshop. hu* ⊘ *Closed weekends* Ⓜ *M4: Móricz Zsigmond körtér.*

DESIGN
Palmetta Design Atelier

CRAFTS | The city base of this design studio run by a couple in the town of Szentendre, showcasing cool, modern Hungarian and European design and homewares, from lamps to cutlery, bowls to pans. ✉ *Bartók Béla út 30, Gellérthegy* ☎ *30/296–6254 the main studio in Szentendre* ⊕ *palmettadesign.hu* Ⓜ *M4: Móricz Zsigmond körtér.*

FOOD & DRINK
Csaphaz

WINE/SPIRITS | Shopping for Hungarian beer to go? This is the place. All the typical Hungarian craft beers are featured, plus novelties and rarer options, and they pour them straight from the tap to the bottle, so they are super fresh. They brew their own, too. The shop is towards the edge of the neighborhood but it's the right place to be if you've worked up a thirst. ✉ *Bartók Béla út 59, Gellérthegy* ☎ *30/545–2620* ⊕ *csaphaz.hu* ⊘ *Closed Sun. and Mon.* Ⓜ *M4: Móricz Zsigmond körtér.*

GALLERIES
Faur Zsófi Galéria

ART GALLERIES | Showcasing a fantastic range of Hungarian artists, this sleek gallery aims to promote them internationally while also welcoming visitors to its HQ. Worth a browse if you want to take the temperature of the modern art scene in the country. ✉ *Bartók Béla út*

25, Gellérthegy ☎ *1/209–3635* ⊕ *www. galeriafaur.hu* Ⓜ *M4: Szent Gellért tér.*

Godot Galéria

ART GALLERIES | A well-chosen selection of contemporary Hungarian artists' work is shown here, in rotating exhibitions. ✉ *Bartók Béla út 11–13, Gellérthegy* ☎ *70/381–6775* ⊕ *www.godot.hu* ⊙ *Closed Sun.*

Gross Arnold Galéria Kávézó

ART GALLERIES | Less a gallery and more a gateway into the beautiful, delicate fairy-tale world of Hungarian artist and etcher, Arnold Gross, this attractive space—with furnishings designed by the artist's son—is both gallery and café. ✉ *Bartók Béla út 46, Gellérthegy* ☎ *70/338–7001* ⊕ *www. grossarnold.com* ⊙ *Closed Sun.* Ⓜ *M4: Móricz Zsigmond körtér.*

GIFTS

⭐ **Prezent**

GIFTS/SOUVENIRS | A properly lovely little place in an area not really known for its shopping, Prezent is everything a modern gift shop should be: interesting, sustainable, and with a focus on local producers. You'll find sweaters, chocolate, and soaps, as well as considerably-less-touristy-than-usual fridge magnets and postcards featuring sketches of the city. ✉ *Döbrentei utca 16, Tabán* ⊕ *prezentbudapest.hu* ⊙ *Closed Tues., Wed.* Ⓜ *Tram 19, 41; bus 5, 16, 105.*

 Activities

PARKS

Buda Arboretum

BIRD WATCHING | A pleasant botanical garden and park that is now part of a university campus, the Buda Arboretum is a good spot for a jog or a walk, particularly in autumn or spring, when the colors are beautiful. ✉ *Villány út 29-43, Gellérthegy* ☎ *1/305–7270* ⊕ *budaiarboretum.szie.hu* Ⓜ *M4: Móricz Zsigmond körtér.*

BELVÁROS (INNER TOWN)

DISTRICT 5

Updated by
Joseph Reaney

 Sights
★★★☆☆

 Restaurants
★★★★☆

 **Hotels**
★★★★★

 Shopping
★★★★★

 Nightlife
★★☆☆☆

NEIGHBORHOOD SNAPSHOT

TOP EXPERIENCES

■ **Walk down Dunakorzó:** This café-lined riverside promenade, which runs south between the Chain Bridge and Elizabeth Bridge, makes for a pleasant stroll day or night.

■ **Stay in luxury:** From the Kempinski to the Ritz-Carlton, this neighborhood is home to Budapest's highest concentration of five-star hotels—so why not treat yourself?

■ **Step back in time:** Visit the Inner City Parish Church, the oldest in Budapest, to discover a thousand years of architectural history (and ruins dating back to Roman times).

■ **Drink in a ruin:** Budapest is famous for its atmospheric ruin bars and Csendes is one of the city's best, with quirky decor including hanging bicycles and mannequin limbs.

■ **Shop 'til you drop:** Splash out on big-name designer brands on Deák Ferenc utca (Fashion Street), or seek out independent boutiques along the Inner Town's smaller streets.

■ **Feel like a Parisian:** You needn't stay at the Párisi Udvar Hotel to stroll through its art nouveau arcade, delighting in its gilded arches, decorative cupolas, and charming cafés and shops.

GETTING HERE

Belváros is extremely well-connected with the rest of the city, with half a dozen Metro stations serving four different lines. The main hub is Deák Ferenc tér where three of those four lines converge. There's also a regular bus connection (Bus 16) to Castle Hill. Traffic and parking can be a challenge.

PLANNING YOUR TIME

If you're staying elsewhere, come here during the day, when you can stroll, shop, and eat at your leisure. There are some lively spots in the evening, particularly along Váci utca, but most head a bit farther east of here (to District 7) for the best bars and clubs.

QUICK BITES

■ **Molnár's kürtőskalács.** This is the place to try a traditional Transylvanian "spit" or "chimney" cake, a cylindrical pastry made from sweet yeasty dough. It's cooked over a charcoal fire then sprinkled with sugar. ⊠ *Váci utca 31, Inner Town* ⊕ *www.kurtoskalacs. com* Ⓜ *M3: Ferenciek tere*

■ **Gentry Coffee & Brunch.** This contemporary café serves some of the best all-day breakfasts in town (try the duck-filled croissant), as well as an excellent choice of coffees, craft beers, and champagnes. ⊠ *Királyi Pál utca 9, Inner Town* ⊕ *www. gentrycoffeebrunch.hu* Ⓜ *M3, M4: Kálvin tér*

■ **Rózsavölgyi Csokoládé.** This boutique Belváros chocolate shop has a tempting selection of artisan bars and truffles, many with unusual flavor combinations, and the sweet treats are wrapped in lovely, arty packaging. ⊠ *Királyi Pál utca 6, Inner Town* ⊕ *www. rozsavolgyi.com* Ⓜ *M3, M4: Kálvin tér*

The Inner Town is the beating heart of Pest, and the city's most visited neighborhood, yet this isn't an area that's brimming with big-ticket sights. Rather, the neighborhood itself is the attraction, with its mix of tiny, stroll-worthy streets and grand avenues lined with stately old buildings—some freshly sparkling after their first painting in decades, others silently but still gracefully crumbling—along with some of the city's best shopping and dining.

The neighborhood is small, and remains more or less equivalent to the historic old town of Pest; its boundaries are Deák Ferenc utca (just below Erzsébet tér, or Elizabeth Square) in the north, Vámház körút (just above Nagy Vásárcsarnok, or the Central Market Hall) in the south, and Múzeum körút (right by the Magyar Nemzeti Múzeum, or Hungarian National Museum) in the east. The Danube marks the Inner Town's western boundary. Pedestrian shopping street Váci utca is at the center of things, with its rich array of antiques stores, luxury boutiques, bookshops, cafés, and restaurants, but perhaps the area's most romantic promenade is the Dunakorzó, which runs parallel to Váci utca along the bank of the Danube.

Belváros also boasts many of the city's biggest foodie highlights, from famous *cukrászdas* and coffeehouses to revered fine dining restaurants, along with its most luxurious and exclusive hotels.

Factor in the easy access to Gellért Hill and the Castle District (just across Elizabeth Bridge) and the rest of the city (via a host of transport connections) and this neighborhood makes a perfect base for any Budapest city break.

◉ Sights

The neighborhood's main attraction is the historic church Budapest-Belvárosi Nagyboldogasszony, but keep your eyes open for other architectural highlights as you stroll the Inner Town's streets.

Budapest-Belvárosi Nagyboldogasszony
(*Inner City Parish Church*)
RELIGIOUS SITE | Located at the Pest end of the Erzsébet híd (Elizabeth Bridge), this is not only the oldest church in Budapest, but the oldest building anywhere on this side of the river (a fact illustrated by the evasive bend in the main road beside it). The relatively understated 18th-century baroque facade belies the long history

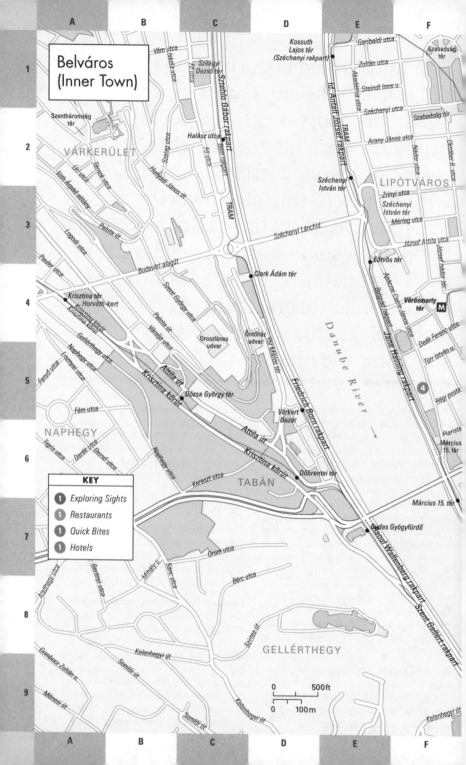

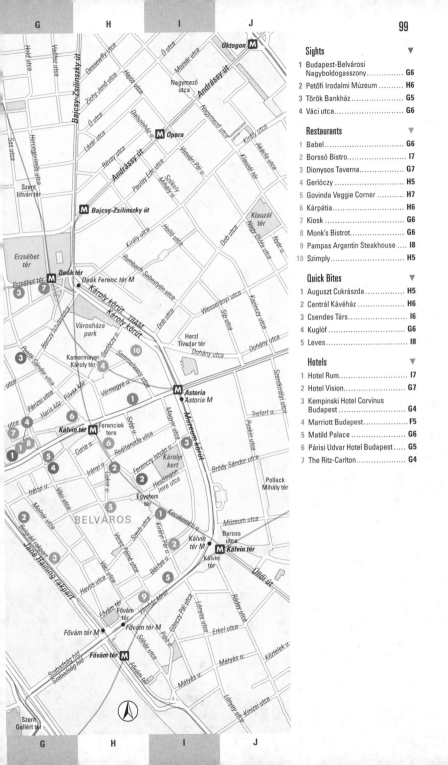

Sights ▼

1 Budapest-Belvárosi
  Nagyboldogasszony............... G6
2 Petőfi Irodalmi Múzeum H6
3 Török Bankház G5
4 Váci utca........................... G6

Restaurants ▼

1 Babel.............................. G6
2 Borssó Bistro....................... I7
3 Dionysos Taverna................. G7
4 Gerlóczy H5
5 Govinda Veggie Corner H7
6 Kárpátia........................... H6
7 Kiosk G6
8 Monk's Bistrot..................... G6
9 Pampas Argentin Steakhouse I8
10 Szimply............................ H5

Quick Bites ▼

1 Auguszt Cukrászda H5
2 Centrál Kávéház H6
3 Csendes Társ...................... I6
4 Kuglóf G6
5 Leves.............................. I8

Hotels ▼

1 Hotel Rum........................... I7
2 Hotel Vision........................ G7
3 Kempinski Hotel Corvinus
  Budapest G4
4 Marriott Budapest................. F5
5 Matild Palace G6
6 Párisi Udvar Hotel Budapest..... G5
7 The Ritz-Carlton.................... G4

and variety of architectural styles you'll find inside, where a medieval Gothic nave stands over the remains of the original 11th century Romanesque basilica (complete with fragments of frescoes) and the ruins of the Roman garrison that it was built upon. You will also find frescoes from the 14th and 15th centuries, a 16th century Islamic *mihrab* (prayer niche)—a holdover from the 150-year Ottoman occupation of Hungary—a 19th century rococo pulpit, and a 20th century high altar. The church contains the relics of Saint Gellért, the bishop who was first buried here in 1046 after pagans pushed him off a hill across the river, as well as those of 11th century Hungarian king Saint László. ⊠ *Március 15 tér, Belváros* ⊕ *www.belvarosiplebania.hu* 🖾 *2,000 HUF, free Sun.* Ⓜ *M3: Ferenciek tere.*

Petőfi Irodalmi Múzeum (*Petőfi Museum of Literature*)
MUSEUM | Founded in 1954 as the national museum of 19th- and 20th-century Hungarian literature, this lovely venue—named after Hungary's most famous poet of the 1848 revolution, Sándor Petőfi—is well worth a visit regardless of what you know (or don't know) about Hungarian creative writing. For one thing, it's in the ravishing neoclassical Károlyi Palota (Károly Palace), which has some grand staircases and stunning rooms filled with period furniture; all free to visit with a museum ticket. And behind the palace is the lovely, flower-filled Károlyi Kert (Károly Garden), a pleasant spot for a post-exhibition amble. ■TIP→ **When entering the palace, look down at the "cobblestone" floor, as closer inspection reveals it's actually made of wood. The owner got fed up with being awakened by horses hooves.** ⊠ *Károlyi utca 16, Belváros* ☎ *1/317–3611* ⊕ *www.pim.hu* 🖾 *800 HUF; temporary exhibitions 1,000 HUF* ⊗ *Closed Mon.* Ⓜ *M3: Ferenciek tere.*

Török Bankház (*Turkish Bank House*)
BUILDING | This eye-catching, glass-covered building, designed in 1906 by architects Henrik Böhm and Ármin Hegedűs, proudly displays Budapest's largest outdoor mosaic. Can't see it? Take a few steps back and crane your neck until you have a good view of the facade's upper gable. It's there you will find the Seccessionist-style mosaic by Hungarian master Miksa Roth, which depicts the Virgin Mary wearing the country's royal crown and wielding a sword before a veritable who's who of Hungarian heroes. ⊠ *Szervita tér, Belváros* Ⓜ *M1, M2, M3: Deák Ferenc tér.*

Váci utca
NEIGHBORHOOD | Running south from Vörösmarty Square to Elizabeth Bridge is Váci utca, Budapest's best-known shopping street and most unabashed tourist zone. This pedestrian precinct with electric 19th-century lampposts has a lot of chain outlets, souvenir stores, and overpriced cafés, but also springs the odd surprise with high-quality china shops, independent bookstores, and folk-craft emporiums. Most notable of all is the architecture, which is consistently beautiful: look out for **Philanthia Virág** at number 9, a tacky flower and gift shop set within a beautiful art nouveau building blessed with original tiles, frescoes, and arches. Other notable art nouveau buildings along Váci utca include the four-story **Thonet House** (no. 11/A) by renowned architect Ödön Lechner, and—somewhat surprisingly—the **McDonald's** on the corner of Régi posta. It was Hungary's first, and remains one of Europe's most beautiful. ⊠ *Belváros.*

🍴 Restaurants

Babel
$$$$ | HUNGARIAN | This atmospheric and intimate Michelin-starred restaurant, which sits in the shadow of the Inner City Parish Church, serves a choice of tasting menus inspired by the beautiful mountainous region of Transylvania in Romania (though it was once part of Hungary). Chef István Veres and his team

Housed in the sumptuous neoclassical Károly Palota, dating from 1840, the Petőfi Irodalmi Múzeum is devoted to Hungary's beloved poet, Sándor Petőfi.

specialize in innovative, flavorful, and playful dishes that put gourmet spins on traditional Carpathian country fare, such as *húsleves* (broth) laced with Tokaj wine and *tojásos nokedli* (egg dumplings) sprinkled with truffles. **Known for:** intimate dining with only a dozen tables; inventive dishes and theatrical presentation; very expensive for Budapest. ⑤ *Average main: 29,900 HUF* ✉ *Piarista köz 2, Belváros* ☎ *70/600–0800* ⊕ *www.babel-budapest. hu* ☉ *Closed Sun. and Mon.; no lunch* Ⓜ *M3: Ferenciek tere.*

Borssó Bistro

$$$ | **FUSION** | The chefs at this cozy high-end bistro combine fresh market ingredients and spoonfuls of imagination to create unique Hungarian-French fusion dishes; think rabbit schnitzel, veal paprika dumplings, and cottage cheese crepes. Everything's beautifully presented, and the friendly servers (or "hosts") are always happy to recommend wines to complement your main. **Known for:** elegant but unpretentious decor; good choice of wines; only open Thursday through Saturday. ⑤ *Average main: 4,500 HUF* ✉ *Királyi Pál utca 14, Belváros* ☎ *1/789–0975* ⊕ *www.borsso. hu* ☉ *Closed Sun.–Wed.; no lunch* Ⓜ *M3, M4: Kálvin tér.*

Dionysos Taverna

$$$$ | **GREEK** | Stone walls and floors, Mediterranean white and blue paint, and a lively terrace will transport you to Santorini. While a bit on the pricey end, this authentic Greek restaurant offers high-quality Greek food and service and a palate break from typical Hungarian fare, which is a popular break apparently as there is often a long wait for a table. **Known for:** Budapest's best Greek restaurant; souvlaki; Piatela Dionysou sharing plate. ⑤ *Average main: 6,000 HUF* ✉ *Belgrád rakpart 16, Belváros* ☎ *1/318–1222* ⊕ *www.dionysos.hu.*

Gerlóczy

$$$ | **EUROPEAN** | The wicker chairs and café tables of this elegant brasserie, on a quiet and leafy square tucked behind Váci utca, are reminiscent of a scene out

of a French movie; the summer terrace is about the prettiest location for lunch in Budapest. At other times of year, visitors can still enjoy the seasonal Hungarian favorites, like *sült libacomb* (crispy goose leg) in winter and asparagus soup in the spring, in the Parisian bistro-style interior. **Known for:** seasonal French and Hungarian dishes; Budapest's fluffiest breakfast croissants; lovely terrace. $ *Average main: 4,000 HUF* ✉ *Gerlóczy utca 1, Belváros* ☎ *1/501–4000* ⊕ *www.gerloczy. hu* Ⓜ *M2: Astoria.*

Govinda Veggie Corner
$$ | VEGETARIAN | The basic Indian-style dishes at Govinda may not be that exciting from a culinary perspective but everything is vegan and made from fresh products coming straight out of Krishna Valley, a communal village of Hare Krishnas near Lake Balaton that dates back to the change in regime. This religious eco-community is almost completely self-sufficient, using solar energy and sustainable subsidies, and supplying their six Hungarian restaurants with vegetables and other stocks. **Known for:** Indian vegan cuisine; puri and homemade chutney; Krishna theme. $ *Average main: 2,500 HUF* ✉ *Papnövelde utca 1, Belváros* ☎ *70/255–2195* ⊕ *www. govinda.hu.*

Kárpátia (*The Carpathia*)
$$$$ | HUNGARIAN | Celebrated Roma musicians play traditional *csárdás* as well as more contemporary tunes in this historic 1877 restaurant with traditional furnishings that include hand-painted walls, heavy curtains, rich wood-paneling, and cushioned red chairs. The menu offers a rather basic fare of traditional, hearty Hungarian cuisine heavy on pork, goose, and beef which you could find elsewhere, but not with this enchanting setting. **Known for:** authentic Hungarian cuisine; elegant old world interior; live folk music. $ *Average main: 6,000 HUF* ✉ *Ferenciek tere 7, Belváros* ☎ *1/317–3596* ⊕ *www. karpatia.hu.*

Kiosk
$$$ | INTERNATIONAL | This restaurant's large outdoor terrace in the heart of the Inner Town makes it a popular lunch stop with tourists throughout the summer, who are also tempted by the great-value midweek lunch menus (2,450 HUF for two courses or 2,950 for three). Come later in the day and you will find a full menu of delicious dishes—from seasonal Hungarian foods like lecsó (pepper stews) to international favorites like burgers, soups, and salads—as well as an unbeatable cocktail menu and (very loud) live music. **Known for:** chic interior and pleasant terrace; delicious homemade lemonades; service can be wilfully slow. $ *Average main: 3,750 HUF* ✉ *Március 15. tér 4, Belváros* ☎ *70/311– 1969* ⊕ *www.kiosk-budapest.com* Ⓜ *M3: Ferenciek tere.*

Monk's Bistrot
$$$ | HUNGARIAN | The decor at this high quality Inner Town restaurant is said to be inspired by the Piarist monastery that once stood here, but with its hip industrial lighting, plushly upholstered furnishings, and sleek open kitchen, it takes quite the imagination to picture monks dining here. Instead, you're likely to find a mix of hip locals and food-loving tourists tucking into the bistro's modern takes on age-old Hungarian dishes. **Known for:** bold and inventive seasonal dishes; extensive wine menu; good value three-course lunches. $ *Average main: 3,500 HUF* ✉ *Piarista köz 1, Belváros* ☎ *30/789–4718* ⊕ *www.english.monks.hu* ☾ *Closed Sun.* Ⓜ *M3: Ferenciek tere.*

Pampas Argentin Steakhouse
$$$$ | ARGENTINE | Meat lovers will be spoiled for choice at this dedicated steak house specializing in imported Argentine beef, where cuts difficult to find in Hungary (like rib eye and New York strip) are aged and lovingly grilled. Steaks can be ordered by weight and come with classic side dishes like jacket potatoes and creamed spinach. **Known for:**

The upper gable of Torok Bankhaz sports a wonderful Secessionist mosaic by Miksa Róth which depicts Hungary surrounded by great Hungarians of the past.

reasonable prices for quality meat; hard-to-find Wagyu burgers; tasty homemade cheesecake to finish. $ *Average main: 10,000 HUF* ☒ *Vámház körút 6, Belváros* ☎ *1/411–1750* ⊕ *www.steak.hu* Ⓜ *M3, M4: Kálvin tér.*

Szimply

$$ | CAFÉ | Fresh, quick breakfasts and light lunches are offered in this cheery little street-side café, open 9–3. The menu is simple but with vegetarian options and attentive service. **Known for:** very popular little spot; fresh and local ingredients; avocado toast. $ *Average main: 2,300 HUF* ☒ *Röser udvar, Budapest* ✥ *just off of Károly körút 22* ⊕ *www.szimply.com* ☽ *Closed Sun.* Ⓜ *M2: Astoria.*

🍽 Coffee and Quick Bites

⭐ Auguszt Cukrászda

$ | CAFÉ | This old-fashioned bakery–café has a loyal following for some of the lightest, most buttery pastries in Budapest. All the classic Hungarian cakes like *rétes* (strudel filled with sour cherries, apples, or cheese) and *dobos torta* (chocolate cream cake with caramel) can be enjoyed here, along with some unique in-house creations. **Known for:** to-die-for cakes and pastries; good coffee selection; located on a busy main road. $ *Average main: 650 HUF* ☒ *Kossuth Lajos utca 14–16, Belváros* ☎ *1/337–6379* ⊕ *www.auguszt. hu* ☽ *Closed Sun. and Mon.* Ⓜ *M2: Astoria.*

⭐ Centrál Kávéház

$$$ | CAFÉ | A classic turn-of-the-20th-century gathering spot for Hungarian writers, this coffeehouse has endured two wars and a communist closure. Today, it offers 19th-century grandeur in 21st-century luxury: coffees are served on silver trays with glasses of mineral water like in the old days, but in air-conditioned comfort. **Known for:** fancy coffee service on silver trays; traditional dishes like borjú paprikás (paprika veal stew); excellent cakes and pastries. $ *Average main: 4,500 HUF* ☒ *Károlyi utca 9, Belváros* ☎ *01/266–2110* ⊕ *www.centralkavehaz.hu* Ⓜ *M3: Ferenciek tere.*

Csendes Társ

$ | CONTEMPORARY | This adorable outdoor-only café is set by the entrance to the lovely Károlyi-kert park, known for its colorful flower beds and manicured lawns. A pleasant spot for breakfast, a light lunch, or for evening drinks in the glow of lanterns, Csendes Társ is open from April to mid-October only. **Known for:** sister café to cool Casendes ruin bar up the street; lovely setting; cash only. ⑤ *Average main: 650 HUF* ⊠ *Magyar utca 16-18, Belváros* ☎ *30/727–2100* ⊕ *www.csend.es* Ⓜ *M2: Astoria.*

Kuglóf

$$ | CAFÉ | Named after a popular Central Eastern European Bundt cake, this bistro's French flair shines in the presentation of its breakfast and cake selection. Enjoy everything from quail eggs and homemade English muffins to spare ribs and cherry pie out on the arched walkway terrace with a view to Március 15 tér (March 15 Square) and the river in the distance. **Known for:** breakfast menu; delicious croissants; outdoor seating with views. ⑤ *Average main: 2,500 HUF* ⊠ *Piarista köz 1, Belváros* ☎ *30/948–1805* ⊕ *www.kuglof.hu* Ⓜ *M3: Ferenciek tere.*

Leves

$ | INTERNATIONAL | As life in Budapest becomes increasingly mobile and fast-paced, this fast food restaurant caters to on-the-go locals with no time to dither by specializing entirely in soup. While the menu is limited to soups, it is not limited: there are soups of all flavor and origin on the always-changing menu. **Known for:** gluten-free soups; varied menu includes Thai, Catalan, and Hungarian soups; cold raspberry cream soup. ⑤ *Average main: 1,200 HUF* ⊠ *Vámház körút 14, Belváros* ☎ *30/527–9495* ⊕ *www.facebook.com/levespont* ☾ *Closed Sun.*

 # Hotels

Hotel Rum

$$ | HOTEL | This smart boutique hotel, located within a 1920s town house in the heart of the Inner Town, offers stylish bedrooms, a superb fine dining restaurant, and one of the city's most popular rooftop bars. **Pros:** great rooftop bar and top-notch restaurant; quiet location within a busy area; showcases modern artworks from a local gallery. **Cons:** breakfast not included; basic "light" rooms are very small; no gym or pool. ⑤ *Rooms from: 43,500 HUF* ⊠ *Királyi Pál utca 4, Belváros* ☎ *1/424–9060* ⊕ *www.hotelrumbudapest.com* ⤳ *40 rooms* ⦿ *No meals* Ⓜ *M3, M4: Kálvin tér.*

Hotel Vision

$$$ | HOTEL | Opened in 2020, Hotel Vision is one of Budapest's most appealing boutique hotels, thanks to its lovely riverside setting, its beautiful art nouveau exterior, and its sleek and stylish bedrooms. **Pros:** romantic river views from suites; free tea and coffee in lobby all day; relaxing wellness area. **Cons:** not all rooms overlook the river; fitness facilities are limited; geometric wallpaper hurts your brain. ⑤ *Rooms from: 45,000 HUF* ⊠ *Belgrád rakpart 24, Belváros* ☎ *20/423–0195* ⊕ *www.hotelvision.hu* ⤳ *91 rooms* ⦿ *No meals* Ⓜ *M3: Ferenciek tere.*

★ Kempinski Hotel Corvinus Budapest

$$$$ | HOTEL | The moment you step inside the Kempinski it's clear you're in one of Budapest's finest five-star hotels, as the lovely lobby area gives way to a charming promenade lined with cafés, bars, takeaway delis, and even a small art gallery, not to mention two exceptional restaurants: the swanky Japanese-fusion Nobu and the steak-focused brasserie ÉS Bisztró. **Pros:** ideal location overlooking Fashion Street; room service from on-site fine dining restaurant Nobu; huge underground parking lot. **Cons:** stone-and-glass exterior makes for a rather cold entrance; breakfast an expensive add-on;

fussy bathroom faucets. $ *Rooms from: 125,000 HUF* ✉ *Erzsébet tér 7–8, Belváros* ☎ *1/429–3777* ⊕ *www.kempinski.com* ⤳ *351 rooms* ⏐◯⏐ *No meals* Ⓜ *M1, M2, M3: Deák Ferenc tér.*

Marriott Budapest

$$$$ | HOTEL | It may be one of the least attractive buildings in Pest, but the Marriott's prime Danube location makes for some breathtaking views: Gellért Hill, the Chain Bridge, and Castle Hill are all visible from every single guest room. **Pros:** spectacular views from every aspect; stylish and modern interiors; free yoga for guests. **Cons:** very ugly building (though guests don't have to look at it); lacks any authentic local flair; bathrooms are a little small. $ *Rooms from: 85,000 HUF* ✉ *Apáczai Csere János utca 4, Belváros* ☎ *1/486–5000* ⊕ *www.marriott.com* ⤳ *364 rooms* ⏐◯⏐ *Free breakfast* Ⓜ *M1: Vörösmarty tér.*

Matild Palace

$$$$ | HOTEL | Built by Princess Marie Clotilde of Saxe-Coburg and Gotha during La Belle Époque, this grand old building is now home to one of the city's most elegant luxury hotels, complete with a dizzying array of drinking and dining options. **Pros:** elegant rooms and sumptuous suites; unique bathrooms inspired by thermal baths; vast rooftop bar open year-round. **Cons:** different room styles means an odd mix of guests; situated on a busy main road; recently opened so still finding its feet. $ *Rooms from: 75,000 HUF* ✉ *Váci utca 36, Belváros* ☎ *1/550–5000* ⊕ *www.marriott.com* ⤳ *130 rooms* ⏐◯⏐ *No meals* Ⓜ *M3: Ferenciek tere.*

★ Párisi Udvar Hotel Budapest

$$$$ | HOTEL | Set with an impossibly ornate, Parisian-style arcade in the heart of Belváros, this Hyatt hotel is a feast for the eyes, with original Gothic and Moorish features combining with a gorgeous art nouveau design. **Pros:** stunning art nouveau building from 1806; top-floor residences among best rooms in Budapest; soothing ZAFIR Spa

has three treatment rooms. **Cons:** basic bedrooms are a little small; service can be slow and surly; arcade can get busy with tour groups. $ *Rooms from: 95,000 HUF* ✉ *Petőfi Sándor utca 2–4, Belváros* ☎ *1/576–1600* ⊕ *www.hyatt.com* ⤳ *110* ⏐◯⏐ *No meals* Ⓜ *M3: Ferenciek tere.*

The Ritz-Carlton

$$$$ | HOTEL | Originally built for an insurance company, this grand palatial building is now home to a popular five-star hotel offering stylish and contemporary rooms, an appealing fitness center and spa, a fine grill restaurant serving Mangalitza pork, and a charming Viennese-style coffeehouse. **Pros:** great location right by a major Metro station; breakfast is beneath a beautiful stained-glass cupola; café has original marble floors and stucco ceilings. **Cons:** can hear street noise and feel Metro from some rooms; swimming pool is beautiful but small; service can be hit and miss. $ *Rooms from: 135,000 HUF* ✉ *Erzsébet tér 9–10, Belváros* ☎ *1/429–5500* ⊕ *www.ritzcarlton.com* ⤳ *200 rooms* ⏐◯⏐ *No meals* Ⓜ *M1, M2, M3: Deák Ferenc tér.*

🌙 Nightlife

BARS AND PUBS

★ Csendes Létterem Vintage Bar & Café

BARS/PUBS | Among Budapest's best ruin bars—drinking holes built within old, abandoned postwar buildings and populated with flea market furniture—Csendes oozes underground atmosphere. *Csendes* means quiet in Hungarian, but this spot is in fact, almost always lively. The junk shop chic decor (think hanging bicycles, vintage knick-knacks, and industrial artworks) brings in the hipster crowds, while the great beer selection, quality bar food, and incredible prices ensure they stick around. Check out their shop, the Csendes Concept Store, just around the corner, which sells handmade Hungarian designer goods from jewelry to ceramics and homemade local food products including cheese, honey, and craft beers. A few doors down, Csendes has a lovely café with a terrace (on the corner of Károlyi Kert). ✉ *Ferenczy István utca 5, Belváros* ☎ *30/727–2100* ⊕ *www. csend.es* Ⓜ *M2: Astoria.*

LIVE MUSIC

Fat Mo's

MUSIC CLUBS | Established Hungarian jazz headliners and young up-and-comers play from Wednesday through Sunday in the small but stylish brick-walled cellar pub. The music is good, but the audience is mainly expats and tourists. ✉ *Nyári Pál utca 11, Belváros* ☎ *70/623–8844* ⊕ *www.fatmo.hu* Ⓜ *M3: Ferenciek tere.*

🎭 Performing Arts

CLASSICAL MUSIC

Pesti Vigadó

DANCE | **FAMILY** | This romantic riverside concert hall, designed by Frigyes Feszl in the mid-19th century but extensively rebuilt after World War II, is the place to come for classical concerts by leading international orchestras, including the Hungarian State Symphony Orchestra. The beautiful 700-seater Main Hall also hosts regular folk dance shows and drama performances, while the rest of the building is given over to temporary art exhibitions and other events. Take the lift to the sixth floor for stunning Danube views from the panoramic terrace. ✉ *Vigadó tér 2, Belváros* ☎ *20/429–4124* ⊕ *www.vigado.hu* Ⓜ *M1: Vörösmarty tér.*

🛍 Shopping

The Inner Town is a shopper's paradise. For designer clothes, head for the pedestrianized Deák Ferenc utca (aka "Fashion Street"); for souvenirs, make a beeline for touristy Váci utca; and for anything else, take a stroll down some side streets.

CLOTHING

Nanushka

CLOTHING | Part designer boutique, part artisan coffee shop, the flagship outlet of this high-end Hungarian fashion brand is well worth a look. Founded by London College of Fashion graduate Sandra Sandor (whose nickname is Nanushka), it has gained a loyal international following for its stylish, feminine, but functional designs. The clothes aren't cheap, but you'll get more bang for your buck than at the big-name luxury brands on nearby Fashion Street. The coffee is fantastic, too. ✉ *Bécsi utca 3, Belváros* ☎ *70/394–1954* ⊕ *www.nanushka.com* ☾ *Closed Sun.* Ⓜ *M1, M2, M3: Deák Ferenc tér.*

Vass Shoes

CLOTHING | If you are looking for a really luxurious indulgence, why not consider a pair of handmade leather shoes, specifically measured to your feet? You can choose from a variety of traditional styles, from cordovan to nubuck. Though wildly expensive when compared to the cost of ready-made shoes, prices are still very competitive with bespoke shoes in Europe and the United States. There's a small selection of ready-to-wear shoes available as well. ✉ *Haris Köz 2, Belváros* ☎ *1/780–7418* ⊕ *www.vass-shoes.com* ☾ *Closed Sun.* Ⓜ *M3: Ferenciek tere.*

CRAFTS

Holló Műhely

CRAFTS | Master wood craftsman László Holló has resurrected traditional motifs and styles of earlier centuries to create the beautiful handicrafts on sale in this shop. You'll find lovely hope chests, chairs, jewelry boxes, candlesticks, Easter eggs, and more—all hand-carved and hand-painted with cheery folk motifs (most commonly birds and flowers in reds, blues, and greens). ✉ *Vitkovics Mihály utca 12, Belváros* ☎ *1/317–8103* ⊕ *www.facebook.com/hollomuhely* ☾ *Closed Sun.* Ⓜ *M2: Astoria.*

Paloma

CRAFTS | Located within an ornate 19th century building centered around a charming courtyard, Paloma brings together a collective of local designers to showcase their handicrafts. The small boutiques are run by the designers themselves and sell all manner of creative designs, including handbags, ceramics, jewelry, stationery, and children's toys. The space also hosts regular contemporary art exhibitons. ⊠ *Kossuth Lajos utca 14, Belváros* ☎ *20/961–9160* ⊕ *www.palomabudapest.hu* ⊙ *Closed Sun.* Ⓜ *M2: Astoria.*

FOOD AND WINE

Szamos Marcipán

FOOD/CANDY | **FAMILY** | Marzipan has always been a favorite in Central Europe, and this well-loved confectioner has spent more than 75 years mastering the art. The store has always been most famous for its marzipan cookies, cakes, and candies, as well as its edible marzipan roses, but today just as many people come for the ice cream. ⊠ *Párizsi utca 3, Belváros* ☎ *30/535–0259* ⊕ *www.szamos.hu* Ⓜ *M3: Ferenciek tere.*

SHOPPING NEIGHBORHOODS

Fashion Street (*Deák Ferenc utca*)
STORE/MALL | This historic street has been recently renovated and redesigned as a sophisticated, high-concept shopping street to complement the traditional pedestrian shopping promenade located just around the corner on Váci utca. Upscale iconic brands meet local fashion favorites as well as small boutiques, restaurants, and bars. This street hasn't quite taken off like other shopping areas but it's still worth a wander across as you head from Deák Ferenc tér to Vörösmarty tér. ⊠ *Deák Ferenc utca 15, Belváros* ⊕ *www.fashionstreet.hu.*

STATIONERY

Bomo Art

BOOKS/STATIONERY | Open since 1997, this charming little stationery store sells hand-bound notebooks, diaries, postcards, writing utensils, wrapping paper, and more besides. The attractive, often Budapest-related graphical designs make them perfect souvenirs or gifts. ⊠ *Régi posta utca 14, Belváros* ☎ *20/594–2223* ⊕ *www.bomoart.com* ⊙ *Closed Sun.* Ⓜ *M1, M2, M3: Deák Ferenc tér.*

Chapter 6

SOUTHERN PEST

DISTRICTS 8, 9

Updated by
Esther Holbrook

 Sights
★★★☆☆

 Restaurants
★★★☆☆

 Hotels
★★★☆☆

 Shopping
★★★☆☆

 Nightlife
★★★★★

NEIGHBORHOOD SNAPSHOT

TOP EXPERIENCES

■ **Nagy Vásárcsarnok:** Get an authentic taste of Hungary at the bustling central market.

■ **Kerepesi Cemetery:** Magnificent tombs and mausoleums fill the beautiful park grounds of Hungary's most famous cemetery.

■ **A Night at the Opera:** Indulge in a decadent night of music and culture at the Erkel Színház for bargain rates.

■ **Soccer:** Check out a local or national soccer match at the city's most popular stadium, the Groupama Aréna, in Ferencváros.

■ **Müpa:** Theater, dance, music, and contemporary art at Budapest's premier culture complex.

■ **The Danube Promenade:** Finish the evening with a panoramic view of the sun setting over the Buda Hills from local hot spot the Bálna.

GETTING HERE

Józsefváros and Ferencváros are a 15-minute walk from the city center and all the major attractions, or a short metro ride to Astoria, Kálvin Tér, Blaha Luzja, or Rákóczi Tér. For a scenic route, take Tram 2 down the riverfront or Tram 47 or 49 from Deák tér to the National Museum or the Nagy Vásárcsarnok.

PLANNING YOUR TIME

Allot a full day, at least, to this area. Avoid the crowds by starting early at the city's grand market, Nagy Vásárcsarnok, for breakfast and all your tasty souvenirs. Head away from the river towards Kálvin tér to the National Museum where relics and exhibitions bring Hungary's history to life. The famous Kerepesi Cemetery feature magnificent mausoleums and statues and an interesting little museum. Taste-test Unicum straight out of the barrel at the Zwack Unicum Museum. Have dinner somewhere off the beaten track on Bródy Sándor utca or find a place along Ráday utca. End the day at Erkel Theatre for a night of opera or check out a performance at the Trafo or the Müpa.

QUICK BITES

■ **Rukkola.** A quick stop for a fresh salad or tasty smoothie on the go. ✉ *Baross utca 1, Józsefváros* ⊕ *www.rukkolabudapest.hu* Ⓜ *M3: Kálvin tér*

■ **Nándori Cukrászda.** Choose from a delectable array of cakes and desserts at this popular mom-and-pop confectionary dating to 1957. Eszterházy, Dobos, and Feketeerdő cakes are some Hungarian classic favorites to try. ✉ *Ráday utca 53, Ferencváros* ⊕ *www.nandori.hu* Ⓜ *Tram 4, 6: Mester utca*

■ **Café Csiga.** This former butcher's shop is a delightfully artsy spot, and a great stop for coffee or a light meal. ✉ *Vásár utca 2, Józsefváros* ⊕ *www.facebook.com/cafecsiga* Ⓜ *Tram 4, 6: Rákóczi tér*

After tourists discovered, descended upon (and then overran) the Jewish District's ruin bars, the working-class Józsefváros and Ferencváros neighborhoods in the 8th and 9th districts, just across the ever-busy Rákóczi Utca, became the city's gritty, pretty, and cool places to be.

A little rough around the edges, this Southeastern enclave is a glorious architectural mash-up of turn-of-the-century villas, squat communist-era buildings, trendy coffee shops, and a mix of classic and underground music venues. There's even a football (soccer) stadium.

You'll find a student vibe and an artsy crowd frequenting counterculture bars, galleries, and vintage stores, and strolling along some of Budapest's finest Paris-esque baroque boulevards. Top attractions in the area include the Nagy Vásárcsarnok—the Central Market Hall, Magyar Nemzeti Múzeum, the National Theatre, and the Zwack Unicum Museum, as well as hidden gems like Budapest's most beautiful library housed in a neobaroque palace. The city's football stadium, Groupama Aréna, is home to Hungary's most successful football club, Ferencvárosi, and tickets are easy to come by for those inclined to really mingle with locals. Stroll by the gorgeous (but closed) art nouveau Iparművészeti Múzeum and linger a while in Mikszáth Kálmán tér, a square lined with bars and cafés and the perfect place to just watch city life go by. Forgo the city's fancier thermal baths in favor of the humble Dandár Gyógyfürdő, where you won't find opulence or throngs of tourists, but you will find affordable prices

and locals enjoying aromatic scrubs. If it's places to linger that you're looking for, Southern Pest has them in spades, including the Bálna, Gozsdu-udvar, and A Grund.

Most of Pest's low-density southeast districts used to be separate towns until their integration into the capital in 1950, and look back on a history of agriculture, Ottoman depredation, and aggressive Socialist development. You see this to the east, at Budapest's Franz Liszt International Airport, which sprawls over the former site of 19th-century vineyards. The hill on which they stood was flattened to make space for the construction, but its old name Ferihegy is still the local vernacular for the airport. To the south, lies the district of Csepel located in the middle of the Danube, technically belonging to neither Buda nor Pest. The first royal seat of Hungary's founding Árpád dynasty in the Middle Ages, Csepel became Budapest's center for heavy industry in the 19th century, and generally speaking still looks the part.

Sights

The Bálna (*The Whale*)
BUILDING | Designed by architect Kas Oosterhuis, and opened in 2013, this

Many famous Hungarian figures—from politicians to scientists to artists—are buried at Kerepesi Cemetery, which is the oldest Christian cemetery in Budapest still in use.

commercial and cultural hub looks pretty much like its name, which means "whale" in English. The interior houses the Budapest Gallery and the Budapest Festival and Tourism Ticket and Information Center, which sells transportation, tour, and entertainment tickets. With several trendy bars and restaurants on its periphery, the Bálna area is a popular meeting point, especially in the summer. On the south entrance, Jónás craft beer house provides a busy, but relaxed, atmosphere to enjoy the view of the river, and the north-facing Esetleg Bisztró is the ideal location from which to catch a stunning sunset over Buda's Gellért Hill. Just a few meters away at neighborhood hangout Nehru Park, locals play football, basketball, and practice skateboarding, but most of all they chill out with a picnic or drink, enjoying this welcome green zone next to the river. The south-facing Buda view of the Citadella is almost as gorgeous as the one of Gellért. ⊠ Fővám tér 11–12, South Pest ⊕ www.balnabuda-pest.hu 🕾 Free.

Dandár Gyógyfürdő (*Dandár Thermal bath*)
HOT SPRINGS | A small and humble spa with a sort of minimalist charm about it Dandár (The Brigade) was once a literal public bathhouse, hence its lack of Ottoman opulence. It was transformed into a thermal spa in the late 1970s and offers wellness services, a sauna, and three indoor pools and two outdoor pools to soothe your weary bones while you mingle with locals playing water chess. ⊠ Dandár utca 5–7, South Pest 🕾 1/215–7084 ⊕ www.dandarfurdo.hu 🕾 2,800 HUF.

Holokauszt Emlékközpont (*Holocaust Memorial Center*)
MUSEUM | Built in 2002 as part of a government initiative focusing on Holocaust research and education, the stark, impressive modern design of the Holocaust Memorial Center, with its high white walls, is somehow evocative of both a fortress and the gates to a city in Holy Land. The interior of the entrance wall is lined from top to bottom with the names of a fraction of the Hungarian

victims of the Holocaust and the permanent exhibition focuses on the Holocaust as experienced by Jewish Hungarians, with a special section on the experience of Roma Hungarians. The Páva Street Synagogue which houses the memorial was once one of the city's largest Jewish congregations; it now displays its significant historical artifacts, and can also be visited when not in service. ✉ *Páva utca 39, Budapest* ☏ *1/455–3333* ⊕ *www.hdke. hu* ⊙ *Closed Mon.* Ⓜ *M3: Corvin-negyed station; tram 4, 6.*

Iparművészeti Múzeum (*Museum of Applied Arts*)

MUSEUM | A gorgeous art nouveau building, closed for renovations until further notice (exhibitions and programs are now being hosted at the György Ráth Villa), the exterior and green roof still merit a visit. Designed by some of Hungarian architects, Ödön Lechner and Gyula Pártos, the building was built specifically for the museum in 1896, making it the third oldest applied-arts museum in the world. The internationally renowned Hungarian ceramics company in Zsolnay was commissioned to provide the tiles, which cover the building inside and out. The result is an incredible work of handcrafted art in which to display beautiful national handicrafts. ✉ *Üllői út 33–37, Budapest* ⊕ *www.imm.hu* ⊙ *Closed until further notice.*

Kerepesi Cemetery (*Fiumei úti nemzeti sírkert*)

CEMETERY | Europe is full of extraordinary cemeteries that function as burial grounds, national memorial spaces, and outdoor art galleries, and Kerepesi Cemetery is one of the most beautiful and impressive. Founded in 1847, this is one of the oldest cemeteries in Hungary and most certainly the most well-known in Budapest as it is the final resting places of Hungary's greatest artists, statesmen, and inventors. Maps are available at the entrance with descriptions of the most famous residents, including Mihály

Vörösmarty, Attila József, Endre Ady, Mor Jókai, Janos Arany, Lajos Kossuth, Ferenc Erkel, Gyorgy Faludy, Miklós Jancsó, and Imre Kertész, to name a few. Wander the tree-lined avenues past the ornate tombs and mausoleums of this stunning graveyard, such as the grandiose lion-guarded one for Lajos Batthyány, or the mausoleum of Ferenc Deák or Lajos Kossuth. The communist-era mausoleum for the Labour movement, designed in 1958 by Olcsai-Kiss Zoltán, may still stir conflicting feelings, but it merits a stop. At 56 hectares (138 acres), this is one of the largest National Pantheons in Europe so you'll want to spend a while. If you are here on a weekday, check out the tiny Kegyeleti Museum (open until 3 pm) located on the grounds. Dedicated to Hungary's death rituals and remembrance of the dead, you'll find some unique artifacts, including Hungarian death masks and Transylvanian wooden gravemarkers. You can also visit the Salgotarjani Street Jewish Cemetery, which occupies the eastern corner—technically part of Kerepesi Cemetery but must be entered from a separate entrance. ✉ *Fiumei út 16–18, Budapest* ☏ *1/323–5231* ⊕ *www.fiumeiutisirkert.nori.gov.hu* 🎟 *Free* Ⓜ *M4: Keleti pályaudvar; tram 24, 28, 37.*

Ludwig Museum

ART GALLERIES—ARTS | The brainchild of Irene and Peter Ludwig, the Ludwig Museum at Müpa is Hungary's only museum dedicated exclusively to contemporary art. Set in the Müpa Budapest cultural center, the Ludwig houses a significant collection of modern international and Hungarian fine art over three floors in the wing closest to the Danube. While focusing on Eastern and Central European art, it also puts a special emphasis on presenting Hungarian art of the 60's to present days in an international context. ✉ *Komor Marcell utca 1, Budapest* ☏ *1/555–3444* ⊕ *www.ludwigmuseum.hu* 🎟 *1,600 HUF.*

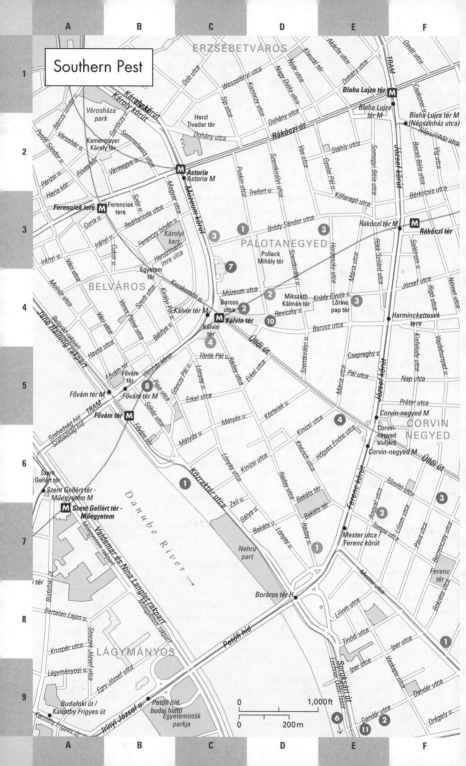

Sights ▼

Restaurants ▼

Quick Bites ▼

Hotels ▼

The Danube Promenade

Budapest may be the pearl of the Danube, but the Danube is the crown it is set in. A walk along the river is a must for any visitor to the city and the Danube Promenade (Dunakorzó) offers spectacular close encounters with the river itself. Traditionally, the korzó running along the Pest side from the Chain Bridge to the Erzsébet Bridge was the preferred Danube stroll, the highlight being a lovely panoramic view to Buda Castle from the delightful Vigadó tér. Recent expansions and improvements have made both sides more accessible and popular with pedestrians and bikers alike, with a crop of new cafés and restaurants to explore along the way. The Danube Promenade experience can start from as far up as Margit Bridge. Heading south on the Pest side, Buda Castle and the Fisherman's Bastion remain the points of convergence until you reach Parliament, just to your left. Take a moment at the Shoes on the Danube memorial commemorating the Hungarian Jews who lost their lives in the Second World War. The Chain Bridge offers more spectacular views of the Castle District all the way down to Fővám tér.

If you decide to start from the Buda side, descend to the bank from the Margit Bridge and head south toward Batthyány tér. Enjoy the views of the Parliament building on the opposite shore, with a steady stream of tour boats bobbing in the foreground. Head south and pass the ornate Várkert Bazár on Ybl Miklós Square to your right. Don't hesitate to detour here to sneak a peek of the view from its rose garden. Farther along, past Döbrentei tér, you'll come upon the imposing Gellért Hill. If you look closely, you will see that the cliffside is riddled with caves and tunnels that are closed to the public. A visit to the Gellért-hegyi sziklatemplom (Gellért Hill Cave Church) offers a hint of what you're missing. Carry on past the University of Technology and Economics to the Petőfi híd, with a view to the Pest side's gigantic white dome known as the Bálna (whale). Eventually you will reach Rákóczi híd and the chic little Kopaszi gát, an inlet that has been made into a cute garden and restaurant space. Head across the river at the Petőfi híd and enjoy a craft beer or glass of wine at the Bálna as you watch the sun set over the Buda Hills.

★ **Magyar Nemzeti Múzeum** (*Hungarian National Museum*)
MUSEUM | The permanent collection here takes you on a stimulating journey into the everyday Hungarian experience, from the recent to the more distant past. Among the highlights are the 20th-century exhibit, including an early movie theater replete with films of the era, an old schoolroom, a 1960s apartment interior, and a host of historical posters—all of which brings you right up to the end of communism and the much-celebrated exodus of Russian troops. Older attractions including masterworks of cabinet-making and woodcarving (e.g., church pews from Nyírbátor and Transylvania); a piano that belonged to both Beethoven and Liszt; and goldsmithing treasures. The museum often hosts interesting temporary installations as well, such as the World Press Photo exhibition housed here every fall. ✉ *Múzeum körút 14–16, Kálvin tér* ☎ *1/338-2122* ⊕ *www.mnm. hu* ✆ *2,600 HUF* ⊘ *Closed Mon.* Ⓜ *M3: Kálvin tér.*

With its cavernous interior, the vast three-level Nagy Vasarcsarnok (Central Market Hall) is a pilgrimage destination for food-lovers and souvenir-hunters.

★ Nagy Vásárcsarnok (*Central Market Hall*)

MARKET | The city's premier market hall, with a stunning gilded exterior, is a treasure chest of Hungarian produce and foodstuffs. This is the oldest (over 120 years) and largest market in town, and a great place to wander and sample specialties like Mangalica ham (Hungarian white swine), Szarvaskolbász (deer sausage), Kovászos uborka (fermented cucumber), and a variety of local handmade cheeses, honeys, Hungarian paprika, and other delectables. Follow your nose for a breakfast of lángo, a Hungarian deep-fried flatbread, and peach strudel from the popular rétes stand. You can stock your suitcase with vacuum-packed products, and look for additional souvenirs on the second floor, where you'll find a mix of lovely and kitsch Hungarian handicrafts, handcarved chess sets, and Rubik's Cubes, as well as a few cheap market eateries. ⊠ *Vámház körút 1–3, Budapest* ☎ *1/366–3300* ⊕ *www.piaconline.hu* ⊙ *Closed Sun.* Ⓜ *H7: Boráros tér and a 10-min walk.*

Salgotarjani Street Jewish Cemetery (*Kerepesi Jewish Cemetery*)

CEMETERY | Dating from 1874, Budapest's oldest Jewish cemetery is technically part of the huge Kerespesi Cemetery but is separated with a tall stone wall. Overgrown with vegetation and in need of repair, these serene grounds are the resting place of aristocratic Jewish Hungarian families and prestigious individuals, with a section dedicated to victims of the Holocaust. Stonemasonry by Hungary's premier architects of the day provide exquisite examples of the conversation between popular artistic movements, such as Szecesszió (Hungarian art nouveau), and Jewish cultural history and identity. ⊠ *Salgótarjáni utca 6, Budapest* ☎ *1/896–3889* ⊕ *www.zsido-temeto.nori.gov.hu* ⊙ *Closed Sat. and on Jewish holidays.*

★ Szabó Ervin Könyvtár (*Metropolitan Szabó Ervin Library*)

LIBRARY | Stately on the outside, spectacular on the inside, this ornate library is located in Wenckheim Palace, one of the

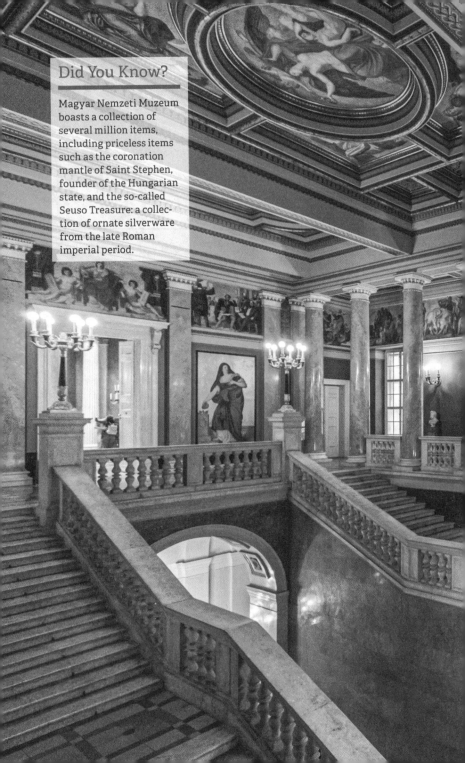

most grand homes in the Palace District when built by a Hungarian aristocrat in the 1800s, and today the city's most beautiful reading rooms. The library moved in in 1931, after the city bought the neobaroque palace. Head straight to the fourth floor to wander the gilded palatial rooms, and take a seat in the former Smoking Room with its carved wood panels and ceiling, ornate spiral staircase, and leather-bound books, or find a velvet chair from which to admire the chandeliers, high ceilings, and elegant finishes in the former Ballroom or the Lady of the House's Room. For bookworms, this is a working library and accessible to the public, so make time to peruse the shelves. Purchase a daily card to get access to some of the library databases and in-house resources or check out their calendar for upcoming public events. It's also just worth coming in to appreciate the setting and have a coffee and a cake at the library café. The library is named for Szabó Ervin, who helped develop the public library system in Budapest. ⊠ Szabó Ervin tér 1, Budapest ☎ 1/411–5000 ⊕ www.fszek.hu ⊠ 1,000 HUF admission to Wenckheim Palace ⊙ Closed Sun. Ⓜ Tram 47, 49; bus 15, 9; trolleybus 83.

★ **Zwack Unicum Museum** (*The House of Unicum*)

WINERY/DISTILLERY | A herbal liquor product made by the legendary Zwack distillery, Unicum is the quintessential Hungarikum (product of Hungary) and this museum is an essential visit. While the Unicum recipe remains a well-guarded secret, visitors can learn about this esteemed company's legacy spanning six generations, a World War, and communist rule, and tour the carefully restored distillery, with systems that are over 100 years old. The final stop on the tour is the Unicum cellar, where visitors are invited for a tasting of classic Unicum or the newer Unicum Plum, a recipe variation created by József Zwack's great-great-great grandchildren Sándor and Izabella Zwack. ■TIP→ FImmaker István Szabó's

1999 movie Sunshine, starring Ralph Fiennes, presents the lives of a Jewish Hungarian family living in Budapest over four generations, and incorporates the Zwack family story in the plot. ⊠ Dandár utca 1, Budapest ☎ 1/476–2383 ⊕ www.zwackunicum.hu ⊠ 2,200 HUF ⊙ Closed Sun.

 Restaurants

★ **Café Jedermann**

$$ | EUROPEAN | Founded by legendary local restaurateur Hans van Vliet, this inviting café and restaurant caters to one and all (Jedermann means "everyone"). The menu is nothing spectacular, but everything is wholesome and freshly made, and the atmosphere is best summed up in buzzwords like off-beat, cool-cat, and jazz bar. **Known for:** affordable all-day breakfast; hearty goulash; live jazz performances and jazz decor. Ⓢ Average main: 3,000 HUF ⊠ Ráday utca 58, Budapest ☎ 30/406–3617 ⊕ www.jedermann.hu.

Építész Pince Étterem

$$ | HUNGARIAN | Once the location of the city's architectural club, this cozy little restaurant tucked away in the Almássy Palace offers reasonably priced traditional Hungarian cuisine in an elegant setting. Enjoy seating outdoors in the delightful garden space in summer or settle into the newly renovated dining room inside. **Known for:** quiet inner city haven; marhapörkölt (goulash); beautiful building and courtyard. Ⓢ Average main: 3,000 HUF ⊠ Ötpacsirta utca 2, Budapest ☎ 1/266–4799 ⊕ en.epiteszpince.hu ⊙ Closed Sun.

Múzeum Kávéház és Étterem

$$$ | HUNGARIAN | This old-timer is a surprisingly affordable option for traditional cuisine served in turn-of-the-20th-century style. A beautifully frescoed ceiling and tables set with sterling silver and Zsolnay porcelain provide an elegant, if somewhat faded, grandeur. **Known for:**

live pianist; Hungarian classics; extensive wine list. $ *Average main: 4,500 HUF* ✉ *Múzeum körút 12, Budapest* ☎ *1/267–0375* ⊕ *www.muzeumkavehaz.hu.*

Pata Negra Tapas Bar

$$$ | TAPAS | The colorful Spanish tiles on the wall, the big legs of ibérico jámon, and a full wall stacked with rioja tip you off to the authenticity of this tapas bar just off Ráday utca. Pata Negra was one of the first tapas spots in town. **Known for:** unpretentious wine bar; jamon, cheese, and great wine; easygoing local feel. $ *Average main: 4,000 HUF* ✉ *Kálvin tér 8, Budapest* ☎ *1/215–5616* ⊕ *www.patanegra.hu.*

Rosenstein Vendéglő

$$$ | HUNGARIAN | FAMILY | This family-run restaurant offers an extensive menu of Hungarian and Jewish Hungarian cuisine, including some vegetarian options. While the decor is your standard traditional Central Eastern European fare—large spaces packed with art objects and memorabilia—the atmosphere is cozy and inviting. **Known for:** Jewish Hungarian cuisine; Hungarian fish soup; restaurant cookbook. $ *Average main: 5,000 HUF* ✉ *Mosonyi utca 3, Budapest* ☎ *1/333–3492* ⊕ *www.rosenstein.hu* ☾ *Closed Sun.*

☕ Coffee and Quick Bites

Black Cab Burgers

$$ | AMERICAN | FAMILY | Hungarians have really embraced burger culture and you can find burgers on the menu almost everywhere now, but most of the time, they're not what you'd expect. Anything goes for a bun and the fillings are sometimes rather unusual. **Known for:** classic hamburgers; cash only; extra charge for condiments. $ *Average main: 2,500 HUF* ✉ *Mester utca 46, Budapest* ⊕ *www.blackcabburger.hu.*

Budapest Bägel

$ | AMERICAN | After the arrival of New York Bagel (in the 13th District), it took another 20 years before bagels became all the rage in Budapest and now it seems that they are popping up around the city. Only a few places have come close to offering an authentic bagel. **Known for:** fresh bagels; long lines; small place with just a few tables outside. $ *Average main: 1,200 HUF* ✉ *Baross utca 4, Budapest* ☎ *30/846–4453* ⊕ *www.budapestbagel.com.*

★ Lumen Café

$$ | INTERNATIONAL | Located in a former chemical factory, Lumen Café's greenery-filled industrial setting with glass-covered ceiling, towering chimney stack, and steel frames makes for one of the city's coolest cafés, and a must-stop in the 8th District. For breakfast with a local flavor, try the Bundás kenyér, the Hungarian version of French toast, or the Hungarian Breakfast, which comes with Hungarian smoked sausage, ham, and eggs. **Known for:** locally roasted coffee and local beers and wines; seasonal menu with lots of vegetarian options; lively cultural programs. $ *Average main: 2,000 HUF* ✉ *Horánszky utca 5, Budapest* ☎ *20/530–0850.*

Hotels

★ Brody House Boutique Hotel

$ | HOTEL | Set on leafy Sándor Brody Utca, Brody House's unassuming and elegant facade belies a beautiful, bohemian interior and one of the city's coolest boutique hotels. **Pros:** feels like a historic home; edgy luxury; access to Brodyland happenings and events. **Cons:** only 10 rooms so it can be hard to get a reservation; some noise carries; no elevator. $ *Rooms from: 28,695 HUF* ✉ *Bródy Sándor utca 10, South Pest* ☎ *1/323–7583* ⊕ *www.brody.house* ⇨ *10 rooms* ◉ *No meals* Ⓜ *M4: Kálvin tér.*

Hotel Corvin

$$ | HOTEL | Tucked into a calm side street in Pest's up-and-coming 9th District, this Hungarian-owned budget hotel is just a few blocks from the Museum of

Applied Arts and busy Ferenc körút. **Pros:** decent budget hotel; good location for sightseeing; convenient to transportation. **Cons:** street-facing rooms noisy; Corvin bathrooms and rooms are bigger; no tea or coffee in rooms. $ *Rooms from: 43,760 HUF* ✉ *Angyal utca 31, Ferenc József körút* ☎ *1/218–6566* ⊕ *www.corvinhotelbudapest.hu* ⇨ *86 rooms* ¶ *Free breakfast* Ⓜ *M3: Ferenc körút.*

Hotel Palazzo Zichy

$$$ | **HOTEL** | For an elegant and chic hotel stay, with flavors of old and modern Budapest, it is hard to beat this boutique conversion of the former palace of Hungarian Count Nándor Zichy. **Pros:** gorgeous building; great breakfast; gym. **Cons:** smallish rooms; not exactly the most central location; room service comes from a nearby pub, not an in-house restaurant. $ *Rooms from: 50,216 HUF* ✉ *Lőrinc Pap tér 2, Southern Nagykörút* ☎ *1/235–4000* ⊕ *www.hotel-palazzo-zichy.hu* ⇨ *75 rooms* ¶ *Free breakfast* Ⓜ *M3: Corvin-negyed, M4: Rákóczi tér.*

Nightlife

BARS AND PUBS

A Grund (*The Grund*)

BARS/PUBS | This large complex of indoor and outdoor spaces set in a dilapidated building is part *romkert* (ruin bar), part culture hub. Students come here for the cheap drinks, and businesses and clubs book the meeting rooms for their membership events, so the place is buzzing almost every night of the week. Brightly colored walls and funky, cozy couches and chairs pepper the interior and lively courtyard. There's not much in the way of food as the small grill station outside has a very basic burger menu—it's all about the beers, cocktails, and games here. The site also features dance and concert spaces, and even a small playground in the back. Laser tag is available by advance booking. ✉ *Nagytemplom utca*

30, Budapest ☎ 20/583–6712 ⊕ *www.agrund.hu.*

Élesztőház

BARS/PUBS | Beer lovers meet Élesztőház (The Yeast House). The friendly staff will happily explain all the beer on offer or engage in a lively discussion over what beer reigns supreme. With a range of light, dark, IPA, APA, and local craft variations, you might want to pull up a stool for a while. The courtyard is perfect on a hot summer night in the city. ✉ *Tűzoltó utca 22, South Pest* ☎ *70/336–1279* ⊕ *www.elesztohaz.hu.*

Jónás Craft Beer House

BREWPUBS/BEER GARDENS | Located at the south side of the Bálna, there is little to be said for the design of this place, but when your view is the Danube overlooking the Citadella in Buda and the outdoor space faces a green city park, you wouldn't notice if there was. The friendly staff, a good selection of beer (some from their own label), a range of other drinks, and a barista in house makes it all the more enjoyable. Stay until sunset for some stunning photo ops. ✉ *Fővám tér 11-12, Budapest* ☎ *70/930–1392* ⊕ *www.balnabudapest.hu.*

Krak'n'Town

BREWPUBS/BEER GARDENS | This swanky craft beer pub describes itself as "a post-apocalyptic vision where the fantasy world of the Victorian era comes to life again," and that pretty much sums it up. This vision resonates with locals as you will see by the lively crowd. The interior features an eclectic mix of antique wallpaper, soviet era souvenirs, and old photos. Most of the action is in the underground cellar, which is open from 5 pm until 3 am. The underground bar features 15 beer taps and a nice selection of wine and shots and there's a second room for music and events. ✉ *József krt. 31a, South Pest* ☎ *30/364–5658* ⊕ *www.krakntown.com.*

MONYO Tap House

BREWPUBS/BEER GARDENS | Featuring swings at the bars and 10 taps of Hungarian and international craft beer, this small local bar is run by a friendly team who has made it the place to hang out since 2005. Sadly, there are only a few snacks available on-site, but it's dog friendly, so who needs food. This spot is extremely popular, so reservations are recommended. Closed on Sunday. ⊠ *Kálvin tér 7, South Pest* ☎ *70/415–7835* ⊕ *www.monyobrewing.com.*

Neked Csak Dezső!

BREWPUBS/BEER GARDENS |"Just Dezső for You!" offers a full menu, a plethora of craft beer on tap and bottled, and new wave coffee in a spacious, stylish, yet understated modern setting. Prices are good and the beer is even better. They also have an open brewery with seven beer tanks. A local favorite and popular hangout. ⊠ *Rákóczi útca 29, South Pest* ☎ *30/177–7424* ⊕ *www.facebook.com/ nekedcsakdezso.*

Púder Bárszínház

CAFES—NIGHTLIFE | This unique, colorful, and charming little theater features a one-room space with seating all facing a tiny stage. It's an intimate space in which to connect with the musicians, actors, and other performers who entertain audiences here regularly. It's got a small menu, too, but just like the bar itself, it's all carefully created. Open from noon to 1 am daily. ⊠ *Ráday utca 8, South Pest* ☎ *1/210–7168* ⊕ *www.puderbar.hu.*

 Performing Arts

FILM

Uránia Nemzeti Filmszínház (*Uránia National Film theater*)

FILM | A stunning art nouveau theater built in 1890, this grand building is just as beautiful inside as it is out. With frequent film festivals featuring English language films and a regular showings of international films here, this might be the most impressive movie theater you will ever visit. Come early and have a coffee and cake at the romantic café upstairs. Bring a notebook, as the opulent setting might inspire you to write a film of your own. ⊠ *Rákóczi út 21, Budapest* ☎ *1/486–3400* ⊕ *www.urania-nf.hu.*

MUSIC VENUES

Auróra Budapest

ARTS CENTERS | A socially active community center dedicated to civil platforms and inclusive spaces, this grungy backstreet venue is also a great place to meet the progressive youth of Hungary, and a fantastic underground-style place to dance the night away. It's got a small room upstairs and a huge basement space downstairs that is perfect for concerts. Marom Hungary, the organization that runs it, originally ran a very similar and very popular venue, Sirály, on Király utca, until the local government shut it down due to a disagreement on the limits of civil participation in politics. Auróra opened in 2014 and has been a happening center of grassroots movements and hip cultural events ever since. Despite its popularity as a venue and a center, in fall 2019 the district did threaten to close them (again) for political reasons, but the newly elected Mayor of Budapest, Gergely Karácsony, interceded on their behalf. Check their website and Facebook page for their regular events. ⊠ *Auróra utca 11, South Pest* ⊕ *www. auroraonline.hu.*

Budapest Park

CONCERTS | Europe's biggest open-air concert stage with state-of-the-art facilities, Budapest Park is one of the top venues for international artists and it's definitely worth checking the schedule of events for outdoor movie nights, poetry readings, cultural events, and local bands if you will be in the city between April and October. If local music is your thing, up-and-coming artists like Quimby, Parno Graszt, and Kiscsillag play here regularly. Located outside the city center, there is no residential curfew on noise here, so the after-parties can take their time. ✉ *Soroksári út 60, South Pest* ☎ *1/434–7800* ⊕ *www.budapestpark.hu* Ⓜ *1095.*

Gólya Presszó

MUSIC CLUBS | This trendy alternative hangout and community center is popular with locals, and while you won't find much in the way of food, inexpensive drinks and a range of unique events like film clubs, lectures, board-game nights, art exhibitions, and concerts keep this place buzzing most nights. ✉ *Orczy út 46-48, Budapest* ☎ *20/801-7522* ⊕ *www.golyapresszo.hu* ☞ *Closed Sun.*

Művelődési Szint (MÜSZI)

ARTS CENTERS | Művelődési Szint (meaning community and art floor), known by everyone just as Müszi, is an independent art and cultural complex and a hub of social and artistic activity, hosting an average of 120 events per month. With 35 resident art studios and four large multifunctional event spaces, the center hosts cultural programs open to the public almost every day and rents out rooms for events and meetings mostly to NGOs, local start-ups, theater groups, grassroots activists, and artists. Located on the third floor of the old communist-era Corvin Department store, look for the green door at the Somogyi Béla street entrance and ring the bell to enter. ✉ *Blaha Lujza tér 1, Budapest* ⊕ *www.muszi.org.*

Muzikum Klub és Bisztró (*Kossuth Kub*)

MUSIC | The old auditorium on the second floor of the Hadik Palota now serves as the stage for a host of Hungarian tribute and other contemporary alternative bands almost nightly. Though the villa was once truly elegant, it's a bit worn and there's no need to dress up here as you are expected to tweak those sneakers on the dance floor. There's a restaurant downstairs and a bar just outside the dance floor. Note: Unless it's a classical concert, you won't find seats here so don't expect too much comfort. Children

are welcome. ✉ *Múzeum utca 7, Budapest* ☎ *20/221–7767* ⊕ *www.muzikum.hu.*

OPERA

Erkel Színház (*Erkel Theater*)

OPERA | Once the city's largest public building, Erkel Színház has been a Hungarian State Opera House venue since 1951, when it was called the Népopera (The People's Opera). The venue generally plays second fiddle to the National Opera House on Andrássy út but while that venue undergoes renovations, Erkel has landed the main role for all major performances. The theater has been nicely spruced up and equipped to host its new responsibility and truly fantastic repertoire. Most operas are performed in their original language, generally Italian, Hungarian, or German, with English subtitles (on a screen above the stage). From the outside, this theater is not much to look at—there is something utilitarian in the exterior form and even the main lobby that, while spacious, lacks the expended grandeur. However, the theater and seating itself presents well. With its one-room form, even the tiered higher levels feel very much like they are in the same space, all with a good view to the stage. Tickets are easily available for sale online, and you can expect to spend about 5,000 to 8,000 HUF for a ticket. Though Hungarians don't tend to be sticklers for time (10 minutes late is the accepted window), the opera is the exception, so arrive early. ■**TIP**➔ **Eat before the performance because all you can find to eat here are Hungarian pretzels, a soft bread sprinkled with sunflower seeds that, while quite nice paired with champagne, may not fit the bill after a day of sightseeing.** ✉ *II. János Pál pápa tér 30, Budapest* ☎ *1/332–6150* ⊕ *www.opera.hu.*

THEATER

★ Művészetek Palotája (*Müpa*)

ARTS CENTERS | In southern Pest, at the foot of Rákóczy (aka Lágymányosi) Bridge, right beside the similarly grand

The Spice of Life

Parika is a popular seasoning in many cuisines but in Hungary it is *the* seasoning. Hungary's two most famous dishes, *gulyás leves* (goulash soup) and *csirke paprikás* (chicken paprikash), are brought to life with the rich, red spice. Meat is cooked with a paprika roux and then mixed with cream to give the dish its light color and rich depth. While its rich flavor is only released in hot oil, many a Hungarian *néni* (great aunt) will warn novice chefs to use paprika judiciously. Removing the pan from heat when adding the delicate spice prevents paprika from burning and turning bitter.

The rose paprika of Hungary is generally considered the finest variety. It is made from choice dark red pods that have a sweet flavour and aroma. A sharper Hungarian variety, *Koenigspaprika*, or king's paprika, is made from the whole pepper. Paprika is available in all Hungarian supermarkets. Varieties to look for include *különleges* (special), which has a pleasantly spicy aroma and is very finely ground; *édes* (sweet), which has a rich color, mild aroma, and is somewhat coarsely ground; *csipo˝s* (hot), which is light brown with yellowish tones, has a fiery flavor, and is coarsely ground; *rózsa* (rose), bright red in color, medium spicy, and medium-ground; and *csemege* (mild), which is light red in color, has a rich aroma, and is medium-ground.

National Theater, this monumental (750,000-square-foot) venue known as Műpa is where the capital's entertainment fans feast on a wide array of musical, theatrical, and dance performances in addition to fine dining. On the outside the Palace of Arts does indeed look palatial, in a very modern sense. The inside, as spacious and as sparkling as it is, contains plenty of intimate, well-cushioned little nooks on all floors on both sides of its Béla Bartók National Concert Hall—which occupies its center and has world-class acoustics—where you can take a seat and ponder life and/ or art. ⊠ District IX, Komor Marcell utca 1, South Pest ☎ 1/555–3300 box office ⊕ www.mupa.hu Ⓜ M3: Üllői út then Tram 2 to Rákóczi híd.

Nemzeti Színház (*National Theater*)
THEATER | Round and colonnaded in front and square in back, Hungary's massive, preeminent national theatrical venue is a spectacular blend of modern and classical, flanked by an even grander neighbor,

the Palace of the Arts. There are nightly performances on at least one of two stages inside the theater.

The spacious square out front and to the side is something to behold—though, admittedly, different folks behold it differently. The large reflecting pool contains a toppled-over, life-size ancient theater facade and three eternal flames. The bow of a ship, which you can walk on, overlooks the pool. Elsewhere scattered about the square—some on benches, others standing—are eight metal statues of late, great Hungarian thespians of the 20th century, each performing a legendary role.

Nearby the theater is a compellingly round structure that's aptly nicknamed the Tower of Babel and that houses a small exhibit gallery. In no time you can walk up the path that winds around its outer perimeter to the top for a modest view of the Buda hills and of the surrounding new architecture on the Pest side. Kids love to get lost in the fascinating little labyrinth of hedges at the foot of the tower. Explore the grounds or come for a show. English subtitles are available for some performances, but it is always best to double-check. ⊠ *District IX, Bajor Gizi Park 1, South Pest* ☎ *1/476–6868 box office* ⊕ *www. nemzetiszinhaz.hu* Ⓜ *M3: Nagyvárad tér, then Tram 24 to Milleniumi Kulturális Központ.*

Trafó Kortárs Művészetek Háza (*Trafó House of Contemporary Arts*)
DANCE | A former electrical transformer station in Pest, the Trafó building today showcases contemporary and alternative dance, theater, and music performances by Hungarian and international companies. English subtitles are often available, but it's best to check ahead. ⊠ *District IX, Liliom utca 41, Budapest* ☎ *1/456–2040* ⊕ *www.trafo.hu* ☞ *Closed Mon.* Ⓜ *M2: Corvin-negyed.*

Shopping

DESIGN
Clique Design Studio
CLOTHING | A traditional showroom on the second floor of a nondescript building, Clique Design Studio functions as a collaborative working space while also showcasing the work of Hungarian designers. You can buy handmade Delacier jewelry, clothing, shoes, and bags directly from young Hungarian designer Dóra Domokos. ⊠ *Baross utca 47, 2nd floor, Budapest* ☎ *30/469–2494* ⊕ *www. clique.hu.*

Stilshop
SHOPPING OVERVIEW | The dreamchild of Stilblog magazine founder, Petra Hoffmann, Stilshop opened in 2017 as a venue where domestic designers could work, present, and sell together. You'll find custom ceramics, home furnishings, bags, paper products, and graphics on offer here. Even if the items on display are a bit out of your price range, you will enjoy checking out the latest in Hungarian fashion and design here. ⊠ *Fővám tér 11–12, Budapest* ☎ *30/920–9201* ⊕ *www. stilshop.hu.*

Activities

SOCCER
Groupama Aréna
SPECTATOR SPORTS | **FAMILY** | Home to the national soccer team and the Ferencváros TC (Fradi) district team, Groupama Aréna is a multipurpose stadium with a capacity of 22,000. Recently renovated, this venue offers modernized facilities and a great way to catch a national or local soccer match and interact with locals. ⊠ *Üllői út 129, Budapest* ☎ *30/525–5498* ⊕ *www.groupamaarena. com.*

Chapter 7

ERZSÉBETVÁROS (ELIZABETH TOWN) AND THE JEWISH QUARTER

DISTRICT 7

Updated by
Esther Holbrook

 Sights
★★★★☆

 Restaurants
★★★★★

 Hotels
★★★☆☆

 Shopping
★★★★★

 Nightlife
★★★★★

NEIGHBORHOOD SNAPSHOT

TOP EXPERIENCES

■ **Ruin Bars:** Explore past and present over a drink, night or day, at Budapest's characteristic and colorful ruin bars.

■ **The Great Synagogue:** Europe's largest synagogue houses a museum, a ghetto-era graveyard, and the history of Zionism itself.

■ **The New York Palace Café:** Enjoy the extravagance of this gold-embossed café, once the haunt of some of Hungary's greatest writers and artists.

■ **Madách Theater:** Experience Hungarian and international productions with English subtitles at one of the city's most popular musical theaters.

■ **Try to escape:** Try breaking out of a locked room at one of the city's escape rooms, an interactive game craze that's caught the imagination of locals.

GETTING HERE

Metro 3 (the blue line) to Deák Ferenc tér or Astoria will get you to District 7's south side and trolley-buses 75 and 79 will drop you off at the Városliget, marking its northern border. The Tram lines 4 and 6 run through this neighborhood, stopping at Király and Wesselényi streets and Blaha Lujza Square. This district is home to most of the city's ruin pubs so it is busy day and night.

PLANNING YOUR TIME

Activity in this neighborhood doesn't pick up until afternoon, so start with a visit to the Great Synagogue, Rumbach Synagogue, or the Kazinczy Synagogue. For more context on the neighborhood's history, take a Jewish District tour. Shop Kiraly utca or look for more unique souvenirs at the Gozsdu udvar weekend market or on Sunday at the Anker't ruin bar flea market. Choose from a wide array of excellent restaurants packed into the lower part of the district and grab a drink afterwards at the endless selection of ruin bars.

QUICK BITES

■ **Fröhlich Kóser Cukrászda.** Dating back to 1953, this is one of the neighborhood's oldest confectioners. Try Jewish classics like Flódni, mákos kifli, and the tasty honey and nut Lekach. ✉ *Nagy Diófa utca 30, Erzsébetváros* ⊕ *www. frohlich.hu* Ⓜ *M2: Astoria*

■ **Pizza Me.** This pizza chain offers fantastic traditional Italian pizza, ranging from meat lovers to vegan options, from noon until past midnight. ✉ *Király utca 20, Erzsébetváros* ⊕ *www.pizzame.hu* Ⓜ *M2: Deák Ferenc tér*

■ **Karaván.** A fast food court open from around noon until 10 pm with something for everyone. ✉ *Kazinczy utca 18, Erzsébetváros* ⊕ *www.facebook. com/streetfoodkaravan* Ⓜ *Trolleybus 74*

Rarely quiet, Budapest's Jewish District and its ruin bars make this part of the city a bustling center of music, food, street markets, and pub crawl culture. Erzsébetváros (Elizabeth Town) was named for the beloved Austro-Hungarian queen Elisabeth or "Sissi" as she is still endearingly referred to by Hungarians, wife of Franz Joseph. Sissi won Hungarian hearts for learning Hungarian, her love of horse-riding, her renowned beauty, and her overall advocacy on behalf of Hungary at the Habsburg courts.

And while it is unlikely that she visited this inner-city working-class neighborhood on her frequent visits to Hungary, Sissi surely would have loved how her namesake neighborhood endured tough times and is now a thriving, lively hub of creativity, and home to some of the city's hottest restaurants and coolest bars.

Before WWII, the inner part of District 7, the Jewish Quarter, was a buzzing neighborhood, teeming with retail stores and kosher restaurants, and home to three synagogues. In the winter of 1944, Nazis and Hungarian fascists turned the Jewish Quarter into a ghetto where thousands died of famine and starvation. The ghetto's walls ran along today's Rumbach, Király, Kertész, and Dohány streets, and the southern gates were the Grand Synagogue and Madách Square. There were curfews and exit passes, brutal forced labor, and during the sieges late in the war, there was absolutely no way out or in. From occupation to its liberation in January 1945, the Jewish population of Budapest was reduced from 200,000 to 70,000 in the ghetto and about 20,000 outside the ghetto, where Jewish residents with diplomatic protection (from the Swiss or Swedish) lived in houses marked with the Star of David.

During the communist era, residents were encouraged to move from this much deteriorated area to the newly built blocks of apartments, known as Panelház or Panel Houses, outside the city center, while older buildings downtown, under the control of the local districts, were essentially abandoned. As people moved, so did the commerce and many street-front businesses fell into further disrepair. At the turn of the 2000s the neglected streets and dilapidated buildings of this historic district attracted entrepreneurial bar managers who took over abandoned and condemned buildings in the area, filling them with scavenged furniture, decorating with the work of local artists, and offering affordable drinks to young and creative locals. Szimpla Kert was the area's first ruin bar and is still one of the city's most famous hangouts and attractions. Within a couple of years, ruin bars were popping up all over here and locals and tourists flooded the area, drawn to the creativity, individuality, and sense of freedom that these crumbling water holes expressed.

However, just as life came back to the district, residents are again moving out. The ruin bars have revitalized this district but some (locals) say they are now 'ruining' it again. The influx of weekending party crowds and guided tours, day and night, has caused noise pollution and dirty streets and generally disrupted life for older inhabitants. Locals are selling their homes to cash in on the booming Airbnb trade and moving to quieter areas in town. While bars like Szimpla Kert can certainly draw the worst of the stag-party crowd, they are still worth visiting: by day to fully appreciate the faded glory and eclectic furnishings, and by night to take in the lively atmosphere. Know that you won't find as many locals as visitors (especially on those two-hour lines in summer) and you won't find the city's most affordable drinks, but there are plenty of lesser known spots to be found in the Jewish Quarter's saturated bar scene. Just be sure to leave time to explore the area's charming streets, hidden courtyards, and rich and tragic history, too.

Sights

Budapest Eye

LOCAL INTEREST | If you have limited time in the city, this ten-minute ride up and over Erzsébet tér offers lovely bird's-eye views of the city. Open every day, all year-round since 2013, what was supposed to be a temporary promotion for the Sziget music festival became a popular attraction of its own. ⊠ *Erzsébet tér, Budapest* ☏ *70/636–0629* ⊕ *www.oriaskerek.com* 🎟 *3,000 HUF.*

★ Dohány utcai zsinagóga (*Dohány Street Synagogue*)

RELIGIOUS SITE | The largest synagogue in Europe and the second-largest working synagogue in the world, this spectacular Moorish Revival-style building, with hints of northern African Islamic design, is appropriately known as the Great Synagogue. This building complex, completed in 1859, was designed to represent the Jewish community's lasting and special place in the life of the nation and its own sad and storied history tells of the Jewish experience in Hungary. The synagogue was bombed by the Hungarian pro-Nazi Arrow Cross Party during WWII and the building was used by the Nazis as a stable for horses. Attached to the synagogue is the Garden of Remembrance with a mass grave for Jews murdered by Hungarian Nazis. The weeping willow memorial features the names of Hungarian Holocaust victims inscribed on the metal leaves while the tomb of Raoul Wallenberg commemorates the Swedish diplomat who saved the lives of thousands of Jews in Budapest during the Holocaust. Severely damaged throughout the war, the building was used for religious purposes again after the war, but it didn't receive much-needed renovations until 1991, with reconstruction lasting until 1998. The museum, an addition made in 1930, was built on the site of the birthplace of Theodor Herzl, the father of Zionism. It features a decent collection of local religious relics and ritual objects,

The Dohány utcai Zsinagóga, also known as the Great Synagogue, is the largest synagogue in Europe and the second-largest in the world, seating 3,000 people.

a Holocaust exhibit, and also hosts visiting exhibitions. A ticket to the Jewish Museum or a full Jewish District tour will grant you access to the synagogue, too. ⊠ *Dohány utca 2, Jewish Quarter* ☏ *70/658–6912* ⊕ *www.greatsynagogue. hu* ☐ *4,000 HUF* ⊗ *Closed Sat. and Jewish High Holidays* Ⓜ *Tram 4, 6; trolleybus 74.*

Elektotechnikai Múzeum (*Hungarian Electrotechnical Museum*)

MUSEUM | FAMILY | Housed in a former transformer station, paved with an art deco stone floor and decorated with Zsolnay tiles, the quirky Elektotechnikai Múzeum merits a visit as much for its setting as for its fascinating collection of early electrical devices, which includes everything from old household appliances to the workings of the electrified fence between Hungary and Austria before the fall of communism. The scientifically inclined will enjoy generating electricity, and even lightning, while design fans will appreciate the collection of vintage signs in the courtyard. The last Saturday

of every month is free for minors and one accompanying adult. ⊠ *Kazinczy utca 21, Budapest* ☏ *1/342–5750* ⊕ *www.mmkm. hu* ☐ *800 HUF* ⊗ *Closed Sun. and Mon.*

Ghetto Wall Memorial

TOUR—SIGHT | Toward the end of WWII, Budapest's Jewish population was herded into a ghetto inside the Jewish Quarter, where thousands died of famine. The ghetto's walls ran along today's Rumbach, Király, Kertész, and Dohány streets, and this small section of the wall along with a plaque are a reminder of the atrocities committed here. Located in the courtyard of a private apartment building, you can peek at the wall through the door or wait until a resident opens the door to go inside. ⊠ *Király utca 15, Jewish Quarter* ✛ *in the back of the courtyard* ☐ *Free* Ⓜ *M3 Deák Ferenc tér and 10-min walk.*

Kazinczy utcai zsinagóga (*Kazinczy Street Synagogue*)

RELIGIOUS SITE | This impressive art nouveau synagogue, tucked in between

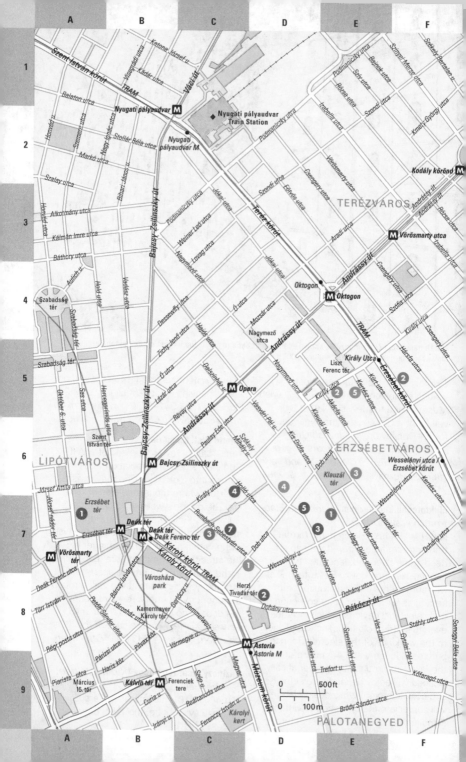

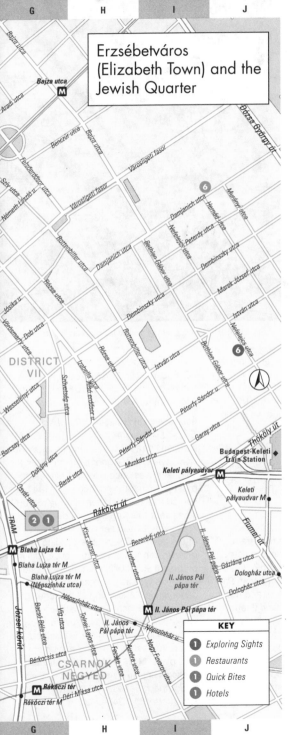

Erzsébetváros (Elizabeth Town) and the Jewish Quarter

Kazinczy utcai zsinagoga is a historic Jewish place of worship with an opulent interior featuring stained-glass windows.

shops, markets, restaurants, and narrow streets has been the epicenter of religious life for Budapest's Orthodox community since its opening in 1913. The interior features pale blue walls and ceiling, stained glass windows painted by famed mosaicist Miksa Róth, and benches adorned with Hungarian folk motifs. ⊠ *Kazinczy utca 29-31, Jewish Quarter* ☎ *1/351–0524* ⊕ *www.maoih. hu* ▨ *800 HUF* ☉ *Closed Sat. and Jewish High Holidays.*

Miksa Róth Museum

MUSEUM | This former home of extraordinary art nouveau and art deco master stained-glass artist, Miksa Róth, whose work can be found on the Hungarian Parliament, St. Stephen's Basilica, and the Liszt Ferenc Academy of Music (Franz Liszt Music Academy), is essentially a three-room residential apartment filled with a collection of his work, objects from his life, and art from the period. To get to this hidden gem, you'll pass through the less touristed streets of District 7, which will give you a feel for "real life" in Budapest. ⊠ *Nefelejcs utca 26, Budapest* ☎ *1/341–6789* ⊕ *www. rothmuzeum.hu* ▨ *750 HUF* ☉ *Closed Mon.* Ⓜ *M2, M4: Keleti pályaudvar.*

Rumbach utcai zsinagóga (*Rumbach Street Synagogue*)

RELIGIOUS SITE | This beautiful Moorish-Revival style-Otto Wagner building dates to 1872 and was once one of Budapest's most prominent synagogues. In 1941, it served as a deporatation site for 16,000 Jews sent to southern Poland, and later in the war hosted services while part of the Jewish Ghetto. The building was recently renovated (some work is still in progress) and it will function as a cultural center as well as a center of religious observance, welcoming all branches of Judaism. The incredibly ornate interior workmanship is now available for viewing in the main hall and in some corridors, where tours,concerts, and exhibitions take place. ■TIP→ **Check the calendar of events to plan a visit around a concert.** ⊠ *Rumbach Sebestyén utca 11–13, Jewish Quarter* ☎ *1/343–0420.*

🍴 Restaurants

Dobrumba

$$ | MIDDLE EASTERN | This charming restaurant just around the corner from all the hustle and bustle of Budapest's Jewish District offers a mouthwatering spread of Middle Eastern and Mediterranean dishes, from patatas bravas to shawarma, and a lively but relaxed atmosphere to go with it. There are a lot of vegetarian options and a nice selection of wine. **Known for:** slow and leisurely service; reservations necessary; fair number of vegetarian options. $ Average main: 3,000 HUF ✉ Dob utca 5, Astoria ☎ 30/194–0049 ⊕ www.dobrumba.hu.

Frici Papa

$ | HUNGARIAN | The humble decor hasn't changed much since this cheap and cheerful spot first opened in 1997, and neither has the menu. Basically, you'll find Hungarian classics and lots of pickled or fried food. **Known for:** affordable Hungarian food; beef stew with egg dumplings; Mákos guba (poppy-seed pudding). $ Average main: 1,000 HUF ✉ Király utca 55, Budapest ☎ 1/351–0197 ⊕ www.fricipapa.hu.

★ Kádár Étkezde

$$ | HUNGARIAN | Known to locals as Kádár bácsi's (Uncle Kadar's place), this home-style family restaurant has been around for a while—long enough to have more than one generation of fans. The walls are decorated with photos of celebrities from years gone by, and the tables are topped with old-fashioned spritzer bottles from which you serve yourself water. **Known for:** Hungarian-Jewish standards; sólet (cholent), a meat and barley stew traditionally served on Saturday; pay-by-the-slice bread. $ Average main: 2,000 HUF ✉ Klauzál tér 9, Jewish Quarter ☎ 1/321–3622 ▭ No credit cards ⊗ Closed Sun. and Mon. No dinner Ⓜ M1: Opera, M2: Blaha Lujza tér.

Kőleves Vendéglő

$$ | HUNGARIAN | Named after the famous Eastern European folktale *Stone Soup*, this restaurant is full of old paraphernalia and character, a great relaxed atmosphere, and flavorful Hungarian food with a modern touch. Don't miss the restaurant's sister beer garden next door: as locals will tell you, no summer is complete without a Fröccs (wine spritzer) at Kőleves Kert. **Known for:** laid-back charm; hearty portions; beer garden next door. $ Average main: 3,000 HUF ✉ Kazinczy utca 41, Budapest ☎ 20/213–5999 ⊕ www.kolevesvendeglo.hu.

M

$$$ | FRENCH FUSION | This no-frills restaurant, not far from the popular kerts (summer bars) in edgy District 7, has a certain charm. The walls are draped in brown paper bags, with things like windows and pictures frames drawn on, and bare tables have single candles and mismatched chairs. **Known for:** popular with students and budget-minded locals; unique style; high-quality seasonal ingredients and menu. $ Average main: 3,200 HUF ✉ Kertész utca 48, Budapest ☎ 70/633–3460 ⊕ www.metterem.hu.

Piroska Vendéglő

$$ | HUNGARIAN | FAMILY | A nostalgic restaurant lost in time, you'll find red-and-white checkered tablecloths, transistor radios, old wooden benches, toilets that were literally once closets, and reliable old-fashioned Hungarian food. The fussy waiters, also a retro feature, take warming up to, but can be easily turned with a smile. **Known for:** retro atmosphere; marhapörkölt (beef stew); always busy. $ Average main: 2,000 HUF ✉ Damjanich utca 40, Budapest ☎ 1/798–2626 ⊕ www.piroska-vendeglo.hu Ⓜ M2, M4: Keleti pályaudvar; bus 5, 7 to Reiner Frigyes park.

Coffee and Quick Bites

★ New York Palace Café

$ | CAFÉ | You don't need to visit every café in the world to decide that the New York Palace Café—often referred to as "the most beautiful café in the world"—definitely deserves its title, or at least ranks very highly on that list. Located within the luxe New York Palace Hotel and built in Italian Renaissance-style, the interiors feature marble columns, stuccoed angels, and sparkling chandeliers dangling from high ceilings adorned by spectacular frescoes. **Known for:** ornate interior; delicious cakes and coffee; long lines. $ *Average main: 6000 HUF* ⊠ *The New York Palace Hotel, Erzsébet körút 9–11, Blaha Lujza tér* ☎ *1/8866-167* ⊕ *www.newyorkcafe.hu* Ⓜ *M2: Blaha Lujza tér.*

★ Massolit Budapest Books and Café

$ | CAFÉ | A popular meeting place with expat writers, Massolit Budapest Bookstore and Café is an excellent place to find a good deal on books by Hungarian and other Central Eastern European writers in English translation, as well as delicious homemade carrot cake, coffee, and some friendly company. It is also a regular venue for book launches, poetry readings, and literary events. **Known for:** English translations of Hungarian books; carrot cake; literary events. $ *Average main: 650 HUF* ⊠ *Nagy Diófa utca 30, Budapest* ☎ *1/788-5292.*

🛏 Hotels

Anantara New York Palace Hotel

$$$$ | HOTEL | Dating to the late 19th century when it was constructed for the New York Insurance Company, and famous for its café—long the haunt of local artists and writers, the opulent New York Palace Hotel is as gilded and glamorous as its famous café suggests. **Pros:** old-world glamour and service; historic and ritzy New York Café; central location. **Cons:** noisy main street; no full swimming pool; some bedrooms do not live up to the lavishness. $ *Rooms from: 78,496 HUF* ⊠ *Erzsébet körút 9–11, Budapest* ☎ *1/886–6111* ⊕ *www.nh-hotels.com* 🛏 *185 rooms* ⦿ *Free breakfast* Ⓜ *M2: Blaha Lujza tér.*

★ Corinthia Hotel

$$$$ | HOTEL | The Corinthia first opened as the luxurious Grand Royal Hotel in time for the Magyar Millennium in 1896, and, despite being destroyed during Hungary's 1956 revolution, it's just as luxurious today. **Pros:** opulent setting without a break-the-bank price; amazing spa and spa package deals; great restaurants. **Cons:** may be too big and too formal for some; non-spa packages don't offer the same value for money; service can be inconsistent. $ *Rooms from: 71,360 HUF* ⊠ *Erzsébet körút 43–49, Blaha Lujza tér* ☎ *1/479–4000* ⊕ *www.corinthia.com* 🛏 *440 rooms* ⦿ *No meals* Ⓜ *M1: Oktogon, Blaha Lujza tér; tram 4, 6 to Király utca.*

Roombach Hotel Budapest

$ | HOTEL | A funky three-star hotel, located in the Jewish District, Roombach offers a trendy colorful design with a homey touch. **Pros:** in the heart of the city; 24-hour open guest bar; clean and orderly. **Cons:** no gym or pool; dark hallways; no baths just showers. $ *Rooms from: 28, 544 HUF* ⊠ *Rumbach Sebestyén utca 14, Jewish Quarter* ☎ *1/413–0253* ⊕ *www.roombach.com* 🛏 *99 rooms* ⦿ *Free breakfast.*

Nightlife

BARS AND PUBS
Apropó Bistro

WINE BARS—NIGHTLIFE | A classic bistro on bustling Király utca, Apropó offers all-day brunch and late-night bites all washed down with an impressive wine selection. The menu is a mix of French, Italian, and Hungarian tapas plates. ⊠ *Király utca 39, Budapest* ☎ *30/193–3000* ⦿ *No dinner on weekends* Ⓜ *Tram 4, 6 to Király utca.*

Csak a jó sör

BREWPUBS/BEER GARDENS | Csak a jó sör (Only Good Beer) offers a wide range of international craft beers, making it a favorite for connoisseurs. A funky combination of bar and shop, at this shop you can browse the shelves or break open one and take a seat and find out more about the history of Hungarian craft beer from the shopkeeper on staff. Just as the name suggests, don't expect much in the way of food here. Open daily 2 to 9 pm. ⊠ *Kertész utca 42, Budapest* ☎ *1/798–0036* ⊕ *www.csakajosor.hu.*

Doboz

DANCE CLUBS | Dobosz means box in Hungarian and this renovated building and garden courtyard space features the eponymous red box installation in front but thinks outside the box with a venue that falls on the swanky end of the ruin bar genre. Part nightclub, part bar, and part art gallery, the massive and trendy interior features a labyrinth of connected spaces opening onto bars and dance floors throughout. Just don't forget to dress to the nines, as there's a dress code to get in. ⊠ *Klauzál utca 10, Budapest* ☎ *20/449–4801* 🍴 *Cover charge: 1,000 HUF for men* Ⓜ *M2: Blaha Lujza tér.*

ELLÁTÓház (*The Hive*)

BREWPUBS/BEER GARDENS | A place to check out local and visiting bands and catch DJ sets, the "Supplier House" is a regular stop on pub crawls. The view of the associated hostel's rooms on the upper levels of the building is both fascinating and weird from the ground floor where the bar and main dance floor are located. Try out one of the local specialties, like a shot of Tatratea, a regional liquor that is all the rage, or have a traditional shot of Unicum (Hungarian herbal liquor) to go with your beer, before hitting the dance floor. ⊠ *Dob utca 19, Király utca* ☎ *20/527–3018* ⊕ *facebook.com/ellatohaz.*

Drink-a Pálinka

No trip to Budapest would be complete without a taste of the fruit spirit pálinka, the local headache-inducing firewater. Look for the Agárdi boutique pálinkas from near Lake Velence. These spirits come in unusual flavors like raspberry and *cigany meggy* (gypsy cherry). All restaurants in Budapest stock the traditional *barackpálinka* (apricot brandy) and *szilvapálinka* (plum brandy). Be forewarned: this strong brandy is not for the weak of stomach.

Fekete Kutya

BARS/PUBS | A cozy bar with a unique atmosphere and a great selection of craft beers, including some on tap, Fekete Kutya is popular with the artistic crowd, young intellectuals, and expats. A small but delectable menu is on offer but you have to fight your way to the bar to order. Try to grab a table in the back and note the wall mural: an homage to the history of modern art, with a Budapest twist. During the warmer months, people spill out to the small outdoor tables underneath the arched alley. ⊠ *Dob utca 31, Budapest* ☎ *20/560–5856.*

Füge Udvar

BREWPUBS/BEER GARDENS | While you may not want to spend all night here, this classic ruin pub and courtyard garden bar is open daily from 4 pm to 4 am, so, you can pop in any time to get a feel for what cool, young Budapest is up to. With its cheap drinks and smoking area, tucked into a leafy courtyard, it's easy to see why it is a favorite with rowdy students and backpackers. ⊠ *Klauzál utca 19, Budapest* ☎ *20/200–1000* ⊕ *www.legjobbkocsma.hu.*

★ Gozsdu Udvar (Gozsdu Courtyard)

BREWPUBS/BEER GARDENS | This complex of seven buildings and their interconnecting courtyards, home to some of Budapest's liveliest bars and restaurants, is the place to be on a night out in the 7th District. Spíler Original gastropub is one of the city's favorite hangouts in the complex. Other places to stop by include sister property Spíler Shanghai, as well as Vicky Barcelona, Spritz Bar, and 4Bro Downtown. On weekends you'll find a flea market here, and the complex also has its own escape room and Christmas market. ☒ Király utca 13, Budapest ⊕ www.gozsduudvar.hu.

Grandio

BREWPUBS/BEER GARDENS | Run by a backpacker's hostel, this cheap and cheerful garden bar (outdoor seating only) occupies a sweet, calm little green space in the heart of the district that will make you forget the hustle and bustle of the nearby streets. Look closely and you will find some exciting relics, including parts of facades from other neighborhood buildings, stored under the awning. ☒ Nagy Diófa utca 8, Budapest ☎ 70/670–0390 ⊕ www.grandio.insta-hostel.com.

Havana Salsa Bar & Restaurant

BARS/PUBS | Located in the historic Fészek Klub, this lively Cuban theme bar and restaurant features some lovely old design elements, live music, and a lively atmosphere. It's a little noisy for a relaxing dining experience but perfect for shared bites over cocktails. The leafy, outdoor courtyard is nice for a summer dinner, featuring live Cuban dance shows, or you can grab a bite to eat in the bar in the front room, or downstairs where the dance floor invites everyone to dance the night away to Latin music. ☒ Fészek Klub, Dob utca 57, Budapest ☎ 20/388–2738 ⊕ www.labodeguitadelmedio.hu.

Hopaholic

BREWPUBS/BEER GARDENS | A quirky little venue with a hip, alternative interior, Hopaholic, the sister bar to Csakajósör, prides itself on its extensive selection of international craft beers. ☒ Akácfa utca 38, Budapest ☎ 1/611–2415 ⊕ www.hopaholic.hu.

Horizont Taproom

BREWPUBS/BEER GARDENS | Horizont, one of the biggest local breweries, and Léhűtő, one of the city's first and most popular local craft beer bars, have joined forces to create a venue dedicated to tastings of quality beers. There is not much here in the way of food, so it's best to go for a beer tasting here before heading elsewhere for dinner. Open daily 9–5. ☒ Holló utca 12–14, Budapest ☎ 70/ 604–4777 ⊕ www.untappd.com.

Kispipa

BREWPUBS/BEER GARDENS | Come here to have a drink in the famous pub where Rezső Seress, Hungarian pianist and composer of the famous 1930's song "Gloomy Sunday," played the piano for the last ten years of his life before committing suicide. It was rumored that after returning from a Nazi labor camp, Seress never left his beloved District 7, heavy stuff to mull over with a beer. While the bar is still true to its original design—seedy, dark, and staffed by grumpy waiters—there's a better variety of craft beers these days, and it's worth a visit to get a feel for gloomy mid-war Budapest. ☒ Akácfa utca 38, Budapest ☎ 1/780–1606 ⊕ www.kispipabar.hu.

Kisüzem

BARS/PUBS | A full house spilling out into the streets on most nights, this is not just a funky bar but also an art gallery and a place to see and be seen for cool types. A relaxed environment where you can rub shoulders with local creative movers and shakers, the prices aren't bad either. ☒ Kis Diófa utca 2, Budapest ☎ 1/781–6705.

Liebling

CAFES—NIGHTLIFE | Considered one of the worst-kept secrets in the neighborhood, this classic salon-style rooftop bar offers a perfect combination of mood music, romantic lighting, and low-key atmosphere, which makes it the perfect end, or beginning, to a 7th District evening. ✉ *Akácfa utca 51, Budapest* ☎ *70/638–5040* ⊕ *www.instant-fogas.com.*

Mika Tivadar Mulató (*Mika*)

BARS/PUBS | Built in 1907 by iron and copper worker Tivadar Mika, this dignified building houses one of the city's most popular ruin bars in a lovely garden courtyard as well as a bar and music venue in the basement. You'll find events including jazz nights, film nights, spoken-word events, and DJ sets most nights, often free of charge. ✉ *Kazinczy utca 47, Budapest* ☎ *20/965–3007* ⊕ *www.mikativadarmulato.hu.*

★ Szimpla Kert (*Szimpla Garden*)

BARS/PUBS | The oldest and best-known of Budapest's uniquely Hungarian romkerts, Szimpla Kert has won various international awards for its wild, exuberant, grungy style, and set the bar for all the ruin bars to follow in its footsteps. Built inside a former stove factory, this maze of dark rooms, eclectic furnishings, local art, and crazy light installations attracts a raucous crowd of locals and tourists working their way through the night with wild abandon. Expect a noisy, lively night here with the occasional patron's dog darting here and there between the tables while its owner sips on a hookah (available to rent). Visit by day to get a better feel for the decor, although you should expect to be joined by a steady stream of camera-toting tour groups as this is one of the city's top attractions. Szimpla also hosts a weekly farmers' market featuring all-natural products on Sunday from 9 am to 2 pm, runs an antique shop next door, and rents bikes. ✉ *Kazinczy utca 14, Budapest* ☎ *20/261–8669* ⊕ *www.en.szimpla.hu* Ⓜ *M2: Astoria.*

Vittula

BARS/PUBS | The quintessential dive bar, Vittula made the news a few years back when actress Jennifer Lawrence threw beer over an annoying fan hassling her here and then talked about the experience on "The Late Show with Stephen Colbert." Technically open from 5 to 11 pm, due to noise regulations, DJ sets played from the extremely small stage in the main room keep the crowds dancing on the street until whenever the actual closing time is. ✉ *Kertész utca 4, Budapest* ☎ *30/938–5486.*

NIGHTCLUBS

Instant (*Fogasház*)

MUSIC CLUBS | Two of Budapest's most popular night clubs joined forces and have since become Instant-Fogas, the unrivaled party hub located in the Jewish Quarter. Packed by midevening, if you are looking to dance, you are in the right space. The building complex includes seven individual venues, each with a distinct atmosphere and their own character and music style. Move from one vibe to the next, taking breaks in between in the connecting covered courtyard bar area. ✉ *Akácfa utca 49–51, Budapest* ☎ *70/638–5040* ⊕ *www.instant-fogas. com* ✉ *Free.*

WINE BARS

Doblo Wine Bar and Shop

WINE BARS—NIGHTLIFE | A charming wine bar offering an excellent selecion of Hungarian wines features live jazz concerts in summer and exudes an all-around romantic atmosphere. Closed Sunday through Tuesday. ✉ *Dob utca 20, Budapest* ☎ *20/398–8863.*

 Performing Arts

DANCE

Rajkó Folk Ensemble (*Rajkó Művészegyüttes*)

DANCE | This fiery group of 60 dancers together with its world-famous orchestra combines ballet and modern dance forms

Did You Know?

Before Szimpla Kert occupied its abandoned building to create the city's original ruin bar, the building was once a brick and furnace factory whose Jewish factory owners were deported during World War II.

with elements of folklore and operetta programs for an impressive musical and dance program. Founded in 1952, you can catch their show at MÜPA, the Duna Palota, the Budapest Bábszínház, and other big stages around town. Check their website for performance locations and schedule. ☒ *Rottenbiller utca 16–22, Keleti Train Station* ☎ *1/322–4841* ⊕ *www.rajko.hu* Ⓜ *M2: Keleti pályaudvar.*

THEATER
Madách Színház

THEATER | With a repertoire of blockbuster international popular musicals, like *Phantom of the Opera* and *Cats,* as well as Hungarian classics, like *Liliomfi,* this 800-seat venue also features performances with English subtitles. ☒ *Erzsébet krt. 29–33, Budapest* ☎ *1/478–2041* ⊕ *www. madachszinhaz.hu.*

Pesti Magyar Színház (*Magyar Theatre*)

THEATER | When high culture was dominated by the German-speaking Hapsburgs and Latin (the official language of Hungary for around 900 years) remained Europe's Lingua Franca for the intelligencia, Pest's Hungarian Theater was the first major Hungarian language theatrical company in the city. The theater venue, designed by Adolf Láng and built in 1897, seats over 1,000 and now features mostly contemporary Hungarian and foreign drama on its main stage. The emphasis is on youth and family programs as well as experimental theater. Check ahead to see if performances have English subtitles as all performances are in Hungarian. ☒ *Hevesi Sándor tér 4, Budapest* ☎ *1/322–0014* ⊕ *www.pestimagyarszinhaz.hu.*

VENUES
Telep-Art Galéria

ART GALLERIES—ARTS | Telep Gallery is a nonprofit, independent gallery space that hosts exhibitions featuring the experimental work of local artists, providing a venue for contemporary members of the community to share ideas. There's a bar on the ground floor that often hosts

engaged conversations about the arts, while the third floor houses a vintage and designer clothing store named Judas. ☒ *Madách Imre utca 8, Budapest* ☎ *1/784–8911.*

Shopping

FASHION
ESZKA Design Store

CLOTHING | Shopping in Budapest, it may seem like Hungarian fashion can't leave its Central European comfort zone, in terms of its preference for black, white, and gray. Costume designer and stylist Kriszta Szakos offers refreshingly vibrant, colorful knitted patterns for clothing and household decor. You can also find her work at Retrock in Anker, but this shop on Nagy Diófa Street offers a much wider range of fashionable attire as well as designer jewelry and clothing by designers Eszter Korcsmár's and Zsófi Hidasi. ☒ *Nagy Diófa utca 9, Budapest* ☎ *20/231–4181* ⊕ *www.eszka.hu* ⊙ *Closed Sat.–Mon.*

Printa

CLOTHING | Printa is a local design house dedicated to offering modern, environmentally conscious fashion with Budapest flair. This store is part design shop, part art gallery, screen-printing studio, and café. You'll find one-of-a-kind pieces, some with vintage, repurposed elements, and be sure to check out their AWARE line and the waste-free products room. ☒ *Rumbach Sebestyén utca 10/a, Budapest* ☎ *30/292–0329* ⊕ *www.printa. hu* ⊙ *Closed Sun.*

HOUSEHOLD GOODS
Szimpla Design Shop

ANTIQUES/COLLECTIBLES | Located next to Szimpla Kert, Budapest's original and most famous ruin bar, this quirky shop is one of the best spots in town to find unique and interesting antiques, clothing, toys, furniture, and decor. As the Szimpla Kert is so famous for its eclectic style and recycled and upcycled wares, it makes complete sense that the Simpla Design Team now peddles their lovingly repaired, restored, and repurposed finds, along with the work of other local designers. A must for treasure hunters. ✉ *Kazinczy utca 14, Budapest* ⊕ *www. en.szimpla.hu* ⊗ *Closed Mon. and Tues.*

PORCELAIN

Hollóházi Porcelán Manufakrúra

CERAMICS/GLASSWARE | Famous for handmade stoneware pieces covered with roses, wildflowers, and multicolored bouquets, the Hollóház Porcelain Factory itself has had a colorful past. Dating to the 1700s, the factory incurred serious damage during WWII and went into state hands in 1948, while the former owner moved to Brazil, never to return. The company would fall in and out of private and national hands many times over the years, until January 2020 when an unknown buyer took full ownership. Shop the range of new and classic Hollóház designs at the shop on Dohány utca. ✉ *Dohány utca 1c, Budapest* ☎ *20/592–5676* ⊕ *www.hollohazi.hu* ⊗ *Closed Sun.*

SHOES

★ Tisza

CLOTHING | For a uniquely Hungarian souvenir, check out this homegrown shoe company named for a beloved river that flows through eastern Hungary. The company is known for its rubber-soled shoes, boots, and sneakers, which were all the rage behind the Iron Curtain in the 1970s. Tisza soles provided the basis for scores of "domestic" shoes then as well, providing workers in Hungary with sturdy and comfortable shoes in which to toil. New designs as well as heritage classics make the sneakers popular with the hipster crowd. You can also find them at Westend Shopping Center but this shop in the 7th District is the original. ✉ *Károly körút 1, Budapest* ☎ *1/266–3055* ⊕ *www. tiszacipo.com* ⊗ *Closed Sun.* Ⓜ *M2: Astoria.*

 Activities

E-Exit Escape Game

LOCAL SPORTS | Whether it's the soviet bloc history, or their landlocked geography, Budapesters really took to the escape room game craze, with a passion that indicated the challenge to get out really resonated. As a result, this city is full of quirky, tough, spooky, sometimes cheesy, and often truly mind-bending escape rooms. It's a fun break from the usual sightseeing and a great, participation-based activity for groups of two-to-six people, though some games allow more. Typically, gamers have one hour to find the clues, usually by solving a range of puzzles and mind games and open all the padlocks and hidden doors they need to get out. Most games come with English and Hungarian instructions, family-friendly options, and games meant more for adult participants. It's best to call and ask for recommendations when you book. For a first experience of a traditional, key and padlock version, try E-Exit's 1984, where, like an interactive museum collection, you will see a lot of antique household items from typical Hungarian life here repurposed as props and clues. Games run from about 5,000-10,000 HUF per person, depending on the number of participants. ✉ *Nyár utca 27, Budapest* ☎ *30/889–3633* ⊕ *www. szabadulos-jatek.hu.*

Chapter 8

VÁROSLIGET (CITY PARK)
DISTRICT 14

Updated by
Esther Holbrook

 Sights
★★★★★

 Restaurants
★★★☆☆

 Hotels
★☆☆☆☆

 Shopping
★☆☆☆☆

 Nightlife
★★☆☆☆

NEIGHBORHOOD SNAPSHOT

TOP EXPERIENCES

■ **Hősök tere:** Budapest's most majestic square features impressive statues of all of Hungary's most iconic figures as well as two of the city's most popular art venues.

■ **Spa day at Széchenyi Fürdő:** Rejuvenate in the warm waters with a view to the grand neobaroque facades at Budapest's largest thermal spa.

■ **One of the World's Oldest Zoos:** Opened in 1866, Budapest Zoo features an impressive array of flora and fauna housed in secessionist houses that were built in the early part of the 20th century. Evening concerts are held here in summer.

■ **Vajdahunyad Castle:** This fairy-tale castle makes for an especially pretty photo op when viewed from the small lake that surrounds it in a rowboat in summer and on ice-skates in winter.

■ **Gundel palacsinta:** Taste Hungary's most famous pancake at the acclaimed Gundel Restaurant.

GETTING HERE

It takes about 30 minutes to walk the length of Andrássy út from the city center, Deak Square, but getting there is a great excuse to take the elegant M1, otherwise known as the *földalatti* (the underground), the city's first metro line. Get off at Hősök tere or Széchenyi Fürdő to end up in the park. If you are coming by car, your best bet for parking is the large lot behind Műcsarnok.

PLANNING YOUR TIME

You'll need a minumum of half a day to take in Városliget, and longer if you plan to soak in the impressive Széchenyi Thermal Baths here. Start with the Museum of Fine Arts (Szépművészeti Múzeum) and the Palace of Art (Műcsarnok), pausing at Hősök tere. Enjoy a stroll through the park, taking in the quirky Museum of Hungarian Agriculture located in the enchanting Vajdahunyad Castle. If time and weather permits, spend a few hours visiting one of the world's most stylish city zoos and rowing on Városligeti lake.

QUICK BITES

■ **Anonymus Étterem.** Take a break from sightseeing with a quick coffee in the fairy-tale settings of the Vajdahunyad Castle and enjoy views to the lake that are almost as delightful an experience as actually rowing around it. ✉ *Kós Károly sétány 1, Városliget* ⊕ *www.facebook.com/anonymusbar* Ⓜ *M1: Széchenyi Fürdő*

■ **Pántlika Bistro.** Have a taste of old-school Hungarian fast food at this charming little retro café that's been a staple here since 1964. ✉ *Opposite Hermina st 47, Városliget* ⊕ *www.pantlika.hu* ⊕ Ⓜ *Trolleybus 70, 72, 74: Erzsébet királyné útja*

■ **Édes Mackó Kürtőskalács-Cukrászda.** Traditional street-food sweets, the Kürtőskalács (chimney cake) are impossible to resist, as is everything else at the Sweet Teddy Bear Chimmney Cake Confectionery. ✉ *Állatkerti krt. 14–16,Városliget* ⊕ *www.vitezkurtos.hu* Ⓜ *Trolleybus 72: Állatkert*

Andrássy út ends at Heroes' Square (Hősök tere), an impressive landmark that acts as the gateway to the enchanting and vast tree-filled Városliget. Budapest's version of Central Park was a private hunting ground for wealthy aristocrats until the mid-19th century, when it was opened to the public.

The preparations for the Millennium Celebrations in 1896 led to major development of the park and the surrounding area, including the addition of the grand Andrássy út, Hősök tere (Heroes' Square), the zoo, and Vajdahunyad Vár (Castle). Many of the park's millennium attractions were so popular that they were kept or rebuilt in stone. Today this leafy park is a welcome family-friendly "escape" from the city, that is not in fact that far from the city center, and offers a variety of cultural, historical, and touristic treasures.

Learn about the world's most famous Hungarians and the history of Hungary between Heroes' Square, Millennium Monument, and the Hungarian War Memorial as you enter the park. Wandering along the winding paths and green hills, you'll find a scenic artificial lake that is a popular rowing spot in summer and doubles as a skating rink in winter. Beside City Park's lake stands Vajdahunyad Vár (Castle), a fantastic medley of Hungary's historic and architectural past, starting with the Romanesque gateway of the cloister of Jak, in western Hungary. A Gothic castle whose Transylvanian turrets, Renaissance loggia, baroque

portico, and Byzantine decorations are all guarded by a spooky modern (1903) bronze statue of the anonymous medieval "chronicler," who was the first recorder of Hungarian history. Designed for the millennial celebration in 1896, it was not completed until 1908. In 2003, a bust of legendary B-movie actor Béla Lugosi was placed in an alcove along the southeast corner, its origins a mystery even today.

The Széchenyi Fürdő, Hungary's best-known thermal spa and Europe's largest medicinal bathing complex, is the park's top attraction, and rightly so. This yellow, copper-domed building in the middle of the park offers arguably the city's best thermal spa experience. It's a must in any weather as the pools maintain their hot temperatures.

Sights

Budapesti Állat-és Növénykert (*Budapest Zoo & Botanical Garden*)
GARDEN | FAMILY | Established in 1866, the Budapesti Állat-és Növénykert was one of the first urban zoos in the world. In the early days, most of the zoo's residents came from the Pannonian

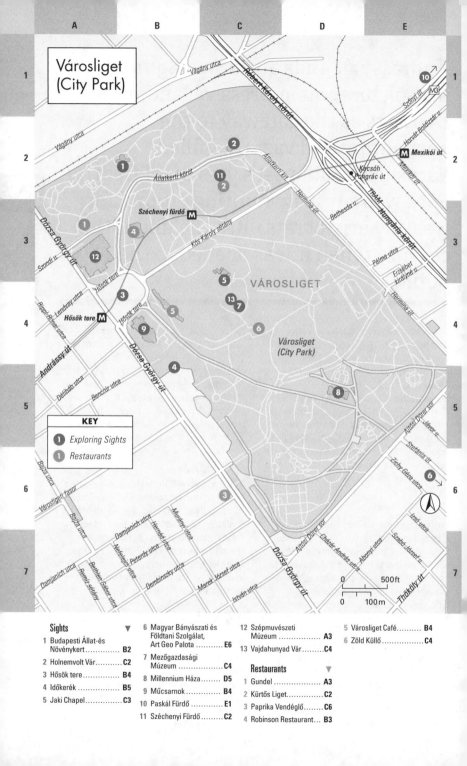

Városliget (City Park)

Basin, with only a handful of more exotic tenants. One of them was a giraffe gifted by Empress Elisabeth of Austria, who was Queen Consort of Hungary at that time. Her husband, Franz Josef, King of Hungary, sent 34 animals to the zoo from Schönbrunn. The lovingly preserved architecture, which seems to be endlessly under renovation, makes for a uniquely elegant urban zoo experience. Don't miss the art nouveau elephant pavilion, decorated with Zsolnay majolica and glazed ceramic animals. In the early 1900s, the elephant house had to be rebuilt at the request of the Turkish ambassador, who thought it resembled a mosque and found it to be offensive. The neighboring lot, once the amusement park immortalized in the classic Hungarian film about the Kádár era, *A Tanú* (The Witness), has been annexed by the zoo and turned into a multistory playhouse complex. Some of the antique relics, like the wooden roller coaster, remain on display. Note that the last tickets are sold one hour before closing, and animal houses don't open until an hour after the zoo gates. ⊠ *Állatkerti körút 6–12, Városliget* ☎ *1/273–4900* ⊕ *www.zoobudapest.com* ✉ *3,300 HUF* Ⓜ *M1: Széchenyi fürdő or Hősök tere.*

Holnemvolt Vár

AMUSEMENT PARK/WATER PARK | Following the property reshuffle after the closing of the city's amusement park, Budapest Zoo now runs a four-story playhouse built like a castle, where each room is designed in the theme of a popular Hungarian children's tale. Opened in May 2018, the Once Upon A Time Castle complex also feature a petting zoo, a riding stable and pony shed, a working hedgehog rescue clinic, a shark aquarium, an antique wooden carousel, and some fairground rides left over from the landmark amusement park. Holnemvolt has two entrances, one from the street and one through Budapest Zoo. ⊠ *Állatkerti krt. 14, City Park* ☎ *1/273–4901* ⊕ *www.zoobudapest.com* ✉ *Free with*

Budapest Zoo ticket Ⓜ *M1: Széchenyi fürdő or Hősök tere.*

★ **Hősök tere** (*Heroes' Square*)

TOUR—SIGHT | A majestic monument akin to Berlin's Brandenburg Gate, the Millennium Monument at the gateway to the city's playground, Városliget, was commissioned to celebrate the country's 1,000th birthday in 1896 but wasn't completed until 1906. Above it all, standing on a 118-foot-tall column, Hungary's patron saint the Archangel Gabriel holds the Hungarian crown in one hand and the apostolic double cross in the other. At the base of the column, the imposing figures of Hungary's founding fathers stand guard on horseback: these are the mythical leaders of the seven tribes whose decendants will one day become the Hungarian nation. Behind them are the full figure statues of their more modern, but equally awe-inspiring counterparts: Hungary's most important rulers since AD 1000 when Szent István allied with the Holy Roman Empire and founded the modern European state of Hungary. The line-up starts on the left with Saint István himself. This square is meant to inspire reverence and it is no coincidence that you can see it from the other end of Andrássy út. The square is a popular meeting point for locals, and is always busy with skateboarders and museum patrons lingering before or after a visit to the surrounding museums. Beware of little old ladies selling imitation furry hats next to the coffin-like memorial for the fallen soldiers of WWI in the middle of the square. However entertaining they may be, their wares are illegal and not the deal they appear to be. ■ **TIP→ If you are here in mid-October look out for the Nemzeti Vágta (National Gallop), a horse race around the square featuring equestrian shows throughout the day. You can purchase grandstand tickets for around 3.000–4.000 HUF or just stand to the side for free.** ⊠ *Hősök tere, City Park* ✉ *Free* Ⓜ *M1: Széchenyi fürdő or Hősök tere.*

8

Városliget (City Park)

Franz Joseph and his wife Queen Elizabeth donated the Budapest Zoo's first giraffe—a pregnant giraffe—in 1868. Since then, a total of thirty giraffes have been born here.

Időkerék (The Timewheel)

TOUR—SIGHT | Located where the statue of Lenin once stood during communism, the Időkerék was erected on May 1, 2004, to commemorate Hungary's admission into the European Union. The design of architect István Janáky, this is Europe's largest hourglass and, before it stopped functioning, this 60-ton hourglass was flipped over every New Year's Eve in order to start its countdown again. These days it's purely decorative. ⊠ *Olof Palme stny. 3, City Park* 🎟 *Free* Ⓜ *M1: Széchenyi fürdő or Hősök tere.*

Jaki Chapel

TOUR—SIGHT | Just like Vajdahunyad Castle, the portal of this church is a replica. The original is located in the village of Ják and Hungary's best example of a Romanesque Church from the 12th century. Featuring a gorgeous facade filled with medieval gothic biblical motifs, statues, and stonework, the chapel is a working Catholic church with regular services, concerts, and the occasional lavish wedding. ⊠ *Vajdahunyad vára, City Park*

⊹ *In the inner courtyard* ☎ *1/251–1359* ⊕ *www.jakikapolna.hu* 🎟 *Free* Ⓜ *M1: Széchenyi fürdő or Hősök tere.*

Magyar Bányászati és Földtani Szolgálat, Art Geo Palota (Geological Institute of Hungary)

MUSEUM | It's enough to go to the Geological Museum just to visit the building, a breathtaking Hungarian secessionist building from 1896 designed by Ödön Lechner. This Maria Teresian yellow building with terra-cotta brick highlights, complete with a globe on the highest spire, is a work of art as well as a functioning institute of geology. While the museum and library feature exhibits and displays, there is little of interest to see here. You can learn about the Hungarian rocks and minerals and see the cute footprints of some prehistoric animals and buy some memorabilia at the gift shop. Guided tours are available in English. ⊠ *Stefánia út 14, City Park* ☎ *1/251–0999* ⊕ *mbfsz. gov.hu* 🎟 *2,000 HUF* ⊙ *Closed Mon.– Wed. and Fri.*

Museums In Progress

Since 2008, the government has promoted its ambitions to construct a Museum Quarter in Budapest. The quarter would span from the upper part of Andrássy út and include the two museums on Hősök tere, plus a host of new or existing museums that would be built or relocated to Városliget. Concerns were immediately raised about the government's motives, and the possibility of meddling in the management of museums should these institutions have exhibits or leadership that are unfavorable to the government, but the most contested point of the plan was the demolition of a significant portion of the green space in City Park. The Liget Budapest Project managing the renovation of City Park has had to revise their work plan as demonstrations, sit-ins, and the election of a new mayor in 2019 (the first from the opposition party in nine years), Gergely Karácsony, succcessfully resisted the plans. It appears that the grand scheme to create a Museum Quarter has been curtailed, but there is a lack of transparency regarding plans, so it remains unclear to what degree plans have been scaled back. The House of the Hungarian Millennium is already complete and the move of the Néprajzi Múzeum is in progress, and a House of Hungarian Music and a Hungarian Museum Restoration and Storage Center are underway, too. The scheme is aiming for completion in 2023, but we'll see what outspoken locals have to say about that.

Mezőgazdasági Múzeum (*Museum of Hungarian Agriculture*)
MUSEUM | FAMILY | Located in the park's enchanting Vajdahunyad Castle, the quirky and slightly faded Museum and Library of Hungarian Agriculture dating to 1907 presents Hungary's agricultural history, an economic mainstay for the country to this day. With 40 collections covering Hungarian agriculture, forestry, animal husbandry, and viniculture through the ages, it's not the flashiest of museums in terms of the displays, but it does have a range of fascinating natural science and cultural anthropological relics on display. Be sure to check out the skeleton of Hungary's most famous, unbeatable racehorse, Kincsem, and the only remaining specimen of the Bakony Pig. The museum also offers tours of the castle's gatehouse and the Apostles' Tower, a fine opportunity to climb the gilded stairs of this gorgeous building and get closer to its glass mosaics by famed artist Miksa Róth. Free entry to children under six years old. ⊠ *Vajdahunyadvár, City Park* ⊹ *Entrance is located in the inner courtyard of the Vajdahunyadvár* ☎ *1/422–0765* ⊕ *www. mezogazdasagimuzeum.hu* ⊠ *1,600 HUF* ⊙ *Closed Mon.* Ⓜ *M1: Széchenyi fürdő or Hősök tere.*

★ **Millennium Háza** (*Millennium House*)
MUSEUM | Hailed as one of the first successes of the Liget Budapest Project, the reconstruction of the long abandoned historical Olof Palme House was completed in October 2020 and given its new name: the Millennium House. The original Zsolnay adornments have been painstakingly restored and new additions placed inside and out; the interior structure was entirely rebuilt. The new grounds include a café space, a stage, a full auditorium, and outside, a rose garden featuring a new Zsolnay water fountain. This exhibition and community space celebrate Hungary's golden age (between

1867–1914) under the Dual Monarchy of Austria-Hungary that saw Budapest prosper and a newly blossoming Hungarian cultural elite begin to flourish. This era was also the heyday of the Városliget as well. Exhibits will focus on the arts, history, literature, and gastronomy of that time. Currently, visitors to the Millennium House can book a guided tour of the building or a History of Városliget tour, which features an interactive exhibit on the golden age of the City Park. ✉ Olof Palme sétány 1, City Park ☎ 1/374–3173 ⊕ www.millenniumhaza.hu ✆ 1,500 HUF for guided building tour ⊙ Closed Mon. Ⓜ M1: Hősök tere, Széchenyi fürdő.

Műcsarnok (*Kunsthalle Budapest*)
MUSEUM | The Műcsarnok contemporary arts hall moved to its current location, a building designed and built specifically to house it, in 1896 as part of the Millennium Exhibition celebrations that changed Budapest's park forever. Its stark neoclassical structure and Greek revival portico set this handsome building apart from its surroundings. Inside, light pours in from the skylights to show off the fine marble work inside. After several incarnations, the space now functions as a Kunsthalle, an artist collective that hosts several cutting-edge temporary art exhibits throughout the year. The building also functions as the headquarters of the Institution of the Hungarian Academy of Arts. ✉ Dózsa György út 37, City Park ✛ To the right, just off Hősök tere ☎ 1/460–7000 ⊕ www.mucsarnok.hu ✆ 2,900 HUF combined ticket ⊙ Closed Mon. and Tues. Ⓜ M1: Széchenyi fürdő or Hősök tere.

Paskál Fürdő (*Paskál Baths*)
HOT SPRINGS | FAMILY | A little off the beaten path and about a ten-minute cab ride from the park, this spa is popular with locals who don't want to contend with visitors at Szechenyi and features indoor and outdoor thermal baths, full-length lap pools, a Finnish sauna, hot and cold plunge pools, as well as some massage and medical treatments. For families, there is even a pool for small children and another for babies. For the older crowd, the connecting indoor-outdoor leisure pool welcomes patrons with a swim-up water bar. Just remember to bring a bank card in or top-up your entry card, as they don't accept cash inside the facilities. ✉ Egressy út 178/f, City Park ☎ 1/252–6944 ⊕ www.paskalfurdo.hu ✆ 3,200 HUF Ⓜ Bus 907: Egressy út.

★ **Széchenyi Fürdő** (*Széchenyi Baths*)
HOT SPRINGS | Széchenyi Thermal Bath, the largest medicinal bathing complex in Europe, is housed in a beautiful neobaroque building in the middle of City Park. There are several thermal pools indoors as well as two outdoor pools, which remain open even in winter, when dense steam hangs thick over the hot water's surface. You can just barely make out the figures of elderly men, submerged shoulder deep, crowded around waterproof chessboards. To use the baths, you pay a standard price (unless you get a doctor's prescription, in which case it's free), plus a surcharge if you prefer having a private changing cabin instead of a locker. Facilities include an outdoor lap pool, Finnish and steam saunas, medical and leisure massage treatments, carbonated bath treatments, and other wellness treatments and wraps. A great way to sweat away last night's *pálinka* (fruit brandy). ✉ Állatkerti körút 9–11, Városliget ☎ 20/435–0051 ⊕ www.szechenyibath.hu ✆ Weekdays 3,500 HUF; weekends 3,900 HUF; cabin 1,000 HUF extra Ⓜ M1: Széchenyi fürdő.

Szépmuvészeti Múzeum (*Museum of Fine Arts*)
MUSEUM | Across Heroes' Square from the Műcsarnok and built by the same team of Albert Schickedanz and Fülöp Herzog, the Museum of Fine Arts houses Hungary's best art collection, rich in Flemish and Dutch old masters. With seven fine El Grecos and five beautiful Goyas as well as paintings by Velázquez

8

Városliget (City Park)

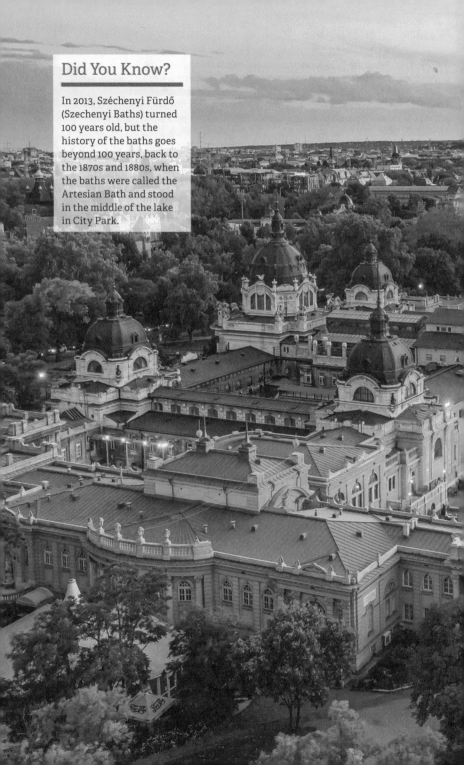

Did You Know?

In 2013, Széchenyi Fürdő (Szechenyi Baths) turned 100 years old, but the history of the baths goes beyond 100 years, back to the 1870s and 1880s, when the baths were called the Artesian Bath and stood in the middle of the lake in City Park.

and Murillo, the collection of Spanish old masters is probably the best outside Spain. The Italian school is represented by Giorgione, Bellini, Correggio, Tintoretto, and Titian masterpieces and, above all, two superb Raphael paintings: the *Eszterházy Madonna* and his immortal *Portrait of a Youth,* rescued after a world-famous art heist. Nineteenth-century French art includes works by Delacroix, Pissarro, Cézanne, Toulouse-Lautrec, Gauguin, Renoir, and Monet. There are also more than 100,000 drawings (including five by Rembrandt and three studies by Leonardo), and Egyptian and Greco-Roman exhibitions. The special exhibits are outstanding and frequent. Labels are in both Hungarian and English; there's also an English-language booklet for sale about the permanent collection. ⊠ *Hősök tere, Városliget* ☎ *1/469–7100* ⊕ *www.szepmuveszeti.hu* ☏ *3,200 HUF* ⊘ *Closed Mon.* Ⓜ *M1: Hosök tere.*

★ **Vajdahunyad Vár** (*Vajdahunyad Castle*)
TOUR—SIGHT | Beside the City Park's lake stands Vajdahunyad Vár, a fantastic medley of Hungary's historic and architectural past, starting with the Romanesque gateway of the cloister of Ják, in western Hungary. A Gothic castle whose Transylvanian turrets, Renaissance loggia, baroque portico, and Byzantine decorations are all guarded by a spooky bronze statue of the anonymous medieval "chronicler," who was the first recorder of Hungarian history. Designed for the millennial celebration in 1896, the permanent structure was not completed until 1908. This hodgepodge houses the surprisingly interesting Mezogazdasági Múzeum (Agricultural Museum), which touts itself as Europe's largest such museum and offers regular arts and crafts events for kids. Plan ahead for tickets to the Vajdahunyad Castle Summer Music Festival featuring some of Hungary's most popular musicians. If time permits, stroll around the castle to spot the Mermaid fountain and the bust of legendary Hollywood B-movie actor

and Hungarian-American Béla Lugosi that was placed in an alcove along the southeast corner in 2003; its origins remain a mystery today. ⊠ *Vajdahunyad Vára, Városliget* ⊕ *www.vajdahunyadcastle. com* Ⓜ *M1: Hősök tere.*

🍴 Restaurants

Gundel
$$$$ | **EASTERN EUROPEAN** | This is probably Hungary's most celebrated restaurant, an officially listed Hungarikum both for its historical significance (opened in 1894) as well as its revival in the 1990s by Hungarian-American restaurateur George Lang. The gorgeous setting in the City Park includes an art nouveau bar designed by Adam Tihany. **Known for:** Gundel pancakes; grand setting; touristy but iconic. ⑤ *Average main: 13,000 HUF* ⊠ *Gundel Károly út 4, Városliget* ☎ *1/889–8111* ⊕ *www.gundel.hu* 👔 *Jacket and tie* Ⓜ *M1: Hősök tere.*

Kürtős Liget
$ | **EASTERN EUROPEAN** | Kürtőskalács (chimney cake) is a traditional Transylvanian spit cake and popular street food, as pervasive in Budapest as Belgian waffles in Western Europe. This charming little shop offers tasty homemade kürtős kalács and classic sweets from an adorable gazebo-style shop in the middle of the park. **Known for:** Kürtős kalács; family recipe; difficult to pass up. ⑤ *Average main: 1,000 HUF* ⊠ *Állatkerti körút 11, Budapest* ☎ *20/969–5352* ⊕ *www. katonenifinomsagai.hu.*

Paprika Vendéglő
$$ | **HUNGARIAN** | While technically in District 7 but at the edge of the park, this kitsch, rustic Hungarian restaurant, with its wooden chairs and tables and village theme, offers a cozy place to have dinner after a long day of walking or bathing at Városliget. Great value for money, the portions are as truly traditional Hungarian-sized as the courses are authentic. **Known for:** traditional village theme;

Vajdahunyad Vár was designed by Ignác Alpár to feature copies of several landmark buildings from different parts of the Kingdom of Hungary, especially the Hunyad Castle in Transylvania.

hearty portions; túrógombóc (sweet cottage cheese balls). $ *Average main: 2,500 HUF ⊠ Dózsa György út 72, City Park ☎ 20/294–7944 ⊕ www.paprikavendeglo.hu.*

Robinson Restaurant

$$$ | FUSION | Robinson can certainly lay claim to one of the more exotic locations in Budapest dining—on wooden platforms atop an artificial lake, looking across to the delightful architectural folly of Vajdahunyad Castle. You can sit outside on the terrace during summer or enjoy the warm pastel interior in colder months. **Known for:** set on a lake; celebrity guests; tried-and-true fare. $ *Average main: 5,000 HUF ⊠ Városliget-tó, Városliget ✛ On the lake ☎ 30/663–6871 ⊕ www.robinsonrestaurant.hu.*

Városliget Café

$$$$ | HUNGARIAN | What this elegant café lacks in menu variety, it makes up for with its simply delightful lakeside view of the Vajdahunyad Castle and great service. Just next door to the ice-skating rink

and boathouse, its wall-to-wall windows assure views for its patrons and the lovely waitstaff are tolerant of weary ice-skaters gutsy enough to come in just for a forralt bor (mulled wine) and a moment of peace in a warm, romantic setting. In summer, the lakeside terrace provides even better views. **Known for:** romantic view of Vajdahunyad Castle; mulled wine in winter; terrace seating. $ *Average main: 5,500 HUF ⊠ Olof Palme sétány 6, Budapest ☎ 30/869–1426 ⊕ www. varosligetcafe.hu.*

Zöld Küllő

$$ | FAST FOOD | FAMILY | The tented garden bar Green Spokes is a great no-fuss place to rest your feet during your trek through Városliget. Offering quick bites, plenty of table space, and an outdoor setting, it's good for large groups and is dog-friendly. **Known for:** cup recycling scheme; leafy rest spot in the park; bicycle- and animal-friendly. $ *Average main: 2,500 HUF ⊠ Paál László út, Városliget ✛ Behind the Vajdahunyad Castle ☎ 30/519–9355.*

 Performing Arts

CONCERTS

★ Vajdahunyad Castle Summer Music Festival

MUSIC FESTIVALS | Concerts are regularly held at Vajdahunyad Castle's outdoor stage and their summer music festival features some of Hungary's most popular and best musicians. Sitting by the lake, among tall ancient trees and listening to music in this fairy-tale castle on a hot summer night, could be just about the most romantic thing you do on your trip—just remember to pack bug spray. ⊠ Vajdahunyadvár, Károlyi udvar, City Park ☎ 1/363–4201 ⊕ www.vajdahunyad.hu Ⓜ M1: Hősök tere.

CIRCUS

Fővárosi Nagycirkusz (Capital Circus of Budapest)

CIRCUSES | FAMILY | The circus folk here say that, as long as Városliget has been around, caravan performers have been entertaining crowds on this very plot of land. First created to attract more people into the vicinity of the public zoo, the city circus became popular in its own right and the result is the Budapest Grand Circus, the only stone structure circus in Central Europe, with seating for over 1,500 audience members. At the Fővárosi Nagycirkusz, colorful performances by local acrobats, clowns, and animal trainers, as well as by international artists, are staged in a small ring. While shows used to be very animal stunt heavy, these days the circus focuses on acrobatic shows using music and dance along with some more humane animal-participation routines. The staircase on the left from the lobby will take you past a small bust of Rodolfó, Hungary's most beloved stage magician from the 20th century. The schedule is subject to change, so it is best to check programs and book tickets in advance online. ⊠ Állatkerti körút 12/a, Városliget ☎ 1/343–8300 ⊕ www.fnc.hu 🎟 1,400–4,500 HUF Ⓜ M1: Széchenyi fürdő.

 Activities

★ Városligeti Műjégpálya és Csónakázótó (City Park Ice Rink and Boat House)

ICE SKATING | FAMILY | Right of Heroes' Square is the distinguished Austro-Hungarian baroque revival pavilion that rents out rowboats for jaunts around the lake in the summer and doubles as the biggest outdoor skating rink in the city in the winter. Opened in 1870, it is one of the oldest ice rinks in Europe. Since its major renovation in 2011, it hosts international sports events for skating, rollerblading, bicycles, and derby cars. Like the setting of a romantic movie, skaters glide along the ice to a backdrop of the scenic Vajdahunyad Castle alight in a warm golden glow. This is as enchanting as it sounds. While this is an outdoor venue on a lake, there's an area marked out for complete beginners, a skate crew out there to keep an eye on things, and adorable sliding seats for rent in the shape of a blue seal; these are worth renting just for the selfies. If you can, try to avoid the rush hours (weekdays after 5 and midday on weekends) as the line to get in can extend into the street and take about 30 minutes to get through. Ice-skating tickets are 2,000 HUF for adults, with special group prices for families. You can rent Bobby the Seal for 500 HUF an hour. For boating in summer, a simple rowboat with seating for four costs 4,000 HUF per hour, or opt for the water bicycle or a bigger boat for just a bit more. ⊠ Olof Palme sétány 5, City Park ☎ 1/363–2673 ⊕ www.mujegpalya.hu Ⓜ M1: Hősök tere.

PARLIAMENT AND AROUND

DISTRICTS 5 AND 6

Updated by
Esther Holbrook

Sights	Restaurants	Hotels	Shopping	Nightlife
★★★★★	★★★★★	★★★★★	★★★★★	★★★★★

NEIGHBORHOOD SNAPSHOT

TOP EXPERIENCES

■ **Parliament:** This majestic neo-Gothic building dating back to 1904 is the third largest parliament building in the world.

■ **A bird's-eye view:** See the city from the top of Szent Stephen's Basilica, Hungary's most famous church and national landmark.

■ **The National Opera House:** Take a backstage tour or splurge and get a box for an Italian opera.

■ **Historic underground:** Travel back in time on the third oldest metro in Europe, the földalatti.

■ **Liberty Square:** Packed with historical symbolism, this square is a testament to the struggle Hungarians have faced to achieve freedom.

GETTING HERE

The metro junction at Deák Ferenc tér is the intersection of three of its four metro lines, so it's hard not to find your way here. Trams 47 and 49 bring you here from Buda. Tram 2 offers captivating views of the river and Buda all the way down the line and Trolleybuses 70 and 78 takes you from Keleti Train Station right to Parliament. Plans to make the city center car-free are a long way from being actualized, but the Herculean challenge of finding parking here will impress upon you why they are considering it.

PLANNING YOUR TIME

In the past, you had to wait for tickets outside, rain or shine, but the new visitor center makes visiting Parliament much easier. It's worth the wait to enter this awe-inspiring building and take a peek into the chambers. Afterward, treat yourself to a Szamos cake and head up the road to the leafy, cheery Falk Miksa utca where antique shops and galleries hawk their wares and coveted finds for the right price. Pass through Liberty Square where you can take in centuries of Hungarian political history. Hop on the M1, Budapest's oldest metro line, and let it take you up Andrássy út. Don't fail to start or end the day with a walk across the Széchenyi Chain Bridge.

QUICK BITES

■ **IÑEZ Bagel Shop.** The best bagels in town are served plain or as a sandwich at this quaint little Colombian bistro open 8 am–3 pm. ✉ *Bajcsy-Zsilinszky út 40, Lipótváros* ⊕ *www.facebook.com/inezbudapest* Ⓜ *M3: Arany János utca*

■ **Fragola.** One of Hungary's best artisanal ice-cream chains, here you can choose from a range of unique flavors like turmeric, fig, and sweet pistachio, or something in their new ultra-healthy vegan line. ✉ *Nagymező u. 7, Terézváros* ⊕ *www.fragolafagylaltozo.hu* Ⓜ *Trolleybus 70, 78 to Andrássy út*

■ **Gerbeaud Coffee House.** Proudly bearing the name of famed confectioner Émile Gerbeaud, who brought the glamour of Paris with him to turn-of-the-century Budapest, this elegant coffeehouse dating from 1858 has remained the pride of the nation ever since. ✉ *Vörösmarty tér 7-8, Lipótváros* ⊕ *gerbeaud.hu* Ⓜ *M1: Vörösmarty tér*

At the center of Lipótváros, named after Habsburg Emperor Leopold II, lies the massive Gothic Revival edifice of the Országház (the "House of the Country"), Hungary's parliament building and one of her most recognizable landmarks. A vibrant center of political, economic, and social life in the city, every street in this neighborhood is lined with points of interest as well as plenty of excellent places to grab something of interest to eat.

A short walk from here leads to the similarly sprawling Szabadság tér (Freedom Square), with such dignified features as the National Bank, the former Stock Exchange Palace (later Hungary's TV headquarters, now empty), the U.S. embassy, a statue of Ronald Reagan, a controversial Soviet War Memorial whose removal—and the alleged legal impossibility thereof—is a regular talking point for Hungarians, as is the equally controversial memorial to the victims of the German invasion. Just a few blocks away is St. Stephen's Basilica, named after the first king of Hungary.

Equally vibrant, Terézváros, the namesake of Queen Maria Theresa, provides ample opportunity to put your finger on the pulse of this dynamic city, embedded in culture and with a booming social scene. Andrássy út, the city's grand promenade, and other major streets here are filled with life throughout the day and, being the capital of a small country, you'll be sure to pass by leading politicians and famous celebrities on their way to coffee, lunch, or work. You might even catch a few movie-star sightings as Hungary is a leading European film production destination. Some of the clubs and bars here stay open until dawn if you are looking to be active when jet-lagged.

 Sights

Andrássy út (*Andrássy Avenue*)
TOUR—SIGHT | Turn-of-the-century Andrássy Avenue links Erzsébet Square with the Városliget and makes for one of Budapest's most pleasant walks with lots of places to stop along the way. From its starting point, on the corner with Bajcsy Zsilinszky út, you can see all the way up to its end point, the spectacular Hősök tere. Lined with spectacular neo-Renaissance mansions and town houses featuring fine facades and interiors, but also green with trees, it was recognized

Budapest on Two Wheels

The city's new bike culture is a source of great pride for Budapesters. In a country where cars and decent roads were once luxury items, Hungarians were used to cycling old metal scrappers across endless potholes in the dark. In a country fiercely dedicated to politics, the extremely successful grassroots movement Critical Mass Budapest was the one platform where people on all sides of the political spectrum found common ground, resulting in new bicyle paths, lanes, legal protection, and safety measures for bicyclists on Budapest roads. Some Critical Mass Budapest protest rides reported up to 80,000 participants, which, if true, would make it one of the biggest Critical Mass movements in the world. Although the city still has a long way to go and some parts of the city remain completely unfit for cycling, the city center is full of designated bike lanes on roads and along pedestrian walkways and there are some pleasant rides to be had along the Dunakorzó (Danube Promenade).

The city runs a bicycle sharing network called BuBi featuring bright green bikes that are available for grab-and-go use at stations across the city. You can even purchase passes and tickets by touch screen at MOL BuBi terminals or via the mobile app. Bike rental is also becoming more popular here, but if you'd feel safer with some local know-how, it is not hard to find guides offering city tours by bicycle, too. Remember that you are still in Central Eastern Europe with its own rhythm and traffic customs and Budapest drivers will be sure to remind you of that!

Bicycle Rental

Best Bike Tours Budapest. This bike rental and tour company offers all-day bike rental with delivery, group and one-on-one bike tours, and bike repair at reasonable prices. ⊠ *Semmelweis utca 14, Budapest* ☎ *30/5200–650* ⊕ *www.bbtb.hu.*

MOL BuBi. BuBi (a combination of the words Budapest and Bicycle) is a bike-sharing partnership between the city and MOL (the Hungarian national oil company). Their bright green bikes are produced by Hungary's most famous bike manufacturer, Csepel, and are available at stations all across the city. You can purchase passes and tickets by touch screen MOL BuBi terminals, via the mobile app, or at a Budapest public transport customer service office, which are usually located in the underground passageways next to the entrance of metro lines. ⊠ *Rumbach Sebestyén utca 19–21, Budapest* ☎ *1/325–5255* ⊕ *www.molbubi.hu.*

Yellow Zebra. Rent a bike, e-bike, or segway, or book a bike tour at this steadfast tour and travel agency, which is also a member of the Cycle Cities, a global network of local bike tour operators. Boat and other city tours are also on offer and they even do bike repair. ⊠ *Lázár utca 16, Budapest* ☎ *20/929–7506* ⊕ *www. yellowzebrabudapest.com* ⌗ *1,000 HUF for bike rental.*

as a World Heritage Site in 2002. Today, it's a high-end shopping promenade filled with cafés and restaurants, embassies, and hotels. It's no accident that the oldest metro line goes all the way up it, with direct stops at the State Opera House and other significant sites in its vicinity. ⊠ *Andrássy út, Parliament* Ⓜ *M1: Vörösmarty utca.*

Central European University (*Közép-Európai Egyetem*)

COLLEGE | Founded just after the fall of communism in 1991 as an international higher education institution based in Budapest and catering to students in the region, CEU is a humanities university that focuses on the idea of Open Society, freedom of dissent, and socially and morally responsible intellectual inquiry. It was recently expelled from Hungary by the government. The law they used to expel the school, known as Lex CEU, was proposed and passed in record time in March 2017 and had conditions that clearly affect only the running of CEU and no other Hungarian insitution, leading to criticism that the move was politically motivated. This led to mass public demostrations for months across the city and began a new wave of opposition movements against the current govenment. CEU has sinced relocated all its teaching facilities to Vienna, Austria. In October 2020, the European Court of Justice ruled that the law used to expel the school violates Hungary's commitments under the WTO and infringes the provisions of the Charter of Fundamental Rights of the European Union relating to academic freedom. Even if CEU will not resume using the Nádor utca campus for its university courses, the fantastic buildings here host lectures (in English and open to the public) on a range of humanities subjects by international scholars. The campus site is made up of a former urban villa owned by the Festetics family and a brand-new, state-of-the-art Bream-certified conference and library facility, with an excellent view of the city

from the roof. Check ahead for event listings. ⊠ *Nádor utca 9–15, Budapest* ☎ *1/327–3000* ⊕ *www.ceu.edu.*

Hopp Ferenc Kelet-Ázsiai Művészeti Múzeum (*Hopp Ferenc Museum of East Asian Art*)

ART GALLERIES—ARTS | Patron of the arts, Ferenc Hopp, bequeathed his home and a 4,000-piece private collection to the creation of a public exhibition space and from 1923 to this day it remains the country's only Asian art museum. Visitors can enjoy visiting a turn-of-the-century aristocrat's home while perusing the collection's currently 30,000 items spanning from Japan to the near East. Visiting exhibitions are always paired thematically with objects existing in the local collection, adding an interesting perspective. The small eastern-Asian-style garden space surrounding the museum is free and open to the public throughout the day. ⊠ *Andrássy út 103, Budapest* ☎ *1/469–7759 Main* ⊕ *www.hoppmuseum.hu* ☜ *1,400 HUF* ☞ *Closed Mon.*

Liszt Ferenc Zeneművészeti Egyetem (*Franz Liszt Academy of Music*)

CONCERTS | Founded by renowned Hungarian composer and pianist Franz Liszt, students have been training at this world-famous music conservatory with the likes of Erno Dohnanyi, Zoltán Kodály, and Béla Bartók among its teachers since 1907. The extravagantly decorated art nouveau concert halls at the Academy were built to enhance musical performance, both acoustically and visually. The interiors are richly decorated, featuring elaborate frescoes, stained glass, mosaics, grand marble stairs, rich woods, and tiled centerpieces featuring Zsolnay tiles. Audiences can even hear the grand hall's beautiful organ, dating back to 1907. The academy is still a working college of music, attracting talent from around the world. There are events running throughout the year but performances are limited during July and August. Opera fans should look out for tickets to the fantastic

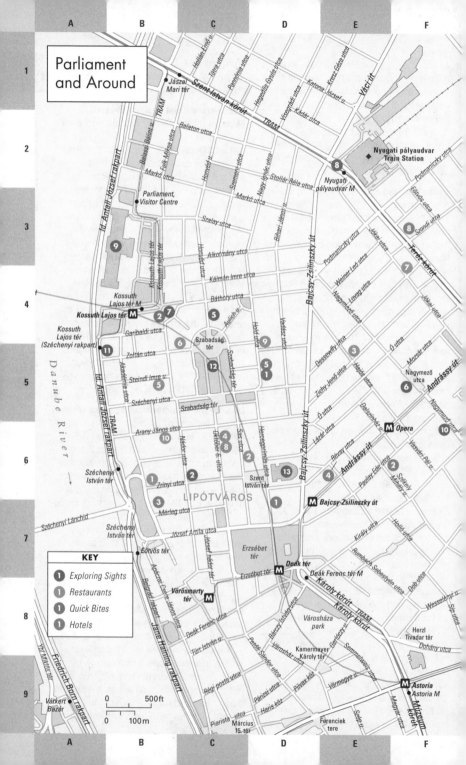

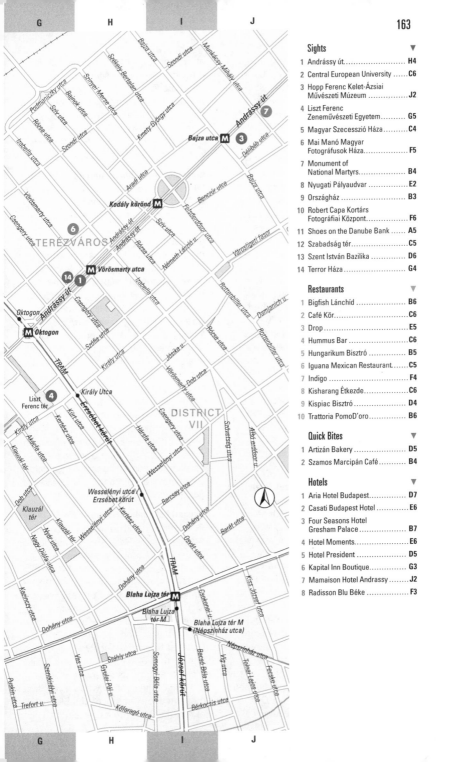

Sights ▼

1 Andrássy út......................... H4
2 Central European University C6
3 Hopp Ferenc Kelet-Ázsiai
  Művészeti Múzeum J2
4 Liszt Ferenc
  Zeneművészeti Egyetem.......... G5
5 Magyar Szecesszió Háza..........C4
6 Mai Manó Magyar
  Fotográfusok Háza................. F5
7 Monument of
  National Martyrs................... B4
8 Nyugati Pályaudvar E2
9 Országház B3
10 Robert Capa Kortárs
  Fotográfiai Központ................ F6
11 Shoes on the Danube Bank A5
12 Szabadság tér.......................C5
13 Szent István Bazilika D6
14 Terror Háza......................... G4

Restaurants ▼

1 Bigfish Lánchíd B6
2 Café Kör............................C6
3 Drop E5
4 Hummus Bar C6
5 Hungarikum Bisztró B5
6 Iguana Mexican Restaurant......C5
7 Indigo F4
8 Kisharang Étkezde.................C6
9 Kispiac Bisztró D4
10 Trattoria PomoD'oro.............. B6

Quick Bites ▼

1 Artizán Bakery D5
2 Szamos Marcipán Café B4

Hotels ▼

1 Aria Hotel Budapest.............. D7
2 Casati Budapest Hotel E6
3 Four Seasons Hotel
  Gresham Palace.................. B7
4 Hotel Moments.....................E6
5 Hotel President D5
6 Kapital Inn Boutique.............. G3
7 Mamaison Hotel Andrassy J2
8 Radisson Blu Béke F3

baroque opera here, tucked away in a tiny but spectacularly designed baroque theater. It's easy to forget not just where you are but *when* you are once the lights dim for the opening act. ✉ *Liszt Ferenc tér 8, Parliament* ☎ *1/321–0690* ⊕ *www.lfze.hu.*

Magyar Szecesszió Háza (*House of Hungarian Art Nouveau*)
MUSEUM | A well-preserved example of Hungarian art nouveau (Szecesszió), the House of Hungarian Art Nouveau is a museum dedicated to the Secession style of art and a coffee shop. The exterior alone is worth making a detour to see, as its gorgeous facade and etchings are truly stunning and Gaudí-esque. Come in for tea and cake served on antique dishes and surrounded by exhibited artistic treasures such as family portraits, porcelain, period furniture, and glassware. There are regular roundtable and lecture events in the lower hall but most of these are in Hungarian. While there is not much in the way of tours, the helpful staff are on hand for questions. ✉ *Honvéd utca 3, Budapest* ☎ *70/643–2331* ⊕ *www.facebook.com/Magyar-Szecesszió-Háza-100208600027839/* ☎ *2,000 HUF* ⊘ *Closed Mon.* Ⓜ *M2: Kossuth Lajos tér.*

Mai Manó Magyar Fotográfusok Háza (*Hungarian House of Photography*)
ART GALLERIES—ARTS | This eight-story neo-Renaissance building was commissioned by photographer Manó Mai and presents a fascinating history of Hungarian photography. Imperial and royal court photographer at the turn of the 20th century, Mai worked and lived here throughout his life. Today, this building features the only intact turn-of-the-century studio house, which has recently been renovated for use. The three-stories of exhibition space display an eclectic selection of photographic works, mostly featuring contemporary artists, but sometimes classic works of art, too. Don't leave without having a coffee and cake at the gorgeous Mai Manó Café on the ground floor—either sit inside enjoying the Moroccan mosaic-tiled walls or sit outside to watch the theater crowds come and go from the Moulin Rouge across the street. ✉ *Nagymező utca 20, Budapest* ☎ *30/167–4034* ⊕ *www.maimano.hu* ☎ *1,500 HUF* Ⓜ *1065.*

Monument of National Martyrs
MEMORIAL | Erected in 2014, the Memorial for Victims of the German Occupation commemorates the Hungarian victims of the German Nazis in WWII. Germany, represented by an eagle, attacks Archangel Gabriel, Hungary's Parton saint. Jewish and opposition leaders have criticized the statue as an attempt to absolve the Hungarian state and Hungarians of their collaboration with Nazi Germany and their complicity in the Holocaust. They have even created their own protest counter-memorial next to it: a collection of Holocaust original and symbolic memorabilia (shoes, suitcases, photos) and a statement in a range of languages asking people to also remember the victims of the Hungarian Arrow Cross Party (Nyilaskeresztes Párt) under whose reign in 1944–1945 thousands of civilians were murdered in Hungary and thousands more sent to concentration camps in Austria and Germany. ✉ *Szabadság tér, Parliament* ☎ *Free.*

Nyugati Pályaudvar (*Nyugati Train Station*)
TRANSPORTATION SITE (AIRPORT/BUS/FERRY/TRAIN) | Nyugati Pályaudvar, constructed by the Eiffel Company, is considered the city's most elegant train station and, to its right, what was once part of the station is perhaps the world's fanciest McDonald's Café, with booths fit for kings. Just one of the perks of wandering around this station, the Royal Waiting Room at Nyugati is not always open, but worth seeing if you get the chance. Maintained in all its splendor, as it was at the turn of the century when it was first presented to Franz Josef and Elizabeth of Austria. Peek into its glassed-in garden

The lavish interiors of Hungary's Országház (Parliament) building are decorated using more than 40 kilograms of 22 to 23 carat gold, including rare gold leaves.

as you turn left, toward the Westend Shopping Center exit. ✉ *Nyugati tér, Parliament* Ⓜ *M3: Nyugati pályaudvar.*

★ Országház (*Parliament*)

GOVERNMENT BUILDING | The most visible symbol of Budapest's left bank is the huge neo-Gothic Parliament, mirrored in the Danube much the way Britain's Parliament is reflected in the Thames. It was designed by the Hungarian architect Imre Steindl and built by 1,000 workers between 1885 and 1902. The grace and dignity of its long facade and 24 slender towers, with spacious arcades and high windows balancing its vast central dome, lend this living landmark a refreshingly baroque spatial effect. The exterior is lined with 90 statues of great figures from Hungarian history, with corbels ornamented by 242 allegorical statues. Inside are 691 rooms, 10 courtyards, and 29 staircases; some 88 pounds of gold were used for the staircases and halls. These halls are also a gallery of late-19th-century Hungarian art, with frescoes and canvases depicting Hungarian history, starting with Mihály Munkácsy's large painting of the Magyar Conquest of 896.

Parliament's most sacred treasure isn't the Hungarian legislature but rather the Szent Korona (Holy Crown), which reposes with other royal relics under the cupola. The crown sits like a golden soufflé above a Byzantine band of holy scenes in enamel and pearls and other gems. It seems to date from the 12th century, so it could not be the crown that Pope Sylvester II presented to St. Stephen in the year 1000, when he was crowned the first king of Hungary. Nevertheless, it is known as the Crown of St. Stephen and has been regarded—even by communist governments—as the legal symbol of Hungarian sovereignty and unbroken statehood. In 1945 the fleeing Hungarian army handed over the crown and its accompanying regalia to the Americans rather than have them fall into Soviet hands. They were restored to Hungary in 1978.

The only way you can visit the Parliament and see the crown is on one of the daily tours. Lines at the visitor center on the north side of the edifice may be long and tickets are in limited numbers, so it's best to purchase tickets in advance (⊕ www.jegymester.hu/parlament). A permanent exhibit about the thousand years of Hungarian legislation is available free through the visitor center until 2 pm. Note that Parliament is closed to the public during ceremonial events and when the legislature is in session (usually Monday and Tuesday from late summer to spring). ⊠ District V, Kossuth tér, Parliament ☎ 1/441–4415 ⊕ latogatokozpont. parlament.hu ⊠ 3,500 HUF (EU citizens), 6,700 HUF (others) ⊘ Closed during plenary sessions Ⓜ M2: Kossuth tér.

Robert Capa Kortárs Fotográfiai Központ

(Robert Capa Contemporary Photography Center)

ARTS CENTERS | Robert Capa was a Hungarian photographer whose images of war made him one of the greatest photojournalists of the 20th century. Born in 1913 in Budapest, Friedmann Endre Ernő began working under the more American-sounding Robert Capa alias when he was working in Paris. In 1936, he was sent to cover the Spanish Civil War and it was here that he took one of his most famous photos, Death of a Loyalist Militia Man, Spain, 1936. Capa is particularly well-known for his photos of World War II and the D-Day landings in Normandy and for being a cofounder of Magnum Photos in Paris. In 1954, Capa was photographing for Life in Thái-Bình, Vietnam, when he stepped on a land mine and was killed. This photography center named for Capa and housed on the second floor of a lovely old downtown villa honors his incredible legacy as an exhibition space that focuses primarily on press and documentary photography and supports the preservation of Hungarian press photography. There is also a small permanent collection featuring Capa's work. The local exhibitions are always extremely

well curated and there are occasional but prestigious international exhibitions here throughout the year. ⊠ Nagymező utca 8, Parliament ☎ 1/413–1310 ⊕ www. capacenter.hu ⊠ 2,000 HUF.

Shoes on the Danube Bank

MEMORIAL | Wander the riverside, just north of the chain bridge, and a simple but powerful memorial presents itself: 60 pairs of 1940s-style men's, women's, and children's shoes cast in iron standing along the riverbank. Shoes on the Danube Bank, designed by film director Can Togay and sculptor Gyula Pauer was erected in 2005 to honor the memory of the countless and nameless victims of the Hungarian Arrow Cross party massacres here. It is estimated that between 1944 and 1945 as many as 200,000 Hungarian Jews were taken from the Budapest ghettos by the "Nyilas," lined up on riverbank spots close to this one, sometimes several people deep, and shot at point-blank range. This haunting tribute to this horrific time in history is appropriately not far from Hungarian Parliament. ⊠ Kossuth Lajos tér, Parliament ⊠ Free Ⓜ M2: Kossuth Lajos tér.

Szabadság tércomm (Liberty Square)

MEMORIAL | The sprawling Liberty Square has represented the pursuit of liberty for Hungarians since its days as the site of a massive troop barracks and the execution of Prime Minister Lajos Batthyány following the failed revolution against the Habsburg Dynasty in 1848. The square is dominated by the former longtime headquarters of Magyar Televizió (Hungarian Television), a former stock exchange building with what looks like four temples and two castles on its roof. Across from it is a solemn-looking neoclassical shrine, the Nemzeti Bank (The Hungarian National Bank). The bank's Postal Savings Bank branch, adjacent to the main building but visible from behind Szabadság tér on Hold utca, is another exuberant art nouveau masterpiece of architect Ödön Lechner, built in 1901 with colorful

Statues to freedom and liberty are nestled among shady walkways and grassy lawns throughout Szabadság tér.

majolica mosaics, characteristically curvaceous windows, and pointed towers ending in swirling gold flourishes.

In the square's center remains a gold hammer and sickle atop a white stone obelisk, one of the few monuments to the Russian "liberation" of Budapest in 1945 that has not been banished to Statue Park. There were mutterings that it, too, would be pulled down, which prompted a Russian diplomatic protest; the monument, after all, marks a gravesite of fallen Soviet troops but also a reminder of how close the city was to falling into Nazi hands.

As if in counterbalance, a memorial statue of Ronald Reagan—one of five that Reagan commissioned himself in his will—was erected in the summer of 2011, standing just left of the Soviet liberation monument. Next to it, at Szabadság tér 12, Stars and Stripes flying out in front and with a high-security presence, stands the United States Embassy. One of the square's most popular stories is how Cardinal József Mindszenty, fearing religious persecution, lived here as a guest of the U.S. government for 15 years during communism. On the south side of the square another monument appeared amid controversy in 2014. The Memorial for Victims of the German Occupation is a state-commissioned statue that commemorates the Hungarian victims of the German Nazis in WWII. Germany, represented by a vicious eagle, is attacking the peaceful form of the Archangel Gabriel, Hungary's parton saint. Jewish and opposition leaders have criticized the statue as an attempt to absolve the Hungarian state and Hungarians of their collaboration with Nazi Germany and complicity in the Holocaust. The latest addition is on the other side of the Soviet obelisk, a statue of former U.S. President George H. W. Bush erected by the Hungarian government in October 2020 to mark the 30th anniversary of the fall of communist rule in Central and Eastern Europe. A political location from its historical beginnings, but a center of leisure life in the city, too, Szabadság tér is also simply a great place to walk or take a break from sightseeing. During major football championships, like the World Cup, it is turned into an outdoor screening area and packed to the gills with locals. About four times a year it is the sight of culinary and seasonal festivals. ⊠ *District V, Szabadság tér, Parliament* Ⓜ *M2: Kossuth tér or M3: Arany János utca.*

★ **Szent István Bazilika** (*St. Stephen's Basilica*)

RELIGIOUS SITE | Handsome and massive, this is one of the chief landmarks of Pest and the city's largest church—it can hold 8,500 people. Its very Holy Roman front porch greets you with a tympanum bustling with statuary. The basilica's dome and the dome of Parliament are by far the most visible in the Pest skyline, and this is no accident: with the Magyar Millennium of 1896 in mind (the lavishly celebrated thousandth anniversary of the settling of the Carpathian Basin in 896), both domes were planned to be 315 feet high and to this day city codes specify that no downtown Pest building may exceed this height.

The millennium was not yet in sight when architect József Hild began building the basilica in neoclassical style in 1851, two years after the revolution was suppressed. After Hild's death, the project was taken over in 1867 by Miklós Ybl, the architect who did the most to transform modern Pest into a monumental metropolis. Wherever he could, Ybl shifted Hild's motifs toward the neo-Renaissance mode that Ybl favored. When the dome collapsed, partly damaging the walls, he made even more drastic changes. Ybl died in 1891, five years before the 1,000-year celebration, and the basilica was completed in neo-Renaissance style by József Kauser—but not until 1905.

Below the cupola is a rich collection of late-19th-century Hungarian art: mosaics, altarpieces, and statuary (what heady days the Magyar Millennium must

have meant for local talents). There are 150 kinds of marble, all from Hungary except for the Carrara in the sanctuary's centerpiece: a white statue of King (St.) Stephen I, Hungary's first king and patron saint. Stephen's mummified right hand is preserved as a relic in the Szent Jobb Kápolna (Holy Right Chapel); press a button and it will be illuminated for two minutes. You can also climb the 364 stairs (or take the elevator) to the top of the cupola for a spectacular view of the city. Extensive renovation work here has, among other things, returned the cathedral from a sooty gray to an almost bright tan. Small-group guided tours in English are offered between 9:30 and 3, but must be reserved in advance. ⊠ *Szent István tér 1, St. Stephen's Basilica* ☎ *1/338–2151* ⊕ *en.bazilika.biz* ⊠ *Church and Szt. Jobb Chapel free (€1 donation requested); cupola 1,000 HUF* Ⓜ *M1: Bajcsy-Zsilinszky út, M2, M3: Deák Ferenc tér or M3: Arany János utca.*

Terror Háza (*House of Terror*)

MUSEUM | For generations during the soviet era, Andrássy út 60 was the well-known site of a secret police interrogation center. People were taken in the night to this location and some never returned. In 2002, the House of Terror Museum opened to tell the story of the regime who used this location to intimidate, interrogate, torture, and kill. The museum has been carefully designed down to the imposing form of the building's awning and the shadow it makes on the sidewalk. The music that accompanies the exhibits is likewise original, composed to create the proper mood. Graphic images and the violent theme make it unsuitable for younger children, but give visitors a sense of the real terror of living in a totalitarian regime. ⊠ *Andrássy út 60, Parliament* ☎ *1/374–2600* ⊕ *www.terrorhaza.hu* ⊠ *3,000 HUF* ☉ *Closed Mon.* Ⓜ *M1: Vörösmarty utca.*

Did You Know?

The mummified hand of St. Stephen who died in 1038 AD is housed in Szent István Bazilika and paraded annually on August 20th, Saint Stephen's Day.

🍴 Restaurants

Bigfish Lánchíd

$$$$ | SEAFOOD | Directly managing imports for the Budaörs Fish Market, this haven of seafood can legitimately stand by its claim to the freshest and best fish in Budapest. There's a daily catch offer as well as mussels, fillets, and grilled fish options but, if you are here to indulge, make sure to get the lobster, too, as it gets the highest reviews all around. **Known for:** best seafood in town; daily catch; nice setting and views if you can get a seat outside. ⑤ *Average main: 8,000 HUF* ✉ *Zrínyi utca 2, Budapest* ☎ *1/782–5085* ⊕ *thebigfish.hu* Ⓜ *M1: Bajcsy-Zsilinszky út.*

Café Kör

$$$ | HUNGARIAN | A cozy little two-room restaurant with turn-of-the-century charm, you'll want to ditch your entourage for this place as tables don't fit more than four comfortably. A handwritten list of the day's menu is written in marker on a flip chart sheet in Hungarian, but menus are available in English, too. **Known for:** upscale Hungarian cuisine; tiny, stylish interior; cash only. ⑤ *Average main: 4,000 HUF* ✉ *Sas utca 17, Budapest* ☎ *1/311–0053.*

Drop

$$$ | ECLECTIC | Ten years ago, a lactose-free, gluten-free restaurant would have had to give its food away for free to survive Budapest's food scene, but the city is ready and even excited about restaurants like Drop these days. This snazzy gluten-free eatery just behind the Opera offers a range of sophisticated dishes that are bound to make the day of meat-eaters who need to pass on the cream and grains. Vegetarians will have to look elsewhere. **Known for:** the best gluten-free burgers; great value; vegan chocolate hazelnut cake. ⑤ *Average main: 4,000 HUF* ✉ *Hajós utca 27, Parliament* ☎ *1/235–0468* ⊕ *www.droprestaurant.com.*

Hummus Bar

$$ | MIDDLE EASTERN | This Hungarian Middle Eastern fast-food chain is the city's go-to for hummus. The first restaurant, long gone now, on Kertesz utca opened up in 2005 and the chain has been a local favorite since. **Known for:** shawarma hummus plate; great vegetarian options; freshly made laffa. ⑤ *Average main: 2,000 HUF* ✉ *Október 6 utca 19, Budapest* ☎ *1/354–0108* ⊕ *www.hummusbar.hu* Ⓜ *M3: Arany János utca.*

Hungarikum Bisztró

$$$ | HUNGARIAN | With its checkered tablecloths and rustic style, this sweet and cheery restaurant has all the charms of its retro theme without the cobwebs. The traditional dishes are served with a modern flair and excellent service, making it feel like the best of both worlds. **Known for:** traditional dishes; retro style and charm; beef goulash. ⑤ *Average main: 3,300 HUF* ✉ *Steindl Imre utca 13, Budapest* ☎ *30/661–6244* ⊕ *hungarikumbisztro.hu.*

★ Iguana Mexican Restaurant

$$ | MEXICAN FUSION | There's always a festive groove at Iguana's, and not just on the occasion of their annual Cinco de Mayo street party. In business since 1997, this is probably the most popular expat restaurant and hangout in town, especially with Americans. **Known for:** expat hangout; classic Mexican dishes; margaritas and tequila. ⑤ *Average main: 3,000 HUF* ✉ *Zoltán utca 16, Budapest* ☎ *1/331–4352.*

Indigo

$$ | INDIAN | Indigo is indisputably one of the best Indian restaurants in town. Mughlai and northern Indian flavor combinations please the palate, and warm rich decorations with traditional Indian designs make the setting very relaxing. **Known for:** local institution since 2005; vindaloos; authentic Indian food. ⑤ *Average main: 3,000 HUF* ✉ *Jókai utca 13, Budapest* ☎ *1/428–2187* ⊕ *www.indigo-restaurant.hu.*

Kisharang Étkezde

$$ | HUNGARIAN | There are only three tables and a counter at this tiny home-style restaurant not far from the basilica. It gets a lunch crowd early and bustles well into the evening with downtown professional types. **Known for:** traditional Hungarian cuisine; strawberry soup; goose-dumpling soup. ⑤ *Average main: 2,000 HUF* ✉ *Október 6 utca 17, St. Stephen's Basilica* ☏ *1/269–3861* ⊕ *www. kisharang.hu* ⊟ *No credit cards* Ⓜ *M3: Arany János utca.*

Kispiac Bisztró

$$$ | HUNGARIAN | Kispiac Bisztró is a tiny gem of a restaurant (its name means "little market") that specializes in huge portions of fresh roasted meat, which come straight from the nearby 5th District market hall. Delicious pork belly, beef ribs, ham hock, or roast duck are the way to go, along with a plate of homemade pickles. **Known for:** meat and more meat; excellent cheesecake; reservations essential. ⑤ *Average main: 3,500 HUF* ✉ *Hold utca 13, Parliament* ☏ *1/269–4231* ⊙ *Closed Sun.* Ⓜ *M3: Arany János utca.*

Trattoria PomoD'oro

$$$ | ITALIAN | Real Italian pizzas made to order in a brick oven attract a hungry business crowd during the week. Weekends find just as many people enjoying pastas like ravioli with Gorgonzola and walnut sauce or the "priest strangler"—homemade pasta in tomato ragout flambéed with Parmesan cheese. **Known for:** large menu of grilled foods and pizzas; good selection of both Italian and Hungarian wines; rustic Tuscan decor. ⑤ *Average main: 3,500 HUF* ✉ *Arany János utca 9, St. Stephen's Basilica* ☏ *1/302–6473* ⊕ *www.pomodorobudapest.com* Ⓜ *M3: Arany János utca.*

😋 Coffee and Quick Bites

Artizán Bakery

$ | BAKERY | This artisanal bakery is known for its fresh-from-the-oven breads, pastries, and great coffee, so don't be surprised to find a line out the door. The cardamom buns, jalapeño rolls, and homemade granola are delicious and worth waiting for. **Known for:** fresh baked bread and pastries; cardamom buns; always busy but worth the wait. ⑤ *Average main: 1,000 HUF* ✉ *Hold utca 3, Parliament* ☏ *30/856–5122* ⊕ *www. artizan.hu* ⊙ *Closed Sun.* Ⓜ *M3: Arany János utca.*

Szamos Marcipán Café

$$ | CAFÉ | Szamos is a household name in Hungarian chocolate confectioners and the shop here, nearby Parliament, is a great place to grab breakfast or a coffee and a chocolate bite to eat in between sights. Try the signature Sacher, Dobos, or Eszterházy torta (cakes). **Known for:** chocolate museum; good breakfast menu; views of the Parliament. ⑤ *Average main: 1,500 HUF* ✉ *Kossuth Lajos tér 10, Parliament* ☏ *30/290–6655* ⊕ *www. szamos.hu* Ⓜ *M2: Kossuth Lajos tér.*

Hotels

⭐ Aria Hotel Budapest

$$$$ | HOTEL | Five-star luxury hotel Aria's music theme starts at the piano footpath at the entrance and extends past the space-age piano, to the subterranean Harmony Spa, throughout the hotel, and to the sky bar. **Pros:** unique music-themed rooms; complimentary wine-and-cheese afternoons; rooftop bar with great views of St. Stephen's Basilica. **Cons:** no views from rooms; small gym; some rooms are nicer than others. ⑤ *Rooms from: 96,846 HUF* ✉ *Hercegprímás utca 5, Parliament* ☏ *1/445–4055* ⊕ *www.ariahotelbudapest.com* ⤴ *49 rooms* ⑪ *Free breakfast.*

Casati Budapest Hotel

$$ | HOTEL | Much about this boutique hotel is small—the sauna, the fitness room, the adjoining hotel bar, Tuk Tuk, and the hotel's carbon footprint—but it's big where it counts, on style, service, and

A Short History of the Gresham Palace

The massive art nouveu palace that is now the Four Seasons Hotel began its life near the turn of the 20th century as, of all things, the headquarters of an insurance company. The London-based Gresham Life Assurance Company hired eminent architect Zsigmond Quittner and almost every prominent craftsman working in Hungary to create the building. Miksa Róth made the beautiful glass mosaics and the stained-glass windows, while the wrought-iron railings of the main staircases and the three large peacock gates opening onto the courtyard were the work of Gyula Jungfer. The Zsolnay Ceramics Factory in Pécs produced the tiles for the walls of the ground-floor passage and the courtyard, and the interior wall and floor tiles. The palace was a luxurious meeting point for British aristocrats, away from the politically charged atmosphere of Vienna and Berlin.

In 1944 the building was severely damaged by the retreating German army. In 1948 Hungary's communist government subdivided the palatial suites into tiny units to house both state offices and residential tenants; the building quickly fell into disrepair. By the 1970s it had been named a national protected landmark, but continued its slow decline; passersby would collect the precious Zsolnay tiles that had crumbled off the facade. After the overthrow of the communists in 1990, the City of Budapest took ownership of the palace. Long-term tenants, including the flamboyant actress Ida Turay, refused to vacate and filed lawsuits against the city, which finally won its case. The building was purchased by a private investment group that, along with Four Seasons, finally received permission to create the hotel. Construction commenced in 2000, and the hotel opened in June 2004.

comfort. **Pros:** central location; charming hotel bar next door; spacious rooms. **Cons:** no restaurant; located on a crowded side street; no guests under 14 years. $ *Rooms from: 39,455 HUF* ✉ *Paulay Ede utca 31, Parliament* ☎ *30/638–1731* ⊕ *www.casatibudapesthotel.com* ⤴ *25 rooms* ❍ *Free Breakfast.*

★ Four Seasons Hotel Gresham Palace

$$$$ | **HOTEL** | It doesn't get much better than this: a centrally located, super-deluxe hotel in a museum-quality landmark with the prettiest views in town. **Pros:** Four-Seasons luxury; lots of amenities; large, marble-filled bathrooms. **Cons:** no real deals to be had here; some rooms have restricted views; guests report some inconsistent service. $ *Rooms from: 179,344 HUF* ✉ *District V, Széchenyi István tér 5–6, St. Stephen's Basilica*

☎ *1/268–6000, 800/819–5053 toll-free in U.S.* ⊕ *www.fourseasons.com* ⤴ *179 rooms* ❍ *No meals* Ⓜ *M1: Vörösmarty tér.*

★ Hotel Moments

$$$ | **HOTEL** | Set on the lower end of fashionable main street Andrassy út, Hotel Moments blends modern comforts and design with the sophisticated interiors and classic elegance of this carefully restored 1880 building—think frescoes, grand staircases, parquet floors, and a glass-topped atrium. **Pros:** great location; character, charm, and elegance; excellent restaurant. **Cons:** most rooms come with showers only; located on a busy street; small gym. $ *Rooms from: €189* ✉ *Andrássy út 8, Parliament* ☎ *1/611–7000*

⊕ hotelmomentsbudapest.hu ⤳ 95
rooms ¶◎¶ Free breakfast.

Hotel President
$$$$ | HOTEL | Just behind Szabadság tér,
tucked away on Hold utca (Moon Street)
the dignified Hotel President offers a
central but quiet location. **Pros:** great
pool; gorgeous rooftop views; convenient
location. **Cons:** no parking in vicinity; small
rooms; rooms lack the character of the
building. ⑤ *Rooms from: 56,000 HUF
⊠ Hold utca 3–5, Parliament ☎ 1/510–
3400 ⊕ hotelpresident.hu ⤳ 152 rooms
¶◎¶ Free breakfast.*

Kapital Inn Boutique
$ | B&B/INN | This home away from home
offers all the feeling of residing in a
traditional Budapest residential apartment, without all the drab interiors and
outdated appliances. **Pros:** rooftop terrace;
tasteful decor; fully equipped kitchen
space. **Cons:** no elevator; no views from
windows; can be difficult to get a reservation. ⑤ *Rooms from: €110 ⊠ Aradi utca
30, Parliament ☎ 30/915–2029 ⊕ www.
facebook.com/kapitalinn ⤳ 14 rooms
¶◎¶ All-inclusive.*

Mamaison Hotel Andrassy
$$ | HOTEL | A classic Bauhaus villa a short
walk from City Park, the Mamaison Hotel
offers contemporary design, an elegant
restaurant, and comfortable rooms
with high ceilings and large, modern
bathrooms. **Pros:** great location; views
of Andrassy út; breakfast on a pleasant
patio. **Cons:** understated atmosphere; no
sauna or gym; some rooms overlook the
parking lot. ⑤ *Rooms from: 32,282 HUF
⊠ Andrássy út 111, Parliament ☎ 1/475–
5900 ⊕ www.mamaisonandrassy.com
⤳ 68 rooms ¶◎¶ Free breakfast.*

Radisson Blu Béke
$$$ | HOTEL | Fully renovated in 2017, the
Radison Blu Béke has been transformed:
rotating doors have been replaced with
sliding ones; the interiors are tastefully
outfitted in whites, golds, and tans;
the historic marble staircase is now

illuminated, and the modern features of
the rooms and dining spaces now com-
pliment the distinguished form of this
historic building. **Pros:** modern, inviting
interior; home to the elegant Zsolnay
Café; parking on-site. **Cons:** unspec-
tacular street views; located on busy
traffic street; no gym. ⑤ *Rooms from:
50,216 HUF ⊠ Teréz körút 43, Parliament
☎ 1/889–3900 ⊕ www.radissonhotels.
com ⤳ 247 rooms ¶◎¶ No meals.*

Nightlife

BARS AND PUBS

Boutiq Bar
BARS/PUBS | The bartenders at this tiny,
dimly lit bordeaux cocktail bar will mix up
whatever drink you have in mind, whether it exists on a menu or in your imagination. For a local twist, try one of their
palinka cocktails. Unfortunately, no credit
cards; this bar is cash only. ⊠ *Paulay
Ede utca 5, Parliament ☎ 30/554–2323
⊕ www.boutiqbar.hu.*

Café Zsivágó
CAFES—NIGHTLIFE | Tatty old antique chairs
and leaning reading lamps, corner nooks
with Victorian curtains, and a shiny,
wooden railing from the second floor that
looks over the gallery: Café Zsivágó is
almost a staged backdrop that insists on
memorable nights. Small local traditional
bands play here regularly on a small
ground floor space in the front and spon-
taneous concerts are held by guests who
fancy playing the old piano in the back
room. For those on shoestring budgets,
there's a decent dry Russian champagne for under 2,000 HUF a bottle. For
everyone else there is a range of lovely
cocktails on offer and a fantastic selection for teetotalers here, too. Just don't
come here hungry, as food options are
slim. ⊠ *Paulay Ede utca 55, Parliament
☎ 30/212–8125 ⊕ www.cafezsivago.hu.*

174

Kaledonia Skót Gastro & Sports Pub
(*Caledonia*)

BARS/PUBS | Caledonia is the city's only Scottish pub and it is no surprise that the rugby and football (soccer) fans take over on game days. It's probably the only place in town that serves haggis, cider on tap, and a wide range of whiskey (also available for takeout). The rustic decor is none too glamorous. The real charm is the enthusiasm of the regulars, who give this place a homey vibe. ⊠ *Mozsár utca 9, Budapest* ☎ *70/789–9130.*

Pótkulcs

BREWPUBS/BEER GARDENS | This popular grungy alternative bar lies behind an unmarked rusty brown door, tucked discreetly in an ivy-covered brick wall. Everything here feels used and well-worn and that's exactly what endears it to locals, who come here for the laid-back atmosphere, live concerts, art exhibits, and a nice, quiet garden out front. The menu is sparse and the kitchen is not open on Sunday, but the fare itself is good, hearty, and homemade. ⊠ *Csengery utca 65/b, Budapest* ✛ *Look for the opening along the ivy-covered wall* ☎ *1/269–1050* ⊕ *www.facebook.com/PotkulcsBudapest.*

360 Bar

BARS/PUBS | One would hardly imagine a rooftop space with views like this exists in the heart of downtown, but the tallest building on Andrassy út offers exactly what it says on the sign: 360-degree bird's-eye views of the city. The food is a bit pricey for what's on offer, but the cocktails here are well made and all worth it for the setting. Check the website for DJ sets and other musical and themed events. If the weather turns sour, fear not; the Sky Bar has nine heated transparent igloos that they put up on rainy days and the winter season. ⊠ *Párizsi Nagy Áruház, Andrássy út 39, Parliament* ✛ *Access is via an elevator just to the right of the Paris Department Store* ⊕ *www.360bar.hu.*

NIGHTCLUBS
Alterego Club

DANCE CLUBS | Budapest's most popular gay bar is regularly only open two nights a week, Friday and Saturday, but on those nights it's where the party's at. While there are a few other gay bars in town, this one is the most inclusive. The evening kicks off in this basement club at 7 pm with a Transvarieté Show and a full set drag show at midnight. The two dance floors feature a different genre of music every week. ⊠ *Dessewffy utca 33, Budapest* ☎ *70/345–4302* ⊕ *www.alteregoclub.hu* 🎟 *2,000 HUF; after midnight 2,500 HUF.*

WINE BARS
Divino

WINE BARS—NIGHTLIFE | This understated and dark two-room bar is all about Hungarian wine, and with 29 winemakers filling up the tables of listings above the main counter, you have your pick of the latest brands trending locally. Complete the experience by having a meat or cheese plate to accompany your wine tasting. The chain has another bar at the Gozsdu-udvar, but the one on Szent István tér is the biggest and busiest. Take a table on their little patio outside and enjoy a view of the Basilika. ⊠ *Szent István tér 3, Parliament* ☎ *70/935–3980* ⊕ *www.divinoborbar.hu.*

🎭 Performing Arts
FOLK DANCING
Aranytíz Cultural Centre

ARTS CENTERS | District 5's municipal culture house offers a wide array of performing arts events open to the public, from theatrical performances and art exhibitions to music and folk dancing in the setting of an eclectic 1880 urban residential villa. This recently renovated center, housing community programs for the neighborhoods of Belváros and Lipótváros, now has six floors that include a dance hall, a meeting room, a multifunctional theater space, an exhibition gallery, and a café as well as a garden space. While everything is intended for local community members and is in Hungarian, there is a lot on offer here and some of it is free of charge. ■TIP→ **Local dance house evenings provide an interactive experience that can help you explore Hungarian cultural life while allowing you to break the ice and get to know some locals.** Look on the website for "néptánc tanfolyam." Sessions cost 1,300 HUF. Weekly dance classes for children ages 3 to 6 take place on Wednesday. ⊠ *Arany János utca 10, Parliament* ☎ *1/354–3400* ⊕ *www.aranytiz.hu.*

LIVE MUSIC VENUES

Akvarium Klub
MUSIC CLUBS | Somewhere in between a snazzy music lounge and a culture-club dive, Akvárium is one of the city's best downtown popular music venues. A top-notch lineup of international, European, and Hungarian musical guests fills the program weekly. Newly renovated, the main music hall features a state-of-the-art sound system and sound insulation that gets good reviews from audiences and due to its location (under the square), there are no city volume restrictions imposed on its concerts. While some of the furniture and layout is a bit on the shabby side, the overall effect is on the mark for a music venue. The glass ceiling in the main room is the bottom of the water fountain located on the neighborhood square above, creating a fantastic, surreal effect, with the help of multicolor lighting. There's a huge outdoor, open-air terrace sprawled out over the concrete steps leading down to the club that is a perfect meetup point for pre-concert drinks or before a night on the town on clear summer nights. Free cultural events often take place out here, too. ⊠ *Erzsébet tér 12, Parliament* ☎ *30/860–3368* ⊕ *akvariumklub.hu.*

Gödör Klub
MUSIC CLUBS | The "Ditch Club" counterculture venue right in the heart of downtown is a bit dark and dingy, which makes it perfect for DJ sets featuring local, European, and international artists. Check out the program for its other music, dance, and culture festival events. ⊠ *Central Passage, Király utca 8–10, Deák Ferenc tér* ✛ *Just off Király utca in the Central Passage* ☎ *20/201–3868* ⊕ *www.godorklub.hu* Ⓜ *M1, M2, M3: Deák tér.*

Pontoon
CONCERTS | Ideal views of the Chain Bridge, fresh air wafting off the Danube, and a relaxed, breezy atmosphere: it's all here at Pontoon. Essentially an outdoor venue located just along the river, sadly it's only open from late spring to early fall. Sit up on the upper deck and enjoy the view or hang out on the clunky plastic chairs on the ground floor just over the water's edge, where the center space is turned into a makeshift stage hosting some of the country's best musicians and DJs. Music from jazz, folk, classical, and Roma to pop, rock, and experimental—there's something for everyone, as well as some welcome relief from midsummer's occasional heat waves at this leafy green venue. ⊠ *Antall József rakpart 1, Budapest* ✛ *Just north of the Pest side of the Chain Bridge* ☎ *30/824–2818* ⊕ *www.facebook.com/pontoonbudapest.*

The Studios (Brody Studios)
GATHERING PLACES | The Studios is the regular events branch of Budapest's one-of-a-kind BrodyLand Group, a lively membership culture club where fine arts, pop culture, and social events mix and mingle to create an atmosphere that is altogether sophisticated, cheeky, and beguiling. Rub shoulders with international actors, eccentric entrepreneurs, and artistic bohemian souls over drinks and intelligent discussion about world affairs, the arts, or whatever's trending at a Studio book launch, film, quiz, or comedy night. All events are in English and patrons are from around the world,

making for some intriguing company. While some events are exclusively open to members only, it is possible for nonmembers to book a spot at some of The Studios's many weekly programs featured on the website. You can also gain access if you are staying at Brody House. ✉ *Vörösmarty utca 38, Budapest* ☎ *1/323–7591* ⊕ *www.thestudios.life.*

MOVIE THEATERS

It was said twenty years ago that, with the arrival of shopping centers and multiplex movie theaters, Budapest's art cinemas would quickly be a thing of the past. Luckily, this is not what happened. With the support of the local community, these theaters joined forces and created a partnership designed to keep each other afloat. Hungarians and expats alike adore the casual and intellectual atmosphere of these worn-down locally run cinemas, coming here to watch popular new releases as well as European and international indie productions.

Művész Mozi (*Művész Movie Theater*)
FILM | The Művész Mozi (art movie theater) is one of the most popular in town. Its understated building has a cute little lobby decked out with worn-out chairs and a fish tank that has been there since the dawn of time. You'll find new releases as well as European and international indie productions and, unlike multiplex theaters, movies are often shown in the original language with Hungarian subtitles. Five stately old theater spaces, each named after an important figure in film history, accommodate a total of up to 500 people in seating that is equally ancient and charming. Its video shop, in the back to the left, has an extensive collection of art, indie, and popular film DVDs for rental and sale (but only some offer English subtitles or dubbing). ✉ *Teréz körút 30, Budapest* ☎ *1/224–5650* ⊕ *www.muveszmozi.hu.*

Toldi Mozi (*Toldi Movie Theater*)
FILM | Toldi, open since 1932, is the primary venue for the Verzio Human

Rights Film Festival in November and participates regularly in other international film festivals as well as occasionally holding film talks and musical concerts. It is also a hub for local activists and arts and creative types who you can find spilling out onto the streets from the lobby bar. Movies here are often shown in the original language with Hungarian subtitles, instead of dubbed. Most of the staff speak at least three or four languages and are happy to provide information about their programs and featured films in English. ✉ *Bajcsy-Zsilinszky út 36–38, Budapest* ☎ *1/224–5650* ⊕ *www. toldimozi.hu.*

OPERA

★ **Magyar Állami Operaház** (*Hungarian State Opera*)
OPERA | Budapest's main venue for opera and classical ballet is located in a magnificent neo-Renaissance building dating from 1884. The work of famed architect Miklós Ybl, it is one of the city's most prominent and iconic landmarks. The exterior features two unique buxom marble sphinxes guarding the driveway that curves upward from the street to the main entrance, a reminder that special guests used to arrive here by horse and carriage. Proceeding inside, the main lobby is flanked by Alajos Strobl's "romantic-realist" limestone statues of Franz Liszt and 19th-century Hungarian composer, Ferenc Erkel, the father of Hungarian opera. The marble staircases and wood-paneled corridors usher guests into gilt lime-green salons, ornate private theater boxes, or the glittering jewel box that is the main auditorium. Helmeted sphinxes bow their heads beneath a dazzling frescoed ceiling by Károly Lotz. Lower down there are frescoes everywhere, with intertwined motifs of Apollo and Dionysus. In its early years the Budapest Opera was conducted by Gustav Mahler (1888–91), and after World War II by Otto Klemperer (1947–50). Badly damaged during the siege of 1944–45, it was restored for its 1984

Magyar Állami Operaház has a reputation for its exceptional acoustics but the building's main draw is its opulent architecture, inside and out.

centenary. Closed again for renovation in the past few years, the opera house has been busy modernizing the orchestra pit and dressing rooms, creating more handicap accessibility, and touching up the ceiling seccos and interior facades. This has been the biggest overhaul the building has seen in over thirty years, delivering an even more spectacular experience. If you want to have a proper look inside, there are daily tours of the opera house in English, which are best booked in advance online or in-person at the box office. Of course, the best way to experience the Opera House is to see a ballet or opera, which is an experience that cannot be recommended highly enough. The main season runs from September to mid-June. Tickets can be purchased online as well as at the box office. While the most coveted of tickets could cost you a couple hundred euros, don't think you are going to have to break the bank to partake; one can sometimes find tickets in the back rows for less than 10 euros. Popular Hungarian productions, like Erkel's patriotic opera *Bánk Bán* and

Béla Bartók's *Blue Beard's Castle,* are still performed regularly but there are also guest performances by international troupes as well as a plethora of classical operas from Italy and around Europe. Most feature subtitles in Hungarian and English, but it is good to double check before purchase. ⊠ *Andrássy út 22, Budapest* ☎ *1/814–7100* ⊕ *www.opera. hu.*

Shopping

BOOKS

★ Bestsellers Bookshop

BOOKS/STATIONERY | From Hungarian classic and contemporary literature to cookbooks and history books, Bestsellers has the best selection of translations of Hungarian literature in the English language available in town. It also sells English language newspapers and magazines and regional literature in translation while also stocking the works of trendy contemporary English-language writers. ⊠ *Október 6 utca 11, Budapest* ☎ *1/312– 1295* ⊕ *www.bestsellers.hu.*

Thanks, It's Vintage

From pricey vintage designer threads to antique vases, unique jewels and pins to Soviet watches, to second-hand books and vintage photos, Budapest is teeming with secondhand, antique, vintage, retro, *turkáló* (grab bag), and *kilós áru* (pay by weight) shopping opportunities.

After the fall of communism, Western-style clothing and goods were all the rage in Hungary. Few people could afford to buy Western fashions new, but fortunately there was an influx of clothing and home goods donations from charitable organizations in the United Kingdom and the Netherlands. There were no established thrift stores in Hungary (nothing could be classified as a charity shop or thrift store during communist rule as, theoretically, everyone was supposed to be equally provided for by the state), so shipments were funneled into shops that became known as "Angol Bolts" (English shops). These stores placed an English and/or Dutch flag out front or in the shop window as code to shoppers. Some shops still bear the union jack in their logo to this day.

While the thrift market never lost popularity in Budapest, thanks to consistently lower salaries than western European counterparts, in the late-2000s it experienced a boom. Perhaps fueled by the popularity of the local "ruin bar" movement and its eclectic "found" aesthetic, suddenly unique, eclectic, and retro furnishings and clothing were all the rage with young Hungarians. Along with vintage Western goods, Hungarian nostalgia took off, too. Today, flea markets and *garázsvásár* (garage sales) are extremely popular and the vintage market is thriving, so there are plenty of treasures to be found.

Popular Shops

Antifactory Vintage Shop. A secondhand shop focusing on a selection of high-quality vintage clothes that appeal to the proprietor's sense of style. Check out their social accounts for updates on what's on offer. ✉ *Paulay Ede utca 43, Budapest* ☎ *20/255–6228* ⊕ *www. facebook.com/antifactory.*

Gardrob. A popular local secondhand shop with its own sense of style, they will also buy unwanted pieces from your wardrobe, if you fancy making room in your suitcase. ✉ *Király utca 42, Budapest* ☎ *30/526–6816* ⊕ *www. facebook.com/kiralygardrob.*

Humana Vintage Butik. One of Hungary's most popular secondhand shops has extended into the boutique trade. You'll find unique, quirky, or just plain bizarre items at rock-bottom prices here. ✉ *Károly körút 8, Budapest* ☎ *30/453–3466* ⊕ *www.humanahaszn-altruha.hu.*

Retrock. A vintage and designer shop that also features creations by a host of local Hungarian designers. It's a designer shop, and not cheap by any means, but filled with fantastic treasures old and new. ✉ *Anker köz 2-4, Budapest* ☎ *30/472–3636* ⊕ *www. retrock.com.*

Szputnyik. This hip, sceney clothing and accessories shop sells new and used (upcycled) items. Carrying fashion brands with eco-friendly policies and offering workshops on how to recycle and upcycle old items, it's not just a store, it's a concept. ✉ *Dohány utca 20, Budapest* ☎ *20/281–5410* ⊕ *www. szputnyikshop.hu.*

CLOTHING

Manier

CLOTHING | With clothes this flashy and conspicuous, it's not a surprise Manier works regularly with the opera house, celebrity musicians, contemporary dancers, and performing artists. Anikó Németh's baroque, rococo, and art deco-inspired collections express the dramatic and bring the wearer out to the forefront. Perusing the shop's selection of frilly dresses, feathery corsets, and colorful coats, those with a flair for the ostentatious will make waves sporting a select piece from this premier designer's shop. ⊠ *Haute Couture Salon, Dalszínház utca 10, first floor, apartment #2, Budapest* ☎ *1/354–1878* ⊕ *www.manier.hu.*

NUBU

CLOTHING | Eastern European fashion featuring dark colors and elegant, minimalist cuts with a focus on sustainability and durability, the clothing line of NUBU is subtle and graceful and definitely carries Hungarian design elements throughout its collection. ⊠ *Andrássy út 15, Budapest* ☎ *70/607–4903* ⊕ *www.nubu.hu.*

Paula

CLOTHING | A selection of labels from three Hungarian female fashion designers branded as slow fashion, Paula features women's clothing, accessories, bags, and a selection of jewelry from Linda Melinda, Vengru, and Rulied. ⊠ *Paulay Ede utca 15, Budapest* ☎ *20/994–5360* ⊕ *www.paulastorebudapest.com.*

FOOD AND DRINK

Cinq Filles Budapest

FOOD/CANDY | Zsolt Unger and Szilárd Demján's signature Cinq Filles chocolatier is filled with a range of designer chocolate, sweets, wine, and champagne, as well as souvenir items. ⊠ *Paulay Ede utca 44, Budapest* ☎ *30/638–9213* ⊕ *www.cinqfillesbudapest.com.*

HOME GOODS AND DESIGN

PointOne

HOUSEHOLD ITEMS/FURNITURE | PointOne is a furniture and home accessories shop featuring internationally known Hungarian interior designers. The showroom just off of Szabadság tér includes fresh concepts by Vitra, Diesel Living, Milliken, and KAZA Concrete. A modern take on traditional styles, the warm dusty colors and smooth rounded shapes are worth a visit for home design fans looking to discover new brands. ⊠ *Szabadság tér 14, Budapest* ☎ *30/181–6100* ⊕ *www. pointone.hu* ☉ *Closed weekends.*

Zsolnay Porcelain

CERAMICS/GLASSWARE | One of Hungary's most esteemed, iconic brands, Zsolnay ceramics have been coveted for over 160 years. Famous artists and architects like József Rippl-Rónai, Victor Vasarely, and Ödön Lechner would settle for nothing less than Zsolnay's distinct Pirogranite tiles. Their bright yellow and green tiles resist damp, cold, and pollution and can be seen on some of Hungary's most beautiful buildings, public objects, fine art, and on the cserépkályha (tile stoves) in Hungary's most prestigious villas. Zsolnay's unique Eosin pieces, created employing an entirely original process that results in an especially colorful and iridescent glaze, are one of the company's highest valued products. Its porcelain tableware, vases, and ornamental objects bear a porcelain glaze that is known the world over. In fact, Vilmos Zsolnay was awarded the French Legion of Honor in 1878 for discovering it. Open daily from 9 to 7, the Budapest shop offers ample opportunity to ogle gorgeous works of art up close (with the added benefit of taking it home if you like). ⊠ *József nádor tér 12, Budapest* ☎ *1/400–7118* ⊕ *www.zsolnay.hu.*

JEWELRY

The Garden Studio

JEWELRY/ACCESSORIES | A retail collective supporting local Hungarian designers, there's a wide range of jewelry, bags, shoes, clothes, ceramics, and household accessories and artwork for sale here. ✉ *Paulay Ede utca 18, Budapest* ☎ *30/848–6163* ⊕ *www.thegardenstudio. hu.*

SHOES AND ACCESSORIES

DRK (*Dorko*)

SHOES/LUGGAGE/LEATHER GOODS | Founded in 2013, Hungarian designer Dorko's sneakers, casual jackets, and sportswear have a cult local following for their regular collaborations with sculptors, street artists, musicians, architects, and tattoo artists. A popular local brand and unique souvenir of Budapest, there is plenty to choose from at their flagship shop on Andrássy út. ✉ *Andrássy út 33, Budapest* ☎ *30/677–7102* ⊕ *www.dorko.eu.*

 Activities

Escape House

LOCAL SPORTS | If you like discovering new places, good old-fashioned mysteries, and problem solving, then you will love Escape House, located in a residential building's basement space since 2013, and one of the best introductions to the Budapest Escape Room phenomenon. It is a classic escape room game with thought-provoking clues including logical, mathematical, general knowledge, and physical tasks that keep players engaged throughout. Once the gamemaster breaks down the rules and objective, you will have one hour to complete the mission. It's best to wear warm, comfortable clothes and shoes, as you will be in a dusty, cold cellar space and only occasionally moving around. Children should be accompanied by adults. Bookings for groups of two to six people can be made in advance online or by phone. ✉ *Csengery utca 66, Budapest* ☎ *70/216–5585* ⊕ *www.escapehouse.hu.*

Mystique Room

LOCAL SPORTS | Dress up like a monk and solve the mystery of the monastery or break into a samurai's house. These are just two of the nine great adventures you can go on at the Mystique Room, a classic Hungarian escape room experience featuring costumes and accessories that bring the story to life. Great for adults and kids alike, you'll have one hour to follow the clues requiring you to use your problem solving, critical thinking skills, and common sense and, if you are lucky, break out of the room in the nick of time. It's best to dress for comfort here, as you will be on your toes, looking for clues in dusty basement rooms. Games usually accommodate two to eight people. Bookings should be made in advance online or by phone. ✉ *Szent István körút 9, Budapest* ☎ *1/786–7394* ⊕ *www. mystiqueroom.hu.*

Chapter 10

MARGITSZIEGET (MARGARET ISLAND) AND NORTHERN PEST

DISTRICT 13

Updated by
Esther Holbrook

 Sights
★★★★☆

 Restaurants
★★★☆☆

 Hotels
★★☆☆☆

 Shopping
★★★☆☆

 Nightlife
★☆☆☆☆

NEIGHBORHOOD SNAPSHOT

TOP EXPERIENCES	QUICK BITES
■ **Margaret Island:** Enjoy an afternoon exploring the medieval ruins in one of Budapest's most popular green spaces. ■ **The Flipper Museum:** Play some of the oldest pinball machines around in this classic pinball museum. ■ **Pozsonyi Street:** Grab coffee at Briós Cafe or have a traditional Hungarian meal at local favorite Pozsonyi Kisvendéglő. ■ **Palatinus Spa:** Beat the heat at one of the city's most popular summer hangouts. ■ **Lehel Market:** Inside this infamously gaudy exterior is one of the best fresh produce markets in town.	■ **Nemsüti.** Hole-in-the-wall vegetarian salad and sandwich bar offering healthy, fresh snacks and light meals. ⊠ *Jászai Mari tér 4b Újlipótváros* ⊕ *www. nemsuti.hu* Ⓜ *Tram 4, 6; trolleybus 75, 76: Jászai Mari tér* ■ **Három Tarka Macska Artisan Bakery.** A very popular local bakery featuring fresh-baked sweet and salty breads and pastries. ⊠ *Pozsonyi út 41, Újlipótváros* ⊕ *www. haromtarkamacska.hu* Ⓜ *Trolleybus 75, 76: Szent István Park* ■ **Lángos Centrum at the Lehel Csarnok.** Don't miss traditional Hungarian fried bread with toppings (and beer) at Budapest's best market. ⊠ *Váci út 9–15, Újlipótváros* ⊕ *www.facebook.com/larumbt* Ⓜ *M3: Lehel tér*

GETTING HERE

A sleepy residential neighborhood with a blast from the past vibe, it is just close enough to the city center to get there by foot but just far enough that you might want to take Tram 2 to Jászai Mari tér or M3 to Nyugati pályaudvar or Lehel tér. Trolleybuses 15, 75, and 76 also pass through here. Margaret Island is not open to regular car traffic. If you are going by car to District 13 proper, please take care: this is a pedestrian-heavy neighborhood with a confusing right-of-way system.

PLANNING YOUR TIME

Once the hunting grounds of kings, then the convent home of revered Saint Margaret, there is history, relaxation, and nature to be enjoyed here. Visit the Palatinus Spa, then rent a four-person pedal car and head north on the pedestrian paths to discover the Japanese garden or the decadent flower beds that surround the old complex of the Grand Margitsziget Hotel. The Pest-side Újlipótváros offers Pozsonyi út filled with independent retailers, Bauhaus-style apartment buildings, as well as the offbeat local watering hole, the Figaró Kert garden café, and the cozy intellectual hub that is Kino Coffeehouse.

More than 2½ km (1½ miles) long and covering nearly 200 acres, Margaret Island was first mentioned almost 2,000 years ago as the summer residence of the commander of the Roman garrison at nearby Aquincum. Later known as the Island of Rabbits (Insula Leporum), it was a royal hunting ground during the Árpád dynasty. King Imre, who reigned from 1196 to 1204, held court here, and several convents and monasteries were built here during the Middle Ages. (During a walk around the island, you'll see the ruins of a few of these buildings.)

Its current name is taken from St. Margaret (1242–71), the pious daughter of King Béla IV, who at the ripe old age of 10 retired to a Dominican nunnery situated here from the 13th to the 16th centuries. Today, it's an island park that's ideal for strolling, jogging (there's a top-notch running track), sunbathing, or just loafing. Vehicular traffic is barred here (except for buses and taxis), so it's pedestrian-friendly and a welcome relief from the city's bustle.

To the east of Margaret Island, across the river in Pest, lies District 13. This entire area was a swampy, industrial zone outside city limits just over 100 years ago. Now, it's one of the largest residential districts with a quaint shopping street and one of the city's most popular green spaces. The northern half is called Angyalföld (Angel's Land). Traditionally a working-class neighborhood, it has been undergoing a recent burst of gentrification ever since Budapest's office construction boom in the 1990s but remains a quiet, out-of-the-way locale, even though it lies just north of the city center.

The Újlipótváros neighborhood in the southern half of the district is a great example of how communities can find a balance between being trendy and keeping their local vibe. Visitors will find excellent examples of Hungarian architecture from the mid-war period, a period of relative independence for Hungary when most of the apartment buildings located here were originally built. As Hungarians find it best not to flaunt their wealth, hidden inside these mostly uniform, respectable but fashionable, Bauhaus-style apartment buildings are a range of unique courtyards and apartments, some with lavish tiling and stained glass and others with lush green gardens. New residential projects like Park West 2 at Lehel tér are targeting young urban dwellers by building modern, smart homes with extras like additional green space and an environmentally friendly transportation infrastructure. Such developments will likely contribute to the growth of this district, while retaining its appeal.

Pozsonyi út is the gem of this neighborhood lined with independent coffee shops, bakeries, bookshops, clothing designers, hat makers, and more. Old mom-and-pop shops are commonplace here and there are some suprising specialty trades, run by the original owners, the likes of which have long vanished elsewhere. Symbols and signs announcing their trade are often hung above sidewalks in front of the main entrances or painted on the walls, adding to the timeless nature of the district.

Szent István Park, originally called Lipótvárosi Park, is as old as the district itself, opening in 1928. It is a popular green space that regularly features free community events like concerts and holiday celebrations where locals of all ages gather. Among its statues is one honoring Raoul Wallenberg, the Swedish diplomat who saved tens of thousands of Jewish Hungarians from the Nazis, many from this neighborhood. The district's Jewish community is an integral part of its history and life. During WWII, many of the yellow star houses, residences where Jews were confined—if they were not interned in the Ghetto in the 7th District—were located here. You can find out more about Budapest's yellow star houses at ⊕ www.yellowstarhouses.org.

Sights

Dagály Termálfürdő

SPA—SIGHT | Located in a working-class neighborhood, this off-the-beaten-path bathhouse was long considered an everyman's bathhouse until the government decided to give it a makeover to use it as a venue to host the 17th FINA Aquatics World Championships in 2017. While many were worried that it would lose its basic charms, the results of the makeover were a delightful surprise to bathers old and new. There are discounts for families, which means it is still very much a part of the community and hasn't lost its roots. Local families come for the green space and to make use of the new facilities, including a large swimming pool, lazy river, playground, basketball court, and sunbeds. Visitors in the know come for the healing waters and authentic bathhouse experience. Located just off the riverfront, it also has a picturesque setting and good view of the Danube from the lookout point. ✉ *Népfürdő utca 36, Budapest* ☎ *30/160–0150* ⊕ *www. mnsk.hu* ☒ *2,500 HUF.*

Flipper Múzeum (*Pinball Museum*)

MUSEUM | **FAMILY** | Part museum space, part gaming center, the carefully curated and maintained Flipper Múzeum was started by avid pinball enthusiasts to inspire pinball enthusiasm in kids of all ages. Admission allows you to play almost all of the 130 machines featured here for free and for as long as you like (some machines are ornamental as they are not working anymore). Look for Terminator, Star Wars, and Mario Brothers pinball games or simple amusment park shooter games dating back to the late 19th century. Offically registered as a museum, it adopts an arcade vibe in the evening as players flip away until midnight most nights. ✉ *Radnóti Miklós utca 18, Budapest* ⊕ *www.flippermuzeum.hu* ☒ *3,500 HUF* ⊙ *Closed Mon. and Tues.*

Set in an unremarkable residential building, the Flipper Muzeum is devoted to classic Pinball.

Imre Nagy Szobor

TOUR—SIGHT | Hungary's Prime Minister at the time of the 1956 Revolution, Imre Nagy was executed by the Russians for his lenience towards the revolters and buried as a traitor. On June 16, 1989, the anniversary of his execution, Nagy was rehabilitated and reburied with full honors, one of the events marking the change in regime. The removal of his statue from Vértanúk ter (Matryrs' Square) in 2018 to make way for the reconstructed Monument of National Martyrs was the talk of the town for months (opposition parties accused Viktor Orbán's right-wing government of historical revisionism). District 13 volunteered to adopt it, placing it here in Jászai Mari tér overlooking the Danube. ☒ *Jászai Mari tér, Budapest* 🚇 *Free.*

Margit híd (*Margaret Bridge*)

BRIDGE/TUNNEL | At the southern end of Margaret Island, the Margaret Bridge is the closer of the two island entrances for those coming from downtown Buda or Pest. Just north of the Chain Bridge, the bridge walkway provides gorgeous mid-river views of Castle Hill and Parliament. The original bridge was built during the 1840s by French engineer Ernest Gouin in collaboration with Gustave Eiffel. Toward the end of 1944, the bridge was blown up by the retreating Nazis while crowded with rush-hour traffic. It was rebuilt in the same unusual shape—forming an obtuse angle in midstream, with a short leg leading down to the island—and has been refurbished in recent years, now sporting a bike path on the north-facing side that pedestrians, joggers, and bicyclists all share on their way to the island. ☒ *Margit-sziget* Ⓜ *M2: Batthyány tér, M1: Nyugati Train Station then Tram 4, 6.*

Palatinus fürdő (*Palatinus Strand Baths*)

SWIMMING | FAMILY | Dating to 1919, Palatinus Thermal and Open-air Bath was the first public outdoor bathhouse in the city and at that time was home to the largest pool in all of Europe. They added the wave pool and the Bauhaus main building designed by Janáky István in 1937. The

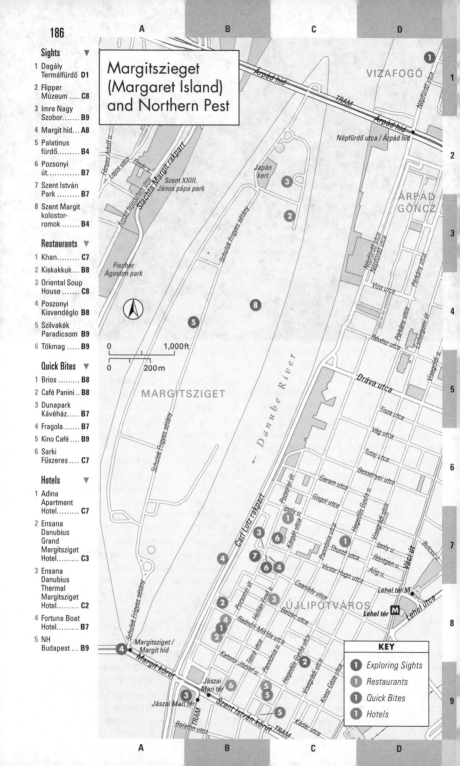

Sights ▼

1 Dagály Termálfürdő **D1**

2 Flipper Múzeum **C8**

3 Imre Nagy Szobor....... **B9**

4 Margit híd... **A8**

5 Palatinus fürdő......... **B4**

6 Pozsonyi út............. **B7**

7 Szent István Park **B7**

8 Szent Margit kolostor-romok **B4**

Restaurants ▼

1 Khan......... **C7**

2 Kiskakkuk... **B8**

3 Oriental Soup House **C8**

4 Poszonyi Kisvendéglo **B8**

5 Szilvakék Paradicsom **B9**

6 Tökmag **B9**

Quick Bites ▼

1 Brios **B8**

2 Café Panini .. **B8**

3 Dunapark Kávéház..... **B7**

4 Fragola....... **B7**

5 Kino Café **B9**

6 Sarki Fűszeres **C7**

Hotels ▼

1 Adina Apartment Hotel......... **C7**

2 Ensana Danubius Grand Margitsziget Hotel......... **C3**

3 Ensana Danubius Thermal Margitsziget Hotel......... **C2**

4 Fortuna Boat Hotel......... **B7**

5 NH Budapest ... **B9**

Margitszieget (Margaret Island) and Northern Pest

entire complex received a refresh and upgrade in 2017. The complex includes full-length lap pools, waterslides, saunas, a geothermal steam room, and ten thermal pools (most of which are open year-round). The grounds are huge, and while there is a café on-site, you might want to pack your own food and drinks to picnic on the lawn. The indoor pools are spacious and open and not as busy as other thermal baths in the city. ⊠ *Margaret Island, Margit-sziget* ☏ *1/340–4500* ⊕ *www.palatinusstrand.hu* Ⓜ *Bus 26.*

Pozsonyi út

PEDESTRIAN MALL | Pozsonyi út has a special place in the Újlipótváros neighborhood. In reaction to developers' plans in the 1990s to turn the district into a shopping mall hub, residents decided to work together to independently turn Pozsonyi into their own premier shopping street. The surprising success of that grassroots initiative resulted in a retail street that doesn't feel like a commercial zone, but a thriving center of local businesses. Support local businesses and the neighborhood's resolve as you wander cute shops and boutiques and stop at great spots for coffee and lunch. ⊠ *Pozsonyi út, Újlipótváros.*

Szent István Park

NATIONAL/STATE PARK | **FAMILY** | Founded in 1928, Szent István Park (originally called Lipótvárosi Park) is as old as the district itself. Full of trees and flower beds, a small playground and a separate dog run, this little park is a popular recreational spot where locals of all ages get together for community events, concerts, and holiday celebrations. Among its statues is one honoring Raoul Wallenberg, the Swedish diplomat who saved tens of thousands of Jewish Hungarians from the Nazis, many from this neighborhood. ⊠ *Szent István Park, Budapest* ☒ *Free* Ⓜ *M3: Lehel tér.*

Szent Margit kolostor-romok (*Ruins of Saint Margaret's Dominican Cloister*) **ARCHAEOLOGICAL SITE** | The ruins of this Dominican Cloister once served as the home of the Holy Saint Margaret, patron saint of the island. According to legend, King Béla IV honored a vow he made to give his child to the church if he was successful in battle against invading forces. He founded this nunnery on the Island as the convent home to his daughter Margaret who lived here from the age of 10 until her death. She was canonized long after her death by Pope Pius XII in 1943. Being an important figure in Hungarian historical lore, Margaret is usually depicted in artwork wearing a nun's habit and holding a white lily and a book. Her grave, marked by a red marble tombstone, can be found in the middle of the excavated building site, to this day covered in fresh wreaths and flowers. ⊠ *Margit-sziget* ☒ *Free.*

🍴 Restaurants

★ Khan

$$$ | **ASIAN FUSION** | Run by three young Vietnamese-Hungarians with a passion for cooking and a background in fashion and design, this trendy Asian-fusion restaurant is a sister restaurant to popular Sáo in the Jewish Quarter. The stylish setting features contemporary art, concrete columns, Vietnamese ceramic bowls, and the menu includes all the expected (slightly overpriced) pan-Asian staples. **Known for:** trendy spot; dumplings, pho, tempura, summer rolls; stylish setting. ⑤ *Average main: 4,000 HUF* ⊠ *Ipoly utca 3, Újlipótváros* ☏ *20/451–1737* Ⓜ *Trolleybus 75: Ipoly utca.*

★ Kiskakukk

$$$ | **EASTERN EUROPEAN** | The art deco facade of the Little Cuckoo restaurant evokes the history of this fashionable residential neighborhood street. The setting today is comfortable; wood-paneled walls and leather-upholstered chairs give the place a sophisticated, albeit homey, feel.

Did You Know?

Margaret Island is named for the Árpád Dynasty princess, Saint Margaret, who spent her life at the Dominican convent here after her father, King Béla IV swore an oath that if Hungary were to be saved from the continued ravages of the Tatars, he would offer up his yet-unborn daughter to the church.

Imre Nagy's statue, long a focal point for Hungarian patriots, was erected in Heroes' Square in 1996 but controversially relocated to Northern Pest in late 2018.

Sunday finds multigenerational Hungarian families enjoying the familiar and attentive service. All the classic Hungarian poultry dishes are well done, including goose and duck leg with cabbage, and there are a few refined dishes, too, such as veal medallions in cream sauce and lamb with rosemary. **Known for:** classic dishes like goose and duck leg with cabbage; large portions; attentive service. $ *Average main: 4000 HUF* ✉ *Pozsonyi út 12, Nyugati Train Station* ☎ *1-786-3439* ⊕ *www.kiskakukk.hu* Ⓜ *M3: Nyugati pályaudvar.*

Oriental Soup House

$$ | **ASIAN FUSION** | The young and dynamic energy in this hopping Vietnamese spot in Újlipótváros feels a million miles (or at least, a few decades) away from some of the more traditional dining options in the area. The menu features a wide variety of pho, and great desserts. Seating is at communal tables with backless wooden stools. Oriental Soup House has two locations, but the one on Balzac utca is a local favorite. Reserve ahead if you want to visit as it is always busy. **Known for:** 11 types of pho; very trendy and busy spot; Vietnamese chè dessert. $ *Average main: 2,000 HUF* ✉ *Balzac utca 35, Újlipótváros* ☎ *70/617-3535.*

Poszonyi Kisvendéglo

$$ | **HUNGARIAN** | Rock-bottom prices ensure a crowd most days for lunch and dinner at this well-loved neighborhood *vendeglo* (restaurant serving home-cooking). Big bowls of *jókai bableves* (bean soup) are sopped up with fresh white bread, and classics like *borjúpaprikás* (veal paprikash) are made the way Hungarian grandmothers used to make them—with plenty of lard. **Known for:** hearty meals; tavern-style atmosphere; great value. $ *Average main: 2,500 HUF* ✉ *Radnóti Miklos utca 38, Újlipótváros* ☎ *1/787-4877* ⊕ *www.pozsonyi-kisvendeglo.eatbu.com.*

Szilvakék Paradicsom

$$$ | **HUNGARIAN** | **FAMILY** | The "Plum Blue Tomato" is the equivalent of a classic '80s restaurant-pub or Hungarian

roadside diner with its warm wood paneling and advertising posters of products from days long gone. Don't expect the waiters to jump to attention (that's just not the Hungarian way), but they will attend to anything you ask, including rearranging tables to accommodate families and larger groups. Enjoy hearty turn-of-the-century cooking with some modern twists, but nothing much for vegetarians on this meat-heavy menu. If the weather is good, you can catch the neighborhood in motion from the big street-facing terrace. **Known for:** gulyásleves (Hungarian soup); family-friendly; nostalgic decor. ⑤ *Average main: 3,500 HUF* ✉ *Pannónia utca 5-7, Budapest* ☎ *1/339–8099* ⊕ *www.bluetomato.hu* Ⓜ *Bus 15, 115: Szent István körút.*

Tökmag

$$ | **VEGETARIAN** | This popular hole-in-the-wall vegan street food joint sometimes has lines all the way out onto the street, a sure sign that you should get on that line. Healthy salads and soups are on offer but it's Tökmag's burgers that have people raving and coming back. Be sure to order a side of tasty deep-fried veggie chips, too. Open daily until 8 pm. **Known for:** beetroot burger ; amazing veggie chips; vegan. ⑤ *Average main: 2,000 HUF* ✉ *Hollán Ernő utca 5, Budapest* ☎ *70/908–9717* ⊕ *www.tokmagvegan.hu* ☉ *Closed weekends.*

☕ Coffee and Quick Bites

Brios

$$ | **BAKERY** | This cool and cheery spot located halfway up beautiful Pozsonyi út is the place to meet for breakfast in District 13. With a range of breakfast plates available all day and unique and healthy salad and sandwich options, it's rarely quiet. The coffee is excellent and if you've got a sweet tooth, be sure to try the fresh-baked pastries before they sell out. **Known for:** fresh-baked pastries; all-day breakfast; outdoor seating on Pozsonyi út. ⑤ *Average main: 2,000 HUF*

✉ *Pozsonyi út 16, Budapest* ☎ *1/794– 6262* ⊕ *www.brios.eatbu.com.*

Café Panini

$$ | **EUROPEAN** | A lovely little eatery just off the waterfront, Panini is perfect for small groups looking for a place to brunch away a couple of hours. There are tables with seating for five to six inside the tidy, no-frills, two-room restaurant, and a couple of tables outside facing the Danube. It's pet-friendly and everything on their menu, from the croque madame to their Waldorf salad, is fresh and tasty. **Known for:** breakfast menu; pleasant atmosphere; Danube views. ⑤ *Average main: 2,400 HUF* ✉ *Radnóti Miklós utca 45, Budapest* ☎ *70/946–8072* ⊕ *www. cafepanini.hu.*

Dunapark Kávéház

$$$ | **EASTERN EUROPEAN** | This gorgeous Bauhaus building nestled on the north side of Szent István Park is home to the favorite local spot for a special occasion meal or dessert. The huge windows of the café and restaurant look out on the Danube bank and Szent István Park, and they also have a terrace, which is the perfect place to linger during the summer. The unique oval shape of the building and elegant space and furnishings throw visitors back to its '30s heyday. Sample pastries at the open bakery in front or sit down for an elegant, traditional lunch with friends. **Known for:** old-world charm; unique Bauhaus architectural style; cakes and coffee. ⑤ *Average main: 3,500 HUF* ✉ *Pozsonyi út 38, Budapest* ☎ *1/786– 1009* ⊕ *dunaparkkavehaz.hu.*

Fragola

$ | **CAFÉ** | **FAMILY** | There are a few ice cream parlors in Budapest worthy of mention and Fragola is one of them. A locally owned shop featuring 120 original homemade flavors, Fragola is famed for the the quality of the ingredients. With 13 locations in town, you don't have to venture to Szent István Park to try it but if you are in the neighborhood, don't pass it by. **Known for:** original flavors; sugar-free and vegan options; tiny benches outside. ⑤ *Average main: 1,200 HUF* ✉ *Pozsonyi út 49, Budapest* ☎ *20/467–2273* ⊕ *www. fragolafagylaltozo.hu.*

Kino Café

$ | HUNGARIAN | An independent movie theater, café, and culture house in one, Kino's outdoor seating has a smart view to the beautiful and impressive baroque revival building next door, Vígszínház. This is the perfect quaint intellectual spot to take a break for a cake and coffee, meet up with friends over a glass of wine, or take in an obscure award-winning documentary film. **Known for:** low-priced all-day breakfast dishes; delicious cakes; movie theater. ⑤ *Average main: 1200 HUF* ✉ *Szent István körút 16, Budapest* ☎ *1/781–9453* ⊕ *www.kinocafemozi.hu* ▭ *No credit cards.*

Sarki Fűszeres

$$$ | BISTRO | This romantic café, a canopy of vines hanging over the art deco facade and surrounded by trees, feels like a charming Parisian corner. A range of gourmet delicatessen counter displays tempting and impressive selection of specialty cheeses, meat, and fresh bread, also available for takeout. Perfect for a traditional European cold plate breakfast, a light lunch, or early dinner. Closing times vary, but it's usually 8 pm, and 3 pm on Sunday. **Known for:** gourmet products; charming setting; great sandwiches and picnics. ⑤ *Average main: 4,000 HUF* ✉ *Pozsonyi út 53–55, Budapest* ☎ *30/347–7037* ⊕ *www.sarki-fuszeres.hu.*

 Hotels

Adina Apartment Hotel

$$ | HOTEL | FAMILY | An international chain that focuses on a homey feel and local experience, the Budapest Adina Hotel is located on an appropriately average street in District 13. **Pros:** free wellness facilities and swimming pool; in-room amenities are great for families or

extended stays; some apartments have double balconies. **Cons:** bathrooms need an update; public spaces a little dull; restaurant is breakfast only. ⑤ *Rooms from: 43,042 HUF* ✉ *Hegedűs Gyula utca 52, Budapest* ☎ *1/236–8800* ⊕ *www. adinahotels.com* ⇄ *21 studios, 58 one-bedroom apartments, 18 two-bedroom apartments* ⦿ *No meals* Ⓜ *M3: Lehel tér.*

Ensana Danubius Grand Margitsziget Hotel

$$$ | HOTEL | This older, much more attractive (at least on the outside) next-door neighbor of the Thermal Hotel on leafy Margitsziget was built in 1873 by Opera House architect Miklós Ybl in neo-Renaissance style. **Pros:** access to Danubius Thermal's spa facilities; tranquil, green oasis; more elegant exterior than the Thermal Hotel. **Cons:** limited transportation options; dated interiors; removed from city sights. ⑤ *Rooms from: 46,629 HUF* ✉ *Margitsziget, Margit-sziget* ☎ *1/889–4752* ⊕ *www.ensanahotels.com* ⇄ *150 rooms* ⦿ *Free breakfast* Ⓜ *M3: Népfürdő utca.*

Ensana Danubius Thermal Margitsziget Hotel (*Thermal Margaret Island Health Spa Hotel*)

$$$ | HOTEL | Bubbling up from ancient thermal springs, curative waters fill the pools of this established spa hotel on the island's northern end. **Pros:** natural thermal springs; bewildering list of relaxing and medicinal spa treatments; stylish rooms. **Cons:** removed from city center; limited transport options; too quiet for some. ⑤ *Rooms from: 46,629 HUF* ✉ *Margit-sziget* ☎ *1/889–4752* ⊕ *www. ensanahotels.com/en/health-spa-hotels/ destinations/hungary/budapest* ⇄ *245 rooms* ⦿ *Free breakfast* Ⓜ *M3: Népfürdő utca.*

Fortuna Boat Hotel

$ | HOTEL | For a change of pace, you can bed down on this retired 1967 vessel, which once plied the waters of the Danube and is now anchored near the Pest side of the Margaret Bridge. **Pros:** unique and original; Danube views; rooftop restaurant. **Cons:** headroom is low; not close to public transport; bathrooms are small. ⑤ *Rooms from: 17,934 HUF* ✉ *Szent István Park, Lower Quay, Budapest* ⊹ *Across the street from Szent István Park* ☎ *70/389–4305* ⊕ *fortunaboat.com* ➴ *40 rooms* �’⊘❘ *No meals* Ⓜ *M2: Jászai Mari tér and an 8-min walk.*

NH Budapest

$$ | **HOTEL** | Extra-thick mattresses, a pick-your-own pillow bar, and free ironing service are some of the welcome extras that set this Spanish-owned business hotel apart. **Pros:** 10-minute walk to central sights; plain breakfast; 5-minute walk to Tram stop. **Cons:** no views; bland decor; needs maintenance. ⑤ *Rooms from: 41,249 HUF* ✉ *Vígszínház utca 3, Budapest* ☎ *1/815-4346* ⊕ *www.nh-hotels.com* ➴ *160 rooms* ❘⊘❘ *No meals.*

 Nightlife

BARS AND PUBS

Figaró Kert

BREWPUBS/BEER GARDENS | From the street, you would hardly imagine just behind the fence is one of the cutest neighborhood garden bars. Inside, cheery fold-up rainbow-colored chairs surround a tiny koi pond, shaded by garden umbrellas and lots of trees overhead. Figaró Kert is a repurposed community lot, and one of the city's best-kept secrets. Though the service is known to be a little cantankerous, prices are good, and the atmosphere is summer chill. Open summer months until 10 pm. ✉ *Katona József utca 13, corner of Borbély utca, Budapest* ☎ *70/365–1078.*

Hippie Island

BARS/PUBS | "Don't worry, feel hippy" entreats this chill restaurant and bar (albeit a little cheesily) with trippy motifs, groovy energy, and a large terrace with views of the Danube. The bar's menu is nothing special but it's decent and priced reasonably. It's all about the drinks (smoothies to alcohol) and the vibes. ✉ *Sirály Csónakház 23600/8, Margit-sziget* ☎ *30/467–2375* ⊕ *www.hippisziget.com.*

Mosselen Belgian Beer Café

BARS/PUBS | This cozy brewery, with Maria-Teresian yellow wallpaper overhead and original wooden parqueting below, all preserved from times bygone, has been serving traditional Flemish-style dishes alongside its excellent range of Belgian and international beers for decades. Try as you may, you won't be able to stay for just one round. Choose from eight beers on tap and forty bottled specialties, and get the mussels, too. ✉ *Pannonia utca 14, Budapest* ☎ *30/452–0535* ⊕ *www.mosselen.hu.*

Patkó Bandi Söröző

BREWPUBS/BEER GARDENS | This authentic Hungarian tavern's namesake, Horseshoe Andi, was a legendary *betyár* (highwayman) of whom Hungarian folklore waxes romantic about his swarthy character's Robin Hood-like feats. The wood-paneled pub is decorated with *puskák* (rifles) and other bandit memorabilia. The crotchety old waitress tries her best at English with foreign guests and is glad for anyone trying their hand at Hungarian. ✉ *Váci út 12, Nyugati Train Station* ☎ *1/239–1128* ⊕ *www.patkobandi.com.*

Zippp Club

MUSIC CLUBS | With a beach-space outdoor volleyball court and a terrace overlooking Buda, this unique nightlife spot caters to Budapest's voguish, young elite. Make an effort for the door here. ✉ *Iharos Sándor, Margit-sziget* ☎ *30/239–8037.*

JAZZ CLUBS

Budapest Jazz Club

MUSIC CLUBS | Budapest's top venue for live jazz music boasts a café and a restaurant in the front, some bar seating in-between, and in the back to the right a huge concert hall with over 150 seats. There are international stars on the bill as well as Hungary's leading jazz musicians:

Bea Palya, Dresch Quartet, Veronika Harcsa, and the Bálint Gyémánt Trio. Performances start at 8 pm. Free entry Monday and Wednesday for open jam sessions at 10 pm. Closed Sunday. ⊠ *Hollán Ernő utca 7, Budapest* ☎ *1/798–7289* ⊕ *www.bjc.hu.*

🎭 Performing Arts

THEATER
RaM Colosseum

CONCERTS | The wildly shaped oval building of the Miklós Radnóti Cultural Center—RaM Colosseum, opened in 2011—is headquarters of ExperiDance Productions, a multimedia performing arts troupe that puts on a range of musical and dance performances. RAM also hosts international and local theater, music, and dance productions. It's pricey and flashy but has got some eye-catching original bills on the repertoire, like the musicals *Nikola Tesla: Infinite Energy* and *The Ballad of the Pearl-Haired Girl.* Almost all performances are in Hungarian but it is still worth a stroll up through the lesser-frequented parts of Budapest's District 13 to a performance at this offbeat theater space. ⊠ *Kárpát utca 23-25, Budapest* ☎ *1/222–5253* ⊕ *www. tbgprod.hu.*

Vígszínház

THEATER | Dating from 1896, The Comedy Theatre is shaped a bit like a Hessian helmet with its grand yellow street-facing entrance and spiked dome over the top. Setting itself apart from its surroundings, this is a prime example of the buildings of its time, with equally grand and stylish interiors that take audiences back to a time of elegance when high culture experiences were a luxury enjoyed by Budapest's upper echelons. With a seating capacity of 1,100, this popular theater remains a well-liked venue for drama (comedy in the Greek sense of the world) and hosts a range of classical and modern Hungarian plays as well as international ones, featuring some of the

country's biggest names in directing and acting. Subtitles in English are available for some productions. ⊠ *Szent István krt. 14, Margit-sziget* ☎ *1/329–2340* ⊕ *www. vigszinhaz.hu.*

VENUES
Margitszigeti Szabadtéri Színpad

ARTS CENTERS | Hosting well-known international troupes as well as featuring some of Hungary's most popular performers and acts, Margaret Island's outdoor stage is the perfect place for those who love to experience professional music, dance, and theater surrounded by the beauty of nature. Ideal for warm spring or fall evenings or even hot summer nights, it is the loudest venue on this refined and genteel island. Even the crickets chirp to the time of the music here. ⊠ *Zielinski Szilárd sétány, Margit-sziget* ☎ *375–5922, 340–4196 Box Office* ⊕ *www.margitszigetiszinhaz.hu.*

🛍 Shopping

MARKETS
★ Lehel Csarnok *(Lehel Market)*

SHOPPING CENTERS/MALLS | Architect László Rajk got a lot of negative attention for his design of this market, unveiled in 2002 and considered one of Budapest's ugliest buildings. But even those who call this gaudy, yellow-and-red building by its nickname, the Kofahajónak (the ship for peasant grannies), cannot deny that Lehel Csarnok is one of the best markets in town for produce, meat, and other local food products. Stroll the aisles for *kolbász* (Hungarian sausage), *körözött* (a spicy cottage cheese spread), *savanyúság* (pickled goods), local honey, cheese, and the freshest fruit around. If you fancy something unique, try the *Ló-* or *Szarvaskolbász* (horse or deer sausage) or *kovászos uborka* (fermented pickles). You will have to try out some Hungarian here, as most vendors are local farmers just doing their business at the local market. When you are done, reward yourself with *lángos*, the

traditional Hungarian fried bread (best covered with sour cream, cheese, and garlic), and a beer at the popular Lángos Centrum. The site has always been popular as a market ground as well as embedded in colloquial controversy. The original open-air market was built over part of a local cemetery in 1890 when the square was called Ferdinánd tér. One hundred years later, when the old complex was finally torn down, construction halted as rumors of a Jewish cemetery underneath were explored. For now, it looks like the ship of the peasant grannies will sail on for many more years to come. ⊠ *Váci út 9–15, Budapest* ☎ *288–6895* Ⓜ *M3: Lehel tér.*

Activities

BICYCLES
Go Mobility
BICYCLING | Go Mobility offer bikes, tandems, go-carts, and monsteRollers for rent. A four-person go-cart costs 4,490 HUF an hour. Easily accessible on the south side of the island, located at the first rotary after you walk down from the bridge, you can hop on a bike and explore the whole island. ⊠ *Margit-sziget* ✛ *By the rotary, in front of the musical fountain* ☎ *30/544–7229* ⊕ *www.gomobility.eu.*

PARKS
Superfly Budapest
PARK—SPORTS-OUTDOORS | Good to know for families at a loss for something to do on rainy days and kids of all ages looking to take a few hours off sightseeing, Superfly indoor trampoline park features basketball, jumping lanes, a ramp, swing, and agility challenges. The giant slide ending in a foam bed is especially fun. Bookings should be made in advance online. Closed Monday. ⊠ *Süllő utca 8, Budapest* ⊕ *superfly.eu/budapest* 🎫 *From 2,000 HUF.*

Chapter 11

ÓBUDA AND
BUDA HILLS

DISTRICTS 2, 3, 12

Updated by
Jennifer Rigby

 Sights
★★★★★

 **Restaurants**
★★★☆☆

 Hotels
★★☆☆☆

 Shopping
★☆☆☆☆

 Nightlife
★★☆☆☆

NEIGHBORHOOD SNAPSHOT

TOP EXPERIENCES

■ **Aquincum:** Amazingly preserved Roman remains, evocatively restored.

■ **Walking in the Buda Hills:** Make like a local and take a hike in the green lungs of the city.

■ **No ordinary metro:** Take the cog railway, the chairlift, or the unique Children's Railway, operated almost entirely by little 'uns.

■ **Fellini Római Kultúrbisztró:** A magical 'cultural bistro' for drinks, dinner, or music on the banks of the Danube.

■ **Veli Bej:** This beautiful, ancient Turkish bath is often overlooked by tourists.

■ **Villa Bagatelle:** Treat yourself to a glorious weekend brunch.

GETTING HERE

Both of these neighborhoods are considered a little off the beaten track, as they are not served by the metro system, but they're still pretty easy to reach. Óbuda is on the suburban railway line/HÉV line, H5, from Batthyány tér to Szentendre, and it only takes 9 minutes from the city center. The Buda Hills are slightly more challenging to access, but there are plenty of buses, and it is only about 30–40 minutes from most of the city to reach some of the best-known hiking trails. The public transport website ⊕ *bkk.hu* is in English, and is great for planning your journey. If you are heading to either neighborhood for an evening meal, take a taxi. Driving and parking are straightforward here as you are outside the city center.

PLANNING YOUR TIME

If you want to mingle with locals, hiking in the hills on the weekend is the way to do it; but if you would rather have the natural beauty to yourself, go during the week. Note that most museums are closed on Monday in Óbuda. Allow time to take the chairlift or cog railway on your way.

QUICK BITES

■ **Kilátó Kávézó.** This old-fashioned café at the foot of the Elizabeth Lookout tower has unsurprisingly great views and good mulled wine in winter. ⊠ *Buda Hills* Ⓜ *János-hegy, Libegő (the chairlift)*

■ **Smokey Monkies.** A mini-chain of fantastically authentic American barbecue. ⊠ *Szentendrei útca 95, Óbuda* ⊕ *www.facebook. com/smokeymonkiesbbq* Ⓜ *H5: Kaszásdűlő*

■ **Trofea Grill.** This branch of the all-you-can-eat buffet restaurant near Fő tér offers decent eats in a pinch. ⊠ *Laktanya utca 5, Óbuda* ⊕ *trofeagrill.com/hu* Ⓜ *H5: Szentlélek tér*

Until its unification with Buda and Pest in 1872 to form the city of Budapest, Óbuda (meaning Old Buda) was a separate town that used to be the main settlement; now it is usually thought of as a suburb. Although the vast new apartment blocks of Budapest's biggest housing project and busy roadways are what first strike the eye, the historic core of Óbuda has been preserved in its entirety.

Living up to the "old" moniker, Óbuda is the site of the ruins of Aquincum, the Roman Empire's border town and capital of the province of Pannonia. Besides the main archaeological dig, numerous pieces of Roman masonry can still be found along motorways and pedestrian underpasses, and the remains of not one, but two amphitheaters (one military, the other civilian) are preserved in public areas. There are also a number of excellent museums, baths, and good restaurants, as well as a natural riverside beach just north of the district where you will find locals lingering at the riverside bars, restaurants, and food trucks. Most of these venues open in spring and close only during wintertime, with some of them being open all year long.

The Buda Hills, meanwhile, cover a vast amount of ground on the edges of the city, and are a wonderful way to get a hit of nature—as well as some great views—while in the Hungarian capital. The residential areas at the foot of the hills are refined and attractive, but the real draw here is the greenery: kilometers of hiking trails in woods and meadows, as well as a couple of interesting caves. Getting up to the top of the hills is all part of the adventure: you can hike, but save your energy and hop on the historic chairlift or cog railway, including the line operated by children.

 ## Sights

★ Aquincum

ARCHAEOLOGICAL SITE | FAMILY | This fascinating complex comprises the reconstructed, extremely evocative remains of a Roman settlement dating from the first century AD. Careful excavations have unearthed a varied selection of artifacts and mosaics, providing a tantalizing inkling of what life was like in the provinces of the Roman Empire. A gymnasium and a central heating system have been unearthed, along with the ruins of two baths and a shrine once operated by the mysterious cult of Mithras. The Aquincum múzeum (Aquincum Museum) displays

the dig's most notable finds: ceramics; a red-marble sarcophagus showing a triton and flying Eros on one side and on the other, Telesphorus, the angel of death, depicted as a hooded dwarf; and jewelry from a Roman lady's tomb. There are reconstructed Roman board games, interactive video games, and a reconstruction of an ancient Roman musical organ in the basement level. The museum also manages the Thermae Maiores or 'Great Bath' complex as part of the Roman Baths Museum, an ancient spa now incongruously located in a pedestrian underpass by Flórián tér station. It's free to visit. ⊠ *District III, Szentendrei út 135, Óbuda* ☎ *1/430–1081* ⊕ *www. aquincum.hu* 🖃 *1,300 HUF Nov.–Mar.; 1,900 HUF Apr.–Oct.* ☉ *Closed Mon. Excavations may be closed due to weather Nov.–Mar.* Ⓜ *M5: Kaszásdűlő.*

Farkasréti Cemetery
CEMETERY | Noted for its spectacular hilltop views of the city, this green and tranquil cemetery is home to some flamboyant memorials and statues—check out the giant griffin, or Griffmadár, designed by Kálmán Veres as a tribute to those who are far away, and the final resting place of numerous Hungarian notables. Look for the tombs of several scientists, academics, and athletes, and note composer Béla Bartók near the main entrance. The mortuary, designed by architect Imre Makovecz to look like a human chest, is worth a look if it is open. ⊠ *Németvölgyi út 99, Buda Hills* ☎ *1/248–3520* ⊕ *www.btirt.hu/temetok/ farkasreti-temeto* Ⓜ *Tram 59; bus 8, 53, 112.*

Flórián tér (*Flórián Square*)
ARCHAEOLOGICAL SITE | The center of today's Óbuda is Flórián tér, where Roman ruins were first discovered when the foundations of a house were dug in 1778. While it does not necessarily merit a visit in its own right, if you're in the neighborhood, it's fairly interesting to contrast the ancient ruins in the center

of the square, carefully excavated two centuries after they were first found, with the racing traffic and cement-block housing projects on the exterior.

The square is now a large, grassy park, which the local authorities regularly promise to spruce up. In the middle, stretching from the square toward Kiscelli utca, is an eerie, black metal angel-like sculpture pointing one hand skyward and holding a wreath in the other. This is the Memorial to the Victims of Road Accidents. In case the title isn't enough, a wrecked car at the foot of the main statue and a list of annual highway death tolls from 1984 to the present further ensures that the point gets across, compliments of the National Police Headquarters' Accident Prevention Committee. ⊠ *District III, Flórián tér, Óbuda* Ⓜ *H5: Szentlélek tér.*

Fő tér (*Main Square*)
PLAZA | Óbuda's old main square is its most picturesque part. There are several good restaurants and interesting museums in and around the baroque Zichy Mansion, which has become a neighborhood cultural center. Among the most popular offerings are the summer concerts in the courtyard (see 'Kobuchi Kert', further on in the chapter) and the evening jazz concerts. Toward the southern end of the square (on the way out to Árpád út and the HÉV) is the elaborate Óbudai Szentháromság Szobor (Óbuda Trinity Statue), built originally in 1740, razed in 1950, and rebuilt in 2000. ⊠ *District III, Kórház utca at Hídfő utca, Óbuda* Ⓜ *H5: Szentlélek tér.*

Gül Baba türbéje (*Gül Baba's Tomb*)
MEMORIAL | A picturesque spot that is also one of the farthest north sites of Islamic pilgrimage in the world, this octagonal tomb houses Gül Baba, an Ottoman-era poet and dervish who took part in, and died shortly after, the Turkish conquest of Buda. He's known as 'Father of the Roses' in Hungary, hence the beautiful rose garden. ⊠ *Mecset utca 14, Óbuda*

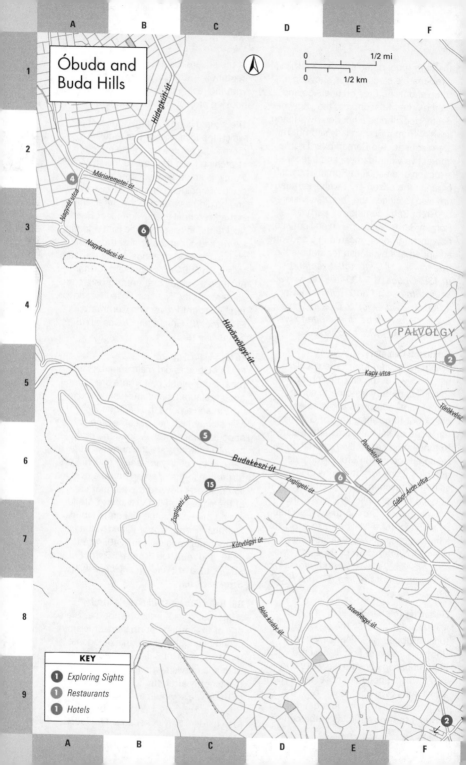

✉ 1/618–3842 ⊕ gulbabaalapitvany.hu
⊘ Closed Mon. Ⓜ H5: Margit híd, budai
hídfő.

Gyermekvasút (Children's Railway)
SCENIC DRIVE | The 12-km (7-mile) Chil-
dren's Railway—so called because it's
operated primarily by children—runs
from Széchenyi-hegy to Hűvösvölgy. The
sweeping views make the trip a treat
for children and adults alike. Depar-
tures are from Széchenyi-hegy and the
journey between terminals takes about
50 minutes. To get to Széchenyi-hegy,
take Tram 56 or 61 from Széll Kálmán tér,
and change to the cog railway (public
transport tickets valid) at the Városmajor
stop. Take the cog railway uphill (also
quite a fun and historic transport option,
with great views) to the last stop and
then walk a few hundred yards down a
short, partly forested road to the left, in
the direction most others will be going.
The railway terminates at Hűvösvölgy,
where you can walk downhill for a few
minutes and catch Tram 56 or 61 back to
Széll Kálmán tér. Various stops along the
railway also act as embarkation points
for hikers into the Buda Hills. ✉ Hegyhát
utca, Buda Hills ✉ 1/397–5392 ⊕ gyerme-
kvasut.hu Ⓜ Tram 56, 61 to cog railway at
Városmajor.

Hercules Villa
ARCHAEOLOGICAL SITE | Near the main
Aquincum ruins—but functioning
separately—a fine third-century Roman
dwelling, Hercules Villa, takes its name
from the myth depicted on its beautiful
mosaic floor. The ruin was unearthed
between 1958 and 1967 and now stands,
rather incongruously, among a large
housing estate. Worth popping your head
in after the Aquincum visit if you feel the
need for more ruins; admission is free.
✉ District III, Meggyfa utca 19–21, Óbuda
⊕ www.aquincum.hu ✉ Free ⊘ Closed
Mon. and Tues. Ⓜ Bus 34, 134, 106, 9,
109.

Hungarian Museum of Trade and Tourism
MUSEUM | The rather dull-sounding name
belies a real gem of a museum, stuffed
with interesting exhibits including
old advertisements, shop signs, and
restaurant items from the communist
era. There are also fascinating details on
the lives of different tradespeople, and
recreated entire shops, cafés, and restaurants from the 19th and 20th centuries.
✉ III Korona tér 1, Óbuda ✉ 1/375–6249
⊕ mkvm.hu ✉ 1,000 HUF ⊘ Closed
Mon. Ⓜ H5: Szentlélek tér.

Kiscelli Múzeum (Kiscelli Museum)
MUSEUM | A short climb up the steep
sidewalk of Remetehegy (Hermit Hill)
will deposit you at this elegant, mus-
tard-yellow baroque mansion. It was built
between 1744 and 1760 as a Trinitarian
monastery. Today, it holds an eclectic mix
of modern design, paintings, sculptures,
engravings, old clocks, antique furniture,
and other items related to the history of
Budapest. Included here is the printing
press on which poet and revolution-
ary Sándor Petőfi printed his famous
"Nemzeti Dal" ("National Song"), in
1848, inciting the Hungarian people to
rise up against the Habsburgs. There
are concerts here every Sunday in July.
✉ Kiscelli utca 108, Óbuda ✉ 1/388–8560
⊕ kiscellimuzeum.hu ✉ 1,600 HUF
⊘ Closed Mon. Ⓜ Tram 17, 19, 41.

★ **Palace of Wonders**
AMUSEMENT PARK/WATER PARK | FAMILY | It
requires confidence to give an attraction a
name like this, but for families, it delivers.
This science-themed, highly interactive
amusement park, museum, and playhouse
features everything from a 9D virtual reali-
ty cinema (that shoots water at 'viewers')
to live science shows, as well as escape
rooms, puzzles, and a mind-bending hall
of illusions that will leave the entire party
questioning what they know about how
the world works. ✉ Buda EG Shopping
Center, Bécsi utca 38-44, Óbuda ✉ 1/814–
8060 ⊕ www.csopa.hu ✉ 3,600 HUF
Ⓜ H5: Szépvölgyi út.

Housed in an old Baroque mansion, Kiscelli Muzeum's permanent exhibitions include a room full of old printing presses and an entire 19th century pharmacy, as well as residential interiors from old Budapest.

★ Pálvölgyi, Szemlőhegyi and Mátyáshegy caves

CAVE | There are about 200 accessible caves in Budapest (some open, some not) but Pálvölgyi and Szemlőhegyi are the most popular. Both provide a long network of underground walking trails through narrow passages filled with crystal formations, stalactites, and stalagmites. The Pálvölgyi Cave stretches around 18 miles, making it the longest cave network in Budapest and one of the longest in Hungary. It is also one of the most beautiful. Breathe in at Szemlőhegyi as this cave is known for its mineral-infused air. The caves must be visited on a guided tour that lasts just under an hour. Pálvölgyi and Szemlőhegyi can be visited on a combined ticket. Mátyáshegy cave, just opposite Pálvölgyi, is a bit more intense, with some climbing required and caving equipment provided, so it is best suited to the fit (and the brave). ■ TIP→ Adventure-seekers should book a 3-hour adventure caving tour (10,000 HUF) with Caving Under Budapest,
which offers the chance to climb and crawl through these caves ⊕ www.caving. hu ⊠ Szépvölgyi út 162/a, Buda Hills ☎ 1/325–9505 ⊕ www.dunaipoly.hu 🎫 2,200 HUF; 3,500 HUF combined with Szemlőhegy; 10,000 HUF for Mátyáshegy ⊙ Closed Mon. Ⓜ Bus 65.

Római amfiteátrum (*Roman Amphitheater*)
ARCHAEOLOGICAL SITE | Probably dating from the second century AD, Óbuda's Roman military amphitheater once held some 16,000 people and, at 144 yards in diameter, was one of Europe's largest. A block of dwellings called the Round House was later built by the Romans above the amphitheater; massive stone walls found in the Round House's cellar were actually parts of the amphitheater. Below the amphitheater are the cells where prisoners and lions were held while awaiting confrontation. ⊠ Pacsirtamező utca at Nagyszombat utca, Óbuda 🎫 Free.

Did You Know?

A professional tour guide will take you crawling, climbing, and creeping through some incredibly tight and narrow spaces at Palvolgy caves, so if you are claustrophobic or unathletic, you may want to ask for a less intense walking tour.

Szent Péter és Szent Pál templom (*Saint Peter and Saint Paul Church*)

RELIGIOUS SITE | Its pale yellow and green metal steeple being one of Óbuda's core landmarks, this church—a tad more impressive on the outside than the inside—was built by the Zichy family from 1744 to 1749 as the successor to a previous church established here by Hungary's first king, Saint Stephen, in 1010. Situated in a peaceful neighborhood a couple minutes' walk from Fő tér and behind the Aquincum Hotel, it features a red-marble altar (1774) and striking wooden statues of Christ and the church's patron saints (1884). ⊠ *Lajos utca 168, Óbuda* ⊕ *peterpalplebania.hu* Ⓜ *H5: Tímár utca station.*

Zichy Mansion (*Óbudai Múzeum, Kassák Múzeum and Vasarely Múzeum*)

MUSEUM | Weather-beaten but beautifully baroque with a pleasingly pink second-floor facade, the 18th century Zichy Mansion is deep in a courtyard at the exalted if neglected-looking address of Fő tér 1. A little cluster of museums in this historic spot make it a de facto cultural center. Permanent exhibitions at the cheerful Óbudai Múzeum include a popular tribute to toys, as well as an immersive tour through Óbuda's history. The mansion is also home to the Kassák Múzeum, which honors the literary and artistic works of a pioneer of the Hungarian avant-garde, Lajos Kassák. Completing the trio, the Vasarely Múzeum is a rambunctious collection of the work of the grandfather of 'op art', Victor Vasarely, who pioneered the funky, geometric patterns that trick the eyes and raise the spirits. The museums host gallery talks and other cultural programs. ■**TIP→ Keep an eye out in the adjacent square, Szentlélek tér, for a group of sculptures by Imre Varga, one of Hungary's leading sculptors. If the group of slightly concerned-looking women with umbrellas whets your appetite, the Imre Varga Collection is just behind the square.** ⊠ *Fő tér 1, Óbuda* ☎ *1/250–1020 Óbudai Múzeum, 1/368–7021 Kassák Museum, 1/388–7551 Vasarely Múzeum* ⊕ *www.obudaimuzeum.hu* ✉ *Óbudai Múzeum: 800 HUF; Vasarely Múzeum 800 HUF; Kassák Múzeum: 600 HUF* ☉ *Óbudai and Vasarely Múzeums: closed Mon. Kassák Múzeum: closed Mon. and Tues.* Ⓜ *H5: Szentlélek tér.*

Zugliget Libegő (*Zugliget Chairlift*)

SCENIC DRIVE | **FAMILY** | If interesting transportation options like the Gyermekvasút (the Children's Railway) are your thing, the Zugliget Libegő (chairlift) in the Buda Hills is also good fun. Transporting passengers between Zugliget and within walking distance of the Erzsébet Lookout Tower, this chairlift takes you above the treetops and up the side of János Hill in about 15 minutes, all the while providing panoramic views of the Buda surroundings. It can be reached by taking bus 291 from Nyugati station to its final stop. The lift operates from 10 am to 7 pm in summer and until 3:30 or 4 pm during the winter. Check the website for special "Night Lift" events (usually in August and September) where you can ride the lift after dark. ⊠ *Zugligeti út 97, Buda Hills* ⊕ *www.bkv.hu* ✉ *HUF 1600 round trip* ☉ *Sometimes closed Mon. for maintenance* Ⓜ *Bus 291 to Zugliget from Nyugati station.*

Spas

Aronia Spa

HOT SPRINGS | Families flock to this wellness center in the Aquincum hotel on winter weekends for its thermal baths and swimming pool, not to mention a seating area that serves healthy meals all day. The spacious resting areas have comfortable lounge chairs nicely set apart, so it never feels too crowded. The big swimming pool keeps the kids happy, and there's a full menu of spa therapies for adults, including several types of massage, a Dead Sea salt bath, and aromatherapy treatments, as well as Finnish saunas. The thermal waters come straight from the nearby Margaret

A Good Walk

Begin your walk on the Margit híd, entering Margit-sziget (Margaret Island) on its southern end. Stroll up the island, toward the Arpád híd, where you can catch the streetcar or just walk over to Óbuda. Once you're there, covering all the sights on foot involves large but manageable distances along major exhaust-permeated roadways. One way to tackle it is to take Tram 17 from its southern terminus at the Buda side of the Margaret Bridge. Óbuda really begins after the third stop; and the fourth stop marks a charming commercial subcenter of this part of town; after this, keep your eyes open to the right, as the tram soon passes by the ruins of the Római amfiteátrum. At the

seventh stop, Szent Margit Korház, get off and walk back a short distance to Kiscelli utca; from there, walk uphill to the Kiscelli Múzeum. Then walk back down the same street all the way past Flórián tér, continuing toward the Danube and making a left onto Hídfo utca or Szentlélek tér to enter Fo tér. A short detour south will get you to Szent Péter és Szent Pál templom. On the south side of the square is the Zichy Mansion, a cultural center and museum. After exploring the square, walk a block or two southeast to the HÉV suburban railway stop and take the train just north to the museum complex at Aquincum and the Hercules Villa, nearby.

Island. ⊠ *Árpád fejedelem útja 94, Óbuda* ☎ *1/436–4130* ⊕ *www.aquincumhotel. com* 🖭 *3,900 HUF weekdays, 4,500 HUF weekends* Ⓜ *H5: Tímár utca; tram 1: Szent Lélek tér.*

Romai Furdo

HOT SPRINGS | FAMILY | These family-friendly outdoor baths, part of the appealing and somewhat surprising stretch of beach on this side of the river, are more lido (public swimming pool) than typical pampering spa, but no worse for that on a hot Budapest summer's day. There is an adventure pool with slides and two other pools, as well as Roman heritage, some of which can be seen dotted around the area. ⊠ *Rozgonyi Piroska utca 2, Óbuda* ☎ *1/388–9740* ⊕ *www. romaistrand.hu* 🖭 *2,500 HUF weekdays, 2,800 HUF weekends* ⊘ *Closed* Ⓜ *H5: Rómaifürdő; D12: BKK ferry to Rómaifürdő.*

Veli bej (*Császár Baths*)

SPA—SIGHT | One of the oldest thermal baths in Budapest—dating to 1575—Veli

bej spa is also one of the most authentic and untouristed. The historic Turkish bathhouse was closed to the public for decades but recent renovations restored it to its original splendor within its original stone building. The central pool of five, underneath a gently lit cupola, is particularly special. The spa complex, also known as Császár Baths, is tucked on the other side of the swimming complex at the Császár Hotel and its healing waters rise from the wells of the nearby Lukács Baths and from Margaret Island. Treatment options include massages, steam baths, and saunas, and there is a café and beauty salon on-site. A small exhibit displays historical finds. *Veli bej is coed, even the locker room.* ⊠ *Árpád fejedelem útja 7, Buda Hills* ⟴ *Behind Császár Hotel's swimming pool complex* ☎ *1/438–8400* ⊕ *www.irgalmasrend.hu/ site/velibej* 🖭 *2,800 HUF* Ⓜ *H5: Margit híd, budai hídfő.*

🍴 Restaurants

These districts offer a handful of good quality neighborhood restaurants, many with lovely outdoor spaces.

Flat White Kitchen

$$ | CAFÉ | Coffee, brunches, and even some swings to sit on: there's a lot to like at Flat White Kitchen, one of this slightly sleepy area's trendiest modern cafés. As its name suggests, coffee is the specialty here, but you'll also find good breakfast, and some eccentric dishes like the Croque a La Flat White, with a wienerwurst, onions, ginger, a fried egg, and salad, among other ingredients. **Known for:** all-day weekend brunches; trendy feel; good cakes and coffee. $ *Average main: 2,000 HUF* ✉ *Szépvölgyi út 15, Óbuda* ☎ *30/420-8415* ⊕ *flat-white.hu* Ⓜ *H5: Szépvölgyi út.*

Fuji Japan

$$$ | JAPANESE | An aura of calm permeates this excellent, long-standing Japanese restaurant in the affluent Rószadomb district of Upper Buda. Comfortable club chairs and big windows make you feel miles away from the hustle and bustle of downtown Pest. Tables are set a comfortable distance apart, so that you can watch the Japanese and Hungarian chefs work their craft in this full-service restaurant. Sushi and sashimi are expertly prepared, as are other Japanese specialties such as teriyaki tenderloin with sesame and mushroom tempura. There's even a separate dining room where you can eat at low tables, in traditional Japanese style. **Known for:** sushi and sashimi; watch chefs at work; popular so reservations are a must for dinner. $ *Average main: 3,000 HUF* ✉ *Csatárka utca 54/b, Buda Hills* ☎ *1/325-7111* ⊕ *www.fujirestaurant.hu* Ⓜ *Bus 11, 19, 91.*

Kéhli

$$$ | HUNGARIAN | This pricey but laid-back, sepia-toned neighborhood tavern is on a hard-to-find street near the Óbuda end of the Árpád Bridge. Practically all the food here arrives in huge servings, which was just the way that Hungarian writer Gyula Krúdy (to whom the restaurant is dedicated) liked it when he was a regular customer. Dishes like the hot pot with marrowbone and toast, or *lecsó* (a stew with a base of onions, peppers, tomatoes, and paprika) are great comfort food on a cool day, and Romani music livens up the place in the evenings. **Known for:** traditional Hungarian food; bone marrow with garlic on toast; Romani music. $ *Average main: 4,000 HUF* ✉ *Mókus utca 22, Óbuda* ☎ *1/368-0613* ⊕ *www.kehli.hu* Ⓜ *H5: Szentlélek tér.*

★ Náncsi Néni Vendéglője

$$$ | HUNGARIAN | FAMILY | "Auntie Nancsi" has built a loyal following by serving up straightforward, homestyle Hungarian dishes in the rustic surroundings of a converted 17th century farmhouse. Chains of paprika and garlic dangle from the low wooden ceiling above tables set with red-and-white gingham tablecloths. Big tables of local families can be found here on summer weekends enjoying well-prepared Hungarian food. Sunday chicken soup and catfish paprika are well-loved by regulars. Try the popular *túrógombóc* (sweet cheese dumpling) dessert; it's the biggest and best in town. There is a garden dining area open during warmer months, when reservations are essential. **Known for:** variety of Hungarian wines; homely local dishes; huge terrace filled with local families. $ *Average main: 3,000 HUF* ✉ *Ördögárok út 80, Buda Hills* ☎ *1/397-2742* ⊕ *www.nancsineni.hu* 🎩 *Jacket required* Ⓜ *Tram 56a, 61.*

Pata Negra Buda

$$$ | TAPAS | Here is a lovely tapas bar with authentic dishes, friendly staff, and a cozy vibe. Pata Negra is not cheap, particularly as you may find yourself ordering rather more than you had planned (it's that good), but it makes for a quality meal out. There's another branch in Pest. **Known for:** prawns with garlic

11

Óbuda and Buda Hills

and croquetas; hearty Spanish red wines and sangria; popular so book in advance. $ *Average main: 5,000 HUF* ✉ *Frankel Leó út 55, Óbuda* ☎ *1/438–3227* ⊕ *patanegra.hu* Ⓜ *H5: Margit híd, budai hídfő.*

Remiz

$$$ | **EUROPEAN** | **FAMILY** | The facade of this upscale, but family-run restaurant in leafy Buda is fashioned out of an old tram depot. The spacious restaurant includes a dining room to suit any season, including a *söröző* (beer cellar), a glass-enclosed room, a richly paneled dining room, and an outdoor terrace. There's a jungle gym and sandbox outside for kids, and that makes the terrace *very* popular in summer. Buda families like the grilled meat cooked on a lava stone, including mouthwatering spare ribs. It's no surprise that the chocolate profiteroles are popular with children as well as their parents. **Known for:** grilled meat, especially spare ribs; chocolate profiteroles for dessert; family-friendly dining. $ *Average main: 4,000 HUF* ✉ *Budakeszi út 5, Buda Hills* ☎ *30/999–5131* ⊕ *www.remiz.hu* Ⓜ *Tram 61; bus 22, 22A, 222.*

Villa Bagetelle

$$ | **BAKERY** | **FAMILY** | One of the city's loveliest breakfast and brunch places, set in a charming refurbished villa in the Buda Hills, Villa Bagetelle offers Hungarian, German, and French specialities that range from simple egg dishes to the full champagne breakfast. There are also tasty lunch options which change by the season, all to be enjoyed either on the terrace, in the winter garden, or in the light-filled villa itself. **Known for:** build-your-own egg breakfasts, with a range of extras; freshly baked sourdough and pastries; good coffee from a Hungarian micro roaster. $ *Average main: 1,790 HUF* ✉ *Németvölgyi út 17, Buda Hills* ☎ *30/359–6295* ⊕ *www.villa-bagatelle. com* Ⓜ *M2: Déli pályaudvar.*

 Hotels

Hotels are a little thin on the ground in these areas, with a couple of stand-out exceptions. Staying around here is all about the peace and quiet, rather than being in the center of things.

Aquincum Hotel

$ | **HOTEL** | Not a looker from the outside, but surrounded by very pretty streets and close to the Danube, the Aquincum is an extremely comfortable and professionally run hotel, with all the mod-cons and facilities you would expect, including a great spa. **Pros:** Aronia spa is excellent; spacious, comfortable rooms; lovely location. **Cons:** a little bland in decor; unattractive from the exterior; removed from the city center. $ *Rooms from: 25,000 HUF* ✉ *Árpád fejedelem útja 94, Óbuda* ☎ *1/436–4100* ⊕ *www.aquincumhotel. com* ⬥ *310 rooms* ⎢⎢ *Free breakfast* Ⓜ *H5: Szentlélek tér.*

★ Bagatelle Gardenhouse

$$$ | **B&B/INN** | Set in a 1936 villa, next door to the delightful Villa Bagatelle bakery and restaurant (run by the same friendly couple), this lovely villa-style hotel offers contemporary design, comfort, and rooms overlooking gorgeous gardens. **Pros:** delicious breakfast; large garden with small pool; impeccable design and style. **Cons:** quieter location is not for everyone; hilly area; some rooms are better than others—ask for a terrace or garden view. $ *Rooms from: 50,000 HUF* ✉ *Németvölgyi út 15, Buda Hills* ☎ *70/365–8775* ⊕ *bagatellegardenhouse. com* ⬥ *6 rooms* ⎢⎢ *Free breakfast* Ⓜ *M2: Déli pályaudvar.*

Császár Hotel

$ | **HOTEL** | This somewhat unremarkable hotel just on the bottom edge of Obuda, heading toward the castle, has two huge selling points: it's in the same building as an Olympic-sized outdoor heated swimming pool that's free for guests and beside the Veli Bej Turkish Baths. **Pros:**

historic Turkish baths and great pool; convenient location; good value. **Cons:** can be very noisy with trams running in front of hotel and pool; a little dated; rooms are a little small. ⓈRooms from: 15,500 HUF ⊠ Frankel Leó utca 35, Óbuda ☎ 20/468–6073 ⊕ www.csaszarhotel.hu ⟿ 45 rooms Ⓞ Free breakfast Ⓜ H5: Margit híd, budai hídfő.

Hotel Papillon
$ | **HOTEL** | This cute little hotel on a very steep street boasts a surprise in its garden: a little swimming pool. **Pros:** hidden pool; lovely roof terrace with views; good value. **Cons:** basic; some rooms have balconies, some don't; very steep street. ⓈRooms from: 12,000 HUF ⊠ Rózsahegy utca 3b, Buda Hills ☎ 1/212–4750 ⊕ hotelpapillon.hu ⟿ 30 rooms ⓄFree breakfast Ⓜ Margit híd, budai hídfő station (Line: H5).

Hotel Tiliana
$$ | **HOTEL** | Probably the best of a clutch of little hotels and pensions in the secluded Buda Hills area, Hotel Tiliana may be removed from the action but it has its own charms. **Pros:** secluded garden location; small spa and pool; good location for exploring the hills. **Cons:** not central; building is not particularly attractive; breakfast is good but a little limited. ⓈRooms from: 24,000 HUF ⊠ Hárshegyi út 1-3, Buda Hills ☎ 1/391–0027 ⊕ www.tiliana.hu ⟿ 49 rooms ⓄFree breakfast Ⓜ Bus 22, 22A, 222.

Hotel Villa Korda
$ | **HOTEL** | This stately old villa, rather fraying at the edges, nonetheless has a lot of charm because of its quiet, green location. **Pros:** spacious rooms; very tranquil; some rooms have lovely views. **Cons:** you'll need to take taxis as public transport is not convenient; no elevator; decor is a little tired. ⓈRooms from: 15,000 HUF ⊠ Szikla utca 9, Buda Hills ☎ 1/325–9123 ⊕ villakorda.hu ⟿ 21 rooms ⓄFree breakfast Ⓜ Bus 65, 29, 111.

Nightlife

Not the most hopping of neighborhoods, but there are a few bars, particularly in summer, that are worth a look if you're in the area. The beachside venues are worth a trip in their own right.

BARS AND PUBS

★ Fellini Római Kultúrbisztró
BREWPUBS/BEER GARDENS | It's a trek to get here (not as bad if you drive or bike it), but it's worth it. This place is a gem: a waterfront "cultural bistro" that's part beach, part music club, part outdoor cinema (on Wednesday), and part good old-fashioned bar and bistro. Open every day all summer, dogs, children, and ducks are all welcome (they even cater to kids wishing to feed the ducks). Dangle your feet in the Danube as you enjoy drinks and then wander to the other venues dotted along the strip of beach. ⊠ Kossuth Lajos üdülőpart 5, Óbuda ⊕ felliniromai.hu Ⓜ H5: Rómaifürdő and a 20-min walk; bus 34.

Marxim
BARS/PUBS | Across the street from Budapest's Millenáris Park, this bar and pizza parlor is a kistch, somewhat tongue-in-cheek tribute to socialism, including graffiti-scrawled walls, chicken wire, and black and red paint smeared everywhere. Try the "Gulag Pizza," covered in spicy red paprika, ham, and corn; it also comes with a bottle of homemade ketchup to pour on top—a popular condiment Hungarians slather on their pizza. ⊠ Kisrókus utca 23, Széll Kálmán tér ☎ 1/316–0231 ⊕ marxim.hu Ⓜ M2: Moszkva tér.

★ Mókus Bisztró
BARS/PUBS | Managing to be both cute and cool at the same time, Mókus (or 'Squirrel') bar has the vague feel of one of Pest's ruin bars, perhaps unsurprisingly, as it is run by the same crew who used to steer one of the hippest venues across the river. Now in Óbuda, this mix of bar, restaurant, gig venue, and beer

11

Óbuda and Buda Hills

garden is *the* place to unwind and feel like a local. ✉ *Mókus utca 1-3, Óbuda* ☎ *70/434–9156* ⊕ *www.facebook.com/ mokusbisztro* Ⓜ *H5: Szentlélek tér.*

WINE BARS
Fioka
WINE BARS—NIGHTLIFE | This popular wine-bar and bistro, with a name that means "chick," Fioka is close to the chairlift and has a lovely garden for a glass or two of Hungarian wine in summer. The food is sprightly and modern. ✉ *Városmajor utca 75, Buda Hills* ☎ *1/ 426–5555* ⊕ *fiokaetterem.hu* Ⓜ *Tram 56A, 61.*

Stelázsi Kávézó, Étterem és Borbár
WINE BARS—NIGHTLIFE | A modern take on a traditional Hungarian coffee shop, restaurant, and wine bar, the atmosphere is warm, the food is authentic and delicious, and the wines come from Hungarian producers via the restaurant's wine cellar. Booking ahead is a good plan. ✉ *Nagyszombat utca 3, Óbuda* ☎ *1/631–3624* ⊕ *stelazsietterem.hu* Ⓜ *H5: Tímár utca.*

 Performing Arts

CLASSICAL MUSIC
★ Budapest Festival Orchestra (*Budapesti Fesztiválzenekar*)
MUSIC | World-renowned conductor Iván Fischer, who is still music director, formed the group with famed Hungarian conductor Zoltán Kocsis in 1983. The orchestra has won international accolades and is hands-down your best bet for classical music in Budapest. International soloists and conductors are often invited to perform with the orchestra. Its home base was previously Liszt Ferenc Music Academy, but since 2005 the orchestra has also performed regularly at the new Béla Bartók National Concert Hall in the *Művészetek Palotája* (Palace of the Arts), and they have monthly Sunday Chamber Music concerts in their rehearsal hall on this side of the river, in Buda. Tickets can be purchased online or at several locations around Budapest, including Ticket Express and the Liszt Ferenc Academy. ✉ *Selmeci utca 14–16, Óbuda* ☎ *1/368–6626 BFO Rehearsal Hall* ⊕ *www.bfz.hu* ⚑ *3,000 HUF for Rehearsal Hall concerts* Ⓜ *H5: Tímár utca.*

VENUES
Bartók Béla Emlékház (*Bartók Béla Memorial House*)
MUSIC | The tiny recital room in this museum, the former home of the famous Hungarian composer, hosts intimate Friday-evening chamber-music recitals by well-known ensembles from mid-March to June and September to mid-December. For fans, the home itself is worth a visit, and the historic atmosphere brings the music to life for everyone. ✉ *Csalán út 29, Buda Hills* ☎ *1/394–2100* ⊕ *www. bartokemlekhaz.hu* Ⓜ *Tram 56, 56A, 61; bus 5, 11, 29.*

Budapest Kongresszusi Központ (*Budapest Convention Center*)
CONCERTS | One of the city's largest-capacity (but least atmospheric) concert venues, this hosts a wide range of events, sometimes with big international names, including some that are part of the Spring Festival. ✉ *Jagelló út 1–3, Óbuda* ☎ *1/372–5400* ⊕ *www.bcc.hu* Ⓜ *Tram 17, 61; bus 8E, 110, 112.*

Kobuci Kert
ARTS CENTERS | An outdoor venue with a great range of folk and contemporary music in a gorgeous old courtyard lit by string lights, this is a good spot to hang with locals for a few drinks and burgers or sandwiches. ✉ *Zichy Mansion courtyard, Fő tér 1, Óbuda* ☎ *70/205–7282* ⊕ *kobuci.hu* Ⓜ *H5: Szentlélek tér.*

Óbudai Társaskör (*Óbuda Society Circle*)
ARTS CENTERS | Music of all stripes, historical talks, and even wine tastings: this little venue offers everything for the Hungarian culture vulture and for tourists, although most offerings are in Hungarian

(less important for the concerts). ⊠ *Kiskorona utca 7, Óbuda* ☎ *1/250–0288* ⊕ *obudaitarsaskor.hu* Ⓜ *H5: Szentlélek tér.*

The Stage

ARTS CENTERS | With a grand title and a slightly odd location—inside the International Business School—performances here include English- and Hungarian-language theater in addition to movies, dance, and concerts. English-only shows are typically once a month, although there is simultaneous translation into English during Hungarian-language events. ⊠ *Tárogató út 2–4, Buda Hills* ☎ *20/350–7356* ⊕ *www.ibs-oc.hu/rendezvenytechnika/szinhaz* Ⓜ *Tram 61; bus 22, 22A, 222.*

🛍 Shopping

Óbuda and Buda Hills don't offer much in the way of shopping—Obuda is all about the ruins and the hills themselves are residential areas, with more trees than shops. There are a few decent malls, but if you want to leave with a souvenir, the best bets in this area are the museum shops.

FOOD AND WINE

Daubner Cukrászda

FOOD/CANDY | **FAMILY** | It's with good reason that this popular confectioner has lines outside the door each morning. Every pastry here is delicate and light. Even a novice can taste the real butter cream in the famous Eszterházy torta, which is a truly magnificent cake. Locals say the Sacher torte is every bit as good as it is in the famous Sacher Hotel in Vienna. It's usually crowded on weekends with families eating ice cream. ⊠ *Szépvölgyi út 50, Buda Hills* ☎ *1/335–2253* ⊕ *www.daubnercukraszda.hu* ⊙ *Closed Mon.* Ⓜ *H5: Nzépvölgyi út.*

MARKETS

MOM Park

SHOPPING CENTERS/MALLS | This serviceable shopping mall, with some nice eateries and a good range of shops, is worth noting because every Saturday, it plays host to Buda's best organic farmers' market. Located just outside the shopping center, there are fruit and vegetable stores, stalls heaving with bread, and local farmers offering juices and other artisan products, as well as Hungarian specialities. Good for stocking up for a picnic in the hills. ⊠ *Alkotás utca 53, Buda Hills* ☎ *1/487–5500* ⊕ *mompark.hu* Ⓜ *M2: Déli pályaudvar.*

Activities

Buda Hills is the city's natural playground. Pack your hiking boots and bathing suit.

HIKING

There are so many magnificent trails in the Buda Hills that you may want to allow an extra few days in the area to enjoy. For those looking for a one-day green escape from the city, most locals tend to head to Normafa—it's the starting point for a lot of good trails and great views. For example, from Normafa, a 30-minute walk also takes you to János Hill, Budapest's highest point and the site of the Elizabeth lookout tower. A hike to Ördögorom (Devil's peak), starting from Farkasreti Cemetery, is another good option. Sashegy is also a lovely neighborhood with a nature reserve on the hill.

PARKS

Budapest Garden

IN-LINE SKATING/ROLLER SKATING | **FAMILY** | This wonderful park right by the river offers bars, street food, sports pitches, a sauna, an outdoor cinema, an obstacle course, a huge trampoline, and special events for kids. It began life as a skate park, and skaters, bladers, and bikers are still catered to, but there's a lot more going on here. ⊠ *Árpád Fejedelem útja*

125, Óbuda ☎ 1/250–4799 ⊕ www.buda-
pestgarden.com Ⓜ H5: Tímár utca.

Millenáris Park
PARK—SPORTS-OUTDOORS | FAMILY | A
former electrical factory turned modern
cultural complex and park, Millenáris Park
now hosts festivals, conferences, exhibitions, and the industrial-chic National
Dance Theater. There's a playground, a
café, a small pond, and, in the biting winters, a huge indoor playground, too. ✉ Kis
Rókus utca 16-20, Óbuda ⊕ millenaris.hu.

★ Római Part
BEACHES | This is a true—and quite
unexpected—hidden gem, just north of
Óbuda proper. Loved by locals but often
unvisited by tourists, it's a 5-km stretch
of riverside beach and promenade that is
perfect for a stroll but also offers sports
venues, open-air bars and restaurants,
and a general countryside vibe. There are
canoe and boat rentals, and biking here
is a joy, even right from the city center.
Lovely in summer, it can also be pleas-
ingly eerie in the depths of winter, too.
✉ Római Part, Óbuda Ⓜ H5: Rómaifürdő.

Chapter 12

SIDE TRIPS FROM BUDAPEST

12

Updated by
Joseph Reaney

 Sights
★★★★★

 Restaurants
★★★☆☆

 Hotels
★★★☆☆

 Shopping
★★★☆☆

 Nightlife
★★☆☆☆

WELCOME TO
SIDE TRIPS FROM BUDAPEST

TOP REASONS TO GO

★ **Step back in time.** Explore 1,000 years of Hungarian history at the immense Esztergom Basilica.

★ **Take the waters.** Drink the sulfuric spring water in Balatonfüred, or soak in a thermal spa in Hévíz.

★ **Sample the wine.** Taste a selection of Hungary's finest vintages in the pretty wine town of Villány.

★ **Meet the locals.** Visit Vác to come face-to-face with perfectly preserved 200-year-old mummies.

★ **Stay in a monastery.** Spend the night in an old monk's cell at Sopron's spectacular abbey-turned-hotel.

1 Szentendre. Gateway to the Danube Bend.

2 Visegrád. A 13th-century fortress.

3 Esztergom. Hungary's first capital.

4 Vác. Best known for its macabre mummies.

5 Hollókő. A UNESCO World Heritage Site.

6 Eger. Stunning architecture.

7 Pécs. Roman ruins and piles of Zsolnay porcelain.

8 Villány. Hungary's southernmost wine region.

9 Kecskemét. A city of vineyards and orchards.

10 Bugac. Center of the Kiskunság National Park.

11 Veszprém. Gateway to the Balaton region.

12 Balatonfüred. An ancient spa resort town.

13 Tihany. A grand hilltop abbey.

14 Badacsony and Szigliget. Trails, castles, and wine.

15 Keszthely and Hévíz. Famed for its magnificent palace.

16 Győr. A lovely northwestern city.

17 Sopron. Hungary's most faithful town.

18 Bratislava. Slovakia's lovely Old Town.

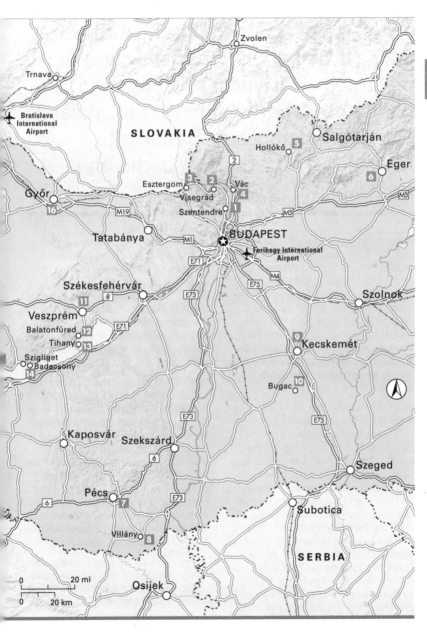

As one of Europe's most beautiful cities, Budapest naturally hogs the limelight. But those who venture a little farther afield—and in this compact country, it *is* only a little—soon find themselves richly rewarded with a host of Hungarian highlights, from ancient castles, majestic palaces, and imposing basilicas to lakeside resorts, thermal baths, and award-winning wine.

Some of the side trips from Budapest, such the towns around the Danube Bend and Hollókő, are within quick and easy reach of the capital so can be visited in a day. At a push, you could even manage them in half a day, though if you have the time it's better to make a day of it with multiple stops. Other Budapest side trips, such as the major (and more distant) cities of Pécs and Sopron, will require a weekend or more to fully explore.

For fans of architecture, there are many reasons to venture outside of Budapest. First there are the castles: Visegrád's enormous 13th-century citadel is the one big must-see, but other picturesque castles and ruins can be found in Eger, Szigliget, and Siklósi (close to Villány). And just across the border lies Bratislava's iconic white renaissance castle. Next there are the abbeys: the world-famous Pannonhalma Abbey near Győr is the country's finest, but the Benedictine Abbey overlooking Lake Balaton in Tihany is pretty special, and there's a majestic monastery-turned-hotel in Sopron, too. Then there are the churches: the enormous Esztergom Basilica is the big-ticket draw, but there are historic cathedrals, churches, and chapels (as well as mosques and synagogues) in pretty much every Hungarian town and city. And that's before we mention all those other gorgeous Gothic, beautiful baroque, remarkable rococo, and incredible Islamic buildings dotted throughout the country.

Outdoorsy types will love to stay on Lake Balaton, with the area's countless opportunities for hiking, biking, fishing, and all manner of water sports, from windsurfing to sailing. Wine lovers will relish a leisurely tour around Villány, home to big-name Hungarian wine producers like Bock and Gere. And foodies will get a real kick out of the countryside's exceptional, traditional Hungarian restaurants, from Macok in Eger to Villa Medici in Veszprém, as well as the never-ending supply of excellent bakery-cafés.

Traveling around Hungary is safe and simple, with the cities and bigger towns easily reached by public transport. However, it is always helpful to have a car for more remote sites. There are fewer tourist facilities and English speakers outside of the capital, but you'll get far more bang for your buck at hotels and restaurants—as well as the satisfaction of really getting to know the country.

MAJOR REGIONS

Within easy reach of Budapest, the **Danube Bend** curves gracefully past a string of postcard-perfect towns. Proximity to the city combined with a high "cute quotient" (think cobblestone squares, candy-colored houses, and a surfeit of crafts shops) makes **Szentendre** the most popular stop, but **Visegrád** (with its pretty 13th-century citadel), **Esztergom** (with its enormous and imposing basilica), and **Vác** (with its macabre mummified remains) are also rewarding destinations. Of course, none of these villages can be classified as well-kept secrets, so expect to encounter crowds.

To the east of Budapest lies **Heves County** and its beautiful capital, **Eger.** One of the country's best-known wine centers, where tasting opportunities abound, Eger is also a popular jumping-off point to explore the world-famous Tokaj wine region. It also appeals to teetotalers thanks to the wealth of baroque and rococo buildings in its well-preserved Old Town. A lovely stop between Budapest and Eger is **Hollókő,** a picture-perfect Hungarian village (and UNESCO World Heritage Site) topped by a dramatic ruined castle.

Head all the way south to reach the beautiful **Baranya County.** Although it only has 145,000 inhabitants, regional capital **Pécs** packs quite a punch, with attractions including Christian sites that run the gamut from a 4th-century mausoleum to a stellar 19th-century basilica, and some of Hungary's best Ottoman architecture. It also has more museums, symphonies, theaters, and ballet companies than you'd expect from a city of this size. A short way south of here lies **Villány,** perhaps Hungary's most appealing wine-growing region thanks to its welcoming wine cellars offering excellent tastings, good food, and even hotel accommodation.

Southwest Hungary is home to one of its most famous attractions: **Lake Balaton.** Central Europe's largest lake is seen as prized real estate in landlocked Hungary, and in summer it seems as if the entire populace congregates here. Stick to the more attractive north shore, where the lakeside boulevards in **Balatonfüred, Tihany,** and **Keszthely** are backed by scenic hills. In places like **Veszprém, Szigliget,** and **Badacsony,** discerning guests have an opportunity to explore traditional hillside villages, hiking trails, and vineyards as well as the waterfront. The upscale spa resorts in **Hévíz** are an added bonus.

To the northwest of Budapest lies the **Small Golden Triangle,** containing three ancient and appealing cities. **Győr** is the largest city in Western Hungary and has 2,000 years of history and conflict etched into its architecture, from its 12th-century cathedral to its beautiful baroque palaces and squares. Pretty **Sopron** also welcomes history buffs, with a remarkably high concentration of antique buildings and monuments (355 to be exact) tucked within its city walls. And **Bratislava,** just across the border in Slovakia, has a spectacular Old Town and grand renaissance castle that showcase a mix of Hungarian, Austrian, German, and Czech influences.

Planning

Getting Here and Around

Most of Hungary's biggest cities and towns are well connected to Budapest by public transport, which is efficient and inexpensive. Intercity travel is most common with buses (run by Volánbusz) and trains (run by MÁV), but the most fun way to reach the Danube Bend is by hydrofoil boat (run by Mahart).

The country's village, town, and city centers are generally quite compact and so eminently walkable. However, there are local bus, tram, and trolleybus services for weary travelers. Getting to more rural or remote areas, including Lake Balaton and the Villány wine region, is trickier by public transport, so it's easiest to have your own car (the only downside is that you'll need to agree on a designated driver during vineyard visits). All the big international car hire brands, including Avis, Hertz, and Sixt, have a presence in Hungary.

BUS
CONTACTS Volánbusz. ⊠ Üllői út 131, Budapest ☎ 1/382–0888 ⊕ www.volan-busz.hu Ⓜ M3: Népliget.

BOAT
CONTACTS Mahart. ⊠ Sales Office, Belgrád rakpart, Belváros ☎ 1/484–4013 ⊕ www.mahartpassnave.hu Ⓜ M3: Ferenciek tere.

TRAIN
CONTACTS MÁV. ☎ 1/349–4949 ⊕ www.mavcsoport.hu.

Hotels

In general, lodging is cheaper outside Budapest, though some establishments in more tourist-heavy destinations may be comparable. There are some fine hotels but few international five-star brands. Staff are less likely to speak English, too—but that's all part of the adventure.

Restaurants

While you can find excellent Hungarian restaurants all over the country, there are less international options once you leave Budapest.

HOTEL AND RESTAURANT PRICES
Hotel prices in the reviews are the lowest cost of a standard double room in high season. Restaurant prices in the reviews are the average cost of a main course at dinner, or if dinner is not served, at lunch. Restaurant and hotel reviews have been shortened. For more information, visit fodors.com.

What it Costs in forints			
$	$$	$$$	$$$$
RESTAURANTS			
under 1,500 HUF	1,500–3,000 HUF	3,001–5,000 HUF	over 5,000 HUF
HOTELS			
under 31,000 HUF	31,000–44,000 HUF	44,001–56,000 HUF	over 56,000 HUF

Tours

There are several tour companies operating out of Budapest that offer trips to the Danube Bend and Lake Balaton, as well as to wine regions like Eger and Villány. It's a little harder to find tours to places like Pécs and Sopron, but these are easily reached by train.

CityRama
EXCURSIONS | As well as offering a host of Budapest city tours, CityRama also offers half- and full-day tours outside the capital, from the Danube Bend to Lake Balaton. It's also possible to order cars or coaches with a driver, which will allow you to travel where you want at your own pace. ⊠ Báthory utca 22, Budapest ☎ 1/332–5344 ⊕ www.cityrama.hu.

Taste Hungary
SPECIAL-INTEREST | This Budapest-based tour company specializes in wine and culinary tours. They offer regular full-day tours to Eger and Villány, as well as a "wine transfer" between Budapest and Bratislava (in either direction). You can

also arrange customized tours with their expert team of guides and sommeliers. ☎ 1/701–1886 ⊕ www.tastehungary.com.

Szentendre

21 km (13 miles) north of Budapest.

A romantic, lively little town with a flourishing artists' colony, this is the gateway to the Danube Bend from Budapest. With its profusion of enchanting church steeples, colorful baroque houses, and winding, narrow cobblestone streets—as well as its myriad art museums—it's no wonder Szentendre attracts swarms of visitors, tripling its population in peak season.

Named for St. Andrew, Szentendre was first settled by Serbs and Greeks fleeing the advancing Turks in the 16th and 17th centuries. They built houses and churches in their own style; rich in reds and blues seldom seen elsewhere in Hungary. From town, a short drive or ferry brings you to the amazingly untouched green paradise that is Szentendrei-sziget (Szentendre Island).

As Szentendre is within easy reach of Budapest, some choose to make it their base while exploring the Hungarian capital. Accommodation is cheaper and the town is empty of tourists by the evening, offering a peaceful night after a long day's sightseeing.

GETTING HERE AND AROUND

If you have access to a car, you can drive to Szentendre from Budapest. It's a relatively short trip (30 minutes), straight up Route 11 on the west bank of the river. There are also three to five local commuter trains (HÉV) an hour from Batthyány Tér Metro station (line M2); the journey takes around 40 minutes.

From mid-April to September, the most interesting way to get to Szentendre is by ferry. Leaving from a dock off Budapest's Vigadó Square at 10 am, the journey takes 1½ hours. Return ferries leave Szentendre at 5 pm, taking just an hour. Round trip tickets cost 3,830 HUF; you'll find a full list of prices and timetables at ⊕ www.mahartpassnave.hu.

Once in Szentendre, ditch the vehicles and simply stroll along the town's lovely cobblestone streets. If this proves tiring (or you wore heels) you can always explore the town by horse-drawn carriage, which you'll see hitched up near the main town square (Fő tér).

 ## Sights

Ferenczy Múzeum

MUSEUM | The museum honors the work of Impressionist Károly Ferenczy (1862–1917), an important leader in the Nagybánya Artist Colony and a Szentendre native. There are a number of his artworks on display, though many of his most famous are in Budapest's Hungarian National Gallery. The exhibition also features the work of his three children, all of whom were popular artists of the early modern era: the expressionist painter Valér, the pioneering tapestry artist Noemi, and the sculptor and graphic artist Beni. ■TIP→ **Pay a little extra for a combined FMC ticket, which also gets you into the Kmetty Múzeum and the Kovács Margit Ceramic Museum.** ✉ Kossuth Lajos utca 5 ☎ 20/779–6657 ⊕ www.muzeumicentrum.hu ☕ 1,400 HUF; combined ticket with Kmetty and Kovács museums 1,700 HUF ⊗ Closed Tues.

Fő tér

PLAZA | Fő tér is Szentendre's colorful main square, the centerpiece of which is an ornate **Memorial Cross** erected by Serbs grateful that their town was spared from a plague. The cross displays a painted crucifixion and stands atop a triangular pillar adorned with a dozen icon paintings. Every single house on Fő tér is a designated landmark. The **Szentendrei Képtár** serves as an information center and also has its own excellent

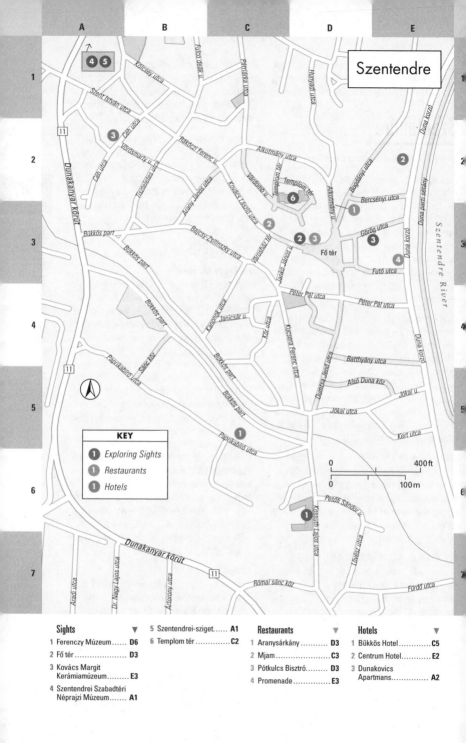

Szentendre

KEY

- **1** Exploring Sights
- **1** Restaurants
- **1** Hotels

collection of local contemporary artists and revolving exhibits of international art. Cross the square and check out the **Kmetty Múzeum**, featuring the work of János Kmetty (1889–1975), a pioneer of Hungarian avant-garde painting. Kmetty tried his hand at everything from Impressionism to Cubism, and his absorbing self-portraits utilize a fascinating mix of styles. Gracing the corner of Görög utca is the Serbian Orthodox church **Blagoveštenska templom**, with its elegant 18th-century edifice built on the site of a wooden church dating from the Great Serbian Migration (around AD 690). Its greatest glory—a symmetrical floor-to-ceiling panoply of stunning icons—was painted between 1802 and 1804. Behind the church lies the **Szerb Egyházi Múzeum**, with its exquisite assemblage of ecclesiastical art and artifacts relating to the history of the church in Hungary. ⊠ *Szentendre.*

Kovács Margit Kerámiamúzeum (*Margit Kovács Ceramic Collection*)

MUSEUM | If you have time for only one of Szentendre's myriad museums, make it this extraordinary exhibition showcasing the works of the renowned Budapest ceramics artist. Kovács, who died in 1977, left behind a wealth of richly textured works that range from ceramic figurines to life-size sculptures and draw inspiration from folk history, Christianity, and 20th century life. Look out for the tiny but wonderful Beggar Woman with Forget-Me-Not Eyes, half-hidden in a wall recess. ⊠ *Vastagh Gyorgy utca 1* ☎ *20/779–6657* ⊕ *www.muzeumicentrum.hu* ⛶ *1,400 HUF; 1,700 HUF combined ticket with Ferenczy and Kmetty museums.*

Szentendrei Szabadtéri Néprajzi Múzeum (*Szentendre Skanzen Village Museum*)

MUSEUM VILLAGE | Szentendre's farthest-flung museum is also the largest open-air museum in the country. Located 5 km (3 miles) northwest of the city center, it is a living re-creation of 18th- and 19th-century village life from different regions of Hungary—the sort of place where blacksmith shops and a horse-powered mill compete with wooden farmhouses and folk handicrafts for your attention. A heritage train takes you around the site. The museum is accessible by bus 230 from stand 7 of the Szentendre terminus of the HÉV suburban railway. Guided tours in English are available if booked in advance. ⊠ *Sztaravodai út 75* ☎ *26/502–537* ⊕ *www.skanzen.hu* ⛶ *2,000 HUF* ⏱ *Closed Mon.*

★ Szentendrei-sziget (*Szentendre Island*)

ISLAND | Looking for some tranquility after squeezing through the crowds in downtown Szentendre? The answer is this lush green island oasis, right across the river but surprisingly untouched and ripe for exploration. At the time of the Hungarian conquest of the Carpathian Basin in AD 896, the flat island—33 km (21 miles) long and up to 3.8 km (2.4 miles) wide—was used as pasture land. It subsequently became a key agricultural, ship-building, and fishing center that helped link the otherwise hilly Danube Bend with Buda to the south. Only after the end of the 120-year Turkish occupation of Hungary in the late 17th century did a loose-knit web of settlements develop, and from the mid-19th century on, resort districts began to spring up for city-weary Budapesters.

Most of Szentendre Island comprises nature preserves and bucolic countryside—this is a rich habitat and stopping-off point for waterfowl—but there are also four villages, from quaint Kisoroszi (with its gorgeous golden beach) on the island's northern tip, to the larger but lovely Szigetmonostor in the south. To get to the island from Szentendre, hop on a ferry from the docks, or cross the bridge at Tahitótfalu, 10 km (6 miles) north of town. ⊠ *Szigetmonostor.*

Templom tér (*Church Square*)

PLAZA | Climb the narrow steps up Váralja lépcső, located near the corner of Fő tér

Szentendre Island, located in the Danube River, is home to a number of villages including Kisoroszi and Horány.

and Görög utca, to reach this cobblestone hilltop square. Once the site of a medieval fortress, it is today home to the baroque **Szentendrei Keresztelő Szent János Plébánia** (Church of St. John the Baptist), famed for its enormous, dark frescoes. But the real reward for the climb comes in the form of spectacular views over the town's angular sile rooftops and steeples, and of the Danube beyond. ✉ *Szentendre.*

 Restaurants

★ Aranysárkány

$$$ | **EASTERN EUROPEAN** | A favorite of early-20th-century Hungarian writer Frigyes Karinthy, the Golden Dragon restaurant has been welcoming locals and tourists for decades. Set within a small, sloped-roof house, it's known for its charming Hungarian decor and its meat- and fish-heavy menu; highlights include the *velős pirítós* (bone marrow on toast), *sárkányerőleves* (dragon's bouillon) with quail eggs, and *mézes-mázas libasteak* (honey-glazed goose steak). **Known for:**

serves international cuisine (not, as the name suggests, Chinese food); extensive wine list with many Hungarian choices; reservations a must in summer. $ *Average main: 4,500 HUF* ✉ *Alkotmány utca 1/a* ☎ *26/301–479* ⊕ *www.aranysarkany. hu* ☽ *Closed Mon.*

Mjam

$$$ | **CARIBBEAN** | This cute little café-restaurant is billed as a Caribbean restaurant, yet among signature dishes like seafood curry and mango salad you'll find a whole host of international fare, from rice noodle soups to roasted duck legs. They also do a mean burger. **Known for:** juicy burgers with homemade sauces; colorful decor; lovely tree-shaded courtyard. $ *Average main: 4,000 HUF* ✉ *Városház tér 2* ☎ *70/440-3700* ⊕ *www. facebook.com/Mjam-1382578311969323* ☽ *Closed Mon. year-round; closed Tues.– Fri. in winter.*

Pótkulcs Bisztró

$$ | **HUNGARIAN** | Whether you are looking for a cozy place for a quick *forralt bor* (mulled wine) on a rainy winter day, or

a hearty meal to tide you over between your museum visits, Pótkulcs Bisztró serves a wide variety of traditional Hungarian dishes. Everything is fresh, homemade, and includes a slight modern-fusion touch. **Known for:** traditional Hungarian paprika-filled stews; friendly staff; local art on the walls (which is for sale). $ Average main: 2,500 HUF ⊠ Fő tér 11 ☎ 70/240–1424 ⊕ www.facebook.com/PotkulcsSzentendre.

Promenade

$$ | **HUNGARIAN** | Endowed with an elegant-country dining room, a 16th-century vaulted wine cellar for tastings, a sprawling garden terrace with stunning views of the Danube, and a menu of enticing farm-to-table dishes, what's not to love? The rather limited menu highlights Hungarian game and fish, with traditional dishes such as venison goulash with potato fritters, crispy roast duck with baked apples, and panfried trout with parsley potatoes. **Known for:** locally sourced game and lamb; few options for vegetarians; extensive menu of 60 Hungarian wines. $ Average main: 2,750 HUF ⊠ Futó utca 4 ☎ 26/312–626 ⊕ www.promenade-szentendre.hu.

🛏 Hotels

Bükkös Hotel

$$$$ | **RESORT** | Offering half-board stays in spacious and stylishly appointed rooms, this romantic, centrally located hotel is renowned for two things: its peaceful and plant-filled rooftop terrace overlooking the Bükkös creek, and its soothing spa facilities, which include a jacuzzi, Finnish saunas, infrared sauna, steam room, and multiple massage treatment rooms. **Pros:** excellent spa with Jacuzzi and saunas; five minutes' walk from Fő tér; tasty breakfast and dinner included. **Cons:** no tea or coffee in standard rooms; minimum two-night stay at peak times; parking costs 2,500 HUF a night. $ Rooms from: 82,000 HUF ⊠ Bükkös

part 16 ☎ 26/501–360 ⊕ www.bukkoshotel.hu ⤴ 22 rooms ⦿ Free breakfast.

Centrum Hotel

$ | **B&B/INN** | As the name suggests, this charming little bed-and-breakfast has a conveniently central (and Danube-facing) location, but remains far enough off the tourist drag to offer some peace and quiet. **Pros:** four-bedroom villa with sauna is a great option for groups; free parking for guests; cheap accommodation option. **Cons:** bedroom decor is quite old-fashioned; thin walls mean you can hear neighbors; breakfast isn't included (extra 1,800 HUF). $ Rooms from: 18,000 HUF ⊠ Duna korzó 5 ☎ 26/302–500 ⊕ www.centrumhotelszentendre.hu ⤴ 9 rooms ⦿ No meals.

Dunakovics Apartmans

$$ | **RENTAL** | **FAMILY** | With five centrally located and individually designed apartments spread across two nearby buildings, Dunakovics is a great option for groups and, in particular, families— it's one of the few hotels in town that actively welcomes kids. **Pros:** each apartment has its own unique style; key code entry means you can come and go as you please; free Dunakavics candies for guests. **Cons:** property is hard to find (look for a small wall sign); not all apartments are to all tastes; no breakfast. $ Rooms from: 39,000 HUF ⊠ Szent István utca 2 ☎ 30/747–7060 ⊕ www.dunakavicsapartman.hu ⤴ 5 apartments ⦿ No meals.

🛍 Shopping

Flooded with tourists in summer, Szentendre is saturated with the requisite souvenir shops, selling dolls dressed in traditional folk costumes, wooden trinkets, and colorful hand-embroidered tablecloths. But look around and you'll find some more authentic shopping options, even along touristy Bogdányi Street.

Bogdányi út

SHOPPING NEIGHBORHOODS | Bogdányi Street is one of Szentendre's main shopping streets, where you'll find the usual tourist fare interspersed with art galleries and folk art, but don't restrict yourself to this one area. Flooded with tourists in summer, Szentendre is saturated with the requisite souvenir shops. Among the attractive (but overpriced) goods sold in every store are dolls dressed in traditional folk costumes, wooden trinkets, pottery, paprika, wine, and colorful hand-embroidered tablecloths, doilies, and blouses. The best bargains are the hand-embroidered blankets and bags sold by dozens of elderly women in traditional folk attire, who stand for hours on the town's crowded streets. Many Szentendre stores stay open all day on weekends, unlike those in Budapest. ⊠ *Bogdányi.*

Ecclesia galéria

CERAMICS/GLASSWARE | This charming little ceramics shop sells all manner of handmade pottery, from plant pots to dinner plates, often with traditional Hungarian folk designs. Head out into the garden to peruse the ceramics at leisure (you can also see it from Templom tér above, if you want to avoid the crowds). ⊠ *Bogdányi út 2.*

Szamos Marcipán Cukrászda

FOOD/CANDY | This quaint little bakery-café and store is the place to indulge your sweet tooth, with a selection of delicious almond-meal candies and other confections; try the orange marzipan bonbons. It also has a small exhibition (500 HUF) with a zany selection of all-marzipan figures: a life-size Princess Diana holds court among animals, flower arrangements, and more. ⊠ *Dumtsa Jenő utca 14* ☎ *26/310–545* ⊕ *www.szamos.hu/uzletek/muzeum-cukraszda.*

Activities

BICYCLING

The waterfront and streets beyond Szentendre's main square are perfect for a bike ride—free of jostling cobblestones and relatively calm and quiet. The town's tourist information center (at Dumtsa Jenő utca 22) offers rentals, or you can bring a bike from Budapest on the train (there are designated bicycle cars). Many people make the trip between Budapest and Szentendre on bicycle along the designated bike path; it runs on busy roads in some places but is mainly pleasant and separate from the road.

Visegrád

20 km (12½ miles) northwest of Szentendre, 40 km (25 miles) north of Budapest.

Visegrád was the seat of the Hungarian kings during the 14th century, when a fortress built here by the Angevin kings became the royal residence. Today, the imposing fortress at the top of the hill towers over the peaceful little town of quiet, tree-lined streets and solid old houses. The forested hills rising just behind the town offer popular hiking possibilities. For a taste of Visegrád's best, climb to the Fellegvár, and then wander and take in the views of the Danube curving through the countryside. Do make time to stroll around the village center a bit—on Fő utca and other streets that pique your interest.

GETTING HERE AND AROUND

Visegrád is best reached by car from Szentendre, as you can go directly up to the citadel and park. To get to the town from Szentendre, simply head northwest on Szarvashegyi út/Szentendrei utca (from Budapest, you'll need to follow Route 11 north to Szentendre before heading northwest from there).

The best public transport option to Visegrád is Bus 880, which leaves every hour from Budapest's Batthyány tér station (90 minutes) and goes via Szentendre (40 minutes). There are also hourly trains from Budapest–Nyugati station (45 minutes), but these drop off at Nagymaros–Visegrád station on the wrong side of the river, so you'll need to walk down from here to catch the hourly car ferry.

If you're coming directly from Budapest in spring or summer, the quickest (and most fun) option is the hydrofoil. Boats leave from a dock off Budapest's Vigadó Square at 9:30 am and the journey takes just one hour. There's also a return ferry at 3:30 pm. A one-way trip costs 4,300 HUF, while a round trip is 6,500 HUF. You'll find a full list of prices and timetables at ⊕ www.mahartpassnave.hu.

Those without a car should pack comfortable shoes for the 40-minute climb up to the citadel—or prepare to pay for a taxi.

Sights

★ Fellegvár (Citadel)

CASTLE/PALACE | Crowning the top of a 1,148-foot hill, Visegrád's dramatic citadel was built in the 13th century and served as the seat of Hungarian kings in the early 14th century. In the Middle Ages, this was where the Holy Crown and other royal regalia were kept, until they were stolen by a dishonorable maid of honor in 1440; 23 years later King Matthias had to pay 80,000 HUF to retrieve them from Austria. Today, the crown is safe and sound in Budapest's Parliament building. There are some interesting exhibits and artifacts inside the castle, including coats of arms, hunting trophies, models of the castle through history, and waxwork recreations of Renaissance feasts and balls, but most people's abiding memory of the site is the breathtaking views it offers of the Danube Bend below. It's certainly ample reward for the strenuous 40-minute hike up, which starts from the back gate of Salamon Tower. Then again, you can always drive up the hill from the

center of Visegrád in five minutes and park (for a fee). ■**TIP→ Only interested in the view? Come after 6 pm for free access to the terrace.** ✉ Fő utca 31 ☎ 26/398–101 ⊕ www.visitvisegrad.hu 🖾 1,700 HUF ⊗ Closed weekdays Jan. and Feb.

Mátyás Király Múzeum (Museum of Matthias Rex)

CASTLE/PALACE | In the 15th century, King Matthias Corvinus had a separate, 350-room palace built on the bank of the Danube below the citadel. It was eventually razed by the Turks, and not until 1934 were the ruins finally excavated. Now, after extensive reconstruction, it's possible to visit about 20 of the rooms—including the royal bed chambers, the kitchen, and the chapel—which are spread throughout the **Királyi palota** (Royal Palace) and its **Salamon torony** (Salamon Tower). Come during summer to see medieval games and craft demonstrations. ✉ Fő utca 23 ☎ 26/597–010 ⊕ www.visegradmuzeum.hu 🖾 1,400 HUF castle; 700 HUF Salamon Tower ⊗ Closed Mon.; closed Oct.–Mar.

Hotels

★ Hotel Silvanus

$$$ | **HOTEL** | Situated high up on Fekete Hill, with commanding forest and Danube views, this is Visegrád's highest-altitude hotel—and one of its finest, incorporating a large wellness center with indoor and outdoor pool, Jacuzzis, saunas, steam rooms, salt chambers, and more. **Pros:** unbeatable views over the Danube Bend; half-board buffet breakfasts and dinners are great; superb pool and spa facilities. **Cons:** some of the decor is a little dated; only accessible by car; parking costs 1,000 HUF a night. ⑨ Rooms from: 55,000 HUF ✉ Panoráma út 2 ☎ 26/398-311 ⊕ www.hotelsilvanus.hu 🛏 151 rooms ۞ All-inclusive.

Thermal Hotel Visegrád

$$$ | **HOTEL** | A half-hour walk from the center of town, this larger than life

Located to the north of the capital city on the enchanting Danube Bend, Visegrád's Fellegvár was built on a hilltop which affords stunning views over the countryside.

hotel isn't much to look at (one might even be tempted to call it a blight on an otherwise idyllic landscape) but it offers a comfortable stay. **Pros:** great views; most rooms have terraces; comfortable. **Cons:** perfectly fine but nothing special; some rooms are a little small; not all rooms face the Danube. *Rooms from: 55,000 HUF* *Lepencevölgy hrsz. 1213* *26/801–900* *www.thv.hu* *164 rooms* *Free breakfast.*

Activities

HIKING

Visegrád makes a great base for exploring the trails of the Visegrád and Pilis hills. A hiking map is posted on the corner of Fő utca and Rév utca, just above the pale-green Roman Catholic Parish Church. A well-trodden, well-marked hiking trail (posted with red signs) leads from the edge of Visegrád to the town of Pilisszentlászló, a wonderful 8½-km (5-mile) journey that takes about three hours, through the oak and beech forests of the Visegrád Hills into the Pilis conservation region. Deer, wild boar, and mouflon roam freely here, and there are fields of yellow-blooming spring pheasant's eye and black pulsatilla.

TOBOGGAN SLIDE

Visegrádi Bobpálya (*Visegrad Bobsled*)
SNOW SPORTS | **FAMILY** | Winding through the trees on Nagy-Villám Hill, high above the town (and just beyond the Silvanus Hotel), is this all-year-round toboggan run, one of the longest slides you've ever seen. You ride on a small cart that is pulled uphill by trolley, then careen down the slope in a small, steel trough that resembles a bobsled run. It's 600 HUF per ride, 3,000 HUF for six, and 4,800 HUF for 10. *Nagyvillám 1* *26/397–397* *www.bobozas.hu* *600 HUF.*

Esztergom

26 km (16 miles) west of Visegrád, 50 km (31 miles) northwest of Budapest.

The impressive Esztergom Basilica, dramatically reflected in the Danube River, takes front and center in this ancient river town. Small though it may be, Esztergom has proved a major force in Hungary's history: St. Stephen, the first Christian king and founder of the nation, was crowned here in AD 1000. This established Esztergom as Hungary's first capital, which it remained for the next 250 years. It also made Esztergom the seat of the Roman Catholic Primate of Hungary, which it has remained for more than a thousand years.

While the town's main attractions can be visited in a day, Esztergom is also home to a fine selection of restaurants and (in particular) bars and music clubs, as well as some decent accommodation options, so consider staying overnight.

GETTING AROUND

You can drive from Visegrád to Esztergom in less than 30 minutes by following the Danube-hugging Route 11 west. There's also a regular bus (number 880) that takes around 45 minutes. From mid-April to September, you can also take a hydrofoil boat trip from Visegrád to Esztergom; it departs at 10:30 am and returns at 3 pm; return tickets cost 4,250 HUF. The boat starts and ends in Budapest and also goes via Vác; there's more information at ⊕ *www.mahartpassnave. hu.*

To reach Estztergom from Budapest by car, simply drive an hour northwest along Routes 10 and 11. There are also hourly trains from Budapest-Nyugati, which take 90 minutes.

Once you're in town, everything can be visited on foot; though prepare for some climbing up and down from the basilica. If you enjoy strolling, leave yourself a little time to explore the narrow streets of Víziváros (Watertown) below the basilica, lined with brightly painted baroque buildings.

Sights

Esztergomi Bazilika

RELIGIOUS SITE | This immense basilica, the largest in the country and visible from miles around, is the seat of the cardinal primate of Hungary. Completed in 1856 on the site of a medieval cathedral and recently restored, the basilica's most wondrous feature is the **Bakócz Chapel** (1506). Named for a primate of Hungary who only narrowly missed becoming pope, the chapel—on your left as you enter—is the most beautiful work of Renaissance architecture in all of Hungary; note its red marble, magnificent carvings, and enormous altar painting. Other highlights to look for are the **sacristy,** which contains a valuable collection of medieval ecclesiastical art; the vast and deep **crypt**, where the cathedral's builders and key priests are buried; and the **treasury**, containing a trove of precious ecclesiastical objects. For a great view of Esztergom, climb the long, winding staircase up to the observation platform in the cathedral's **cupola,** or take a stroll around the back of the building to the impressive **Szent István megkoronázása** (St. Stephen's Coronation) sculpture. Each section of the basilica's interior requires an entrance fee, from 300 to 900 HUF, so your best bet is to purchase the combination ticket. ⊠ *Szent István tér 1, Esztergom* ☎ *33/402–354* ⊕ *www. bazilika-esztergom.hu* 🎫 *1,500 HUF combo ticket.*

Keresztény Múzeum (*Christian Museum*)

MUSEUM | Considered by many to be Hungary's finest art gallery, the Christian Museum is located in the Primate's Palace in the pretty riverside Víziváros district. It's home to the country's greatest collection of medieval Hungarian religious art, as well as Dutch, German, and Italian master paintings; the 14th- and 15th-century Italian collection is unusually large for a museum outside of Italy. The museum's showstopper is the intricately carved 15th-century Holy Sepulchre of Garamszentbenedek, depicting the 12 Apostles clustered around Christ's tomb, which was wheeled through the town during Easter processions. You can reach the museum from the basilica via the steep Macskalépcső, or Cat Stairs. ⊠ *Mindszenty tér 2, Esztergom* ☎ *33/413–880* ⊕ *www.kereszteny-muzeum.hu* 🖻 *900 HUF* ⊘ *Closed Mon., Tues., Jan., and Feb.*

Vármúzeum (*Castle Museum*)

MUSEUM | Situated right beside the basilica, the Castle Museum is housed in the former Royal Palace, built in the 12th century when Esztergom was the country's capital but later ransacked by the Turks. Today, it's an intriguing jumble of modern and medieval, with a historic collection of archaeological finds from the area, including pottery and artifacts dating from the 11th century. Visitors can also explore the remaining rooms of the Royal Palace, including the gorgeous chapel with its 13th-century frescoes. ⊠ *Szent Istvan ter 1, Esztergom* ☎ *33/415–986* ⊕ *www.varmegom.hu* 🖻 *1,600 HUF* ⊘ *Closed Mon.*

 Restaurants

★ Csülök Csárda

$$$ | HUNGARIAN | With its hearty Hungarian fare, rustic atmosphere, and unbeatable location in full view of the basilica, the Pork Knuckle Tavern has long been popular with locals and visitors alike. Knuckles are, of course, the specialty here, and if you've never tried this succulent dish, now's your chance. **Known for:** pork knuckle in many varieties and forms; basic tavern atmosphere; few options for vegetarians. ⑤ *Average main: 3,500 HUF* ⊠ *Batthyány Lajos utca 9, Esztergom* ☎ *33/412–420* ⊕ *www.csulokcsarda.hu.*

Mediterraneo

$$ | HUNGARIAN | Nothing about the menu accounts for the name, but this pleasant eatery is popular for generous portions of homey, unpretentious traditional Hungarian dishes. Meat lovers will appreciate a hearty steak or veal chops, fish fans will favor the baked salmon with steamed veggies, and vegetarians and vegans will find a limited selection of salads and side dishes. **Known for:** homey Hungarian fare (despite the name); meatless salads and sides but few other veggie options; central location with views of the bridge. ⑤ *Average main: 2,950 HUF* ⊠ *Helischer József út 2, Esztergom* ☎ *33/311–411* ⊕ *www.facebook.com/MediterraneoVendegfogado.*

★ Prímás Pince

$$$ | HUNGARIAN | Its dramatic setting under soaring vaulted ceilings in the old basilica's cellar is just one of this contemporary dining room's many attractions. Add an enticing menu of Hungarian and international dishes, the city's best wine selection (with information boards on all of the country's distinct wine-growing regions), and surprisingly low prices, and you've got the top choice in town. **Known for:** spectacular cellar setting with shimmering chandeliers; dishes like roast duck leg and baked trout; draws crowds but never feels crowded. ⑤ *Average main: 3,750 HUF* ⊠ *Szent István tér 12, Esztergom* ☎ *33/541–965* ⊕ *www.primaspince.hu* ⊘ *No dinner Sun.*

Hotels

Hotel Adalbert - Szent Tamás Ház

$ | HOTEL | The newer and smarter outpost of the long-established Hotel Adalbert, St. Thomas House is set within an old monastery building within sight of the basilica, and offers a selection of simple but comfortable rooms and apartments. **Pros:** simple but stylish decor; free parking and secure storage for bikes; super-friendly staff. **Cons:** no tea and coffee facilities; some rooms are small;

crucifixes hanging everywhere may put some off. $ *Rooms from: 19,000 HUF* ✉ *Batthyány Lajos utca 6, Esztergom* ☎ *33/541–972* ⊕ *www.hoteladalbert.hu* ⛱ *56 rooms* ⦿❘ *Free breakfast.*

Portobello Hotel
$$$ | **RESORT** | **FAMILY** | Billing itself as a "Wellness and Yacht Hotel," this resort-style building overlooks the Little Danube (a tiny tributary of the main river) and is directly connected to the Aquasziget water park with its multiple swimming pools, flumes, and wellness areas—making it a perfect option for families. **Pros:** access corridor to a fun water park; breakfast included and half board available; bikes available to rent. **Cons:** the green glass-covered exterior isn't very appealing; water park often busy with nonguests; minimum three-night stay in summer. $ *Rooms from: 49,000 HUF* ✉ *Táncsics Mihály utca 5, Esztergom* ☎ *30/335–6518* ⊕ *www.portobello.hu* ⛱ *95 rooms* ⦿❘ *Free breakfast.*

 ## Nightlife

All in Music Café
MUSIC CLUBS | The centrally located All in Music Café is Esztergom's go-to spot for an instant party and features both live music and an enormous selection of wine and brandy. ✉ *Bajcsy-Zsilinszky út 37, Esztergom.*

Kaleidoszkop Ház
MUSIC CLUBS | This many-faceted art gallery and cultural center hosts a Friday-night series of live concerts featuring indie bands, jazz, folk, and contemporary experimental music by Hungarian and European talents. Concerts are held in the garden in warm weather and in the center's spacious vaulted cellar in the cooler months. ✉ *Pázmány Péter utca 7, Esztergom* ☎ *30/334–6024* ⊕ *www. kaleidoszkophaz.hu.*

★ Pálinka Patika
BARS/PUBS | As the name suggests, this charming little bar specializes in *pálinkas*

(Hungarian fruit brandies) with more than 120 different varieties on offer. Sit inside to enjoy the retro decor, including the apothecary-style cabinets, or sit out on the terrace to people-watch as you drink. ✉ *Széchenyi tér 25, Esztergom* ☎ *30/336–3474* ⊕ *www.palinkapatika. com.*

Vác

42 km (26 miles) east of Esztergom, 42 km (26 miles) north of Budapest.

Located on the Danube's east bank, the sleepy town of Vác is well worth a short visit. Its attractive main square is towered over by the pale yellow baroque facade of the Fehérek temploma (Church of the White Friars), and is also home to Memento Mori, the town's macabre headline attraction. Yet visitors who wander onto Vác's narrow cobblestone side streets will be rewarded further with pretty baroque buildings in matte yellows and reds.

The promenade along the Danube is a wonderful place to stroll or picnic, looking out at the glistening river or back toward the pretty historic town. The main entrance to the riverfront area is from Petróczy utca, which begins at the cathedral on Konstantin tér and feeds straight into the promenade. If you arrive by train in late April or early May, you'll be greeted outside the station by a lovely pink promenade of cherry blossoms.

GETTING HERE AND AROUND
To reach Vác by car from Esztergom, you will need to cross the river. The quickest way (just over an hour) is to drive over the bridge in Esztergom, heading north on Route 564 then east on Route 12, but this involves a foray into neighboring Slovakia. A simpler, if slightly longer, option is to head east along Route 11 to Tahitótfalu, then hop on a car ferry across to Vác; if you're lucky with ferry crossings, this can take as little as 1¼ hours.

There are no direct bus or train connections from Esztergom to Vác. But from mid-April to September, a hydrofoil boat sails from Esztergom to Budapest every day, with a stop at Vác. It departs at 3 pm and takes 50 minutes; a single ticket costs 3,300 HUF.

If you're coming from Budapest, you can drive north along the river-hugging M2 highway (40 minutes), or take a regular direct train from Budapest-Nyugati (25 minutes).

 Sights

★ **Memento Mori**

MUSEUM | The fascinating (if somewhat macabre) discovery of the Memento Mori was made in 1994 during renovation work on the Church of the White Friars, when workers happened upon the largely forgotten, sealed entrance to a crypt that had been used by the Dominicans to bury clergy and local burghers from 1731 to 1801. Inside were numerous ornately decorated coffins with surprisingly well-preserved, still-clothed mummies and their burial accessories, including rosaries and crucifixes. The coffins have now been moved to a nearby cellar on the same square, with three open caskets displaying the eerie mummified remains of a nine-year-old girl, a woman in her 50s, and a man in his 60s. The museum starts with some interesting above-ground exhibits on the discovery, as well as the history of church and the town at large, before a steep staircase leads downstairs to the cold exhibit room. ⊠ *Március 15 tér 19, Vác* ☎ *27/200–868* ⊕ *www.muzeumvac. hu* 🖾 *1,400 HUF* ⊗ *Closed Mon.*

Nagyboldogasszony-székesegyház (*Assumption Cathedral*)

RELIGIOUS SITE | A short walk from Vác's main square, this 18th-century cathedral is an outstanding example of Hungarian neoclassicism. It was built between 1763 and 1777 by Archbishop Kristóf Migazzi to the designs of the Italian architect Isidor Carnevale; the most interesting features are the murals by the Austrian Franz Anton Maulbertsch, both on the dome and behind the altar. Exquisite frescoes decorate the walls inside. Due to break-ins, you can view the interior only through a locked gate, except during the twice-daily masses. ⊠ *Schuszter Konstantin tér 11, Vác* ☎ *27/814–184.*

Vácrátóti Nemzeti Botanikus Kert (*National Botanical Garden*)

GARDEN | FAMILY | Around 14 km (9 miles) southeast of Vác, on the road to Gödöllő, lies Hungary's biggest and best botanical garden. Home to more than 12,000 plant species, the arboretum's top priority is botanical research, and the collection falls under the auspices of the Hungarian Academy of Sciences. You're welcome to stroll along the paths and sit on benches in the leafy shade. The greenhouse opens a bit later and closes earlier than the surrounding garden. ⊠ *Alkotmány utca 2–4, Vác* ☎ *28/360–122* ⊕ *www. botanikuskert.hu* 🖾 *1,000 HUF.*

 Restaurants

Adullam Coffee House

$ | CAFÉ | Venture down an unassuming side street off the main square and you will stumble across this tiny subterranean cellar café. It's situated at the bottom of what was once a public well, and the exposed brick walls, vaulted ceilings, and candlelit tables make a lovely setting for sipping a coffee or soda. **Known for:** the very definition of a hidden gem; Adullam was a biblical cave and means "refuge" in Arabic; good selection of coffee and sodas. ⑤ *Average main: 350 HUF* ⊠ *Március 15. tér 8, Vác* ☎ *30/370–6488* ⊕ *www.adullam.hu.*

Hotels

★ Natura Hill

$$ | HOTEL | If you've come to the Danube Bend to enjoy the stunning natural landscapes and river views, book a stay at this gorgeous hillside hotel (which also happens to have the region's finest restaurant). **Pros:** stylish rooms and apartments; slow-living concept restaurant offers innovative tasting menus; zero plastics and no-waste philosophy; **Cons:** hard to reach (but totally worth it); breakfast only included if you book directly; no TVs in rooms won't suit everyone. ⑤ *Rooms from: 42,000 HUF* ⊠ *Off Szarvas utca, Vác* ☎ *30/599–5732* ⊕ *www.naturahill.hu* ⇱ *11 rooms* ⍟ *Free Breakfast.*

Hollókő

77 km (66 miles) northeast of Vác, 97 km (48 miles) northeast of Budapest.

UNESCO lists this tiny village in the hills close to the Slovakian border as one of its World Heritage Sites because of its unique medieval structure and its indigenous Palóc cultural and handcrafting traditions, still practiced by its 400 inhabitants today. The most famous of these traditions is its Easter celebration, when villagers dress in colorful embroidered costumes and thousands of visitors descend upon the village.

Pocket-size though it may be, Hollókő (which literally translates as "Raven Stone") is authentically enchanting. Old whitewashed, wattle-and-daub houses, some of them built in the 17th century, cluster together on narrow cobblestone pathways. And directly above them loom the hilltop ruins of a 13th-century castle.

GETTING HERE AND AROUND

You will need a car to reach Hollókő. To get here from Vác, head north on Route 2, which merges into Route 22 as it heads east to Szécsény. From here,

follow Kossuth út down into Hollókő. From Budapest, head west on the M1 then north on Route 21.

On arrival in the village, you will probably be directed up to a parking area on the hillside a short walk from the village's historical center (which is closed to traffic). Expect to pay around 400 HUF an hour for the privilege.

🍴 Restaurants

Muskátli vendéglő

$$ | HUNGARIAN | Named for the bright red and pink flowers lining its windowsills, the Geranium Restaurant is a cozy little eatery on Hollókő's main street. It's a great stop for quick and tasty lunches, with specialties including *palócgulyás* (a rich local goulash thick with chunks of pork, potatoes, and carrots) and *nógrádi palócpecsenye* (pork cutlets bathed in mustard-garlic sauce). **Known for:** traditional Hungarian decor and outfits; tasty strapachka (mini dumplings) with curds or cabbage; closes by 6 pm so no dinner. ⑤ *Average main: 2,900 HUF* ⊠ *E Kossuth utca 61, Hollóko* ☎ *30/206–5968* ⊕ *www. muskatlivendeglo.hu* ⍟ *Closed Mon. and Tues.*

Eger

87 km (54 miles) east of Hollókő, 132 km (82 miles) northeast of Budapest.

With vineyard surroundings and more than 175 of Hungary's historic monuments—a figure surpassed only by Budapest and Sopron—the picture-book baroque city of Eger is ripe for exploration. The city, which lies in a fertile valley between the Mátra Mountains and their eastern neighbor, the Bükk range, has borne witness to much history, heartbreak, and glory. It was settled quite early in the Hungarian conquest of the land, and it was one of five bishoprics created

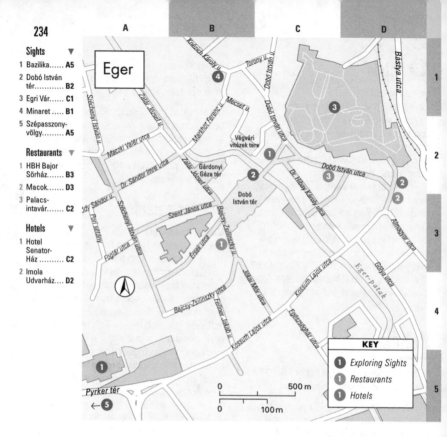

Eger

KEY

① Exploring Sights
① Restaurants
① Hotels

0 — 500 m
0 — 100 m

by King Stephen I when he Christianized the country almost a millennium ago.

In 1552 the city was attacked by the Turks, but the commander, István Dobó, and fewer than 2,000 men and women held out for 38 days against 80,000 Turkish soldiers and drove them away. One of Hungary's great legends tells of the women of Eger pouring hot pitch onto the heads of the Turks as they attempted to scale the castle walls (the event is depicted in a famous painting now in the National Gallery in Budapest). Despite such heroism, however, Eger fell to the Turks in 1596 and became one of the most important northern outposts of Ottoman power until its reconquest in 1687.

Today, restored baroque and rococo buildings line Eger's cobblestone streets, making for excellent strolling and

sightseeing. Wherever you wander, make a point of peeking into open courtyards, where you may happen upon otherwise hidden architectural gems.

GETTING HERE AND AROUND

Driving to Eger from Hollókő takes around 1½ hours; simply head east on Routes 21 and 23. From Budapest, it only takes 15 minutes longer: follow the M3 east for around 108 km (67 miles) then head north on the M25.

Another easy option from Budapest is the train, with direct service every hour from Budapest-Keleti station. The journey takes a little over two hours. Check train schedules at ⊕ www.mav-start.hu.

Once in the downtown area (about a 20-minute walk from the train station), you'll find most attractions are within walking distance. A fun alternative way to get around is the Kisvonat (⊕ *www.kisvonatok.hu*), a miniature land train that leaves from Március 15 tér every hour for a 40-minute tour of Eger's historical sights. It costs 1,200 HUF per person.

Sights

Bazilika

RELIGIOUS SITE | The grand, neoclassical Eger Bazilika, built in the center of town early in the 19th century, is the second-largest cathedral in Hungary after Esztergom (which was built later by the same architect, József Hild). It is approached by a stunning stairway flanked by statues of four saints—Stephen, László, Peter, and Paul—and filled inside and out with 22 carved biblical reliefs; all the work of Italian sculptor Marco Casagrande. From June through October, delightful half-hour organ recitals are held every day in the church; it's at noon on weekdays and 12:45 pm on Sunday. ⊠ *Pyrker János tér 1* 🕿 *36/420–970* ⊕ *www.eger-bazilika.plebania.hu* 🖃 *Free (suggested donation 300 HUF).*

Dobó István tér

PLAZA | Eger's picturesque main square is marked by two intensely animated statues produced in the early 20th century by a father and son: *Dobó the Defender* is by Alajos Stróbl, and the sculpture of a Magyar battling two Turks is by Stróbl's son, Zsigmond Kisfaludi-Stróbl. Dobó tér's famous statues flank the pale-pink **Minorita templom**. With its twin spires and finely carved pulpit, pews, and organ loft, this Minorite Church is considered one of the finest baroque buildings in Central Europe. ⊠ *Eger.*

★ Egri Vár (*Eger Castle*)

CASTLE/PALACE | **FAMILY** | Built after the devastating Tatar invasion of 1241–42, Eger's castle is inspired by the mighty fortresses seen by Béla IV in Italy and the West. Within the castle walls, an imposing Romanesque **cathedral** was built, and then later rebuilt in Gothic style, though

today only its foundations remain. Inside, you can explore the castle's **catacombs,** hewn in the 16th century by Italian engineers. It was by racing back and forth through this labyrinth of underground tunnels and appearing at various ends of the castle that the hundreds of defenders tricked the attacking Turks into thinking there were thousands of them. The Gothic-style **Püspök Ház** (Bishop's House) contains the castle history museum and, in the basement, a numismatics museum where coins can be minted and certified (in English). Other highlights here include the **statue of St. Stephen** watching over the city; a popular **art gallery** displaying Italian and Dutch Renaissance works; and (for an extra fee) a **wax museum**, depicting characters from the Hungarian historical novel *Eclipse of the Crescent Moon.* ▪**TIP→ Not interested in the exhibitions? Come after 5:30 pm in high season (or 3:30 pm in low season) when they're closed and you'll pay half the entrance fee.** ⊠ *Vár 1* 🕿 *36/312–744* ⊕ *www.egrivar.hu* 🖃 *2,000 HUF; evening ticket 1,000 HUF.*

Minaret

RELIGIOUS SITE | A long-standing reminder of Ottoman rule in Hungary, this 40-meter-high minaret was originally built in the early 1600s as part of the larger Djami of Kethuda mosque. Today it stands all alone, capped with an obvious Christian cross. Meanwhile, the platform once used for the Muslim call to prayer is instead crowded with tourists, who have climbed the 97 spiral stairs to enjoy fine panoramic views of the city. ⊠ *Knézich Károly utca* 🕿 *70/202–4353* ⊕ *www.minareteger.hu* 🖃 *400 HUF.*

Szépasszony-völgy

WINERY/DISTILLERY | Eger wine is renowned within and beyond Hungary, and the place to sample the best vintages is the Szépasszony-völgy (literally "Valley of the Beautiful Woman"), a wine-growing area on the southwestern edge of Eger's city limits. More than 200 small wine cellars (some of them literally holes-in-the-wall) stand open and inviting in warm weather, and a few are open in winter, too. You may be given a tour of the cellar, and wines will be tapped from the barrel into your glass by the vintners themselves at the tiniest cost (but it's prudent to inquire politely how much it will cost before imbibing). Make sure you sample the area's best-known variety, *Egri Bikavér* (Bull's Blood of Eger), a full-bodied red wine, as well as other outstanding vintages like the delightful dry white Leányka, the dark red dessert wine Medoc Noir, and the sweeter white Muskotály. ⊠ *Szépasszpny Völgy*.

🍴 Restaurants

HBH Bajor Sörház

$$ | GERMAN | For substantial German-style cuisine and frothy beer, head for the popular HBH Bavarian Brewery, which has a great location just off Dobó tér. The cuisine ranges from traditional Hungarian fare such as veal paprikash to Bavarian-style knuckle of ham. **Known for:** beer brewed under a Bavarian license; hearty tavern fare; boistrous atmosphere. 💲 *Average main: 3,000 HUF* ⊠ *Bajcsy-Zsilinszky út 19* 📞 *36/515–516* ⊕ *www.hbh-eger.hu.*

★ Macok

$$$ | HUNGARIAN | Considered one of the best restaurants not only in Eger but in the whole of Hungary, Macok is the city's most coveted dining experience. Yet it isn't formal and stuffy: this is a playful, colorful, and elegant bistro offering a menu full of upscale comfort food, including confit duck leg with cabbage-flavored pasta, Angus sirloin steak with toasted potatoes, and risotto with porcini mushrooms. **Known for:** best dining option in Eger; great location at the foot of the castle; wines from the renowned St. Andrea vineyards. 💲 *Average main: 4,500 HUF* ⊠ *Imola Udvarház, Tinódi Sebestyén tér 4* 📞 *36/516–180* ⊕ *imolaudvarhaz.hu.*

Palacsintavár

$$ | EASTERN EUROPEAN | This hip little cellar establishment, adorned with funky wall (and ceiling) art from Dalí prints to cigarette packs, is *the* place to have your fill of Hungary's famous rolled-up pancake, the *palacsinta*. You can choose from any of more than two dozen varieties, from the "Boss's Favorite" (with a filling of pork knuckle, beans, cabbage, and sour cream) to the "Spring Pancake" (sheep's cheese with dill and chives), to banana pancakes with vanilla cream. **Known for:** both savory and sweet pancakes; cellar is pleasantly cool on a hot summer day; food can be a little salty. 💲 *Average main: 2,300 HUF* ⊠ *Dobó István utca 9* 📞 *36/413–980* ⊕ *www. palacsintavar.hu.*

Hotels

★ Hotel Senator-Ház

$ | HOTEL | This little inn, a lovely 18th-century town house, sits on Eger's main square. **Pros:** historical building has lots of character; infrared sauna available to guests; bike rental included in price. **Cons:** service in restaurant can be slow; can hear street noise from some rooms; no elevator. 💲 *Rooms from: 18,750 HUF* ⊠ *Dobó tér 11* 📞 *36/411–711* ⊕ *www. senatorhaz.hu* 🛏 *11 rooms* 🍴 *Free breakfast.*

Imola Udvarház

$$ | HOTEL | The rooms and apartments at Eger's most upmarket small hotel are pricey by local standards, but the excellent location, stylish decor, and superior facilities justify the premium rates. **Pros:** good value single rooms available for solo travelers; free garage parking for guests; on-site store sells fine local wines. **Cons:** hot options at breakfast are limited; service can be hit-and-miss; beds may be a little firm for some. 💲 *Rooms from: 26,000 HUF* ⊠ *Tinódi Sebestyén tér 4* 📞 *30/207–8085* ⊕ *www.imolaudvarhaz. hu* 🛏 *15 rooms and apartments* 🍴 *Free breakfast.*

The Cella Septichora is a UNESCO World Heritage Site and a series of tombs from the late Roman and Paleochristian eras.

Pécs

346 km (215 miles) southwest of Eger, 200 km (124 miles) southwest of Budapest.

Pécs (pronounced "paytch"), the southern capital of *Transdanubia* (the area south and west of the Danube), dates back to the Roman period. For centuries it was a frontier province and an important stop along the trade route; today it is far richer in Roman ruins than the rest of Hungary. The city played an important role during the Middle Ages as well; in 1009 St. Stephen set up a diocese in Pécs to help cement Christianity among the Magyar tribes. In fact, it was a thriving city right up until the Turkish Conquest in 1543, and the Turks' 143-year rule left its own distinct imprint on the city. While the Habsburgs later destroyed or converted many of the Ottoman buildings, Pécs is home to many of Hungary's most important remaining Turkish-era sites. The latter half of the 19th century was most notable for the rise of local hero Vilmos Zsolnay, whose Secession-style ceramics company would go on to define the city and become one of Hungary's national treasures.

Today Pécs is a vibrant and dynamic university town, rich with historic (and often UNESCO-listed) sites, including early Christian tombs, a magnificent basilica, two mosques, and a handsome synagogue—as well as a half-dozen museums. What's more, Pécs's status as European Capital of Culture in 2010 led to an extreme makeover and the creation of new attractions like the remarkable Zsolnay Cultural Quarter. Add it all together, and you can easily justify a two- or three-day stay here.

GETTING HERE AND AROUND

Driving to Pécs from Budapest involves a straight trip down the M6 and takes two hours. From Eger, you will need to drive west to Budapest on the E71/M0, before joining the M6 south (four hours in total).

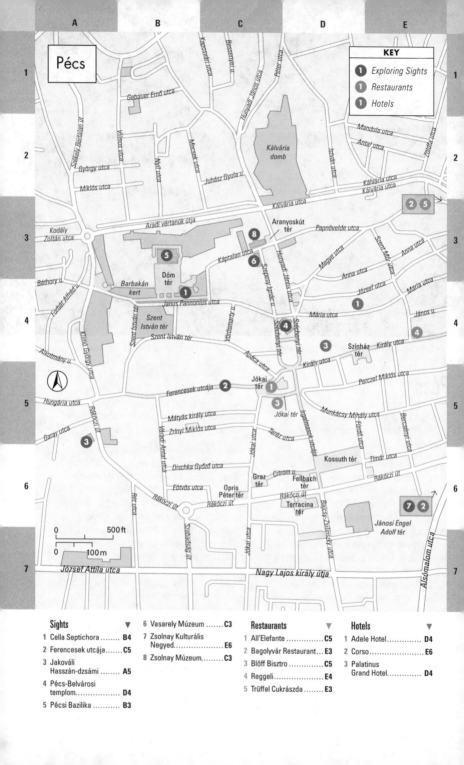

Pécs

KEY
- ❶ Exploring Sights
- ❶ Restaurants
- ❶ Hotels

Trains leave from Budapest-Keleti every hour and take between three and four hours. From Eger, add on another train to Budapest, and another two hours.

Pécs itself is best explored on foot, as some of the downtown area is blocked off to cars. The city is small enough to tour in a day but rich enough with attractions that you could spend a leisurely weekend exploring the area. Take time to meander through the side streets for glimpses of the Zsolnay tiles that adorn random buildings throughout the city.

◉ Sights

Most of the city's biggest sights are located downtown, the area within the old city walls. But one of its newest—the remarkable Zsolnay Cultural Quarter—is a 20-minute walk east of the center. If you have time, it's also worth exploring the hillside district of Tettye, home to the medieval ruins of a bishop's palace as well as stunning city views.

★ Cella Septichora

ARCHAEOLOGICAL SITE | Situated in a serene little park in front of Pécsi Bazilika, this subterranean museum—and UNESCO World Heritage Site—is home to a series of burial chambers, many with remarkably well-preserved religious murals. The burial site dates back to when Pécs was a Roman outpost called Sopianae, though it was located just outside the city walls (as was the custom). Today, the excavated crypts are linked with a series of suspended metal walkways to help preserve them from damage. Two are of particular note: the beautifully decorated **Wine Pitcher Burial Chamber,** with its paintings of vines and drinking vessels (best seen from above); and the chapel-like **Peter and Paul Burial Chamber,** covered in Christian symbols and colorful frescoes (best seen from below). A ticket for Cella Septichora also gets you into the nearby **Early Christian Mausoleum,** a tomb with stunning murals of Adam

and Eve, Daniel in the Lion's Den, and the Resurrection. ■ TIP→ **Download the "VisitorGuide" app for a free audio guide of the museum**. ✉ *Sétatér 7621, Pécs* ☎ *72/224–755* ⊕ *www.pecsorokseg.hu* ✉ *1,900 HUF (inc. Early Christian Mausoleum)* ⊘ *Closed Mon.*

Ferencesek utcája

NEIGHBORHOOD | This pedestrianized street in the heart of downtown Pécs is a particularly pleasant place for a stroll. Walking west to east (toward Széchenyi tér), you'll see the beautiful baroque **Szent Ferenc-templom** (St. Francis Church), which dates back to 1760; **A Pécsi Villamos,** a lovely old yellow tram with an exhibition on street vehicles; **Memi Pasa Fürdője** (Memi Pasha's Baths), the ruins of a 16th-century Turkish bathhouse; and **Jókai tér,** a pleasant Mediterranean-style public square with one of the city's best *cukrászdas* (cake shops). ✉ *Pécs.*

Jakováli Hasszán-dzsámi (*Yakovalı Hasan Paşa Mosque*)

RELIGIOUS SITE | Just beyond the ancient city wall to the west and unceremoniously sandwiched by two larger and more modern buildings, this beautiful 16th-century Turkish mosque is the only Ottoman-era religious building in Hungary with its original minaret and architecture intact. The interior has a museum with a few artifacts from the Turkish period and some Iznik ceramics; however, it is currently closed for restoration with no firm date for reopening. ✉ *Rákoczi út 2, Pécs.*

★ Pécs-Belvárosi templom (*Inner Town Parish Church*)

RELIGIOUS SITE | Crowning the city's main square, Széchenyi tér, this delightful 16th-century Turkish mosque-turned-church is a Pécs landmark. Dating from the years of Turkish occupation (1543–1686) when it was known as the Mosque of Pasha Qasim, the building was converted into a Catholic church in 1702; a fact you might infer from the cross that surmounts the gilded crescent atop the dome. Despite the fierce religious war raging on its walls—Christian statuary and frescoes beneath Turkish arcades and *mihrabs* (prayer niches)—this church remains the largest and finest relic of Turkish architecture in Hungary. Look out in particular for the enormous painting above the gallery, showing the defeat of the Turks: while triumphalist, the defeated soldiers are depicted rather sympathetically. ⊠ *Széchenyi tér, Pécs* ☎ *30/373–8900* ⊕ *www.pecsiegyhaz-megye.hu/en/attractions/mosque-of-pa-sha-gazi-kassim* ⌨ *1,800 HUF.*

Pécsi Bazilika (*Pécs Basilica*)
RELIGIOUS SITE | Also known as Sts. Peter and Paul's Cathedral, though it was promoted to basilica rank after Pope John Paul II's visit in 1991, this is one of Europe's most magnificent churches with foundations dating back 1,000 years. At the beginning of the 19th century, Mihály Pollack directed the transformation of the exterior, changing it from baroque to neoclassical; its interior remained Gothic. Near the end of the 19th century, Bishop Nándor Dulánszky decided to restore the cathedral to its original, Árpád-period style—the result is a four-spired monument that has an utterly breathtaking interior frescoed from floor to ceiling in shimmering golds, silvers, and blues. It's so light and colorful that it feels brand-new. Climb the **lookout tower** for a beautiful view over Pécs, including the nearby city walls. ⊠ *Dóm tér 2, Pécs* ☎ *72/513–030* ⊕ *www.pecsiegyhaz-megye.hu* ⌨ *1,900 HUF.*

Vasarely Múzeum
MUSEUM | **FAMILY** | The pioneer of Op Art (who left Hungary as a child and spent the rest of his life in Paris), Victor Vasarely was born Gyozo Vásárhelyi in 1908 in this house, which has been turned into something wild, as much a fun house as a museum. The first hall is a corridor of 3D visual tricks devised by his disciples, at the end of which hangs a hypnotic canvas of shifting cubes by Jean-Pierre Yvaral. Upstairs, the illusions grow

profound: a zebra gallops by while chess pieces and blood cells seem to come at you. ⊠ *Káptalan utca 3, Pécs* ☎ *30/934–6127* ⊕ *www.pecs.varosom.hu* ⌨ *1,500 HUF* ⊘ *Closed Mon.*

★ **Zsolnay Kulturális Negyed** (*Zsolnay Cultural Quarter*)
NEIGHBORHOOD | You can easily spend half a day exploring this sprawling complex, a city within a city that was opened in 2010 to mark Pécs's status as European Capital of Culture. Built on the site of the old Zsolnay porcelain factory, which was established by Miklós Zsolnay in the 19th century, the streets and squares are adorned with a host of colorful ceramic-tiled features, from industrial chimneys to charming pavilions. Many of the buildings are home to Zsolnay-related exhibits, including the **Pink Exhibition,** showcasing the factory's early rose-tinted output like the decorative Lotus series; the **Golden Age Collection,** a series of more than 600 pieces revealing Zsolnay's evolution towards the Art Nouveau style; and the **Live Manufactory,** where brand-new ceramic creations are molded, painted, and fired. The quarter also has a shopping street, some excellent cafés and restaurants, and even rental apartments. As well as Zsolnay exhibits, it's also home to **1861 Kesztyűmanufaktúra,** the factory, shop, and exhibition space of luxury glove brand Hamerli, as well as the **Bóbita Bábszínház** (Bóbita Puppet Theater) and a **Planetárium.** ■TIP→ Head to the cigar room of the Zsolnay Restaurant to see one of Zsolnay's most beautiful and innovative creations; a gorgeous black-and-gold fireplace. ⊠ *Felsővámház utca 52, Pécs* ☎ *72/500–350* ⊕ *www.zsolnayn-egyed.hu.*

Zsolnay Múzeum
MUSEUM | **FAMILY** | If you haven't had your fill of Zsolnay, make a beeline for this museum. Occupying the upper floor of the oldest surviving building in Pécs, which dates from 1324 and has been built and rebuilt over the years in

When Pécs was awarded the title of European Capital of Culture in 2010, the former Zsolnay family factory and the surrounding grounds were rebuilt, and now include attractions, shops, and restaurants.

Romanesque, Renaissance, and baroque styles, this museum is a merry show-and-tell waltz through a revolution in pottery that started in 1851. That's when local merchant Miklós Zsolnay bought the site of an old kiln and set up a stone-ware factory for his son Ignác to run. Ignác's brother, Vilmos, a shopkeeper with an artistic bent, bought the factory from him in 1863, imported experts from Germany, and (with the help of a Pécs pharmacist for chemical glaze experiments and his daughters for hand-painting) created the distinctive namesake porcelain. Today, the museum's collection includes Vilmos's early efforts at Delft-blue handmade vases, cups, and saucers; his two-layer ceramics; examples of the gold-brocade rims that became a Zsolnay trademark; and table settings for royal families. Look up on your tour to see the unusual Zsolnay chandeliers lighting your way. ⊠ *Káptalan utca 2, Pécs* ☎ *72/514–045* ⊕ *www.jpm.hu* 🖅 *1,500 HUF* ☉ *Closed Mon.*

🍴 Restaurants

All'Elefante

$$$ | PIZZA | This bustling Italian restaurant and pizzeria, with a huge terrace that opens onto the bustling Jókai tér (Jókai Square), is a perennial Pécs favorite. The menu includes some 20 kinds of pizza, all cooked in an authentic wood-burning stove, along with a huge choice of pastas, risottos, and salads. **Known for:** the best pizza in Pécs; delicious home-made lemonades; can get very busy on weekends. ⑤ *Average main: 3,500 HUF* ⊠ *Jókai tér 6, Pécs* ☎ *72/216–055* ⊕ *www.elefantos.hu.*

★ Bagolyvár Restaurant

$$$ | HUNGARIAN | For dinner with a view, it's hard to beat the Owl Castle, an unusual, pseudo-cellar restaurant that is not only above ground but situated high up on the hill in the Tettye district of Pécs. Take a seat in the brick-vaulted interior to enjoy the carved columns, decorative furnace, and folksy bric-a-brac, or sit out on the terrace surrounded by orchards—the fruit from which is used to make those potent house *pálinkas* (fruit brandies)—for spectacular city views. **Known for:** 900,000-brick interior with folksy decor; gorgeous city views from terrace; steep drive or a bus then 10-minute uphill walk. ⑤ *Average main: 4,500 HUF* ✉ *Felsőhavi dűlő 6, Pécs* ☎ *72/513–213* ⊕ *www. bagolyvarpecs.hu.*

Blöff Bisztró

$$ | MEDITERRANEAN | It doesn't look like much from outside, but this conveniently located downtown diner has gained a loyal following for its simple but satisfying cuisine. The menu mainly comprises delicious grilled meat and fish dishes, though there are some other Balkan specialties on offer, including *lepények* (a pizza-like pastry stuffed with meat or cheese). **Known for:** tasty (and meaty) Balkan cuisine; stylish and cozy interior; service can be curt or even downright rude. ⑤ *Average main: 2,600 HUF* ✉ *Jókai tér 5, Pécs* ☎ *72/497–469* ⊕ *www.facebook. com/Bloff-Bisztro-122505751420351* ⊘ *No dinner Sun.*

Reggeli

$$ | MODERN EUROPEAN | Billing itself as a breakfast and coffee specialist, Reggeli serves a nutritious and delicious brunch menu every day from 8 am to 3 pm. Order a coffee or cold-press juice then take your pick from the lengthy, egg-heavy menu, which includes American pancakes, French toast, and English breakfasts. **Known for:** best breakfasts and brunches in town; decor is a hipster's dream; lots of veggie and vegan options. ⑤ *Average main: 1,600 HUF* ✉ *Király utca 23-25, Pécs* ☎ *72/529–910* ⊕ *reggelipecs.business.site* ⊘ *No dinner.*

★ Trüffel Cukrászda

$ | BAKERY | This out-of-the-way bakery, a good 20-minute walk from the center, has display cabinets crammed with mouthwatering confections, from honey cream slices to chocolate profiteroles, apple poppy cake to smoked cheese scones. Inside, it appears to be just a small take-out place, but stroll around the back to discover a lovely, sprawling terrace and garden, complete with kids' play area. **Known for:** a bit of a walk from downtown Pécs; lemon ice cream is to die for; tasty vegan cakes available. ⑤ *Average main: 700 HUF* ✉ *Hársfa út 34, Pécs* ☎ *70/409–6661* ⊕ *www.truffel.hu.*

Hotels

Adele Hotel

$ | HOTEL | This charming boutique hotel, a two-minute walk from Széchenyi tér, is set within a protected building dating back over 200 years, yet it's one of the city's most modern and elegant accommodation options. **Pros:** convenient central location; great little wellness center in the cellar; delicious breakfasts with fresh orange juice (a rarity here). **Cons:** sauna gets busy so pre-booking advised; room service has an additional fee; nude photographs in public areas are tasteful but might bother some. ⑤ *Rooms from: 28,500 HUF* ✉ *Mária utca 15, Pécs* ☎ *72/510–226* ⊕ *www.adelehotel.hu* 🛏 *25 rooms* ⚬ *Free breakfast.*

Corso

$ | HOTEL | Popular with couples, this out-of-the-center hotel has a wide choice of comfortable and well-equipped bedrooms with large bathrooms, but it's the surprisingly affordable suites that make this place stand out. **Pros:** great value suites with saunas and terraces; decorative Zsolnay ceramics outside and in; has a wheelchair-accessible room. **Cons:** a 15-minute walk from the downtown; no gym or wellness (though they partner with a nearby resort); breakfast isn't included. ⑤ *Rooms from: 15,000 HUF* ✉ *Koller utca 8, Pécs* ☎ *72/421–900* ⊕ *www.corso.accenthotels.com* 🛏 *81 rooms* ⚬ *No meals.*

★ Palatinus Grand Hotel

$ | HOTEL | While art nouveau architecture is found throughout Hungary, for some pure art deco, check out this hotel in downtown Pécs. **Pros:** stunning art deco entrance and grand ballroom; excellent breakfast with attentive service; standard rooms are very good value. **Cons:** rooms are poor compared to public areas; shower gel dispensers instead of bath products; can get busy (and loud) with wedding parties. ⑤ *Rooms from: 28,000 HUF* ✉ *Király utca 5, Pécs* ☎ *72/889–400* ⊕ *www.palatinusgrandhotel.hu* ➷ *100 rooms* ❙❍❙ *Free breakfast.*

Nightlife

Tüke Borház

WINE BARS—NIGHTLIFE | Located in the hillside Tettye district, this charming wine bar features a lovely terrace with panoramic views of the center and beyond. There's a huge selection of hard-to-find Hungarian wines here, with around 90% coming from small, local winemakers (within 50 miles) and the rest from other regions of the country. Depending on the season, you can enjoy your wine with barbecued steaks or cold cuts. ✉ *Böck János utca 39, Pécs* ☎ *20/317–8178* ⊕ *www.tukeborhaz.hu.*

🎭 Performing Arts

Pécsi Nemzeti Színház (*National Theater of Pécs*)

CONCERTS | This pretty baroque theater is the main venue for regular performances by the Pécs Symphony Orchestra and the theater's own opera and modern ballet companies. ✉ *Színház tér 1, Pécs* ☎ *72/512–660* ⊕ *www.pnsz.hu.*

Villány

34 km (21 miles) southeast of Pécs, 216 km (314 miles) south of Budapest.

The sleepy town of Villány, a short detour south of Pécs and nestled in the low, verdant Villányi Hills, is the center of one of Hungary's most famous wine regions. Roman ruins uncovered in the region attest to a long history of wine production here, and today the Villány-Siklós wine region covers more than 2,000 hectares. Its exceptional red wines are heralded both here and abroad, with local varietals like Kékoportó and Kékfrankos complemented by Merlots and Cabernets that give the French a run for their money. The town itself is clustered with friendly *pincék* (cellars) and *panziók* (pensions) offering wine tastings, and most owners will be happy to tell you about winemaking in the region as you taste.

GETTING HERE AND AROUND

Getting to Villány is easiest by car. From Pécs, simply head southeast on Route 578 (35 minutes). From Budapest, drive straight down the M6, then briefly switch to the M60 before taking exit 6 and following signs into the village (2¼ hours).

There is a direct bus from Pécs, but this is infrequent and takes over an hour. There's also a train (40 minutes), though finding your way into town from the station can be a headache: you'll need to go left on the main road that passes by the station (i.e., in the direction of the train) and keep walking for around 20 minutes as the road curves right and finally enters the surprisingly small, wine-cellar-dominated town center. Trains from Budapest-Keleti go via Pécs (4¼ hours in all).

◉ Sights

★ Bock Pince

WINERY/DISTILLERY | One of Villány's most celebrated wine producers, the Bock family has been in business here for more than 200 years. Today, they produce more than a million bottles a year to sell them all over the world. A visit here is a chance to sample Bock's selection of spectacular (mostly red) wines, from award-winning classics to untraveled vintages, during one of the twice-daily tastings. Visitors can also get a glimpse behind (or rather under) the scenes with a tour of the atmopheric wine cellar every day at 2 pm and 5 pm. The main feature of the cellar is an extaordinary central vault (known as the "Bock Chapel") that looks like a Turkish baths and has some bizarre acoustics: stand in the middle to have your own voice reflected back at you, or talk to a friend across the room with just a whisper. As well as welcoming day-trippers, Bock Pince also has 33 comfortable and stylish bedrooms—unusually, the standard rooms are nicer than the deluxe ones—with prices starting from 26,000 HUF a night. ⊠ Batthyány Lajos utca 15, Villány ☎ 72/492–919 ⊕ pince.bock.hu.

Siklósi vár (Siklósi Castle)
CASTLE/PALACE | Situated 13 km (8 miles) west of Villány—though still within the famous Villány-Siklós wine region—this enormous 13th-century castle is well worth a half-day detour. First mentioned in 1294, when it was the property of the Soklyosi family, the castle now stands at the southernmost point of Hungary, just 10 km (6 miles) from the Croatian border. A single ticket (1,900 HUF) will get you into all the castle's exhibitions, including the prison and torture chamber, the medieval weapons exhibition, and the wine museum, or you can opt for a 90-minute English-language tour (7,000 HUF). ⊠ Vajda János tér 8, Villány ☎ 72/579–090 ⊕ www.siklosivar.hu ☜ 1,900 HUF ⊙ Closed Mon. in Jan. and Feb.

Villányi Bormúzeum (Villány Wine Museum)
MUSEUM | If you wish to learn about the local wine before imbibing, stop in at this fascinating museum. Set within a former grape press-house, the museum details the history of the Villány-Siklós region's viticulture over the last 2,000 years, with exhibits ranging from Roman artifacts to 19th-century coopers' tools. The impressively deep cellar is a great place to cool off on a hot day. ⊠ Bem József utca 8, Villány ☎ 30/335–5343 ⊕ www.villany.hu ☜ 600 HUF.

Hotels

Crocus
$$$ | **HOTEL** | Owned by the renowned Gere Winery, this beautiful Villány resort offers a slice of luxury and a whole heap of peace and quiet in the heart of town. **Pros:** hotel has a peaceful garden and vineyards; award-winning fine dining restaurant; funky wine barrel light fittings in hallways. **Cons:** some rooms have an older (and less appealing) style; gets very busy in harvest season; minimum two-night stay in summer. ⑤ Rooms from: 55,000 HUF ⊠ Diófás utca 4-12, Villány ☎ 72/492–195 ⊕ crocus-hotel.gere.hu ➳ 34 rooms ⑩ Free breakfast.

★ Palkonyha
$ | **HOTEL** | The small lakeside village of Palkonya is renowned for its streets lined with tiny, turf-covered wine cellars, and this charming little hotel and restaurant—a pun on "Palkonya" and "konyha" (kitchen)—is within easy reach of all of them. **Pros:** traditional Swabian architecture; "slow food" restaurant serving five-course meals; has a swimming pool and sauna. **Cons:** restaurant open weekends only; a short drive from Villány; breakfast costs 2,900 HUF extra. ⑤ Rooms from: 16,000 HUF ⊠ Fő utca 76, Villány ☎ 30/630–0401 ⊕ www.palkonyha.hu ➳ 6 rooms ⑩ No meals.

Kecskemét

191 km (118 mi) southwest of Debrecen, 85 km (53 mi) east of Budapest

With a name roughly translating as "Goat County," this sprawling city of 120,000 smack in the middle of Hungary never fails to surprise unsuspecting first-time visitors with its elegant landmark buildings, interesting museums, and friendly, welcoming people. As far back as the 14th century, Kecskemét was a market town, and under Turkish rule in 1439 it was a *khas* (exclusive) city, which meant it received favorable treatment and was spared much of the devastation rendered on other Hungarian cities at the time. Thus, Kecskemét was able to flourish as other cities were destroyed and deserted. That said, as a votive pillar in front of the Katona József Theater attests, an 18th-century plague claimed the lives of two-thirds of the city's population.

A 10-minute walk from the train station will get you to the splendid and verdant main square, Szabadság tér (Liberty Square). This soon becomes Kossuth tér, which is marred only by two faceless but incredibly well-kept cement-block buildings, one of which houses the city's McDonald's (a true sign this is not just a dusty prairie town anymore); the other with lovely flowers all over its balconies. Home of the elite Kodály Institute, where famous composer and pedagogue Zoltán Kodály's methods are taught, the city also maintains a fairly active cultural life.

Although raising goats was an economically viable livelihood early on for many in this region of formerly none too fertile soil, Kecskemét and environs ironically came to distinguish itself eventually not so much for goats as for fruit. Although climatic conditions and the soil today are not nearly as ideal as they once were for producing apricots, Kecskemét still milks its reputation as the fruit center of the Great Plain for all it's worth—in particular when it comes to producing barack pálinka, a smooth yet tangy apricot brandy that can warm the heart and blur the mind in just one shot. Ask for home-brewed házi pálinka, which is much better (and often stronger) than the commercial brews.

A short drive from town takes you into the expansive sandy grasslands of Kiskunság National Park, the smaller of the two protected areas (the other is Hortobágy National Park) of the Great Plain. You can watch a traditional horse show, do some riding, or immerse yourself in the experience by spending a night or two at one of the inns out on the prairie.

FESTIVALS AND EVENTS

Tavaszi Fesztivál

(*Spring Festival*) Kecskemét's annual Tavaszi Fesztivál (Spring Festival) is held from mid- March to early April, and includes concerts, dance performances, theater productions, and art exhibits by local and special guest artists from around the country and abroad.

 Sights

Cifrapalota (*Ornamental Palace*)

BUILDING | Kecskemét's most famous building is the Cifrapalota (Ornamental Palace), a unique and remarkable Hungarian-style art nouveau building built in 1902. A three-story cream-colored structure studded with folksy lilac, blue, red, and yellow Zsolnay majolica flowers and hearts, it stands on Liberty Square's corner like a cheerful cream pastry. Once a residential building, it now houses the Kecskeméti képtár (Kecskemét Gallery), with an excellent display of artwork by Hungarian fine artists as well as occasional international exhibits and some space devoted to local history and traditions. The ceiling of the main room on the second floor is something to behold, not least its peacocks: imagine what it was like for the family that lived here. ✉ *Rákóczi út 1, Kecskemét* ☎ *76/481-350* ⊕ *muzeum.kecskemet.hu/cifrapalota* 💰 *700 HUF.*

PIAC

MARKET | Kecskemét is Hungary's fruit capital, and it's worth experiencing the region's riches firsthand by visiting the bustling market, where—depending on the season—you can indulge in freshly plucked apples, cherries, and the famous Kecskemét apricots. Provided there is no sudden spring freeze, apricot season is around June through August. It's about 2 km from the city center. ✉ *Along Budai utca ✛ near corner of Nagykörösi út.*

Szent Miklós templom (*Church of St. Nicholas*)

RELIGIOUS SITE | The oldest building on Kossuth tér is the Szent Miklós templom (Church of St. Nicholas), known also as the Barátság templom (Friendship Church) because of St. Nick's role as the saint of friendship. The church, the oldest in the city, was built in Gothic style in either the 13th or 15th century (a subject of debate). What is not debated is that it was rebuilt in baroque style during the 18th century. Once you pass through the elaborate wrought-iron gate and through an attractive little courtyard out front, note the interior's apricot hues, which are typical of many an edifice in downtown Kecskemét. ⊠ *Kossuth tér 5, Kecskemét* ⊕ *kecskemet.hu* ⊠ *Free.*

Szórakoténusz Játékmúzeum és Muhely (*Szórakoténusz Toy Museum & Workshop*)

MUSEUM | FAMILY | The unusual, one-of-a-kind Szórakoténusz Játékmúzeum és Muhely (Szórakoténusz Toy Museum & Workshop) chronicles the history of Hungarian toys with almost 18,000 archaeological pieces such as stone figures and clay toys from medieval guilds. The museum also hosts changing international exhibits. In the workshop, artisans create traditional toys and invite you to try to make toys yourself. Next door to the toy museum (in the same building) is the small Magyar Naív Muvészek Múzeum (Hungarian Naive Art Museum), where you can see a collection of this simple style of painting and sculpting created by Hungarian artists. You can get here via a 5-minute walk to a less than inspiring neighborhood of concrete apartment blocks on the outskirts of downtown. ⊠ *Gáspár András utca 11, Kecskemét* ☎ *76/481-469* ⊕ *www.szorakatenusz.hu* ⊠ *450HUF.*

Városház (*Town Hall*)

HOUSE | Built between 1892 and 1896 by Ödön Lechner in the Hungarian Art Nouveau style that he created, the Városház

(Town Hall) is one of its finest examples. Window frames are arched here, pointed there, and the roof, peppered with tiny copper- and gold-color tiles, looks as if it has been rained on by pennies from heaven. In typical Lechner style, the outlines of the central facade make a curving line to a pointed top, under which 37 little computer-driven bells in a screened-in balcony of sorts add the finishing visual and aural touch: every hour from 9 AM to 4 PM (hours may vary on Fridays and weekends), they flood the main square with the ringing melody of the "Rákóczi March," a patriotic 18th-century tune later orchestrated by Berlioz and adapted by Liszt in one of his Hungarian Rhapsodies. Note also the goat occupying center stage in the city's coat of arms on the building's facade. The building's Dísz Terem (Ceremonial Hall), on the second floor, is a spectacular palace of glimmering gold-painted vaulted ceilings, exquisitely carved wooden pews, colorful frescoes by Bertalan Székely (who also painted the frescoes for Budapest's Matthias Church), and a gorgeously ornate chandelier that floats above the room like an ethereal bouquet of lights and shining brass. The hall is open only to tour groups that have made prior arrangements. ⊠ *Kossuth tér 1, Kecskemét* ⊕ *kecskemet.hu.*

🍴 Restaurants

Kisbugaci Étterem

$ | HUNGARIAN | This cozy, csárda-style eatery tucked away on a side street a 10-minute walk from the main square is warm and bright. The inner area has wood paneling and upholstered booths; the outer section has simple wooden tables covered with locally embroidered tablecloths and matching curtains. **Known for:** traditional Hungarian fare; old-school feel; large portions. ⑤ *Average main: 1200 HUF* ⊠ *Munkácsy utca 10, Kecskemét* ☎ *76/322-722* ⊕ *kisbugaci.hu.*

Bugac

46 km (29 miles) south of Kecskemét, 120 km (74 miles) southeast of Budapest.

The Bugac puszta, declared by UNESCO as a bioreserve for its unique flora and fauna, is the central and most-visited section of the 127,200-acre Kiskunsági Nemzeti Park (Kiskunság National Park)—the smaller sister of Hortobágy National Park (farther northeast); together they compose the entire Great Plain. Bugac puszta's expansive, sandy, impossibly flat grassland scenery has provided Hungarian poets and artists with inexhaustible material over the centuries. Although the dry, open stretches may seem numbingly uniform to the casual eye, the Bugac's fragile ecosystem is the most varied of the entire park; its primeval juniper trees, extremely rare in the region, are the area's most protected and treasured flora. Today Bugac continues to inspire visitors with its strong equestrian traditions and the fun but touristy horse shows and tours offered within its boundaries. The park's half-hour traditional horse show takes place twice daily, around 11 and 2. You can also wander around the area and peek into the Kiskunság National Park Museum, which has exhibits about pastoral life on the prairie. ■ TIP→ **Note that areas of the park farther away from Bugac can be accessed for free; the park center in Kecskemét has maps (with English text) that describe the various short trails (whose signs also include English text).**

🍴 Restaurants

★ Bugaci Csárda

$$ | HUNGARIAN | Bugac's most famous and popular restaurant is a tour-bus magnet, but is still considered a mandatory part of a puszta visit. It's at the end of a dirt road just past the park's main entrance, in a traditional whitewashed, thatch-roof house decorated inside with cheerful red-and-white folk embroideries.

Known for: hearty Hungarian classics; picnic tables outside; kitschy. Ⓢ *Average main: 3,000 HUF* ⊠ *Rte. 54, Nagybugac 135, Bugac* ✚ *at the entrance to Kiskunság National Park* ☎ *30/4166439* ⊕ *www.bugacpuszta.hu/karikas-csarda-bemutatkozas.html* ⊙ *Closed Mon.–Wed.*

Veszprém

208 km (129 miles) north of Villány, 115 km (71½ miles) southwest of Budapest.

Lake Balaton, the largest lake in Central Europe, stretches 80 km (50 miles) across western Hungary. Its vast surface area contrasts dramatically with its modest depths, which average out at 10 feet. As the most popular playground of this landlocked nation, the lake's sandy beaches can be packed on a hot summer's day, though many family groups and partygoers set up camp in Siófok on the southern side of the lake. We have focused on Balaton's northern shores, which offer its most interesting cultural attractions.

Most culture-focused tours of Lake Balaton begin in hilly Veszprém, even if it is a little removed from the lake itself. One of Hungary's oldest cities, Veszprém was established during the 11th century during the rule of St. Stephen, but it was destroyed by the Turks during their occupation—and then again during Hungarian-Austrian independence battles. The city was rebuilt in the early 18th century, but its castle was never reconstructed. Nevertheless, its Castle Hill remains home to historic churches, museums, and statues, while the area around has some lovely pedestrian squares with cafés and outdoor seating. Veszprém will be the official European Capital of Culture in 2023, so expect to see construction and renovation works in preparation for a bumper year of cultural events.

GETTING HERE AND AROUND

The only reasonable way to reach Veszprém from Villány is by car (2¾ hours): head north on the M6, then west on Routes 61, 64 and 710. However, most visitors come from Budapest, which is an easier and quicker drive southwest on the M7 and Route 8 (1½ hours). It's also possible to get to Veszprém by direct bus every hour from Budapest's Népliget station (2½ hours).

The city center (including Castle Hill) is largely pedestrianized, so park your car in one of the designated lots and continue on foot.

 Sights

Herendi Porcelánművészeti Múzeum (Herend Porcelain Museum)

MUSEUM | Hungary's reputation for creating fine pieces of porcelain was sparked by the purchase of a dinner set by Britain's Queen Victoria in 1851 (the chosen pattern of colorful and detailed butterflies and flowers was later coined the "Victoria" collection). Some 600 mold-makers, potters, and painters are still trained here to craft Herend's high quality dinnerware, decorative items, and figurines, while the porcelain-prone public are welcomed to share the experience in the Porcelanium Visitor Center. You can see how products are made in the Minimanufactory and check out a treasure trove of precious pieces in the Museum of Porcelain Art. In the adjoining Apicius Restaurant and Café you can even experience dining off their collection of dinnerware. The town of Herend lies 16 km (10 miles) northwest of Veszprém on Route 8, and regular buses ply the route all day (40 minutes each way). ⊠ Kossuth Lajos utca 140, Herend 🖼 88/523–190 ⊕ www.herend. com/visit-herend/information 🎫 3,500 HUF ⊙ Closed mid-Dec.–Mar.

Várhegy (Castle Hill)

NEIGHBORHOOD | The cobblestone Vár utca, north of Szabadság tér, runs through the most picturesque part of town. It also has most of the sights worth seeing in Veszprém. The **Hosök kapuja** (Heroes' Gate) at the entrance commemorates those who died during World War I and has a small exhibit on Hungary's history. Farther up, **Szent Mihály-bazilika** (St. Michael's Basilica) is a beautifully light and colorful cathedral that's been rebuilt many times since the 11th century. Nearby, the **Gizella kápolna** (Gisele Chapel), named for St. Stephen's wife, is home to gorgeous Byzantine-style frescoes of the apostles from the 13th century. From here, walk to the top of the hill to see giant stone **statues of St. Stephen and Gisele,** as well as lovely views out to a rocky outcrop with a crucifix; a popular Easter procession stop. On the way back down the hill, stop in to see **Ferences-templom** and **Piarista templom,** two churches with very different depictions of St. Stephen (his outfits reflect the fashions of the time), as well as some interesting museums and galleries, including **Vass László** and **Dubniczay Palota.** Finally, just before you are back at Szabadság tér, you'll pass by the half-medieval and half-baroque **Tűztorony** (Fire Tower). ⊠ Vár utca, Veszprém.

🍴 Restaurants

Elefánt

$$ | ITALIAN | Situated on Óváros tér at the foot of Castle Hill, this charming little bistro offers an extensive menu of Italian favorites, including pizzas, pastas, and risottos, alongside some distinctly Hungarian grilled and fried meat dishes. If you come at lunchtime, you'll also find a great value three-course daily menu on offer, typically priced between 2,500 and 3,000 HUF. **Known for:** tasty poppy seed bread pudding; lovely street terrace in summer; central location means slightly higher prices. ⑤ Average main: 2,500 HUF ⊠ Óváros tér 5, Veszprém 🖼 88/329–695 ⊕ www.elefantetterem. hu.

★ Oliva

$$ | MEDITERRANEAN | In the heart of downtown Veszprém, this restaurant is a little tricky to find—look for the covered alley off the southeastern edge of Óváros Tér—but it's as charming as they come, with dim lighting and stylish decor, fine Mediterranean-inspired cuisine, and unfailingly friendly staff. The interior of the establishment is decorated in soft Mediterranean colors, including olive-green banquettes and funky artworks, while the lovely, leafy terrace has live music several nights a week. **Known for:** creative Mediterranean dishes; colorful decor and inviting terrace; attached hotel includes an outdoor Jacuzzi. ⑤ *Average main: 2,990 HUF* ✉ *Buhim utca 14–16, Veszprém* ☎ *88/403–875* ⊕ *www.oliva. hu.*

★ Villa Medici Restaurant

$$$$ | HUNGARIAN | Tucked away in a pretty valley to the west of Castle Hill, Villa Medici is widely considered to be one of the region's best restaurants—and for good reason. The setting is simply beautiful, whether you dine in the beautifully appointed interior, featuring walls lined with original artworks, or out on the charming lamplit garden terrace, set around a lily pond. **Known for:** beautifully presented set menus; formal service and smart casual dress code; a 10-minute walk from center. ⑤ *Average main: 10,800 HUF* ✉ *Kittenberger Kálmán utca 11, Veszprém* ☎ *88/590–072* ⊕ *www. villamedici.hu.*

Nightlife

Papírkutya

BARS/PUBS | Billing itself as a "kultúr bisztró," the Paper Dog not only serves hot meals and ice cold drinks from early until late, but also prides itself on being a cultural hub, with regular performances of live music, theater, and even performance poetry. The glass-fronted bar displays a vast selection of rums, and there's a quirky, arty vibe throughout the place, from the off-the-wall paintings to the Shrek-themed pinball machine. ✉ *Szabadság tér 9, Veszprém* ☎ *20/241– 0074* ⊕ *www.facebook.com/papirkutya. veszprem.*

Balatonfüred

19 km (12 miles) south of Veszprém, 124 km (77 miles) southwest of Budapest.

Fed by 11 medicinal springs, Balatonfüred first gained popularity as a health resort (the lake's oldest) where people with heart conditions and fatigue would come to take (or, more accurately, to drink) a cure. The waters, said to have stimulating and beneficial effects on the heart and nerves, are still an integral part of the town's identity and consumed voraciously, but only the internationally renowned cardiac hospital has actual bathing facilities.

Today Balatonfüred, also known simply as Füred, is one of the Balaton's most popular destinations. Above its busy boat landing, beaches, and promenade lined with great plane and poplar trees, the twisting streets of the Old Town climb hillsides that are thickly planted with vines. The climate and landscape also make this one of the best wine-growing districts in Hungary. Every year in July the most elaborate of Lake Balaton's debutante cotillions, the Anna Ball, is held here.

GETTING HERE AND AROUND

From Veszprém, it's a 30-minute drive south along Route 73 to reach Balatonfüred. Regular buses also connect the two urban areas via the same route (45 minutes).

From Budapest, it's a 1¾-hour drive down the M7 and along Route 710. There are no direct public transport links between the capital and Balatonfüred, so you're best off coming via Veszprém.

Sights

★ **Baláca római villagazdaság** (*Villa Romana Baláca*)
ARCHAEOLOGICAL SITE | Take a short detour off the road from Veszprém to Balatonfüred to find this impressive archaeological site, once a large Roman farmstead covering a sprawling 55 hectares. The site today barely covers two, but this includes a partially reconstructed central residential building, as well as the ruins of baths and burial sites and a host of carved stone monuments. Head down into the cellar of the main building to see four well-preserved mosaic floors, and keep an eye out for an almost-complete peacock frieze. The whole site is brought to life through models and interactive exhibits. Baláca is set a little way back from the road, so look for a small concrete car park; it's a five-minute walk from here to the entrance. ⊠ *Nemesvámos-Baláca, Veszprém* ✦ *On the road between Nemesvámos and Veszprémfajsz* ☎ *88/265–050* ⊕ *www. balaca.hu* 🎟 *800 HUF* ☉ *Closed Mon.*

Gyógy tér
PLAZA | The center of town is this small square, where the bubbling waters from five volcanic springs rise beneath a slim, colonnaded pavilion. The square's centerpiece is the neoclassical **Well House of the Kossuth Spring**; from here you can sample the water, which has a pleasant, surprisingly refreshing taste, despite the sulfurous aroma. Note that there's a strict, 30-liters-per-person limit (good luck trying to break that rule). All the buildings on the square are pillared like Greek temples. At No. 3 is **Horváth Ház**, a former sanatorium that hosted the first of what was to become the Anna Ball in 1825. The ball now takes place every July in another colonnaded building on the square, and also a former sanatorium, the **Anna Grand Hotel**. On the north side of the square is the **Balatoni Pantheon**: aesthetically interesting tablets and reliefs honoring Hungarian and foreign notables who took the waters here. From Gyógy tér, you can stroll east along Blaha Lujza utca to see several landmarks, such as the **Blaha Lujza Ház**, a neoclassical villa built in 1867 (and, later, the summer home of the eponymous actress), and the sweet little 19th-century **Kerek templom** (Round Church). ⊠ *Balatonfüred.*

Tagore sétány (*Tagore Promenade*)
PROMENADE | Trees, restaurants, and shops line this busy waterfront promenade, which is named after the Nobel Prize–winning Bengali poet Rabindranath Tagore. Why? Because he came to one Balatonfüred's sanitoriums in 1926 to get treatment for a heart condition. You will find a bust of Tagore in front of a lime tree along the promenade; the poet planted it himself following his recovery. The promenade begins near the boat landing and runs for nearly a kilometer (½ mile) to the east. ⊠ *Balatonfüred.*

Vaszary galéria
MUSEUM | With connections to both Kolos Ferenc Vaszary (1832–1915), the former Archbishop of Esztergom and Prince-Primate of Hungary who summered in Balatonfüred, and his renowned painter nephew János Vaszary, this eye-catching 19th-century building houses the town's best art gallery. Come to see everything from paintings by Old Masters to works by contemporary artists. There's also a lovely art-filled garden terrace with a good café. ⊠ *Honvéd utca 2–4, Balatonfüred* ☎ *87/950–876* ⊕ *kultura.balatonfured.hu* ☉ *Closed Mon.*

🍴 Restaurants

★ **Bistro Sparhelt**
$$$$ | MODERN EUROPEAN | This modern European bistro is considered one of Hungary's best restaurants, so it's well worth the 25-minute walk from the lakeside. The stylish, stripped-back interior— all exposed brick walls, wooden-beamed ceilings, and distressed leather chairs— makes the perfect setting for a culinary

adventure. **Known for:** popular poppy-seed soufflé; exposed brick walls and wooden beams; terrace dining in the summer. $ *Average main: 5,500 HUF* ✉ *Szent István tér 7, Balatonfüred* ☎ *70/639–9944.*

Kedves Cukrászda

$ | **BAKERY** | Need something to take the taste of Kossuth Spring water out of your mouth? Stroll to this nearby café and patisserie, once a popular haunt of actress Lujza Blaha (who lived opposite), to sample its fine selection of homemade cakes, pastries, and pies. **Known for:** the city's oldest bakery café; delicious home-made cakes (try the plum pie); tree-shaded terrace in summer. $ *Average main: 600 HUF* ✉ *Blaha Lujza utca 7, Balatonfüred* ☎ *20/471–2073* ⊕ *www.facebook.com/KedvesCukraszda* ⊘ *Closed Mon.*

Hotels

★ Anna Grand

$$$$ | **HOTEL** | This centuries-old sanitorium-turned-hotel is Balatonfüred's grandest accommodation option, though its rooms vary dramatically in quality. **Pros:** spacious and well-appointed suites; fantastic swimming and spa facilities; Anna Café serves scrumptious cakes. **Cons:** suites face the street (though it's quiet at night); fitness center costs extra to use; older rooms are far less appealing. $ *Rooms from: 67,000 HUF* ✉ *Gyógy Tér 1, Balatonfüred* ☎ *87/581–200* ⊕ *www.annagrandhotel.hu* ⇄ *108 rooms* ⧫ *Free breakfast.*

Nightlife

★ Petrányi Pince

WINE BARS—NIGHTLIFE | The village of Csopak, just to the northeast of Balatonfüred, is at the heart of the region's wine-growing industry, and a number of local producers—from Jásdi to Szent Donát—now offer wine tastings on their properties. The best of the bunch is Petrányi thanks to its large hillside terrace with sweeping views of the lake,

its great selection of wines for tasting (mostly from their own vineyards, which spread out below), and its menu of delicious Hungarian and international dishes. Ask nicely and you might get a tour of the chapel-like cellar, complete with a hidden room once used to hide bottles from the taxman. ✉ *Balatonfüred* ☎ *30/515–7953* ⊕ *www.petranyipince.hu.*

SpiccBistro

BARS/PUBS | This fashionable end-of-the-pier bar is a lovely place to enjoy a drink, especially in the evening. Watch the sun set over the lake as you sip one of many locally produced wines, from signature Olaszrizlings to sparkling rosés, or just a homemade lemonade. The food is good, too. ✉ *Balatonfüred vitorláskikötő, Balatonfüred* ☎ *20/418–3132* ⊕ *www.facebook.com/spiccbistro.*

Tihany

8 km (5 miles) south of Balatonfüred, 130 km (81 miles) southwest of Budapest.

The famed town of Tihany, with its twisting, narrow cobblestone streets and hilltop abbey, sits on a peninsula of the same name. Joined to the mainland by a narrow neck and jutting 5 km (3 miles) into the lake, Tihany Peninsula is not only a major tourist resort—it is, after all, Hungary's closest approximation of a Mediterranean or Adriatic experience—but perhaps the most historic part of the Balaton area. In 1952 the entire peninsula was declared a national park, and because of its geological rarities, it became Hungary's first nature conservation zone. Explore its smooth Belso Tó (Inner Lake), 82 feet higher than Lake Balaton, as well as its endless lavender fields (aided by the sun coming from three directions) and historic caves.

The town itself is best known for its Benedictine Abbey, but you can easily spend half a day here strolling its winding streets, enjoying stunning lake views, and eating lavender-flavored ice cream.

GETTING HERE AND AROUND

Tihany is easily reached by car (15 minutes) or by bus (30 minutes) from Balatonfüred, both via Route 71 and the lakeside street Lepkesor. If you are driving from Budapest, follow directions to Balatonfüred then simply continue on Route 71.

Once in town, park in the lot behind the Tihany Posta (post office) and explore on foot.

Sights

Barátlakások (*Friar's Caves*)
CAVE | This network of hillside caverns, carved out of the basalt rock between the 11th and 14th centuries but only rediscovered in the 20th century, was once home to a group of Greek Orthodox hermit-monks. A mix of living quarters, chapels, and dining rooms, the caves have since been restored and stabilized with columns, making them safe to visit. You'll find them on the eastern slopes of Óvár hill; follow the green hiking route through the forest from Tihany town, or park your car at the *kiinduló pont* (starting point) and walk 300 meters downhill to the biggest cave. ■ **TIP→ Access is via a steep woodland path, so you'll need hiking boots and should avoid visiting during or after heavy rain.** ⊠ *Kecskeköröm utca 28, (starting point car park), Tihany.*

★ **Bencés Apátság** (*Benedictine Abbey*)
RELIGIOUS SITE | On a hilltop overlooking the Old Town is this twin-spired abbey, whose foundations were laid by King András I in 1055. Today, his body lies in the 11th century crypt, along with a replica of the abbey's charter, the oldest written source of the Hungarian language (the original is in Pannonhalma). The contrast between the simple crypt, where a small black crucifix hangs over the king's tomb, and the abbey's lavish 18th century baroque interior—all gold, gilded silver, and salmon—is vast. The altar, abbot's throne, choir parapet, organ case, and pulpit were all the work of Sebestyén Stuhloff, and it's said he immortalized his doomed sweetheart as the angel kneeling on the right-hand side of the altar to the Virgin Mary. A magnificent organ, adorned by stucco cherubs, can be heard during evening concerts in summer. In a baroque house adjoining—and entered through—the abbey is the **Bencés Apátsági Múzeum**. The best exhibits are in the basement lapidarium: relics from Roman colonization, including mosaic floors; a relief of David from the 2nd or 3rd century; and 1,200-year-old carved stones. Get a joint ticket for the abbey and museum from the modern visitor center, where you can watch a short introductory video. ⊠ *András tér 1, Tihany* ☎ *87/538–200* ⊕ *www.tihanyiapatsag.hu* 🎫 *1,000 HUF (abbey and museum).*

Skanzen Tihany
MUSEUM VILLAGE | Tihany's open-air museum of ethnography assembles a group of old structures across a small area west of the abbey. The main two buildings are the Smallholder's House, an unplastered dwelling with basalt walls, a thatched roof, verandas, and white-framed windows dating back to the 18th century, and the Fisherman's House, the former home of the Fishermen's Guild, with all kinds of angling tools and even an ancient boat on display. ⊠ *Pisky sétány 12, Tihany* ☎ *30/749–7182* 🎫 *350 HUF* ⊘ *Closed Mon. and Oct.–Apr.*

🍴 Restaurants

★ **Apátsági Rege Cukrászda**
$$ | **CAFÉ** | Whatever you do in Tihany, don't miss this extraordinary hilltop bakery-café. Not only does it have the best coffee and cake anywhere in town, with many of the brews and bakes incorporating Tihany's signature crop lavender, but its terrace offers breathtaking views across the shimmering blue waters of Lake Balaton. **Known for:** extraordinary

lake views from the terrace; lavender espressos and lavender cheesecake; can get very busy in the summer. $ *Average main: 2,500 HUF* ✉ *Kossuth Lajos utca 22, Tihany* ⊕ *www.apatsagicukraszda.hu.*

Malackrumpli

$$$ | **HUNGARIAN** | Literally translated as "pig potatoes," this popular bistro in the heart of Tihany mainly uses ingredients from its own farm—and yes, that includes pork and potatoes. While the dishes on offer are invariably simple and hearty staples, from beef goulash and chicken paprikash to burgers and pizzas, they are also uncommonly high quality and beautifully presented. **Known for:** signature Mangalica pork sausage pizza; only open on weekends; expensive by local standards. $ *Average main: 3,490 HUF* ✉ *Kossuth Lajos utca 14, Tihany* ☎ *30/636–5577* ⊕ *www.malackrumpli.hu* ⊙ *Closed Mon.–Thurs.*

Hotels

Club Tihany

$$$ | **RESORT** | **FAMILY** | Picture Club Med transposed to late-1980s Central Europe, and you'll have some idea of what to expect at this 32-acre lakeside resort 3 km (2 miles) south of town. **Pros:** fantastic family holiday resort; large swimming pool with views over the lake; candlelit spa sessions every evening. **Cons:** half the rooms and suites have no A/C; expect a scramble for the breakfast buffet; parking costs 1,000 HUF a night. $ *Rooms from: 52,000 HUF* ✉ *Rév utca 3, Tihany* ☎ *87/538–564* ⊕ *www.clubtihany.hu* ↪ *490 rooms* ⦿ *No meals.*

Shopping

PaprikaHáz

FOOD/CANDY | This whitewashed, thatched-roofed building is difficult to miss, as it's almost completely covered in hanging bundles of red peppers. Naturally, the food store inside specializes in pepper products, from paprika powder to chili beer, but it also does a good line in lavender confections. ✉ *Kossuth Lajos utca 18, Tihany.*

Badacsony and Szigliget

39 km (24 miles) west of Tihany, 168 km (104 milies) southwest of Budapest.

One of the northern shore's most treasured images is of Mt. Badacsony (1,437 feet), simply called the Badacsony, rising from the lake. The mysterious, coffinlike basalt peak of the Balaton Highlands is actually an extinct volcano flanked by smaller cone-shape hills. The masses of lava that coagulated here created bizarre and beautiful rock formations. At the upper edge, salt columns tower 180 to 200 feet like organ pipes in a huge semicircle.

As well as making Badacsony a popular hiking area, this unique volcanic landscape has also resulted in rich soils, ideal for wine growing. There are vineyards everywhere, producing much-loved Badacsony white wines like Rizlingszilváni, Kéknyelu, and Szürkebarát. Proud producers claim that "no vine will produce good wine unless it can see its own reflection in the Balaton."

Just to the west of Badacsony lies Szigliget, a tranquil town with fine thatched-roof wine-press houses and a small beach, all overlooked by an enormous fortress.

GETTING HERE AND AROUND

To get to Badacsony from Tihany, simply drive west on Route 71 for around 40 minutes. It's also possible to get here by bus, though this requires a connection in Balatonfüred, so takes close to two hours.

If you're driving from Budapest, simply follow directions to Balatonfüred then continue along Route 71 for another 40 km (25 miles). Szigliget is 7 km (4½ miles) farther west along Route 71.

◉ Sights

Avasi templomrom (*Avas Church*)
ARCHAEOLOGICAL SITE | These church ruins on the outskirts of Szigliget, right at the intersection with the road to Badacsony, are what is left of the village's oldest building. These Romanesque remains date back to the Árpád dynasty (855–1301), but the herringbone-like stones in the church walls suggest the site is even older, dating back to at least Roman times. Visit the Avas Church today to see the remaining 12th-century basalt tower with a stone spire. ⊠ *Réhelyi út 67, Szigliget.*

Kisfaludy kilátó (*Kisfaludy Lookout Tower*)
VIEWPOINT | The steep climb to the lookout tower on Mt. Badacsony's summit is an integral part of the Badacsony experience and a rewarding bit of exercise. The trek to the tower, which climbs 455 meters—437 for the hill and a further 18 for the tower—begins behind the Kisfaludy Ház, a restaurant just above the Szegedy Róza-ház. Here stands the Rózsakő (Rose Stone), a flat, smooth basalt slab with many carved inscriptions; local legend has it that if a boy and a girl sit on it with their backs to Lake Balaton, they will marry within a year. Follow the trail marked in yellow up to the foot of the columns that stretch to the top. Steep flights of stone steps will take you through a narrow gap between rocks and basalt walls until you reach a tree-lined plateau. From here, simply follow the blue triangular markings along a path to the lookout tower. Even with time out for rests and views, the whole ascent should take less than an hour. ⊠ *Egry sétány 21, Badacsonytomaj* ☎ *87/571–270* ⊕ *www. badacsonykilato.hu.*

Szegedy Róza-ház
MUSEUM | Built in 1790, this charming baroque wine-press house features a thatched roof, gabled wall, six semicircular arcades, and an arched and pillared balcony running the length of the four raftered upstairs rooms. It was here that Sándor Kisfaludy, a writer from Budapest, met hometown girl Róza Szegedy—the start of a fairy-tale love story. The house now serves as a memorial museum to both of them, furnished much the way it was when Kisfaludy was doing his best work immortalizing his two true loves, the Badacsony and Róza, who became his wife. Róza herself was heavily involved with wine-making, and her homemade vermouth was famous throughout Hungary. ⊠ *Kisfaludy Sándor utca 17, Badacsonytomaj* ☎ *70/382–9210* ⊕ *www.szegedyrozahaz.hu* ⊠ *900 HUF* ⊙ *Closed Tues.*

Szigliget óvár
ARCHAEOLOGICAL SITE | Towering over the village of Szigliget, atop a 239-meter-high hill, is the ruin of the 13th-century Óvár (Old Castle). Unlike many of Hungary's fortresses, this one was so well protected that it was never taken by the Turks; in fact, it was demolished in the early 18th century by Habsburgs fearful of rebellions. A steep path starting from Kisfaludy utca brings you to the top of the hill, where you can explore the ruins and take in the breathtaking views. ⊠ *Hegyaljai út 7, Szigliget.*

◍ Restaurants

★ Hableány
$$$ | HUNGARIAN | A restaurant since the late 1800s but most recently refurbished in summer 2019, Hableány remains a Badacsony favorite for its delicious Hungarian dishes incorporating fresh, local ingredients—think smoked catfish with sour cabbage, Mangalica pork shoulder with beetroot, and wild boar stew with mushrooms. As well as a bistro, the building incorporates a state-of-the-art winery; you can take the factory tour, sample a glass at the wine bar, or pick up a take-out bottle in the wine shop. "Hableány" means "mermaid," and there's a large mural outside that depicts the local legend of a hill god who fell for a

mermaid; he leapt into the lake, creating a splash that extinguished the volcanic Mt. Badacsony. **Known for:** elegant interior and inviting terrace; includes a modern winery plus wine bar and shop; mermaid mural outside relates to local legend. *§ Average main: 3,950 HUF ⊠ Park utca 26, Badacsony ☎ 30/792–9131 ⊕ www. hableanybadacsony.hu.*

Halászkert

$$$ | HUNGARIAN | The festive Fish Garden has won numerous international awards for its fine Hungarian cuisine. Inside are wooden rafters and tables draped with peachy-pink tablecloths; outside is a large terrace with umbrella-shaded tables. **Known for:** delicious catfish stew with strapachka (mini dumplings); very friendly and attentive service; the attached hotel is uninspiring. *§ Average main: 3,200 HUF ⊠ Park utca 1, Badacsony ☎ 87/531–008 ⊕ www.hotelhalaszkert. hu.*

Hotels

Bonvino

$$$ | HOTEL | With a strong focus on wine and wellness, this conveniently located Badacsony hotel is renowned for its well-stocked wine bar, with more than 100 different vintages including local varietals like Kéknyelű, and its extensive spa facilities, including a large pool, Jacuzzi, and range of massage treatments. **Pros:** free wine tastings for guests three times a week; extensive wellness facilities; e-bikes available to rent. **Cons:** rooms are comfy but uninspired; grape-pattern carpets look more like billiard balls; minimum two-night stays in summer. *§ Rooms from: 49,900 HUF ⊠ Park utca 22, Badacsony ☎ 87/532–210 ⊕ www.hotelbonvino.hu ➧ 48 rooms ⦿I All-inclusive.*

Hotel Neptun

$ | HOTEL | Directly above Bonvino, this attractive mansion-turned-hotel offers a choice of modern, stylish, and colorful rooms, as well as a large family apartment. **Pros:** designer rooms and apartments; wine tasting at nearby Fata Pince included; free parking for guests. **Cons:** bathrooms have frosted glass walls; hot options limited at breakfast; restaurant only open weekends. *§ Rooms from: 27,900 HUF ⊠ Római út 170, Badacsony ☎ 87/431–293 ⊕ www.hotelneptunbadacsony.hu ➧ 15 rooms ⦿I Free breakfast.*

Nightlife

Istvándy

WINE BARS—NIGHTLIFE | This little bar, a short walk from the center of Badacsony, is a great stop for a glass of wine. Sit in the garden to enjoy a lake panorama with your drink, or head inside for the cellar experience, often with live music. The wines come from the Istvándy pincészet (winery) about 5 km (3 miles) north of here. *⊠ Római út 155, Badacsony ☎ 30/650–2476.*

★ Laposa borterasz

WINE BARS—NIGHTLIFE | This gorgeous wine terrace, situated high in the hills above Badacsony with spectacular views of Lake Balaton, is just about the most romantic spot imaginable for a wine tasting—particularly at sunset. Try three types of Laposa estate wine for 2,200 HUF, or six for 3,300 HUF. There's also a small menu of delicious meals and platters available. It's a popular spot in summer, so it's best to pre-book a table (as well as a taxi, unless you fancy the steep, 30-minute walk each way). *⊠ Bogyay Lajos út 1, Badacsonytomaj ☎ 20/777–7133 ⊕ www.laposaborterasz. hu.*

Keszthely and Hévíz

15 km (9 miles) west of Badacsony, 196 km (122 miles) from Budapest.

With a beautifully preserved historic center, a spectacular baroque palace, and a relative absence of honky-tonk, Keszthely is far more classically attractive than other large Balaton towns. It also holds regular cultural events, including an annual summer arts festival, continuing the cultural tradition begun by Count György Festetics two centuries ago. The water around Keszthely's beaches appears disconcertingly cloudy, but it's nothing to worry about: it's simply sediment churned up by water flowing from the nearby Kis-Balaton (Little Balaton) into the main lake.

Seven kilometers (4½ miles) northwest of Keszthely is Hévíz, one of Hungary's biggest and most famous spa resorts. Centered around the largest natural curative thermal lake in Europe, which offers warm water bathing all year round, this charming little town has a fine selection of high quality hotels—most of which have extensive spa facilities. So while Keszthely is a great place to spend the afternoon, either strolling around town or wading along the Balaton shore, Hévíz is a far superior place to spend the night.

GETTING HERE AND AROUND
To reach Keszthely from Badacsony (via Szigliget), simply drive west along the lakeside Route 71 for 30 minutes. There are also regular direct buses that follow the same route (50 minutes).

From Budapest, the only real option is to drive. Head southwest along the M7—you'll find yourself skirting the south side of Lake Balaton—before turning off at exit 170 and following Routes 76 and 71 into Keszthely. The journey takes around two hours.

From Keszthely, it's a 10-minute drive or a 30-minute bus ride into Hévíz. Both towns are small enough to explore on foot.

Sights

Baba Múzeum (*Doll Museum*)
MUSEUM | Supposedly the largest of its kind in Central Europe, Keszthely's Doll Museum exhibits some 450 porcelain figurines dressed in 240 types of colorful folk dress. The building has a pastoral look, created not only by the figurines—which convey the multifarious beauty of village garb—but also by the ceiling's huge, handcrafted wooden beams. On the two upper floors are wooden models of typical homes, churches, and ornate wooden gates representative of all regions in and near present-day Hungary that Magyars have inhabited since conquering the Carpathian basin in 896. The museum's pièce de résistance is the life work of an elderly peasant woman from northern Hungary: a nine-yard-long model of Budapest's Parliament building, patched together over 14 years from almost four million snail shells. ⊠ *Nádor utca 1, Keszthely* ☎ *30/855–6533* ⊕ *www.babamuzeum-keszthely.hu* ⊠ *600 HUF.*

★ **Festetics Kastély**
CASTLE/PALACE | Keszthely's magnificent Festetics Palace is one of the finest baroque complexes in Hungary. Begun around 1745, it was the seat of the enlightened and philanthropic Festetics dynasty, which had acquired Keszthely six years earlier. Surrounded by manicured **gardens** with fine sculptures and a **nature reserve park** filled with rare plants, the palace's distinctive churchlike tower and more than 100 rooms were added between 1883 and 1887. A tour of the interior starts with an interactive Festetics family tree, followed by a series of remarkable rooms including the historic **Helikon Library,** home to 52,000 volumes and family history records, and the atmospheric **chapel** with its gorgeous stained glass windows and coin-covered floor. As you walk around, keep an eye out for some items that were forced into exile during communism but have

Did You Know?

The gorgeous grounds of Festetics Kastély include a protected nature reserve with a French and an English garden, fountains and statues, and a palm house where you can find the most unique tropical hibiscus collection in Europe.

recently found their way home, including a beautiful black-and-gold desk made by Louis XIV's carpenter, and a Hungarian ceremonial outfit on display in front of a portrait of a family member wearing it. A standard ticket (2,900 HUF) includes the palace plus one exhibition—choose from the **Palm House,** the **Coach Collection,** the **Hunting Exhibition,** and the **Model Railway**—while a deluxe ticket (4,400 HUF) gets you in everywhere. ✉ *Kastély utca 1, Keszthely* ☎ *83/314–194* ⊕ *www.helikonkastely.hu* 🎫 *2,900 HUF (palace and one exhibition)* ⊘ *Closed Mon. Oct–Apr.*

★ **Hévízi Tófürdő** (*Thermal Lake of Hévíz*) **SPA—SIGHT** | When it comes to public bathing facilities, few can match the beauty and novelty of this thermal lake in the heart of Hévíz. Covering nearly 60,000 square yards, the water never grows cooler than 33°C (91.4°F) in summer and 30°C (86°F) in winter, allowing for year-round bathing. It's also richly laced with sulfur, alkali, calcium salts, and other curative components, making a dip highly recommended for those with spinal, rheumatic, gynecological, and articular disorders (the water can also be drunk to help digestive problems and receding gums). Squeamish bathers should be forewarned that along with its photogenic lily pads, the lake naturally contains assorted sludgy mud and plant material. It's all supposed to be good for you, though—even the mud, which is full of iodine and is claimed to stimulate estrogen production in the body. Nonswimmers can also enjoy the lake, as there's special hydrotherapy equipment available. You can buy a day's entry ticket for cover either two or three hours (3,500 or 4,500 HUF), or a 10-hour lake pass if you're staying for several days (10,000 HUF). ⚠ **Bathing for more than three hours at a time is not recommended.** ✉ *Dr. Schulhof Vilmos sétány 1, Hévíz* ☎ *83/501–708* ⊕ *www.hotelspaheviz.hu* 🎫 *3,500 HUF.*

🛏 Hotels

Hotel Bonvital

$ | RESORT | It may have a smaller wellness area than most Hévíz hotels, but the adult-only Bonvital makes up for it with a convenient central location near Lake Hévíz, a choice of modern and spacious rooms, and one of the most popular and elegant restaurants in town. **Pros:** all rooms above standard have balconies; elegant on-site Brix Bistro; only 200 meters from Lake Hévíz. **Cons:** small spa with no thermal water; half-board is the only option; brown-heavy room decor feels a little musty. ⑤ *Rooms from: 28,000 HUF* ✉ *Rákóczi utca 16–18, Hévíz* ☎ *83/900–120* ⊕ *www.bonvital.accenthotels.com* 🛏 *90 rooms* ⦿ *All-inclusive.*

Lotus Therme

$$$$ | RESORT | This excellent spa and wellness hotel, which lies in 17 hectares of land south of the center, makes for a relaxing and invigorating stay. **Pros:** outdoor pool is warm year-round; stylish wine bar with pool table; bikes and e-bikes available to rent. **Cons:** decor is very 90s (though still more modern than some Hévíz hotels); a 20-minute walk to the center; very expensive. ⑤ *Rooms from: 88,500 HUF* ✉ *Lótuszvirág utca 1, Hévíz* ☎ *83/500–500* ⊕ *www.lotustherme.net* 🛏 *232 rooms* ⦿ *All-inclusive.*

Zenit Hotel Balaton

$$$ | RESORT | Located 5 km (3 miles) east of Keszthely, this hillside resort is more than a match for most of Hévíz's wellness hotels, with facilities including a 15-meter swimming pool, a kids' pool with slide, indoor and outdoor Jacuzzis, and massage treatments that incorporate locally sourced grape-seed oil and even red wine. **Pros:** comfortable rooms with balcony; Bock Bisztró has a lovely lake-view terrace; geothermal energy used to heat and cool the building. **Cons:** TVs in rooms are small and old; reception staff could be more helpful; no options other than half-board. ⑤ *Rooms from:*

49,000 HUF ✉ Helikon utca 22, Keszthely ☎ 20/801–0568 ⊕ www.hotelzenit.hu ⤳ 47 rooms ⊙l All-inclusive.

Győr

129 km (80 miles) north of Keszthely, 121 km (75 miles) west of Budapest.

The largest city in western Hungary, Győr is often called the "Town of Rivers," as it's situated at the confluence of the Rába, Rábca, and Mosoni-Duna rivers in the heart of Hungary's Kisalföld (Little Plain). Just over halfway between Budapest and Sopron, and almost exactly halfway between Budapest and Vienna, it's a pleasant and convenient stop for any long-distance travelers. The same, unfortunately, has been true for invaders: throughout its 2,000-year history, Győr has seen occupations by Romans, Tatars, Teutons, and Huns. And even though a former city fortress was built by Italian engineers, it was not strong enough to hold back the Turks, who took the city in 1594.

Downtown Győr, where the three rivers meet, is packed with baroque buildings and museums. Highlights include a 12th-century cathedral and several art museums with renowned collections. If your timing is right, you could also catch a performance by the Győri Balett, the country's most renowned ballet company.

GETTING HERE AND AROUND

Driving to Győr from Keszthely takes around two hours; simply head north on Route 84, before joining the M86. There are also direct trains, which run every two hours, but these follow a more circuitous route and take 2¾ hours. Coming from Budapest? Drive west on the M1 (1¼ hours) or hop on an hourly train from Budapest-Keleti station (1½ hours).

Győr's main attractions, restaurants, and hotels are all in the center, which you can explore on foot; there are few reasons to venture out to the industrial suburbs.

◉ Sights

Esterházy-palota (*Esterházy Palace*)
MUSEUM | This historic palace, with its decorative entranceway just off the northwest corner of Széchenyi tér, was once owned by the famous Esterházy family. Today it's part of the Rómer Flóris Művészeti és Történeti Múzeum (Rómer Flóris Museum of Art and History) and home to its Radnai Collection. This includes everything from József Rippl-Rónai's resplendent Still Life with Mask to József Egry's light-pervaded Lake Balaton landscapes, alongside many other outstanding examples of 20th-century Hungarian painting, sculpture, and graphic art. ■ **TIP→ Buy a single entry ticket (800 HUF) rather than a combined ticket (2,500 HUF) as even if you visit every exhibit, the savings are negligible.** ✉ *Király utca 17, Gyor* ☎ *96/322–695* ⊕ *www.romer.hu* ▣ *800 HUF ⊙ Closed Mon.*

Jedlik-csobogó
FOUNTAIN | This small but eye-catching drinking fountain, created by local glass artist László Hefter in 2012, depicts a turquoise soda bottle spurting water into a small tiled pool. A glance at any drinks menu in Hungary reveals an obsession with soda water, and this fountain commemorates its inventor (or, at least, the man who first mass produced it) Ányos Jedlik. The bottle itself weighs a toe-crushing 365 kilograms (804 pounds), one for each day of the year. ✉ *Jedlik Ányos utca 9, Gyor.*

Káptalandomb (*Capital Hill*)
NEIGHBORHOOD | This charming neighborhood, which lies at the confluence of the three rivers, is the ancient heart of Győr. With its maze of fences and wonderfully curved gates surrounding baroque-style homes, it's a lovely area to simply stroll around, but two buildings in particular are worth a closer look. The first is the

Püspökvár (Bishop's Palace), the long-time residence of the Győr bishops. With sections that date right back to the 13th century—though it was built on the walls of an even-older Roman fort—the palace is now open as an exhibition space and lookout tower (entry costs 1,000 HUF). The second is the **Székesegyház** (Cathedral) with its heady mix of Romanesque, Gothic, and baroque features. Step inside to see the bishop's throne, which was a gift from Empress Maria Theresa; the frame of a painting depicting the Blessed Virgin and infant Jesus, which is considered a rococo masterpiece; and the 15th-century bust of St. László in his namesake chapel, which is an excellent example of medieval Hungarian gold-smithing. ⊠ *Gyor.*

★ **Pannonhalmi Főapátság** (*Pannonhalma Abbey*)
RELIGIOUS SITE | Perched divinely above the countryside on a hilltop roughly 20 km (12½ miles) southeast of Győr, this giant 1,000-year-old Benedictine abbey still gleams like a gift from heaven. During the Middle Ages it was an important ecclesiastical center, the location of Hungary's first school, and perhaps the first place the Holy Scriptures were read on Hungarian soil. It's still a working monastery and school; 60 monks and 320 students live here.

Come by car (there's no other way) from Győr to explore the abbey, either by yourself—make sure you pick up an audio guide at reception—or on one of the frequent English-language guided tours. While the abbey's architecture is predominantly baroque, the main **basilica** is in the early Gothic style, while the 180-foot-high **bell tower** is distinctly neo-classical. Don't miss the incredibly decorative **Porta Speciosa** (ornate entrance) or the spectacular **library** with its more than 300,000 volumes, including some priceless medieval documents like the 11th-century deed to the abbey of Tihany.

A short uphill walk from the abbey takes you to the **Millennium Monument,** erected in 1896 to mark the Magyars' settlement of the Carpathian Basin 1,000 years earlier, while a downhill stroll leads to the upmarket restaurant-with-a-view **Apátsági Viator.** ⊠ *Vár 1, Pannonhalma* ☎ *96/570-100* ⊕ *www.pannonhalmifoapatsag.hu* ⌨ *2,500 HUF (incl. audio guide); 3,200 HUF guided tour in English* ⊘ *Closed Mon. Oct.–May.*

Széchenyi tér
PLAZA | Győr's main square, ringed by historic buildings, hotels, restaurants, and bars, is the life and soul of the town. It's the setting for most of the city's major cultural events, including the famous " **Baroque Marriage,** " a traditional August ceremony where baroque music is played and participants dress up in ornate wedding outfits and perform. While in the square, check out the attractive, twin-turreted **Loyolai Szent Ignác bencés templom** (Benedictine Church of St. Ignatius of Loyola) and the nearby **Mária-oszlop** (Mary's Column), built in 1686 to commemorate the recapturing of the city from the Turks. It depicts the Virgin wearing the Hungarian crown and holding the infant Jesus in her arms. ⊠ *Gyor.*

🍴 Restaurants

★ **Lamareda**
$$$ | **HUNGARIAN** | This elegant Győr restaurant is widely considered one of the best in Hungary, renowned for its refined dining room—all dangling chandeliers and white tablecloths—and its distictive dishes, which take the conventions of Hungarian cuisine and give them subtle Mediterranean twists. Think beef tenderloin strips with pappardelle and porcini, duck breast with pumpkin and *pommes Anna*, and red tuna steak with garlic linguine and spinach. **Known for:** extensive and exclusive wine list; delicious flódni (a layered cake with plum jam and poppy seed); knowledgeable service staff.

$ *Average main: 4,600 HUF* ✉ *Apáca utca 4, Gyor* ☎ *96/510–982* ⊕ *www. lamareda.hu.*

West Kiraly BRGR

$$$$ | BURGER | Probably the best burger joint in town, West Kiraly BRGR has a huge menu of perfectly grilled patties, from a bacon-and-truffle-cheese beast to a red-salmon-and-Gorgonzola creation. All the burgers are available in three different sizes, according to appetite, while there are also sandwiches and ciabattas available. **Known for:** delicious eight-hour-cooked pulled pork burger; whole-wheat and gluten-free buns available; very expensive by local standards. $ *Average main: 7,000 HUF* ✉ *Király utca 1, Gyor* ☎ *30/228–8700* ⊕ *www.kiralybrgr.west-yburger.hu.*

Hotels

Hotel Capitulum

$$ | HOTEL | Győr is not blessed with luxury five-star accommodations, but this convenient city center business hotel is one of the city's better options. **Pros:** convenient city center location; good breakfast buffet; private underground parking garage. **Cons:** decor a little dated in places; toiletries are a bar of soap and sachet of shampoo; street noise can be heard at night. $ *Rooms from: 38,000 HUF* ✉ *Sarkantyú köz 11, Gyor* ☎ *96/512–358* ⊕ *capitulum.hu* ➴ *44 rooms* ⦿❙ *Free breakfast.*

🎭 Performing Arts

Győri zsinagóga

CONCERTS | Built in the 1860s in the neo-Romanesque style (and since renovated with a splash of art nouveau), this beautiful old synagogue building hosts regular concerts, as well as other cultural events like the MEDIAWAVE International Film and Music Festival. ✉ *Kossuth Lajos utca 5, Gyor* ☎ *20/425–2660.*

Sopron

92 km (57 miles) west of Győr, 214 km (133 miles) west of Budapest.

Lying in the far northwest of Hungary, close to the Austria border and within easy reach of Vienna, Sopron is one of Central Europe's most picturesque cities, packing a frankly incredible array of historic monuments into a very small area.

Sopron is often called Hungary's most faithful town, as its residents voted to remain part of Hungary (rather than join Austria) in 1921 after World War I. Today's city of 60,000 was a small Celtic settlement more than 2,300 years ago. During Roman times, as Scarabantia, it stood on the main European north–south trade route, the Amber Road, and also happened to be near the junction with the east–west route used by Byzantine merchants. In AD 896 the Magyars conquered the Carpathian basin and later named the city Suprun, after a medieval Hungarian warrior; after the Habsburgs took over the territory during the Turkish wars of the 16th and 17th centuries, they renamed it Ödenburg. The city suffered greatly during World War II, until it was "liberated" by the Soviet Red Army in April 1945. Decades of communist rule followed, until protests on the nearby Hungary-Austria border in 1989 helped to instigate the fall of the Berlin Wall.

Despite the centuries of upheaval, Sopron's historic core has survived and been painstakingly restored; the city even won a 1975 Europe Prize Gold Medal for Protection of Monuments. Today, the horseshoe-shaped Belváros (Inner Town), a wondrous mix of Gothic, Baroque, and Renaissance architecture protected by city walls (one set built by Romans, the other by medieval Magyars), attracts visitors from far and wide. It makes for a great stopover between the Hungarian and Austrian capitals.

GETTING HERE AND AROUND

The easiest way to get to Sopron is by train, with regular services leaving from Győr (1 hour) and Budapest-Keleti (2½ hours). Driving from Győr is easy: simply head west on the M85/Route 85 for around 1½ hours. Driving from Budapest means heading west on the M1 to Győr, then joining the M85 (2½ hours in total).

Sopron is a small city, so it's easy to navigate on foot. Most of the city sights are in Belváros, but even those outside are still within walking distance. To get to attractions outside the city, like Eszterházy Palace and Széchenyi Mansion, you can take a bus or drive.

VISITOR INFORMATION

CONTACTS Tourinform. ⊠ *Szent György utca 2, Sopron* ☎ *99/951–975* ⊕ *www. turizmus.sopron.hu.*

Sights

Esterházy-kastély (*Esterházy Palace*)
CASTLE/PALACE | A 30-minute drive east of Sopron in the town of Fertőd, and near the southern shore of Neusiedl Lake, this magnificent yellow baroque and rococo palace is often referred to as the Hungarian Versailles. Built between 1720 and 1760 as a residence for the Hungarian noble family, it was badly damaged in World War II but has since been painstakingly restored. Step through the intricate wrought-iron gate entrance to discover the palace's 126 lavishly decorated rooms, including the Banqueting Hall with its ceiling fresco of Apollo in his chariot, the beautiful library with almost 22,000 volumes, and the enormous Sala Terrena with its heated marble floor. There's also a three-story-high concert hall, where classical concerts are held throughout the summer as part of the International Haydn Festival; Joseph Haydn was the court conductor to the Eszterházy family here for 30 years. Before you leave, take a walk around the ornamental French-style gardens. ⚠ **Not**

to be confused with Schloss Esterházy in Eisenstadt, also a 30-minute drive but north, not east. This was the family's main residence; see the Eisenstadt section for more. ⊠ *Joseph Haydn utca 2, Fertod* ☎ *99/537–640* 🖰 *2,500 HUF.*

Fő tér (*Main Square*)
PLAZA | The city's attractive main square is dominated by the early Gothic **Soproni Nagyboldogasszony templom** (Blessed Mary Benedictine Church), better known as the Goat Church for reasons both fantastical—it's said the church was financed with treasure found by a billy goat—and practical—goats feature on the coat of arms of the *actual* church financiers. It's a real mishmash of styles, with a Gothic choir, a rococo main altar, and a Baroque red-marble pulpit, along with recently discovered medieval tombs. Outside stands the 18th-century **Szentháromság-szobor** (Holy Trinity Column), Hungary's finest plague memorial and among the first anywhere to feature a twisted column.

Facing the square are three very different but equally fascinating museums. **Fabricus Ház** (Fabricius House) is a beautiful Baroque mansion with exhibits on ancient city history: highlights include the remains of a Roman bathhouse and the 1,200-year-old Cunpald Goblet. The **Storno Ház** (Storno House) is Sopron's finest Renaissance-era building with a collection of furniture, porcelain, sculptures, and paintings belonging to the Stornos, a rags-to-riches dynasty of chimney sweeps-turned-art restorers. The **Fehér Angyal Patikamúzeum** (Angel Pharmacy Museum) is a real-life 17th-century apothecary that now houses a collection of period pharmaceutical tools, books, potions, and lotions. ⊠ *Sopron.*

Mária-oszlop (*Mary's Column*)
PUBLIC ART | With its finely sculpted biblical reliefs, the column is a superb specimen of Baroque design. It was erected in 1745 to mark the former site of the medieval Church of Our Lady,

The 13th-century Fire Tower has a 200-step spiral staircase to a balcony that offers lovely views of Sopron and the countryside.

which was destroyed by Sopron citizens in 1632 because they feared the Turks would use its steeple as a strategic firing tower. ☒ *Várkerület 62, Sopron.*

Ó-zsinagóga (*Old Synagogue*)
RELIGIOUS SITE | This medieval synagogue is now a religious museum complete with stunning stained-glass windows, a stone *mikvah* (a ritual bath for women), and old Torahs on display. Built around 1300, the synagogue endured several incarnations over the centuries, including a stint as a hospital (in the 1400s) and a residential building (in the 1700s); the existing facade dates from 1734. The synagogue was once at the heart of the city's Jewish ghetto, and a plaque honors the 1,640 Jews of Sopron—85% of the city's total population—who were murdered by the Nazis. ☒ *Új utca 22, Sopron* ☎ *99/311–327* ✉ *800 HUF* ☉ *Closed Mon. and Oct.–Mar.*

Széchenyi kastély (*Széchenyi Mansion*)
HOUSE | This pretty manor house, situated 13 kilometers (eight miles) southeast of Sopron, is the family seat of the Széchenyi family. Mostly completed in the neoclassical style but heavily rebuilt after World War II, the property is now home to the Széchenyi Museum, which tells the family's story through reconstructed rooms and period furnishings. The star of the show is Count István Széchenyi, known as the "Greatest Hungarian" for his achievements as a politician, writer, reformer, and generous patron: his money helped establish the Hungarian Academy of Sciences and build the Chain Bridge in Budapest. You'll find an immodest number of István portraits throughout the property, as well as interactive exhibits on some of his projects. ■ **TIP→ Information within each room is scarce for non-Hungarian speakers, so be sure to pick up an English-language brochure on your way in.** ☒ *Kiscenki utca 7, Sopron* ☎ *30/4471–1248* ⊕ *www.szechenyiorokseg.hu* ✉ *1,400 HUF* ☉ *Closed Mon.*

Szent György utca (*St. George Street*)
NEIGHBORHOOD | This beautiful Inner Town street runs south from Fő tér to Orsolya tér, where there's an interesting fountain showing Jesus using his crucifix to pierce a snake with an apple. As you walk down the street, you will come across an eclectic mix of architecture coexisting in a surprisingly harmonious fashion. The **Erdody Vár** (Erdody Palace) at No. 16 is Sopron's richest rococo building. Two doors down, at No. 12, stands the **Eggenberg Ház** (Eggenberg House), where the widow of Prince Johann Eggenberg held Protestant services during the harshest days of the Counter-Reformation and beyond. Today, it's home to the **Macskakő Múzeum**, an interactive children's museum about the everyday lives of people living in ancient times. But the street takes its name from **Szent György templom** (St. George's Church), a 14th-century Catholic church so sensitively "Baroqued" some 300 years later that its interior is still as soft as whipped cream. ⊠ *Sopron.*

★ **Tuztorony** (*Fire Tower*)
BUILDING | This symbol of Sopron's endurance—and entranceway to the Inner Town—is 200 feet high, with foundations dating to the days of the Árpád dynasty (9th–13th centuries) and perhaps back to the Romans. The tower is remarkable for its uniquely harmonious blend of architectural styles: it has a Romanesque base rising to a circular balcony of Renaissance loggias topped by an octagonal clock tower that is itself capped by a brass Baroque onion dome and belfry. The upper portions were rebuilt after most of the earlier Fire Tower was, ironically, destroyed by the Great Fire of 1676, started by students roasting chestnuts in a high wind (today a double-headed eagle weathervane helps to predict wind direction; it's said that if the eagles face north and south it's going to rain). On the inside of the gate, you'll find a depiction of "Hungaria" receiving the loyalty of Sopron's kneeling citizens. Climb the 200-step spiral staircase to the top of the tower for lovely views of the town and surrounding countryside. It's from here that tower watchmen warned of approaching enemies and tolled the alarm for fire or the death of a prominent citizen. And occasionally, musicians would serenade the townsfolk from here. ⊠ *Fő tér 5* ☎ *99/311–327* ⊕ *www.tuztorony.sopron.hu* ⊠ *1,400 HUF.*

Várfalsétány (*Bailey Promenade*)
ARCHAEOLOGICAL SITE | Starting near the Fire Tower and following the route of Sopron's medieval town walls, the Bailey Promenade makes for a lovely stroll. The oldest part of city walls were built in the 14th century but some sights along the way are even older: look out for ancient gate foundations, remnants of the Roman town of Scarbantian. Some sections of the promenade close overnight. ⊠ *Sopron.*

 Restaurants

Corvinus
$ | HUNGARIAN | Set on the ground floor of the historic Storno House on Sopron's delightful cobblestone main square, Corvinus combines a café, pub, pizzeria, and restaurant all in one. Among the traditional Hungarian specialties are a meaty soup with a baked-on pastry cap, and roast venison goulash with porcini mushrooms. **Known for:** in beautiful 500-year-old building; cheese-heavy vegetarian options; good value for central location. ⑤ *Average main: 2,000 HUF* ⊠ *Fő tér 8, Sopron* ☎ *99/505–035* ⊕ *www.corvinusetterem.hu.*

El Gusto
$$ | INTERNATIONAL | This attractive and popular café-bistro is a great stop for breakfast, brunch, lunch, and dinner or just a takeaway coffee and ice cream. Enjoy an international menu of soups, salads, pizzas, paninis, and burgers (along with a few local specialties) in the simple Scandi-style interior, or else sit outside on the pleasant street terrace.

Known for: simple but warm decor; burgers and pizza; excellent coffee and cakes. ⑤ *Average main: 3,250 HUF* ✉ *Várkerület 79, Sopron* ☏ *70/3723–961* ⊕ *www. elgusto.hu.*

★ Erhardt

$$$ | HUNGARIAN | On a quiet side street a block from Várkerület, away from the main tourst drag, this excellent restaurant serves delicious, inventive dishes in a choice of beautiful settings: take your pick from the wood-beamed rooms upstairs, the beautiful 18th century brick-vaulted wine cellar below, or the leafy garden terrace outside. The menu features high quality, overwhelmingly meaty and fishy Hungarian fare, like roasted duck breast and paprika catfish (though vegetarian options like delicious barley-stuffed peppers do exist). **Known for:** curd-cheese dumplings with fruit; choice of beautiful settings; combined dinner and wine tasting for 11,600 HUF. ⑤ *Average main: 5,500 HUF* ✉ *Balfi· út 10, Sopron* ☏ *99/506–711* ⊕ *www. erhardts.hu.*

Hopsz

$$ | CAFÉ | Offering something a little different, this cool café and grill is a real bright spot in a rather drab part of town. Sit in the achingly-hip interior—all funky artworks, bold patterns, and bright prints—to enjoy a menu of delicious international dishes, or sit out on the plant pot–covered terrace in summer. **Known for:** cool interior with eclectic artworks; great food early 'til late; a 10-minute walk from the center. ⑤ *Average main: 2,800 HUF* ✉ *Gyár utca 1-3, Sopron* ☏ *99/333–355* ⊕ *www.hopszsopron.hu.*

Jégverem Fogadó

$$ | HUNGARIAN | A short walk from the Inner Town, this charming restaurant is a perennial favorite for its cozy, rustic interior of wooden-beamed ceilings, cast iron light fittings, and checkered tablecloths, as well as for its "guzzle guts" menu of homemade Hungarian specialities, often with an inventive twist.

In warm weather, you can also sit outside in the lovely, leafy courtyard. **Known for:** gigantic portions; poppy seed bread and butter pudding; bargain lunch menus. ⑤ *Average main: 3,000 HUF* ✉ *Jégverem utca 1, Sopron* ☏ *99/510–113* ⊕ *www. jegverem.hu.*

 ## Hotels

Hotel Wollner

$$ | HOTEL | Tucked inside the city center, this quiet and charming 18th century peach-colored hotel has been restored to its original splendor, with comfortable rooms boasting arched ceilings, comfy beds, and spacious bathrooms. **Pros:** a property with oodles of history; convenient Inner Town location; the garden incorporates medieval town wall. **Cons:** traditional furnishings not to all tastes; no elevator or A/C; no parking facilities. ⑤ *Rooms from: 34,000 HUF* ✉ *Templom utca 20, Sopron* ☏ *99/524–400* ⊕ *www.wollner.hu* ⤶ *18 rooms* ⑩ *Free breakfast.*

Pannonia Hotel

$$ | HOTEL | This elegant, antique-filled hotel has a long and illustrious past, starting in the 17th century as the Golden Hind, when it welcomed stagecoaches traveling between Vienna and Budapest. **Pros:** convenient central location; big rooftop terraces with views; rooftop basketball court. **Cons:** some stains on carpets; no tea and coffee in rooms; breakfast isn't included. ⑤ *Rooms from: 26,000 HUF* ✉ *Várkerület 75, Sopron* ☏ *99/312–180* ⊕ *www.pannoniahotel. com* ⤶ *79 rooms* ⑩ *No meals.*

★ Sopronbánfalvi Kolostor Hotel

(*Pauline-Carmelite Monastery of Sopronbánfalva*)

$$$ | HOTEL | If you're looking for a memorable stay in Sopron, look no further than this extraordinary 12th-century monastery-turned-hotel. **Pros:** this is a truly one-of-a-kind stay; an audio guide introduces the property; Refektórium restaurant is one of Sopron's finest. **Cons:** some rooms have single beds; hotel services are limited; a 40-minute walk (or 10-minute taxi) from the center. $ *Rooms from: 46,000 HUF* ✉ *Kolostorhegy utca 2, Sopron* ☎ *99/505–895* ⊕ *www.banfalvakolostor. hu* 🛏 *20 rooms* 🍽 *All-inclusive.*

Nightlife

Cézár Pince

WINE BARS—NIGHTLIFE | Come for the wine, stay for the decor: this beautiful 17th-century wine cellar sits beneath a gorgeous Gothic building that once played host to the Diet of Hungary (the medieval kingdom's parliament). Today, you can sample a good selection of local vintages, along with a wide choice of meat and cheese platters. ✉ *Hátsókapu utca 2, Sopron* ☎ *99/311–337* ⊕ *www. cezarpince.hu.*

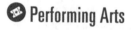 Performing Arts

★ Fertőrákosi Barlangszínház (*Fertőrákos Cave Theater*)

CONCERTS | For a unique entertainment experience, it's hard to beat this cave theater, carved out of a limestone quarry eight kilometers (five miles) northeast of Sopron. The 760-seat theater has amazing natural acoustics, which make for memorable classical music performances, pop and rock concerts, and musical theater productions. Arrive an hour early to enjoy the walking trail around the quarry, with lovely lookout points over the southern shore of Lake Neusiedl and a fun paleontological exhibition. ✉ *Fő utca 1, Fertőrákos, Sopron* ☎ *99/530–404* ⊕ *www.fertorakosikofejto.hu.*

Shopping

ART

Septem

ART GALLERIES | With its name stylized as "SEP7EM" on its sign above the door, this cozy little art gallery and shop showcases works by contemporary Sopron artists, as well as prints of classic Hungarian artworks. All are available to buy. ✉ *Kolostor utca 7, Sopron* ⊕ *www. septem.hu* ⊘ *Closed Sun. and Mon.*

CERAMICS

Esterházy Márkabolt

CERAMICS/GLASSWARE | This small shop is devoted to the renowned Herend hand-painted porcelain (the company first gained international acclaim when England's Queen Victoria ordered a dinner set for Windsor Castle in 1851). ✉ *Várkerület 98, Sopron* ☎ *99/508–712* ⊕ *www.herend.com* ⊘ *Closed Sun.*

Zsolnay Porcelán Márkabolt

CERAMICS/GLASSWARE | If you can't make it to the less expensive factory outlet in Pécs, you can purchase exquisite Zsolnay porcelain here. A tiny room lined with glass cabinets displays the delicate wares. ✉ *Előkapu 11, Sopron* ☎ *99/505–252* ⊕ *www.zsolnay.hu.*

COSMETICS

L'Apotheca Kozmetika

PERFUME/COSMETICS | This cute little boutique sells organic cosmetics—including face creams, shower gels, and body lotions—crafted to recipes by local pharmacist Tömea Glöckner. ✉ *Színház utca 4, Sopron* ☎ *20/298–7494* ⊕ *www. lapotheca.com* ⊘ *Closed Sun.*

WINE

Natura Vinotéka

WINE/SPIRITS | Situated on Várkerület, the main shopping street that partly circles the outside of the Old Town, this is a good place to look for fine Sopron wines, whether the peppery red kékfrankos or the spicy white zöld veltelini. ✉ *Várkerület 24, Sopron* ☎ *30/986–6488* ⊕ *www.sopronivinoteka.hu* ⊘ *Closed Sun.* Ⓜ *9400.*

Bratislava, Slovakia

88 km (55 miles) northeast of Sopron, 200 km (125 miles) northwest of Budapest.

Slovakia may be one of the world's youngest nations, but the country—and its capital Bratislava—has a long and illustrious history. Settled since the Neolithic era, Bratislava and the area around has spent much of this time as a component of a larger state, from the Roman Empire to the Kingdom of Hungary, the Habsburg Monarchy to Czechoslovakia. In 1993, Slovakia became an independent state, and since then Bratislava has blossomed into a thriving, modern European capital—while still retaining its charming historic center.

The city's most visible attraction is its enormous white Renaissance castle, perched on a rocky hill overlooking the Danube. But head down to ground level and you'll find there are plenty of other charms to this city, from the extensive Old Town that combines medieval and Gothic architecture to the thriving restaurant and nightlife culture that seriously rivals Budapest. Most of the top attractions are free (or very cheap) to experience, but if you want to dig a little deeper, it's worth picking up a **Bratislava Card.** This will give you entry into 16 museums and galleries in the city and around, including the Museum of Viticulture and Devín Castle, as well as a one-hour guided tour of the Old Town and free public transportation. The card is valid for 24, 48, and 72 hours, at €20, €25, and €28 respectively. Pick it up at the tourist information or on the Visit Bratislava website.

GETTING HERE AND AROUND

Bratislava has a small international airport served by budget airlines including Ryanair and Wizzair; a 40-minute bus brings you in the city center. For long-haul destinations and national carriers, fly to and from Vienna.

To reach Bratislava from Sopron, drive northeast through Austria on the B50 and A6 (1½ hours) or take a train via Vienna (2½ hours). From Budapest, drive 2 hours northwest on the M1/E60 then M15/E75, or take a long-distance bus (3–4 hours).

Once you're in town, ditch the car: the Old Town is almost completely pedestrianized, and small enough to walk around, while regular buses and trams will take you to destinations farther afield.

AIRPORT INFORMATION Bratislava Airport. *(Letisko M. R. Štefánika)* ✉ *Ivanská cesta, Bratislava* ☎ *02/330–333–53* ⊕ *www.bts.aero.*

RESTAURANT AND HOTEL PRICES

What it Costs in Euros			
$	$$	$$$	$$$$
RESTAURANTS			
under €10	€10–€15	€16–€20	over €20
HOTELS			
under €80	€80–€105	€106–€135	over €135

VISITOR INFORMATION

CONTACTS Visit Bratislava. ✉ *Klobučnícka 2, Bratislava* ☎ *02/544–194–10* ⊕ *www.visitbratislava.com.*

◉ Sights

★ **Bratislavský hrad** *(Bratislava Castle)*
CASTLE/PALACE | With roots dating back more than a millennium—it was first mentioned in 907 for its role in a battle between Bavarians and Hungarians—Bratislava Castle was significantly rebuilt in the Renaissance style in the mid-16th century. It's this enormous, rectangular form with four stocky towers that you can see today (though it incorporates architectural features from throughout its history, and the dazzling white paint

job is distinctly 20th century). Walk up the (steep) castle hill and pass through one of the four entrance gates (probably **Viedenská brána** or **Leopoldova brána**) for incredible views of the town and the Danube below. The grounds are free to enter, so you can soak up the vistas as long as you like; make sure you visit the beautiful **Baroková záhrada** (Baroque Garden) while you're at it. You only need to pay if you want to head inside, either for the **SNM-Historical Museum**, which is a little sparse but does include access to the **Crown Tower** via a narrow passageway, or any of the regularly changing temporary exhibits. ⊠ *Zámocká 2, Bratislava* ☎ *02/204–831–10* ⊕ *www. bratislava-hrad.sk.*

Devínsky hrad (*Devín Castle*)
CASTLE/PALACE | Located on the confluence of the Morava and Danube rivers that form the border between Slovakia and Austria, just 10½ kilometers (6½ miles) west of Bratislava, lies this extraordinary ruined castle. Built on the top of a high crag, the enormous Devín Castle is one of the oldest in the region, first mentioned in written sources in 864. You can learn about the history of the castle and the village (all the way back to Neolithic times) in a fascinating exhibition within the castle walls. Enjoy the sweeping views from the top of the ruined Upper Castle, and take a snap of the famous **Maiden's Tower**, a tiny watchtower precariously balanced on a lone rock that has spawned countless legends of imprisoned women leaping to their deaths. In summer, there are kid-friendly medieval-themed events held in and around the castle. To reach Devín, take Bus 29 from Bratislava (30 minutes) or drive west out of the city on Devínska cesta. ⊠ *Muránska 1050/10, Bratislava* ☎ *02/657–301–05* ⊕ *www.muzeum. bratislava.sk* ⊠ *€5* ⊘ *Closed Mon.*

Grasalkovičov palác (*Grassalkovich Palace*)
GOVERNMENT BUILDING | This grand Rococo-style summer residence was built in 1780 for Count Anton Grassalkovich, advisor to Empress Maria Theresa (who was crowned in Bratislava in 1761). Today, it's the official residence of the President of the Slovak Republic so it isn't possible to see inside, but come at 1 pm any day of the week to witness the ceremonial Changing of the Guard. You can also head around the back of the palace to explore the lovely Prezidentská záhrada (Presidental Garden), a public park that's an oasis of manicured lawns, sculpted hedges, and gorgeous flower displays. It also has a number of avant garde sculptures, including the playful *Fountain of Youth* by Slovak sculptor Tibor Bártfay. ⊠ *Hodžovo námestie 2978/1, Bratislava* ☎ *02/578–881–55* ⊕ *www. prezident.sk.*

Hlavné Námestie
PLAZA | Bratislava's main square is the beating heart of the city, home to some of its most interesting history, architecture, and artworks. The centerpiece of the square is **Maximiliánova fontána** (Maximilian's Fountain), erected in 1572 as a public water supply. The knight on top is said to bow once a year, on New Year's Eve, though only for those pure of heart and born in Bratislava. The square is ringed by a number of beautiful Gothic and Baroque buildings, many of which are now embassies. The most notable of these is the **Stará radnica** (Old Town Hall), which is actually a mishmash of different houses built at various stages from the 14th century onwards; look for the cannonball embedded in the town hall's tower. Opposite, on the corner outside Café Mayer, is the **Schöne Náci** (Nice Nazi) statue, depicting a famous local eccentric who cheerfully wandered the streets in top hat and tails. As well as the permanent fixtures, the square also hosts regular markets, concerts, and political events. ⊠ *Bratislava.*

Hviezdoslavovo námestie (*Hviezdoslav Square*)

PLAZA | This charming, tree-shaded promenade is named for renowned Slovak poet Pavol Országh Hviezdoslav and lined with some of the city's grandest buildings—now mainly embassies, hotels, and restaurants. The "square" starts with a **statue of Hviezdoslav** and ends at **Morový stĺp**, a beautiful Baroque trinity column. Just east of Hviezdoslav Square is the old **Slovenské národné divadlo** (Slovak National Theatre) building, while just around the corner crowds gather to see the popular **Čumil** (Rubberneck) sculpture; a cheeky bronze chap peeping out from under a manhole cover. ⊠ *Bratislava.*

Kostol svätej Alžbety (*Blue Church*)

RELIGIOUS SITE | Bratislava's most striking Secession (art nouveau) style building, the Church of St. Elizabeth is noted for its powder blue exterior, which extends all the way up to its 120-foot round tower. The unusual color scheme continues throughout the early-20th-century building, from the blue ceramic roof tiles, mosaics, and maiolica (tin-glazed pottery) decorations outside, to the baby blue pews and arches inside. The church once functioned as the chapel of the school opposite, which is evident in the two buildings' similar design elements (though the school has a rather more traditional color scheme). ⊠ *Bezručova 2, Bratislava* ⊕ *www.modrykostol.fara.sk.*

Michalská brána (*Michael's Gate*)

MUSEUM | The last gate standing from Bratislava's original 13th century city walls, Michael's Gate was rebuilt in the Baroque style in 1758; that's when the onion dome was added. Look up to the top of the tower to see the dome, as well as a statue of the archangel Michael slaying a dragon; or look down to see a bronze plate showing the distances to different world capitals. Also of note is the remarkably skinny house on the northwest side of the gate, now a fast food joint. For a small fee, you can climb the tower for views over the city; your ticket also includes entry to the small Museum of Arms within the gate, as well as the nearby Pharmacy Museum, a fascinating exhibition on 16th century medicine. ⊠ *Michalská ulica 22, Bratislava* ☎ *02/544–330–44* ⊕ *www. muzeum.bratislava.sk* ✉ *€4.50 (tower and museum)* ⊗ *Closed Mon. (tower and museum).*

Primaciálny palác (*Primate's Palace*)

CASTLE/PALACE | This gorgeous Neoclassical building, constructed between 1778 to 1781 for the Archbishop József Batthyány—"primate" is a title given to a bishop; nothing to do with monkeys—played a vital role in European history in 1805. That's when the palace's Hall of Mirrors was used to sign the fourth Peace of Pressburg, which effectively brought an end to the Holy Roman Empire. Today, you can visit the beautiful hall, elegantly furnished with period pieces, as well as the picture gallery with portraits of Hungarian rulers. Somewhat surprisingly, the palace also contains a rare collection of exquisite English tapestries from the time of King James I (1566–1625). ⊠ *Primaciálne námestie 2, Bratislava* ☎ *02/593–563–94* ⊕ *www. visitbratislava.com/places/primatial-palace* ⊗ *Closed Mon.*

Slovak National Collection of Wines

WINERY/DISTILLERY | Attached to the Museum of Viticulture—which traces the long history of winemaking in the Bratislava and Lower Carpathians region—is this beautiful 16th century wine cellar offering regular tastings. The national collection is made up of Slovakia's "Top 100 Wines," which are chosen from more than 600 entries each year; you can find everything from Tokajs to ice wines. Choose to sample two, four, or eight of the collection's wines and a professional someliér will guide you through the experience. Alternatively, opt for the self-guided, all-you-can-drink "72 wines in 100 minutes" tasting. All tastings are available for individuals or groups, but it's best to call ahead to ensure an English-speaking guide. ⊠ *Radničná 577/1, Bratislava* ☎ *918–664–992* ⊕ *www.salonvin.sk* ⊙ *Closed Sun.–Mon.*

★ St Martin's Cathedral (*Katedrála svätého Martina*)

RELIGIOUS SITE | The enormous golden crown and cushion on top of this beautiful Gothic cathedral reveals that this was once a coronation church. In fact, it was *the* coronation church for Hungarian (and later Austrian) monarchs for more than 250 years; 19 different royals were crowned here between 1563 and 1830, including Empress Maria Theresa. The church was also one of the city's lines of defense, which explains the chunky walls, the arrow-slit windows, and the exceptionally tall (lookout) tower. Luckily, the interior is more delicate and decorative, with dramatic rib vaults, colorful stained glass windows, and a grand altar showing St. Martin in a traditional Hungarian hussar dress. Next to the cathedral lie the remains of the **Neologická Synagóga** (Neological Synagogue), demolished by the communist government in the 1970s, and overlooked by the glorious facade of the **Lekáreň u Salvátora** (Pharmacy Salvator). ⊠ *Rudnayovo námestie 1, Bratislava* ☎ *02/544–313–59* ⊕ *www.dom.fara.sk.*

🍴 Restaurants

★ Albrecht

$$$$ | FRENCH | One of the city's most elegant fine dining experiences, Restaurant Albrecht near Bratislava Castle serves sumptuous, strictly seasonal French cuisine using the highest quality locally sourced ingredients; menus often list individual farms and producers. Head chef Jaroslav Žídek is known for his elaborate, multicourse tasting menus, but you can also order the dishes à la carte: opt for the tuna ceviche to start, the lamb back with sheep-cheese ravioli for main, and the plum dumplings to finish.

Known for: multicourse tasting menus; great value lunch menu; five minutes by taxi from the Old Town. $ *Average main:* €30 ⊠ *Mudroňova 4237/82, Bratislava* ☎ *902–333–888* ⊕ *www.hotelalbrecht.sk/restauracia* ⊙ *Closed Sun.*

Roxor

$$ | BURGER | Melt-in-the-mouth eco-farm beef, crunchy double-cooked fries, and crisp craft beers are the order of the day at this excellent burger joint. There are half a dozen burger options to choose from, including veggie mushroom and vegan patty ones; all are cooked medium as standard and served with tasty sides like rosemary or garlic fries, kimchi, and coleslaw. **Known for:** Bratislava's best burgers; homemade pineapple-curry mayo; a little way out of the Old Town. $ *Average main: €15* ⊠ *Šancová 19, Bratislava* ☎ *02/210–205–00* ⊕ *www.roxorburger.sk.*

Zylinder

$$$ | AUSTRIAN | With dishes based on traditional Austro-Hungarian recipes, this well-located café and restaurant makes a pleasant stop for lunch or dinner. Expect everything from traditional Austrian schnitzel and *tafelspitz* (boiled beef served with minced apples) to Hungarian beef goulash and *somlói galuska* (sponge trifle), as well as Slovakian specialties like *halušky* (small potato dumplings with sheep cheese, sautéed bacon, and sour cream). **Known for:** tasty beef broth with noodles; great location on Hviezdoslav Square; big portions and good value for area. $ *Average main: €16* ⊠ *Hviezdoslavovo námestie 19, Bratislava* ☎ *903–123–134* ⊕ *www.zylinder.sk.*

☕ Coffee and Quick Bites

★ Konditorei Kormuth

$$ | CAFÉ | It may look unassuming from the street, but step inside and it becomes immediately apparent why this is considered one of Europe's most beautiful cafes. The walls and ceilings throughout the interior are plastered in majestic Renaissance-style frescoes, while seemingly every nook and cranny of the old building is filled with antiques, some dating back to the 16th century. **Known for:** stunningly decorative interior; delicious cakes and pastries; entrance fee. ⑤ *Average main: €10* ✉ *Sedlárska 363, Bratislava* ☏ *02/544–325–37* ⊕ *www.konditoreikormuth.sk* ۞ *Closed Mon.–Tue.*

Koun

$ | **FAST FOOD** | In recent years, Bratislava has been taken over by ice cream stores, and today it's hard to find an Old Town street without a high-quality gelato option. But if you have to choose only one scoop while you're in town, opt for Koun (pronounced "cone"). **Known for:** incredible lemon cake ice cream; sunny decor and even sunnier staff; half-hidden on a side street off Hviezdoslav Square. ⑤ *Average main: €5* ✉ *Paulínyho 1, Bratislava* ☏ *948–687–795* ⊕ *www.koun.sk* ۞ *Closed Mon.*

Hotels

Loft Hotel

$$ | **HOTEL** | Standing out from the Old Town crowd with its industrial-style decor incorporating exposed brick walls, distressed wooden floors, shabby leather sofas, and retro advertising prints, Loft offers a different kind of hotel experience. **Pros:** sixth floor rooms have gorgeous garden views; free snacks and wine for guests; popular Fabrika brewpub downstairs. **Cons:** industrial decor isn't to all tastes; underground parking is €20 a day; wood floors can be noisy. ⑤ *Rooms from: €85* ✉ *Štefánikova 864/4, Bratislava* ☏ *901–902–680* ⊕ *www.lofthotel.sk* ⇥ *111 rooms* ❢❢ *No meals.*

★ Marrol's Boutique Hotel

$$$ | **HOTEL** | A romantic boutique gem in the heart of the Old Town, Marrol's is set within a 19th century burgher's house and oozes period charm, with its opulent

chandeliers, deep leather armchairs, and charming wood paneling. **Pros:** free minibar full of drinks; lovely plant-covered Summer Terrace; underground parking available. **Cons:** breakfast is nothing special; service isn't always with a smile; noise in corridors carries. ⑤ *Rooms from: €110* ✉ *Tobrucká 6953/4, Bratislava* ☏ *02/577–846–00* ⊕ *www.hotelmarrols. sk* ⇥ *54 rooms* ❢❢ *Free breakfast.*

Roset Hotel

$$$ | **HOTEL** | Built in 1903 in the Secession (art nouveau) style, this sophisticated hotel, which is conveniently located by the Old Town, offers 27 spacious and elegant suites, a spa with fitness center, sauna, and Jacuzzi, and the time-honored Tulip Café. **Pros:** beautiful turn-of-the-century building; in-suite massages available; incorporates famous old literary café. **Cons:** breakfast is underwhelming; mattresses are a little hard; some rooms need sprucing up. ⑤ *Rooms from: €115* ✉ *Štúrova Ulica 10, Bratislava* ☏ *917–373–209* ⊕ *www.rosethotel.sk* ⇥ *27 rooms* ❢❢ *Free breakfast.*

Nightlife

Grand Cru Wine Gallery

WINE BARS—NIGHTLIFE | This popular Old Town bar is the perfect place to sample some high-quality Slovakian wines. Amiable owner Martin Pagáč is always on hand to talk you through individual vintages and answer questions. ✉ *Zámočnícka 404/8, Bratislava* ☏ *908–656–259* ⊕ *www.facebook.com/ GrandCruWineGallery.*

KC Dunaj

DANCE CLUBS | Set within a communist-era shopping mall but now reclaimed by a younger, hipper crowd, this lively bar and club venue hosts regular live concerts, club nights, theater events, and more. ✉ *Nedbalova 435/3, Bratislava* ☏ *904–330–049* ⊕ *www.kcdunaj.sk.*

★ **Kláštorný pivovar**
BREWPUBS/BEER GARDENS | For a great-tasting, great-value beer, you won't beat the home brew at this popular brewpub—it's just €3.70 for a whole liter of Monastic Beer served straight from the tap. Enjoy it with tasty Slovak pub food like grilled sausages, baked pork knuckle, and *halušky* (potato dumplings with sheep's cheese). ✉ *Námestie SNP 469/8, Bratislava* 🕾 *907–976–284* ⊕ *www.klastornypivovar.sk.*

UFO
BARS/PUBS | Situated at the top of the observation tower on the UFO bridge, this swanky bar offers the chance to enjoy delicious cocktails, spirits, and wines while overlooking the Danube and the city below. There's also a well-regarded restaurant here, but beware: the sky-high setting also means sky-high prices. ✉ *Most SNP 1, Bratislava* 🕾 *02/625–203–00* ⊕ *www.u-f-o.sk.*

Performing Arts

Slovenské národné divadlo (*Slovak National Theater*)
THEATER | Whether at the grand, 18th-century, Neo-Renaissance building in the heart of the Old Town, or at the shiny, art-filled, 21st century building downriver, the Slovak National Theater knows how to put on a show. The regular, high-quality operas, ballets, and drama performances are typically around €20 a ticket. ✉ *New Slovak National Theater, Pribinova 17, Bratislava* 🕾 *02/204–722–89* ⊕ *www.snd.sk.*

Shopping

BEER
100 Pív
LOCAL SPECIALTIES | A small bottle shop on the edge of the Old Town, 100 Pív has hundreds of beers available to buy, with a big focus on local craft breweries. There are always some beers on tap, so you can try before you buy. ✉ *Medená 111/33, Bratislava* 🕾 *948–405–409* ⊕ *www.100piv.sk.*

FASHION
NOX Vintage
CLOTHING | A favorite with lovers of vintage and retro fashion, this Old Town store has rack upon rack of clothes, bags, and shoes, as well as a few items of furniture and homeware. ✉ *Ventúrska 3, Bratislava* 🕾 *905–861–879* ⊕ *www.facebook.com/NOXvintage* 🕙 *Closed Sun.*

GIFTS AND SOUVENIRS
Slávica
GIFTS/SOUVENIRS | You'll find everything from clothing and jewelry to art prints and ceramics from local producers at this hip design store near Laurence's Gate. ✉ *Laurinská 19, Bratislava* 🕾 *917–968–736* ⊕ *www.slavicadesign.sk.*

Index

Photo Credits

Front Cover: Yarchyk/iStockphoto [Description: The historical architecture of the capitol city Budapest, Hungary with a reflection in the waters of the Danube river.]. **Back cover, from left to right:** Daniel Korzeniewski/Shutterstock, Cujochan | Dreamstime.com, ZGPhotography/Shutterstock. **Spine:** Ihor Pasternak/Shutterstock. **Interior, from left to right:** krivinis/Shutterstock (1). Claudio Trasforini/New York Cafe (2). **Chapter 1: Experience Budapest:** Razak.R/Shutterstock (6-7). CK Travels/Shutterstock (8). New York Cafe (9). Áment Gellért/MAGYAR NEMZETI GALERIA (9). Bergics Balazs/Bock Cellar (10). Free Budapest Walking Tours (10). Andocs/Shutterstock (10). Práczki Istvan (10). pgaborphotos/Shutterstock (11). Kewuwu | Dreamstime.com (11). Razak.R/Shutterstock (12). Roman Sigaev/Shutterstock (12). Praczky Istvan (12). maziarz/Shutterstock (12). Attila Nagy (13). Balázs Attila/Mtu gov hu (14). Kateryna_Moroz/Shutterstock (14). Oleg Zorchenko/Shutterstock (14). Brendan Riley/Shutterstock (14). posztos/Shutterstock (15). Crisfotolux | Dreamstime.com (15). Courtesy of BFTK (18). vitfoto/Shutterstock (18). angeluisma/iStockphoto (18). ALLEKO/iStockphoto (19). Dar1930/Shutterstock (19). Práczky István/Courtesy of BFTK (20). Práczky István/Courtesy of BFTK (20). Tito Slack/Shutterstock (20). Práczky István/Courtesy of BFTK (21). Práczky István/Courtesy of BFTK (21). Ungorf | Dreamstime.com (22). AlizadaStudios/iStockphoto (23). acceptfoto/iStockphoto (24). Práczky_István (24). Práczky István (24). T photography/Shutterstock (24). quisait/iStockphoto (25). posztos/Shutterstock (25). Valentyna Gupalo/iStockphoto (25). VSM Fotografia/Shutterstock (25). Budapestinfo.hu (26). Uskarp | Dreamstime.com (27). **Chapter 3: Várkerület (Castle District), District 1:** Craig Hastings/Shutterstock (59). ZGPhotography/Shutterstock (64). ZGPhotography/Shutterstock (66). Zoltangabor | Dreamstime.com (68-69). **Chapter 4: Gellérthegy (Gellért Hill) and Tabán, Districts 1, 11:** ZGPhotography/Shutterstock (77). Alzamu | Dreamstime.com (83). pinkcigarette/Flickr (84). Craighastings4 | Dreamstime.com (88). **Chapter 5: Belváros (Inner Town), District 5:** Alzamu | Dreamstime.com (95). Celestine Gandu/Shutterstock (100). posztos/Shutterstock (102). Javier Valero Iglesias/Flickr (104). **Chapter 6: Southern Pest, Districts 8, 9:** Ccat82 | Dreamstime.com (109). posztos/Shutterstock (112). Hermsdorf/iStockphoto (117). posztos/Shutterstock (118-119). **Chapter 7: Erzsébetváros (Elizabeth Town) and the Jewish Quarter, District 7:** Attila Csipe/iStockphoto (127). Thanate Tan/Flickr (131). dnaveh/Shutterstock (134). Fabiomichelecapelli/iStockphoto (140). **Chapter 8: Városliget (City Park), District 14:** Evgeniya Biriukova/dreamstime (143). VictoriaSh/Shutterstock (148). Nikitin Mikhail/Shutterstock (150). Photogeza | Dreamstime.com (152-153). Razak.R/Shutterstock (155). **Chapter 9: Parliament and Around, Districts 5 and 6:** Mazur Travel/Shutterstock (157). Tupungato-Shutterstock (165). Fabiomichelecapelli/iStockphoto (167). Luciano Mortula - LGM/Shutterstock (169). posztos/Shutterstock (177). **Chapter 10: Margitszieget (Margaret Island) and Northern Pest, District 13:** Alexey Oblov/Shutterstock (181). Chaikovsky | Dreamstime.com (185). GTS Productions/Shutterstock (188-189). Wulwais | Dreamstime.com (190). Titoslack | Dreamstime.com (195). **Chapter 11: Óbuda and Buda Hills, Districts 2, 3, 12:** Dani Lugo/Shutterstock (197). Skovalsky | Dreamstime.com (200). posztos/Shutterstock (205). Tupungato/Shutterstock (206). **Chapter 12: Side Trips from Budapest:** Filip Fuxa/Shutterstock (215). Gabor Tokodi/Shutterstock (224). Geza Kurka Photos/Shutterstock (228). Botond Horvath/Shutterstock (237). Berni0004 | Dreamstime.com (241). Lkonya | Dreamstime.com (253). Istvan Csak/Shutterstock (258-259). Boris Stroujko/Shutterstock (265). **About Our Writers:** All photos are courtesy of the writers.

Every effort has been made to trace the copyright holders, and we apologize in advance for any accidental errors. We would be happy to apply the corrections in the following edition of this publication.

Notes

MAPS

Chapter 1

EXPERIENCE
BUDAPEST

20 ULTIMATE EXPERIENCES

Budapest offers terrific experiences that should be on every traveler's list. Here are Fodor's top picks for a memorable trip.

1 Thermal Baths

Soaking and relaxing in Budapest's most beautiful thermal baths at Széchenyi or Gellért is an essential local experience. *Ch. 4, 8*